INFORMATION SECURITY *and* CYBER LAWS

INFORMATION SECURITY *and* CYBER LAWS

SARIKA GUPTA

Asstt. Prof.

MCA. M.Tech, MBA, Ph.D(CSE)

CSE/IT Deptt. Dronacharya College of Engineering

Greater Noida, Uttar Pradesh (INDIA)

ER. GAURAV GUPTA

Manager Client Services

Rightwave Info. Solution Pvt. Ltd.

NOIDA

KHANNA BOOK PUBLISHING CO. (P) LTD.

Publisher of Engineering and Computer Books

4C/4344, Ansari Road, Darya Ganj, New Delhi-110002

Phone : 011-23244447-48 **Mobile:** +91-9910909320

E-mail : contact@khannabooks.com

Website : www.khannabooks.com

Dear Readers,

To prevent the piracy, this book is secured with HIGH SECURITY HOLOGRAM on the front title cover. In case you don't find the hologram on the front cover title, please write us to at contact@khannabooks.com or whatsapp us at +91-99109 09320 and avail special gift voucher for yourself.

Specimen of Hologram on front Cover title:

Moreover, there is a SPECIAL DISCOUNT COUPON for you with EVERY HOLOGRAM.

How to avail this SPECIAL DISCOUNT:

Step 1: Scratch the hologram
Step 2: Under the scratch area, your "coupon code" is available
Step 3: Logon to www.khannabooks.com
Step 4: Use your "coupon code" in the shopping cart and get your copy at a special discount
Step 5: Enjoy your reading!

Price: ₹ 465.00

ISBN: 978-93-81068-24-3

Information Security & Cyber Laws *by* Sarika Gupta & Gaurav Gupta

First Edition: 2013
Revised Reprint: 2023, **2025**

To view complete list of books, Please scan the QR Code:

Published by:
Khanna Book Publishing Co. (P) Ltd.
CIN: U22110DL1998PTC095547

Visit us at: **www.khannabooks.com**
Write us at: **contact@khannabooks.com**

Printed in India.

This book is dedicated to-

OUR FAMILY

Preface

It gives us great pleasure in presenting the first edition of this book to our esteemed readers. "**Information Security and Cyber Law**" is written with several goal in mind. It is designed to provide all essential information you'll need to learn **ISCL**. It can be used as a test-cum-reference book by students of B.Tech (CS/IT) / MCA and M.Tech.

I am sure that the text's user friendly approach will encourage the students to read the book and will make them understand the concept in easy way.

We always welcome emails with comments and suggestions from researchers, academicians, students and other to improve the quality of this book.

Sarika Gupta
Gaurav Gupta
togupta.gupta@yahoo.co.in

Acknowledgements

I take this opportunity to express my deep sense of gratitude to Dr. Ajay Matto (CEO, DCE group) and Prof. R.N.Sharma (Principal, DCE group) for their constant inspiration and encouragement. I am also greatful to Prof. Aswani (Administrator, DCE group) and Prof. Kaul (Registrar, DCE group) for their kind support.

I also want to express my heartiest thanks to Prof. Anil Chopra (Head CSE/IT/MCA), S.K. Srivastava for their valuable suggestions, support, guidance and encouragement.

Last but not the least, I would like to thank Mr. Chand s Nagar of Limited Colors, who designed the book. Thanks are also due to Mr. Puneet Khanna and Mr. Mukul Seth of Khanna Publishing Co. Pvt. Ltd., for managing the publishing agreement and production process.

Sarika Gupta

Gaurav Gupta

togupta.gupta@yahoo.co.in

Acknowledgements

I take this opportunity to express my deep sense of gratitude to Dr. Ajay Mittal (CEO, DCE group) and Prof. R.N. Sharma (Principal, DCE group) for their constant inspiration and encouragement. I am also grateful to Prof. Aswani (Administrator, DCE group) and Prof. Kaul (Registrar, DCE group) for their kind support.

I also want to express my heartiest thanks to Prof. Anil Chopra (Head CSE/IT/MCA) and S.K. Srivastava for their valuable suggestions, support, guidance and encouragement.

Last but not the least, I would like to thank Mr. Chand Sahgal of Ink Inteca Colors, who designed the book. Thanks are also due to Mr. Puneet Khanna and Mr. Manoj Sethi of Khanna Publishing Co. Pvt. Ltd. for managing the publishing agreement and production process.

Sarika Gupta

Gaurav Gupta

[illegible]gupta@yahoo.co.in

Contents

UNIT-1

UNIT-3

UNIT-4

UNIT – 1

1. What is Information
2. What is Security

CHAPTER 1

What is Information

Information, in its most restricted technical sense, is an ordered sequence of symbols. As a concept, however, information has many meanings. Moreover, the concept of information is closely related to notions of constraint, communication, control, data, form, instruction, knowledge, meaning, mental stimulus, pattern, perception, and representation.

In general, raw data that has been verified to be accurate and timely, is specific and organized for a purpose, is presented within a context that gives it meaning and relevance, and which leads to increase in understanding and decrease in uncertainty. The value of information lies solely in its ability to affect a behavior, decision, or outcome. A piece of information is considered valueless if, after receiving it, things remain unchanged.

1.1 WHAT IS A SYSTEM

The term "system" originates from the Greek term systema, which means to "place together." Multiple business and engineering domains have definitions of a system. This text defines a system as:

System is an integrated set of interoperable elements, each with explicitly specified and bounded capabilities, working synergistically to perform value-added processing to enable a User to satisfy mission-oriented operational needs in a prescribed operating environment with a specified outcome and probability of success.

There are some another definition of system as

1.1.1 Definition of System

1. A group of interdependent items that interact regularly to perform a task.
2. An established or organized procedure; a method.
3. A computer system refers to the hardware and software components that run a computer or computers.

4. An *information system* is a system that collects and stores data.
5. On Macintoshes, *System* is short for *System file*, an essential program that runs whenever you start up a Macintosh. The System provides information to all other applications that run on a Macintosh. The System and Finder programs together make up the Mac OS.
6. *System* often simply refers to the operating system.

1.2 CLASSIFICATION OF SYSTEM

Classification of systems can be done in many ways.

1.2.1 Physical or Abstract System

Physical systems are tangible entities that we can feel and touch. These may be static or dynamic in nature. For example, take a computer center. Desks and chairs are the static parts, which assist in the working of the center. Static parts don't change. The dynamic systems are constantly changing. Computer systems are dynamic system. Programs, data, and applications can change according to the user's needs.

Abstract systems are conceptual. These are not physical entities. They may be formulas, representation or model of a real system.

1.2.2 Open Closed System

Systems interact with their environment to achieve their targets. Things that are not part of the system are environmental elements for the system. Depending upon the interaction with the environment, systems can be divided into two categories, open and closed.

Open systems: Systems that interact with their environment. Practically most of the systems are open systems. An open system has many interfaces with its environment. It can also adapt to changing environmental conditions. It can receive inputs from, and delivers output to the outside of system. An information system is an example of this category.

Closed systems: Systems that don't interact with their environment. Closed systems exist in concept only.

1.2.3 Man Made Information System

The main purpose of information systems is to manage data for a particular organization. Maintaining files, producing information and reports are few functions. An information system produces customized information depending upon the needs of the organization. These are usually formal, informal, and computer based.

Formal Information Systems: It deals with the flow of information from top management to lower management. Information flows in the form of memos, instructions, etc. But feedback can be given from lower authorities to top management.

Informal Information systems: Informal systems are employee based. These are made to solve the day to day work related problems. Computer-Based Information Systems: This class of systems depends on the use of computer for managing business applications. These systems are discussed in detail in the next section.

1.3 ANALYTICAL REPRESENTATION OF A SYSTEM

As an abstraction we symbolically represent a system as a simple entity by using a rectangular box as shown in Figure 1. In general, inputs such as stimuli and cues are fed into a system that processes the inputs and produces an output. As a construct, this symbolism is acceptable; however, the words need to more explicitly identify WHAT the system performs. That is, the system must add value to the input in producing an output.

We refer to the transformational processing that adds value to inputs and produces an output as a capability. You will often hear people refer to this as the system's functionality; this is partially correct. Functionality only represents the ACTION to be accomplished; not HOW WELL as characterized by performance. This text employs capability as the operative term that encompasses both the functionality and performance attributes of a system.

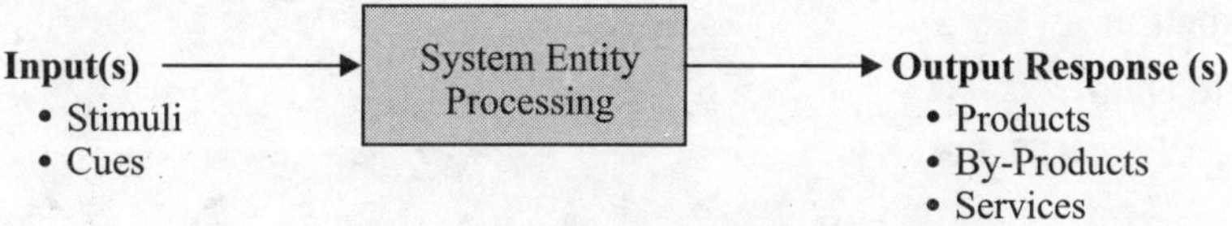

Figure 1.1: Basic System Entity Construct

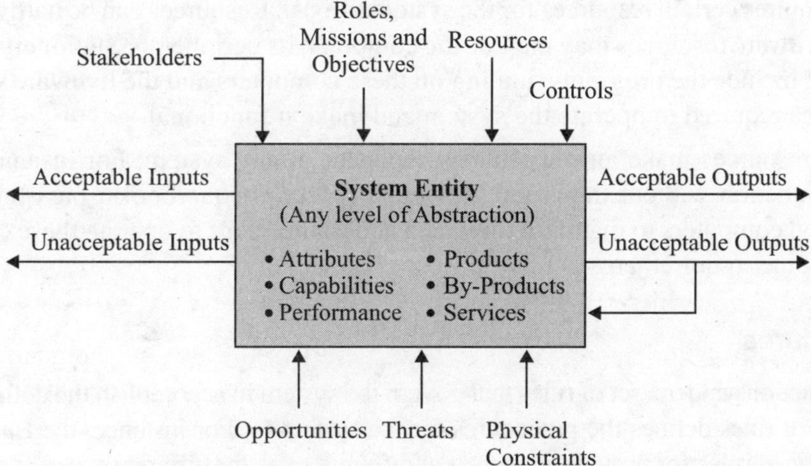

Figure 1.2: Analytical System Entity Construct

The simple diagram presented in Figure 1.1 represents a system. However, from an analytical perspective, the diagram is missing critical information that relates to how the system operates and performs within its operating environment. Therefore, we expand the diagram to identify these missing elements. The result is shown in Figure 1.2. The attributes of the construct which include desirable/undesirable inputs, stakeholders, and desirable/undesirable outputs serve as a key checklist to ensure that all contributory factors are duly considered when specifying, designing, and developing a system.

1.4 SYSTEM COMPONENTS AND CHARACTERISTICS

A big system may be seen as a set of interacting smaller systems known as subsystems or functional units each of which has its defined tasks. All these work in coordination to achieve the overall objective of the system. Systcm cngineering requires development of a strong foundation in understanding how to characterize a system, product, or service in terms of its attributes, properties, and performance.

As discussed above, a system is a set of components working together to achieve some goal. The basic elements of the system may be listed as:

- Resources
- Procedures
- Data/Information
- Intermediate Data
- Processes

1.4.1 Resources

Every system requires certain resources for the system to exist. Resources can be hardware, software or live ware. Hardware resources may include the computer, its peripherals, stationery etc. Software resources would include the programs running on these computers and the liveware would include the human beings required to operate the system and make it functional.

Thus these resources make an important component of any system. For instance, a Banking system cannot function without the required stationery like cheque books, pass books etc. such systems also need computers to maintain their data and trained staff to operate these computers and cater to the customer requirements.

1.4.2 Procedures

Every system functions under a set of rules that govern the system to accomplish the defined goal of the system. This set of rules defines the procedures for the system to. For instance, the Banking systems have their predefined rules for providing interest at different rates for different types of accounts.

1.4.3 Data/Information

Every system has some predefined goal. For achieving the goal the system requires certain inputs, which are converted into the required output. The main objective of the System is to produce some useful output. Output is the outcome of processing. Output can be of any nature e.g. goods, services or information.

However, the Output must conform to the customer's expectations. Inputs are the elements that enter the system and produce Output. Input can be of various kinds, like material, information, etc.

1.4.4 Intermediate Data

Various processes process system's Inputs. Before it is transformed into Output, it goes through many intermediary transformations. Therefore, it is very important to identify the Intermediate Data. For example, in a college when students register for a new semester, the initial form submitted by student goes through many departments. Each department adds their validity checks on it.

Finally the form gets transformed and the student gets a slip that states whether the student has been registered for the requested subjects or not. It helps in building the System in a better way. Intermediate forms of data occur when there is a lot of processing on the input data. So, intermediate data should be handled as carefully as other data since the output depends upon it.

1.4.5 Processes

The systems have some processes that make use of the resources to achieve the set goal under the defined procedures. These processes are the operational element of the system.

For instance in a Banking system there are several processes that are carried out. Consider for example the processing of a cheque as a process. A cheque passes through several stages before it actually gets processed and converted. These are some of the processes of the Banking system. All these components together make a complete functional system.

Systems also exhibit certain features and characteristics, some of which are:

- Objective
- Standards
- Environment
- Feedback
- Boundaries and interfaces

Objective

Every system has a predefined goal or objective towards which it works. A system cannot exist without a defined objective. For example an organization would have an objective of earning maximum possible revenues, for which each department and each individual has to work in coordination.

Standards

It is the acceptable level of performance for any system. Systems should be designed to meet standards. Standards can be business specific or organization specific.

For example take a sorting problem. There are various sorting algorithms. But each has its own complexity. So such algorithm should be used that gives most optimum efficiency. So there should be a standard or rule to use a particular algorithm. It should be seen whether that algorithm is implemented in the system.

Environment

Every system whether it is natural or man made co-exists with an environment. It is very important for a system to adapt itself to its environment. Also, for a system to exist it should change according to the changing environment. For example, we humans live in a particular environment. As we move to other places, there are changes in the surroundings but our body gradually adapts to the new environment. If it were not the case, then it would have been very difficult for human to survive for so many thousand years.

Another example can be Y2K problem for computer systems. Those systems, which are not Y2K compliant, will not be able to work properly after year 2000. For computer systems to survive it is important these systems are made Y2K compliant or Y2K ready.

Feed Back

Feedback is an important element of systems. The output of a system needs to be observed and feedback from the output taken so as to improve the system and make it achieve the laid standards. In fig 1.1, it is shown that a system takes input. It then transforms it into output. Also some feedback can come from customer (regarding quality) or it can be some intermediate data (the output of one process and input for the other) that is required to produce final output.

Boundaries and Interfaces

Every system has defined boundaries within which it operates. Beyond these limits the system has to interact with the other systems. For instance, Personnel system in an organization has its work domain with defined procedures. If the financial details of an employee are required, the system has to interact with the Accounting system to get the required details.

Interfaces are another important element through which the system interacts with the outside world. System interacts with other systems through its interfaces. Users of the systems also interact with it through interfaces. Therefore, these should be customized to the user needs. These should be as user friendly as possible.

1.5 WHAT IS AN INFORMATION SYSTEM (UPTU 2010–11)

An **information system** (IS) is any combination of information technology and people's activities using that technology to support operations, management, and decision-making. In a very broad sense, the term information system is frequently used to refer to the interaction between people, algorithmic processes, data and technology. In this sense, the term is used to refer not only to the information and communication technology (ICT) an organization uses, but also to the way in which people interact with this technology in support of business processes. In another words an information system is a system that collects and stores data and a system is a group of interdependent items that interact regularly to perform a task. Information system deals with data of the organizations. The purposes of Information system are to process input, maintain data, produce reports, handle queries, handle on line transactions, generate reports, and other output. These maintain huge databases, handle hundreds of queries etc. The transformation of data into information is primary function of information system.

Information Systems (IS) is an academic/professional discipline concerned with the strategic, managerial and operational activities involved in the gathering, processing, storing, distributing and use of information, and its associated technologies, in society and organizations. As an area of study, IS bridges the multidisciplinary business field and the interdisciplinary computer science field that is evolving toward a new scientific discipline.

As such, information systems inter-relate with data systems on the one hand and activity systems on the other. An information system is a form of communication system in which data represent and are processed as a form of social memory. An information system can also be considered a semi-formal language which supports human decision making and action.

Information systems are the primary focus of study for the information systems discipline and for organizational informatics.

Computer based information system, following a definition of system, is:

- a technologically implemented medium for recording, storing, and disseminating linguistic expressions,
- as well as for drawing conclusions from such expressions.

which can be formulated as a generalized information systems design mathematical program

Geographic Information Systems, Land Information systems and Disaster Information Systems are also some of the emerging information systems but they can be broadly considered as Spatial Information Systems. System development is done in stages which include:

- Problem recognition and specification
- Information gathering
- Requirements specification for the new system
- System design
- System construction
- System implementation
- Review and maintenance

1.6 DIFFERENCES BETWEEN SYSTEM AND INFORMATION SYSTEM (IMPORTANT)

System is the interrelated component that work together for common purpose/goals and Information system is a collection of components that work together to produce useful information for decision making.

1.7 TYPES OF INFORMATION SYSTEMS (EXPECTED)

Information systems are constantly changing and evolving as technology continues to grow.

Information systems differ in their business needs. Also depending upon different levels in organization information systems differ. Three major information systems are

1. Transaction processing systems
2. Management information systems
3. Decision support systems

Figure 1.3 shows relation of information system to the levels of organization. The information needs are different at different organizational levels. Accordingly the information can be categorized as: strategic information, managerial information and operational information.

Strategic information is the information needed by top most management for decision making. For example the trends in revenues earned by the organization are required by the top management for setting the policies of the organization. This information is not required by the lower levels in the organization. The information systems that provide these kinds of information are known as Decision Support Systems.

1.7.1 Transaction Processing Systems

TPS processes business transaction of the organization. Transaction can be any activity of the organization. Transactions differ from organization to organization. For example, take a railway reservation system. Booking, canceling, etc are all transactions. Any query made to it is a transaction. However, there are some transactions, which are common to almost all organizations. Like employee new employee, maintaining their leave status, maintaining employees accounts, etc.

This provides high speed and accurate processing of record keeping of basic operational processes. These include calculation, storage and retrieval.

Transaction processing systems provide speed and accuracy, and can be programmed to follow routines functions of the organization.

1.7.2 Management Information Systems

These systems assist lower management in problem solving and making decisions. They use the results of transaction processing and some other information also. It is a set of information processing functions. It should handle queries as quickly as they arrive. An important element of MIS is database.

A database is a non-redundant collection of interrelated data items that can be processed through application programs and available to many users.

1.7.3 Decision Support Systems (UPTU 2010–11)

These systems assist higher management to make long term decisions. These type of systems handle unstructured or semi structured decisions. A decision is considered unstructured if there are no clear procedures for making the decision and if not all the factors to be considered in the decision can be readily identified in advance.

These are not of recurring nature. Some recur infrequently or occur only once. A decision support system must very flexible. The user should be able to produce customized reports by giving particular data and format specific to particular situations.

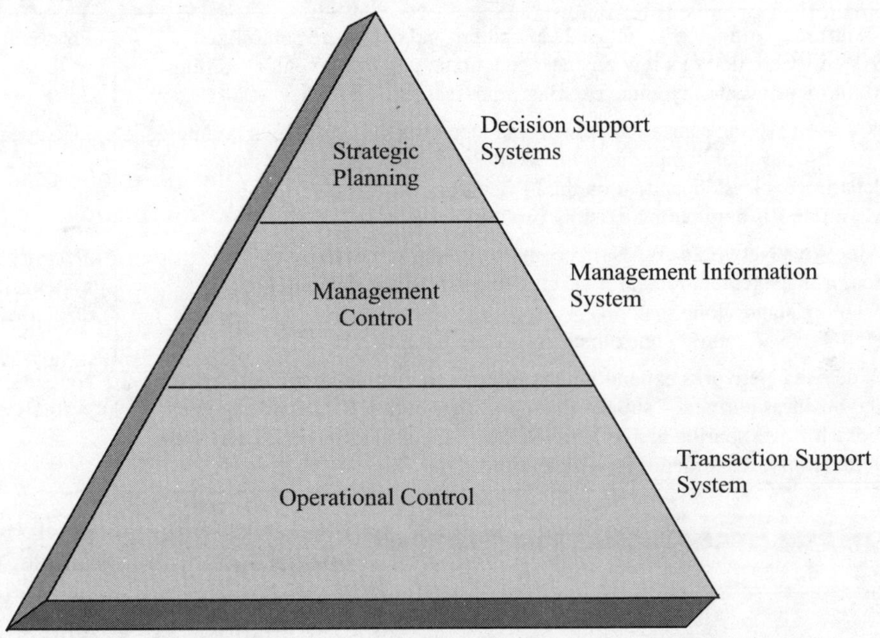

Figure 1.3: Relation of information systems to levels of organization

The second category of information required by the middle management is known as managerial information. The information required at this level is used for making short term decisions and plans for the organization. Information like sales analysis for the past quarter or yearly production details etc. fall under this category. Management information system (MIS) caters to such information needs of the organization. Due to its capabilities to fulfill the managerial information needs of the organization, Management Information Systems have become a necessity for all big organizations. And due to its vastness, most of the big organizations have separate MIS departments to look into the related issues and proper functioning of the system.

The third category of information is relating to the daily or short term information needs of the organization such as attendance records of the employees. This kind of information is required at the operational level for carrying out the day-to-day operational activities. Due to its capabilities to provide information for processing transaction of the organization, the information system is known as Transaction Processing System or Data Processing System. Some examples of information provided by such systems are processing of orders, posting of entries in bank, evaluating overdue purchaser orders etc.

1.8 HISTORY OF INFORMATION SYSTEM

The History of Information Systems in Business

Table 1.1

Year	Main activities	Skills required
1970s	Mainframe computers were used Computers and data were centralized Systems were tied to a few business functions: payroll, inventory, billing Main focus was to automate existing processes	Programming in COBOL
1980s	PCs and LANs are installed networking Departments set up own computer systems End-user computing with Word Processors and Spreadsheets makes departments less dependent on the IT department Main focus is automating existing processes	PC support, basic
1990s	Wide Area Networks (WANs) become corporate standards Senior management looks for system integration and data integration. No more stand-alone systems. Main focus is central control and corporate learning	Network support, systems integration, database administration
2000s	Wide Area Networks expand via the Internet to include global enterprises and business partners – supply chain and distribution Senior management looks for data sharing across systems. Main focus is efficiencies and speed in inventory, manufacturing, distribution	Network support, systems integration

1.9 SUMMARY OF INFORMATION SYSTEMS

Table 1.2

Catagories of Information System	Characteristices
Transaction Processing System	Substitutes computer-based processing for manual procedures.Deals with well-structured processes. Includes record keeping applications.
Management information system	Provides input to be used in the managerial decision process. Deals with supporting well structured decision situations. Typical information requirements can be anticipated.
Decision support system	Provides information to managers who must make judgments about particular situations. Supports decision-makers in situations that are not well structured.

1.10 GLOBAL INFORMATION SYSTEMS (UPTU-2010)

In a global economy, organizations are increasingly selling online in multiple markets, as well as coordinating work teams distributed across geopolitical, cultural, and language boundaries. These factors play an important role in informing the design of effective and appropriate human-computer interfaces. we explore issues in interface localization, and the challenge of designing for multiple markets and audiences. We use a high-speed low cost analysis of different national and linguistic versions of the home pages of Yahoo! and Google to illustrate the power and speed of this approach.

There is a variety of definitions and understandings of a Global Information System (GIS, GLIS), such as

- A global information system (GLIS) is an information system which is developed and / or used in a global context.
- A global information system (GLIS) is any information system which attempts to deliver the totality of measurable data worldwide within a defined context.

Many organizations are exploiting the opportunities of networked technologies to sell their products and services not just in domestic markets but internationally. Just as domestic e-commerce can open up dramatic cost savings and potential for new niches and modes of selling, so too can international e-commerce. While creating immense opportunities for growth and diversification, the resultant pressures from new international competitors are also impelling many organizations to expand not just their sales but also their operations from a domestic to a multinational perspective.

Online systems are especially valuable for multinational organizations whose members are geographically distributed and may be culturally diverse. These online systems can help fill the "structural holes" in networks to get richer information and solve problems more quickly.

But how to design a system that people from many different cultures are able to use and be happy to do so. The fundamental issues are the same whether one is designing public interfaces with which to interact with customers, or the internal system through which the organization's members are to interact with each other. Guided by this strategy, a multi-national organization may develop a "global" system with a standardized user interface, enjoying considerable economies of scale. At its most crude, this would mean a uniform interface in a single language (most likely English) with minor modifications to conform to local legal requirements. This will rarely be feasible. However, a straightforward translation of the interface is unlikely to be sufficient either. The "global system" will probably not be embraced globally because the cultural embeddedness within information systems can not make "one-size-fits-all".

Example 1

McDonald's saying, "One taste, worldwide" evokes the image of a globally standardized system for food preparation and distribution, resulting in a uniform, consistent flavor which ignores variation across cultures; the McDonald's culture is somehow independent of the surrounding environment where its restaurants are located. However, the reality of eating at a McDonald's is quite the opposite; it has adjusted its "recipe to suit varying cultural preferences. As with its different national menus, McDonald's has carefully customized its different national websites to appeal to its user group in each target culture, in order to make sure that its marketing is as effective as possible in different cultural environments . The case of McDonald's illustrates the importance of creating culturally sensitive systems which are capable of adapting to local needs and preferences while adhering to standards of quality and service. However, we must also acknowledge the opportunity costs of providing such diversity compared to a consistent uniform global solution that can enjoy both greater economies of scale and reduce the complexities of synchronizing incremental changes across numerous slightly different manifestations. We will explore that tension in the challenges of developing multiple user interfaces in different cultural contexts.

Specific dimensions of information systems are always based on assumptions inherent in the cultural backgrounds of their designers. If these systems are used by people with cultural backgrounds which differ from those of the designers, features intended to facilitate utilization may actually inhibit this process.

Example 2

With a vision of "one global firm", Accenture tried to use a standard global knowledge

sharing system, but it was less successful in motivating its consultants in East Asia to contribute knowledge than its Western consultants. This was mostly due to the requirement that all contributions be in English, which was off-putting to Asian consultants who felt that their English writing skills were inadequate, or that it was too much work to create perfect English text, or were embarrassed about potential errors. Additionally, it is uncommon for Asians to write something and submit for sharing on a voluntary basis.

Example 3

Japanese employees preferred to wait until instructed directly to contribute their own knowledge because posting something voluntarily is associated with self-promotion and thus it is not an appreciated behavior in Japanese culture. Similarly, when Microsoft released its localized Japanese version of the Windows 3.0 operating system in Japan, it was met with a lukewarm reception and sluggish sales. After studying the work habits and local culture of Japanese users, the completely redesigned Windows 3.1 quickly exceeded the sales of its predecessor. This experience helped Microsoft further build culturally sensitive products which gained rapid adoption in both Chinese and South Korean markets.

1.11 COMPONENTS OF INFORMATION SYSTEMS

The main components of information systems are computer hardware and software, databases, telecommunications systems, human resources, and procedures.

1.11.1 Computer Hardware

The term hardware refers to machinery. This category includes the computer itself, which is often referred to as the central processing unit (CPU), and all of its support equipments. Among the support equipments are input and output devices, storage devices and communications devices. Today even the smallest firms, as well as many households, own or lease computers. These are usually microcomputers, also called personal computers. Large organizations typically employ multiple computer systems, from a few powerful mainframe machines (or even more powerful supercomputers) and minicomputers to widely deployed personal computers. Together with computer peripheral equipment, such as magnetic disks, input-output devices, and telecommunications gear, these constitute the hardware of information systems. The cost of hardware has steadily and rapidly decreased, while processing speed and storage capacity have increased vastly.

1.11.2 Computer Software

The term software refers to computer programs and the manuals (if any) that support them. Computer programs are machine-readable instructions that direct the circuitry within the hardware parts of the CBIS to function in ways that produce useful information from data. Programs are generally stored on some input / output medium-often a disk or tape.

Computer software falls into two broad classes: system software and application software. The principal system software is known as the operating system. It manages the hardware, files, and other system resources and provides a systematic and consistent means for controlling the computer, most commonly via a graphical user interface (GUI). Application software is programs designed to handle specialized tasks; many of these programs are sold as ready-to-use packages. Examples include general-purpose spreadsheet and word processing programs, as well as "vertical" applications that serve a specific industry segment for instance, an application that schedules, routes, and tracks package deliveries.

1.11.3 Databases

Data are facts that are used by program to produce useful information. Like programs, data are generally stored in machine-readable from on disk or tape until the computer needs them.

Many information systems are primarily delivery vehicles for databases. A database is a collection of interrelated data (records) organized so that individual records or groups of records can be retrieved that satisfy various criteria. Typical examples of databases include employee records and product catalogs. Particularly valuable are customer databases that can be "mined" for information in order to design and market new products more effectively. Anyone who has ever purchased something with a credit card in person, by mail order, or over the Web is included within some of the numerous customer databases.

1.11.4 Telecommunications

Telecommunications are used to connect, or network, computer systems and transmit information. Various computer network configurations are possible, depending on the needs of an organization. Local area networks (LANs) join computers at a particular site, such as an office building or an academic campus. Wide area networks (WANs) connect machines located at different sites, and often within different organizations. The Internet is a network of networks, connecting millions of computers located on every continent. Through networking, personal computer users gain access to information resources, such as large databases, and to human resources, such as coworkers and people.

1.11.5 Human Resources and Procedures

1.11.5.1 People

There are many roles for people in information systems. Common ones include

- Systems Analyst
- Programmer
- Technician
- Engineer
- Network Manager
- MIS (Manager of Information Systems)
- Data entry operator

1.11.5.2 Equipment

When you think "equipment", immediately think "Hardware AND Software"

1.11.5.3 Procedures

A procedure is a series of documented actions taken to achieve something. A procedure is more than a single simple task. A procedure can be quite complex and involved, such as performing a backup, shutting down a system, patching software. Qualified people are a vital component of any information system. Technical personnel include development and operations managers, systems analysts and designers, computer programmers, and computer operators. In addition, workers in an organization must be trained to utilize the capabilities of information systems. Hundreds of millions of people around the world are learning about information systems as they use the Web.

Procedures for using, operating, and maintaining an information system are part of its documentation. For example, procedures need to be established to run a payroll program, including when to run it.

1.12 CATEGORIES OF IS

1.12.1 Operational Support

At the operational level are transaction processing systems through which products are designed, marketed, produced, and delivered. These systems accumulate information in databases that form the foundation for higher-level systems.

In today's leading organizations, the information systems that support various functional units marketing, finance, production, and human resources are integrated into what is known as an enterprise resource planning (ERP) system. ERP systems support the entire sequence of activities, or value chain, through which a firm may add value to its goods and services. For example, an individual or other business may submit a custom order over the Web.

1.12.2 Support of Knowledge Work

A large proportion of work in an information society involves manipulating abstract information and knowledge, rather than directly processing, manufacturing, or delivering tangible materials.

Such work is called knowledge work. Three general categories of information systems support such knowledge work: professional support systems, office information systems, and knowledge management systems.

Professional Support Systems

Professional support systems offer the facilities needed to perform tasks specific to a given profession. For example, automotive engineers use computer-aided engineering (CAE) software together with "virtual reality" systems to design and test new models for fuel efficiency, handling, and passenger protection before producing prototypes, and later they use CAE in the design and analysis of physical tests. Biochemists use special three-dimensional modeling software to visualize the molecular structure and probable effect of new drugs before investing in lengthy clinical tests.

Office Information Systems

The main objectives of office information systems are to facilitate communication and collaboration between the members of an organization and to facilitate them between organizations. Placing an organization's documents and messages in an electronic format which can be classified, indexed, and stored for easy retrieval enables individuals to access information on demand. One type of office information system, known as a workflow system, is used to route relevant documents automatically to all appropriate individuals for their contribution. Other types of office information systems handle digital messages in the form of electronic mail, facsimile, and voice mail.

Management Support

Management Reporting Systems

A large category of information systems comprises those designed to support the management of an organization. Those systems rely on data obtained by transaction processing systems, as well as data acquired outside the organization (such as business intelligence gleaned on the Internet) and data provided by business partners, suppliers, and customers.

Information systems support all levels of management, from those in charge of short-term schedules and budgets for small work groups to those concerned with long-term plans and budgets for the entire organization.

Decision Support Systems

All information systems support decision making, however indirectly, but decision support systems are expressly designed for this purpose. The two principal varieties of decision support systems are model-driven and data-driven.

In a model-driven decision support system, a preprogrammed model is applied to a limited data set, such as a sales database for the present quarter. During a typical session, an analyst or sales manager will conduct a dialog with this decision support system by specifying a number of "what-if" scenarios.

Executive Information Systems

Executive information systems make a variety of critical information readily available in a highly summarized and convenient form. Senior managers characteristically employ many informal sources of information, however, so that formal, computerized information systems are of limited assistance. Nevertheless, this assistance is important for the chief executive officer, senior and executive vice presidents, and the board of directors to monitor the performance of the company, assess the business environment, and develop strategic directions for the future.

1.13 ACQUIRING INFORMATION SYSTEMS

Information systems are a major corporate asset, with respect both to the benefits they provide and to their costs. Therefore, organizations have to plan for the long term before acquiring and deploying information systems. On the basis of long-term corporate plans and the requirements of various individuals from data workers to top management, essential applications are identified and project priorities are set. For example, certain projects may have to be carried out immediately to satisfy a new government reporting regulation or to interact with a new customer's information system.

1.13.1 Acquisition from External Sources

There are three principal ways to acquire an information system from outside the organization. The most common method is to purchase or lease a software package that is usually customized internally or by an outside contractor. Instead of an expensive purchase or rental, an organization may decide to use the services of an application service provider (ASP), a firm that makes applications available over the Web.

1.13.2 In-house Development

When an information system is developed internally by an organization, one of two methods is used: life-cycle development or rapid application development (RAD).

Large organizational systems, such as transaction processing systems and management reporting systems, are generally developed and maintained through a systematic process, known as a system life cycle, that consists of six stages: feasibility study, system analysis, system design, programming and testing, installation, and operation and maintenance. The first five stages concern system development proper; the last stage involves long-term exploitation.

1.14 MANAGING INFORMATION SYSTEMS (VERY IMPORTANT)

1.14.1 Information System Infrastructure and Architecture (UPTU 2010–11)

A well-designed information system rests on a coherent foundation that supports modifications as new business or administrative initiatives arise. Known as the information system infrastructure, the foundation consists of core telecommunications networks, databases, software, hardware, and procedures. Managed by various specialists, information systems frequently incorporate the use of general information and telecommunication utilities, such as the Internet. Owing to business globalization, an organization's infrastructure often crosses many national boundaries. Creating and maintaining such a complex infrastructure requires extensive planning and consistent implementation to handle strategic corporate initiatives and transformations.

1.14.2 Organization of Information Services

An information services unit is typically in charge of an organization's information systems. Where information services are centralized, this unit is responsible for planning, acquiring, operating, and maintaining information systems for the entire organization. In decentralized structures the central unit is responsible only for planning and maintaining the infrastructure, while business and administrative specialists provide systems and services for their own units. Additionally, a variety of intermediate organizational forms are possible.

1.15 THE IMPORTANCE OF INFORMATION SYSTEMS

In today's highly technological world, Information in an organization is very important, it is more important, than other assets. The systems and resources processing such Information are also of major importance.

Secondly, ICT Systems have gradually taken over decision making responsibilities from human beings. Increased volumes, changing technology and widening expertise may lead to risks such as the following:

- Loss of data due to accidents, deliberate intervention, etc.
- Loss of confidentiality due to insecure access to information
- High cost of recovery in case of breakdowns
- Inefficient acquisition and development of software applications
- Inefficient use of ICT systems due to lack of training
- Business interruption
- Loss of information integrity

To provide connection and information distribution between employees, to customers and suppliers, and to other third parties while providing protection to sensitive data as required by law or company policy.

Information Systems (IS) have a variety of important functions, ranging from allowing businesses to keep track of customers, products, and trends, to public health organizations keeping track of patients, doctors, medicine, and illnesses.

It is surprising facts that there are many more companies still do not use the Internet. It is even more surprising that some of them are still using their twenty-year-old computer information system.

Company information system is a set of interrelated component that collect, process, store, and disseminate information to support companies' managerial team in decision making, coordinating, controlling, and analyzing.

Upgrading the computer information system is not an option in this technology-driven era; it is a requirement. Companies that use an up-to-date information system to gather, assimilate, and evaluate internal as well as external information are gaining competitive advantage over other firms. Management is quicker to cater to customer's needs and complaints. With the growth of communication networks, there are almost no barriers between the firm's management, employees, customers and suppliers. Networked computing systems have made new modes of work possible.

A sophisticated computer information system enables companies to monitor employees, to keep managers and employees informed, to coordinate activities among divisions, or even to sell their products to customers via the internet. Moreover, in the era of information technology like this, information has become valuable organizational asset just like human resources and inventories.

Furthermore, a good information system can facilitate direct communication between firm and suppliers, manufacturers, dealers, and marketers. Together, they can create a value chain as though they were in one organization.

In the meantime, the widespread use of information freeway is inviting unwelcome threats. Today, companies are plagued by hackers; competitors, thieves, spies, hired agents, or even from disgruntled employees. Therefore, firms have taken measures to safeguard their system such as installing complex computer firewalls to detect hackers or purchasing expensive and advance encryption software.

More and more people are working from their homes nowadays. Information technology has become so sophisticated it allows people to choose to work from home. Teleconferencing and video conferencing enable employees to beam in whenever needed. In addition to that, information technology can allow a firm to reduce costs. Taking Ernst &Young for example, the company has successfully reduced its office space by 2 million square feet by allowing their employees to work from home.

In conclusion, information system enables companies to react, respond, cater, store, retrieve, disseminate, and control their new valuable asset that is information. In the years to come, a good information system within a company will be no longer an option; it will become a compulsory in determining success.

1.15.1 Information is an Asset for Organizations (UPTU 2010-11)

Information is an asset for today's organizations and individuals. Information may be less or more important and very often has a monetary value. The disclosure, improper modification, or unavailability of information may incur expenses (loss) or missed profits for the organization or the individual. Therefore, most organizations and individuals protect information to a certain extent. IT security is the science of protecting information assets from threats. An information asset is an atomic piece of information that has meaning to the organization or the individual. Information assets have an owner. The information assets of a business organization are owned by a business owner, and those of an individual are owned by the actual individual. Organizations delegate the responsibility of protecting information assets to the IT department, the Information Security department, or the Information Risk Management department; individuals typically protect their own resources, but they may interact with other individuals and organizations, and may seek advice or transfer protection responsibilities to other individuals and organizations.

Whoever is managing protection is considered a custodian of the information asset; however, the owner is still responsible for valuating information, posing requirements for information protection, ensuring that information is protected by following defined procedures for information protection and auditing the protection mechanisms in place.

The custodian is responsible for defining security protection mechanisms that meet the requirements of the information owner.

Both organizations and individuals typically have three main requirements to information asset protection:

1. Confidentiality: information protection from disclosure to unauthorized individuals and other organizations.

   Information that represents a patent, a trade secret, most types of military information, or financial information are examples of information that typically needs protection from disclosure. The company payroll information is normally a resource that requires protection from unauthorized disclosure.

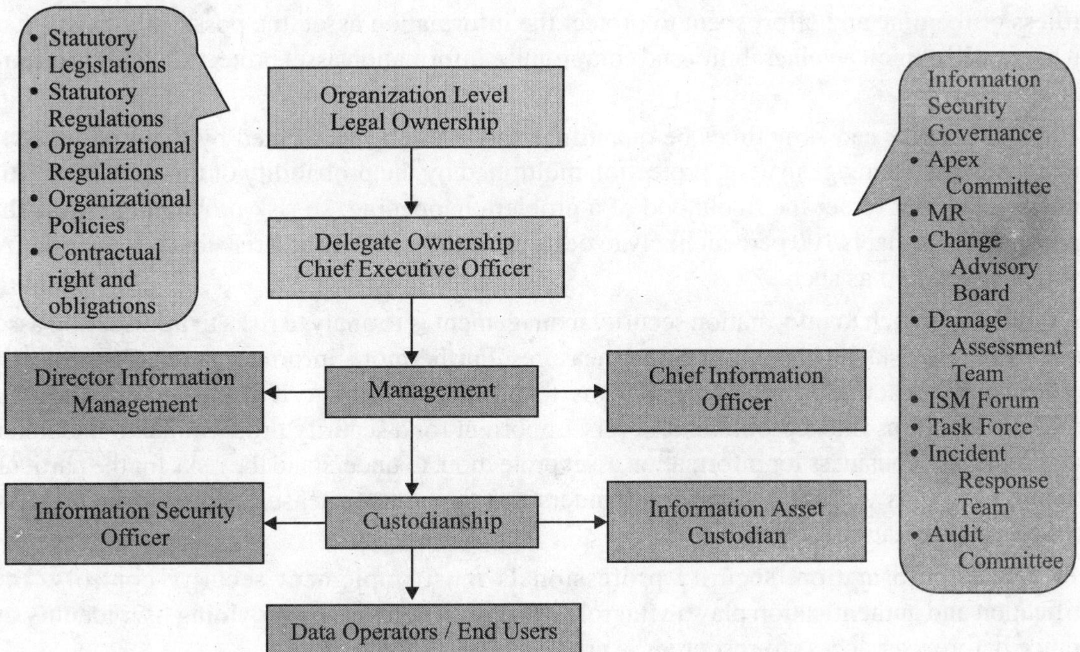

Figure 1.4: Information Asset Management Roles

2. Integrity: information protection from accidental or intentional modification that may affect data validity.

   Financial transactions are a typical example of an information asset that requires integrity protection. If an individual wants to transfer $1000 and someone modifies the amount to $20,000, it does make a difference.

3. Availability: information and services that expose information to organizations and individual users must be available when users need them.

If an online Web banking application uses very secure technologies for user authentication, information encryption, and signing but the site is down and not available to users who need it, then it will hardly meet protection requirements. In an ideal world, a custodian will apply the best technologies in terms of countermeasures to protect confidentiality, integrity, and availability of information assets. However, IT costs money in terms of hardware, software, training, labor, and other resources required to provide protection, confidentiality, integrity, and availability. Targets may be set accordingly so that protection is cost effective in relation to the information asset being protected. Regardless of the level of protection, and mainly due to unclear requirements set by the information asset owners, by failing to implement protection for properly defined requirements, as well as due to hardware, software, and configurations thereof that may have security flaws, information assets may be vulnerable to one or more security threats that will typically compromise information asset confidentiality, integrity, or availability.

Threat agents such as malicious individuals (or attackers) may give rise to threats and exploit vulnerabilities. If vulnerabilities exist in the protection scheme and they are very likely to exist regardless of the time and effort spent to protect the information asset the possibility exists that a threat agent will exploit a vulnerability and compromise information asset protection. This is referred to as risk

The level of risk can sometimes be quantified and is often represented by the product of the value of a potential damage to asset protection multiplied by the probability of this occurring. Risk is not a problem but rather the likelihood of a problem happening, so risk probability is less than 100 percent. A risk that is 100 percent likely to occur is a problem such as a risk that has materialized and should be treated as such.

A typical approach to information security management is to analyze risks to information assets and mitigate these risks by imposing countermeasures. Furthermore, information security protection will also devise reactive (contingency) plans to minimize damage if for some reason a risk materializes and turns into a problem. It is very important for a security professional to understand the requirements of business for information asset protection, to understand the risks for the particular information asset, as well as to devise and understand the countermeasures for information asset protection from threats.

To protect information, security professionals must implement security controls. User identification and authentication play a vital role in security controls by providing user identity and assurance before user access to resources is granted to an individual.

1.16 BENEFITS OF AN INFORMATION SYSTEM

The following are benefits of information systems:

- central access
- easy backup
- central distribution of information
- easy record-keeping
- easy tax preparation
- easy customer trait identification
- Let outline some advantages to start with and we'll go from there... OK!
- Streamline business operations and production.
- Manage mass build-to-order parts.
- Global visibility of plant operations and performance
- Streamline information sharing and collaboration
- Increase efficiency and reduce wastes
- Maintain plant organization and control
- Improve business and production processes
- Reduced Costs
- Increased Quality
- Increased Visibility
- Improved Customer Service and Supplier Responsiveness
- Form or improve your employee benefit system.

1.16.1 Where Information Systems Used

Information system is used in information technology, networks applications and developments. Lets have a brief discussion of each them as given below. Information systems are used in marketing. They are used for computer terminology and computer technology. Marketing is done mainly by computers anymore, so information systems are vital to have. Information systems are an important part of the technology of the 21st Century. The systems keep track of employees, profits, losses, buildings, inventory and any other area of business

1.16.2 Introduction to Information Systems - Technology

The factors influencing information systems engineering. Influential 'Information Systems Development: Methodologies, Techniques and Tools'.

Databases are at the heart of modern commercial application development. Their use extends beyond this to many applications and environments where large amounts of data must be stored for efficient update and retrieval.

1.16.2.1 *Technology*

- Introduction to Computer Hardware.
  - — Computers Systems.
  - — Computer Peripherals.
- Introduction to Computer Software.
  - — Application Software.
  - — System Software.
- Introduction to Database Management..
  - — Database Management.
  - — Technical Foundations of Database Management.

1.16.3 Introduction to Information Systems - Networks

All businesses use telecommunications and the Internet as a matter of course these days, it has become the *norm* and a must for business operations in this day and age.

Are there viable alternatives, if so, how effective would they be within the current market constraints?

1.16.3.1 *Networking*

- Introduction to Business Telecommunications.
  - — Overview of Business Telecommunications and Networks.
  - — Technical Telecommunications Alternatives.
- The Internet and Electronic Commerce.
  - — The Internet and Business.
  - — Fundamentals of Electronic Commerce.
- Intranets, Extranets, and Electronic Collaboration.
  - — Intranets and Extranets in Business.
  - — Enterprise Collaboration Systems.

1.16.4 Introduction to Information Systems - Applications

Information and data storage are crucial to any business operation. The choice of applications to provide such a service seems endless.

Are they worth the cost and time of implementation with the strategic advantage they give?

1.16.4.1 *Applications*

- Information Systems for Business Operations.

— Business Information Systems.

— Transaction Processing Systems.

- Information Systems for Managerial Decision Support.

— Management Information and Decision Support Systems.

— Artificial Intelligence Technologies in Business.

- Information Systems for Strategic Advantage.

— Fundamentals of Strategic Advantage.

— Strategic Applications and Issues in Information Technology.

1.16.5 Introduction to Information Systems - Development

Developing and managing information systems utilizing information technology, making secure and ethical changes to business.

The question of social acceptance to advancing methods of operation on the global scale and the impact it will have.

1.16.5.1 Development and Management

- Developing Business Solutions with Information Technology.

— Developing Information System Solutions.

— Implementing Business Change with Information Technology.

- Enterprise and Global Management of Information Technology.

— Managing Information Resources and Technologies.

— Global Information Technology Management.

- Security and Ethical Challenges of Information Technology.

— Security and Control Issues in Information Systems.

— Ethical and Societal Challenges of Information Technology.

1.17 DIFFERENTIATING IS FROM RELATED DISCIPLINES

Similar to computer science, other disciplines can be seen as both related disciplines and foundation disciplines of IS. But, while there may be considerable overlap of the disciplines at the boundaries, the disciplines are still differentiated by the focus, purpose and orientation of their activities.

In a broad scope, the term **Information Systems** (IS) is a scientific field of study that addresses the range of strategic, managerial and operational activities involved in the gathering, processing, storing, distributing and use of information, and its associated technologies, in society and organizations. The term information systems is also used to describe an organizational function that applies IS knowledge in industry, government agencies and not-for-profit organizations. ***Information Systems*** often refers to the interaction between algorithmic processes and technology. This interaction can occur within or across organizational boundaries. An information system is not only the technology an organization uses, but also the way in which the organizations interact with the technology and the way in which the technology works with the organization's business processes. Information systems are distinct from information technology (IT) in that an information system has an information technology component that interacts with the processes components

What is the difference between examples of information systems and types of information systems?

Types of IS include Transaction Processing Systems (TPS), Management Information Systems (MIS), Decision Support Systems (DSS), Enterprise Resource Planning (ERP) and Customer Relationship Management Systems (CRM).

Examples of IS would be Air Miles making use of CRM to track customer's purchasing history and preferences. As well as a company using the Internet to keep track of transactions coming in over the years.

1.18 LEVELS OF INFORMATION SYSTEM

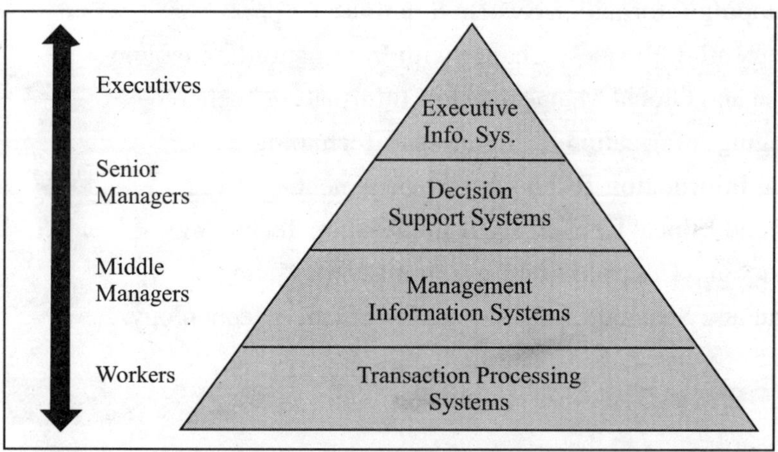

Figure 1.5

1.19 PURPOSE OF INFORMATION SYSTEM

Information system deals with data of the organizations. The purposes of Information system are to process input, maintain data, produce reports, handle queries, handle on line transactions, generate reports, and other output. These maintain huge databases, handle hundreds of queries etc. The transformation of data into information is primary function of information system.

These types of systems depend upon computers for performing their objectives. A computer based business system involves six interdependent elements. These are hardware (machines), software, people (programmers, managers or users), procedures, data, and information (processed data). All six elements interact to convert data into information. System analysis relies heavily upon computers to solve problems. For these types of systems, analyst should have a sound understanding of computer technology.

1.20 BASICS OF IS (IMPORTANT)

The Basics of IS are

1.20.1 Hardware

Hardware is the parts of the information system (i.e. the parts of the computer) which can be touched.

- Peripheral devices
  - — A peripheral devices is any input or output device connected to a computer.
  - — Input devices are components such as a mouse, keyboard, scanner and modem
  - — Output devices are components such as monitors, printers and modems.
- Storage
  - — Storage is crucial for any information system. Without storage we could not save any of our work and this would make an information system next to useless.
  - — There are a range of storage devices including hard drives, optical disks (including CD and DVD), zip drives, floppy drives, magnetic tape
- Processor
  - — The processor is the part of the computer which actually controls the computer and manages the flow of data. This refers to the CPU (central processing system)

1.20.2 Software

- — Software refers to the programs run on the computer.
- — There are two types of software: system software and application software.
- — System software deals with the management of the processes of running the computer such as Windows and Mac OS
- — Application software is used when a specific task is done on the computer such as a word processor, spreadsheet or game program.

- Word processors
  - — Word processors are application programs which allow text editing.

— Many word processors allow users to manipulate graphics and do a number of other tasks as well as writing documents.

- Spreadsheet
  - — A spreadsheet is an application program which allows numerical calculations and the sorting and displaying of numerical data.
  - — A spreadsheet is divided into rows and columns.
  - — Columns run vertically (up and down) just like the Greek columns.
  - — Rows run across
- Database
  - — Databases are application programs which are used to collect, store and process data into information.

1.20.3 Data

— Data is the raw unprocessed facts.

— Data becomes information after it is sorted and organized.

- Data structure
  - — Ways of organizing data is called data structures
  - — Some ways of organizing data is arrays, files and records.
  - — Spreadsheets organize data into rows and columns. One block of information (at the intersection of a row and column is called a cell. Spreadsheets have the same organization as a two dimensional array.
  - — Databases organize information into files, records, fields and entries (flat file database structure)
- Arrays
  - — Array: an array is an arrangement of data into a table like structure similar to a spreadsheet. This is a two dimensional array.
  - — Look at the table below. In cell A3 is d. In A7 is John. Notice with a cell reference the row is said first "A" followed by the column "3" thus we end up with A3.

    Very importantly an array must have the same data type.
- Database
  - — A database will be saved as a file.
  - — Inside that file will be a record which is composed of several fields and each field will contain an entry.
  - — For example in the school database there would be a file with all of the students names. If we chose an individual student to look up we look up the record on that student. The student's name is one field. The address is another field.

1.20.4 Methods of Data Access

- A file can be accessed either directly because we have an address such as in our earlier array or sequentially.
- A sequential file is probably stored in some kind of ascending or descending order but the computer must look at every bit of information in the order in which it is stored until the correct entry is located. Sequential access is very slow.
- A direct access file is located very quickly because the computer uses a form of index and addressing system to locate the correct entry.

1.20.4.1 Data preparation

- Data preparation involves the preparation of data for use in a database.
- This involves its collection, organizing, sorting and data entry into the computer.

1.20.4.2 Data validation

- Data validation takes place when the data is entered into the computer.
- It is normally built into the software and will do a type check or range check of data try to ensure the data is correct.
- For example if I entered my name by mistake where it asked for data of birth, data validation tells the program that it was supposed to be numbers but I have entered text. Likewise if it was expecting 4 numbers but I entered in 7 then the program would know that I have made a mistake.

1.20.4.3 Verification

- Verification of data is part of the maintenance of a database. It is to check that the data is still accurate.
- Have any of the details in the database changed?
- For example: Has a persons address or phone number changed?

1.20.4.4 Data manipulation

- Data manipulation involves the sorting or statistical manipulation of that data to derive other information.
- Data manipulation is one of the key uses for a database or spreadsheet.
- When large databases do this commercially and mine the data for other information held within it this is referred to as "data mining" and is worth a lot of money.

1.20.4.5 Application

- This involves how databases, spreadsheets and other software applications are used in the real world.

1.20.5 Maintaining Data of an Organization

- This involves the entire process of entering new data and making sure that verification of the data in the company system is accurate.
- An organization will use databases to store personnel information and payroll information.
- Data verification is crucial to the successful use of the information system.

1.20.6 Using a Database System

- Database systems are very useful for companies.
- Orders, invoicing, human resources and payroll are probably the main uses that businesses make of information systems.
- An order form will give the details of goods that a company has ordered to buy.
- An invoice will be generated when the goods are delivered.
- Inventory management is another use for an information system. This will keep track of all the property or goods a company has in stock.

1.20.7 People

- People are referred to as users or participants and are a critical element of any information system.
- People design, construct, maintain and operate information systems.
- Unfortunately as information systems become more reliable the number of people required is reducing.

1.20.8 Providers of Information Services

The people directly involved in an information system includes:

- **Systems analysts**: design information systems
- **System managers**: manage the operation of the system.
- **Computer programmers**: create the software the information system uses.
- **Computer operators**: Look after the basic requirements of a computer system. (This is one category of It job which is quickly disappearing as users become more IT literate)
- **Data entry operators**: Enter the data into the system

1.20.9 Users of Information

- Users are those affected by the system. There are three types of users: direct users, indirect users and intermediary users.

- **Direct users**: Direct users are those who will directly interact with the system. They will either enter or retrieve information but either way they will physically be using the system themselves.
- **Indirect users**: They will not directly use the system. When we buy groceries or hire a video the customer does not enter the information into the system.
- **Intermediary Users**: Intermediary user is a direct user who interacts with the information system on behalf of the indirect users. Looking at the video store example again the shop assistant who is the direct user acts as an intermediary user on behalf of the customer who is an indirect user.

1.20.10 Abuse of Information Systems

- Information needs to be safeguarded.
- People will try to "hack" (break into) systems and steal information.
- This activity is not only illegal but is also criminal.
- The information stolen can be sold and then money may be stolen out of people's accounts, credit card details can be used and even people's identities are stolen (people will pretend to be other people).
- Firewalls and a variety of other anti hacking tools are used in an effort to stop hacking.

1.20.11 Reason Why do Organizations Need Information Systems

Computers are essential today. We check our email with it, find answers to questions, watch media, bank and more using computers. There for we need systems that can organize, and serve information when people around the world request it. Servers do the task. Each website has a server. A computer that host the website. When you type google.com the server who host that website receives data from your computer and sends data back. Letting you access the servers data. Thus you see Google's homepage. Without servers there would be no websites.

Information is the life blood of any organization. Damaged or lost data can cause disruptions in normal business activities leading to financial losses, law suits, etc. Information systems, which comprise hardware, software, data, applications, communication and people, help an organization to better manage and secure its critical corporate, customer and employee data.

An information system is also a system but differs from other kinds of systems because its objective is to monitor and document the operations of other systems, which we can call target systems. An information system owes its existence to the target system. For example, production activities would be the target system for a production scheduling information system, human resources would be the target system of a human resource information system, and so on. We could say that every reactive system may have a subsystem that can be considered as an information system whose objective is to monitor and control such a system. The main functions of an information system may be input, processing, output, storage and control at work place.

1.21 CHANGING NATURE OF INFORMATION SYSTEM

In the past decade, the nature of IS has undergone a dramatic change, from mainframe-based IS to client / server computing to today's web-based information system, with the Internet having made the revolution.

The four powerful worldwide changes that have altered the business environment are:

1. Globalization;
2. rise of the information economy;
3. transformation of the business enterprise;
4. emergence of the digital firm.

1.22 FUNCTION OF IS

An Information System (IS) is the system of persons, data records and activities that process the data and information in a given organization, including manual processes or automated processes. Usually the term is used erroneously as a synonym for computer-based information systems, which is only the Information technologies component of an Information System. The computer-based information systems are the field of study for Information technologies (IT); however these should hardly be treated apart from the bigger Information System that they are always involved in.

The focus of Info Systems are on the development of solutions for business problems rather than simply describing them.

Information systems strongly focuses on explaining empirical phenomena of the real world. IS has often been called an "explanation-oriented" approach in contrast to the "solution-oriented" BI approach. IS researchers try to explain why things in the real world are the way they are and conduct a lot of empirical surveys whereas a BI researcher tries to develop IT solutions for problems they have observed or assumed. Academics in BI, for example, are often fond of applying new technologies to business problems and doing feasibility studies by building software prototypes. BI students are also taught this constructive approach. Their ability to not only explain reality, but rather shape it, is what makes them very attractive employees for companies as well as good candidates for entrepreneurs in the business IT field.

We have identified that information systems is an interdisciplinary subject that must be seen as more than just computerized information collection, storage, processing and distribution. However, in order to justify this argument, we must also identify what other functions information systems perform.

We can identify five functions of information systems including the information processing function described earlier.

1.22.1 Information Processing and Usability Function

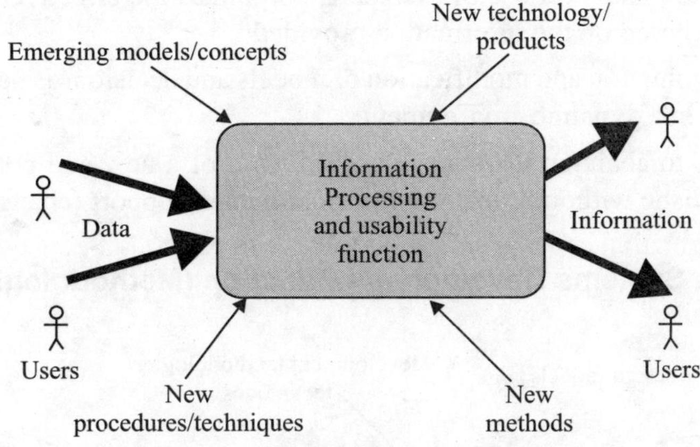

Figure 1.6

1.22.2 Educating and Learning Function

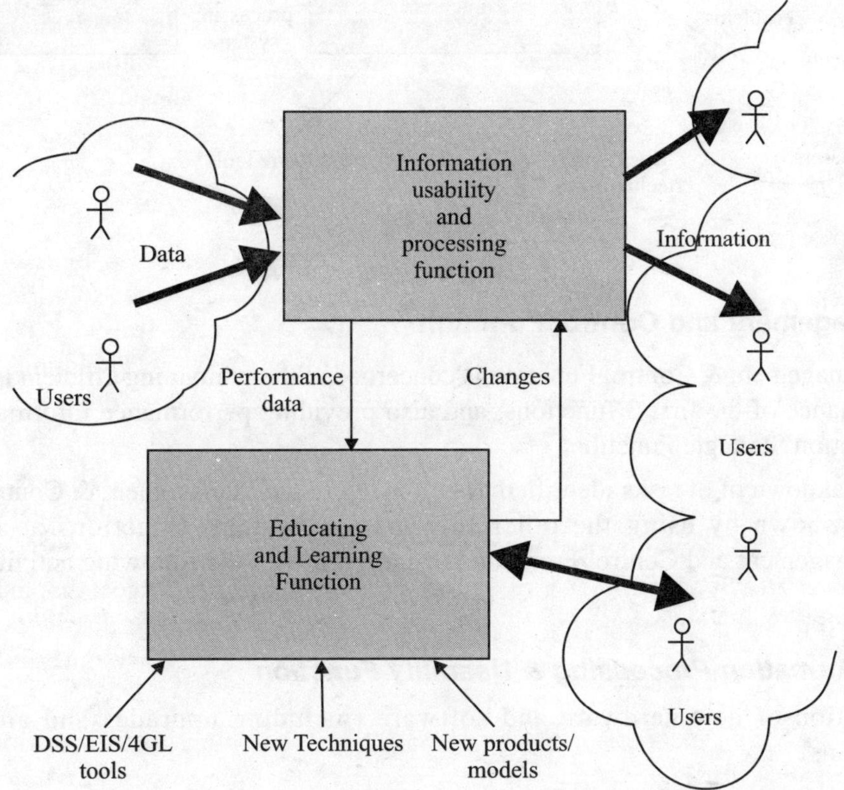

Figure 1.7

- Systems should provide learning opportunities for inexperienced and naive users.
- Enabling users to make best use of systems incorporates the effectiveness of the decision-making process based on the information provided.
- Continuous examination and modification of models and decisions is necessary where users have to operate in a dynamic environment.
- Expecting users to abandon the status quo in favour of a new and potentially threatening system is unrealistic without transition information and support (change management).

1.22.3 Information Systems Development Function (Methodologies)

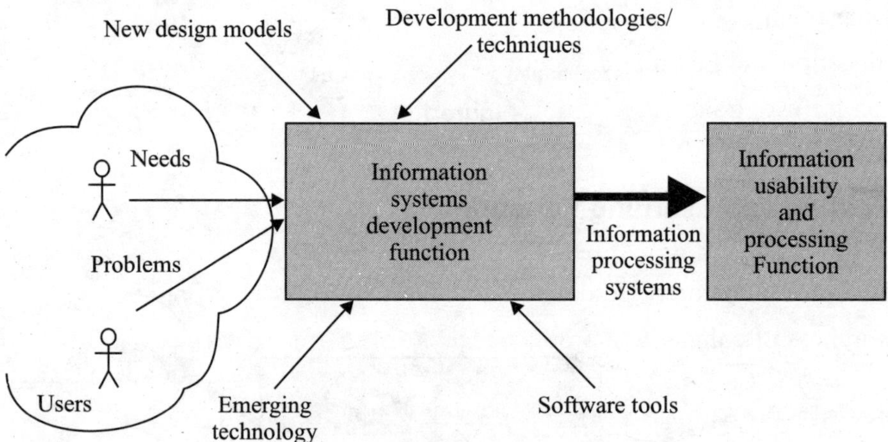

Figure 1.8

1.22.4 Management and Control Function

- The Management & Control Function is concerned with maintaining efficient and effective performance of the first 3 functions, and also providing performance information for the Information Strategic Function.
- The breakdown of of tasks identified as belonging to the Management & Control Function can be shown by using the other Information Systems Functions as heading so the Management and Control Function is concerned with the following activities, relative to the:

1.22.4.1 Information Processing & Usability Function

- acquisition of new hardware and software (including upgrades and amendments/ extensions)
- budget management

- cost analysis
- guidelines and policies (both statutory and permissive)
- supplier and service contracts
- task prioritisation
- quality control, safety standards and service performance
- communication and procedural controls for client and user requests , complaints, revisions and amendments.
- target-setting and monitoring (i.e. MTBF, MTTR, down-time, lead-time, production targets)
- user management
- User Education and Learning Function :
- provision for user training/retraining
- budgetary control
- co-ordination of training effort with requirements of other Information System functions
- timetabling
- promotion/promulgation of guidelines, standards, policies and controls
- user awareness of competitive products, new technology and models

1.22.4.2 Information Systems Development Function

- Project Management
- Policy on performance and delivery targets
- Decisions on standardisation, controls, constraints
- Amendment/upgrade to systems on basis of user feedback, competitive factors, new methods/ technologies, etc.

1.22.5 Strategy & Planning Function

As we have already identified, the Management and Control Function provides performance data to the Information Strategic Function, which in turn provides the Management and Control Function with the strategy by which the system evolves. The relationship is that the Management and Control Function is informed by strategy developed by the Information Strategic Function in relation to the following activities:

- The Manager
- Budgeting Time Constraints
- Production Planning

- Auditing
- Quality Assurance
- Law
- Market Factors
- Competitive Products
- Capital
- Available Manpower
- Skills Distribution
- Technology
- Location
- Infrastructure
- Economic Trends
- Management Techniques

From this list we can see that the Information Strategic Function provides the following necessary facilities for the Information Systems Functional Model:

- Supports corporate strategy
- Executive Information Support
- Comparison of strategic position with marketplace and broader markets
- Aid in development of existing market/product-base and lateral movement
- Aid in deriving corporate strategy
- Altering balance of power with suppliers, competitors, etc
- Identification of new marketplaces, products, approaches, etc.

An information system is strategic if it changes an organizations products or service or the way it competes

- Our consideration of the Information Systems Functional Model leads to the conclusion that the discipline of Information Systems is an interdisciplinary and multi-disciplinary subject. We can identify five specific areas of study :
  1. Information Technology
  2. Information Systems Functions
  3. Organizational Studies
  4. Social Implications of Information Systems
  5. Systems Integration

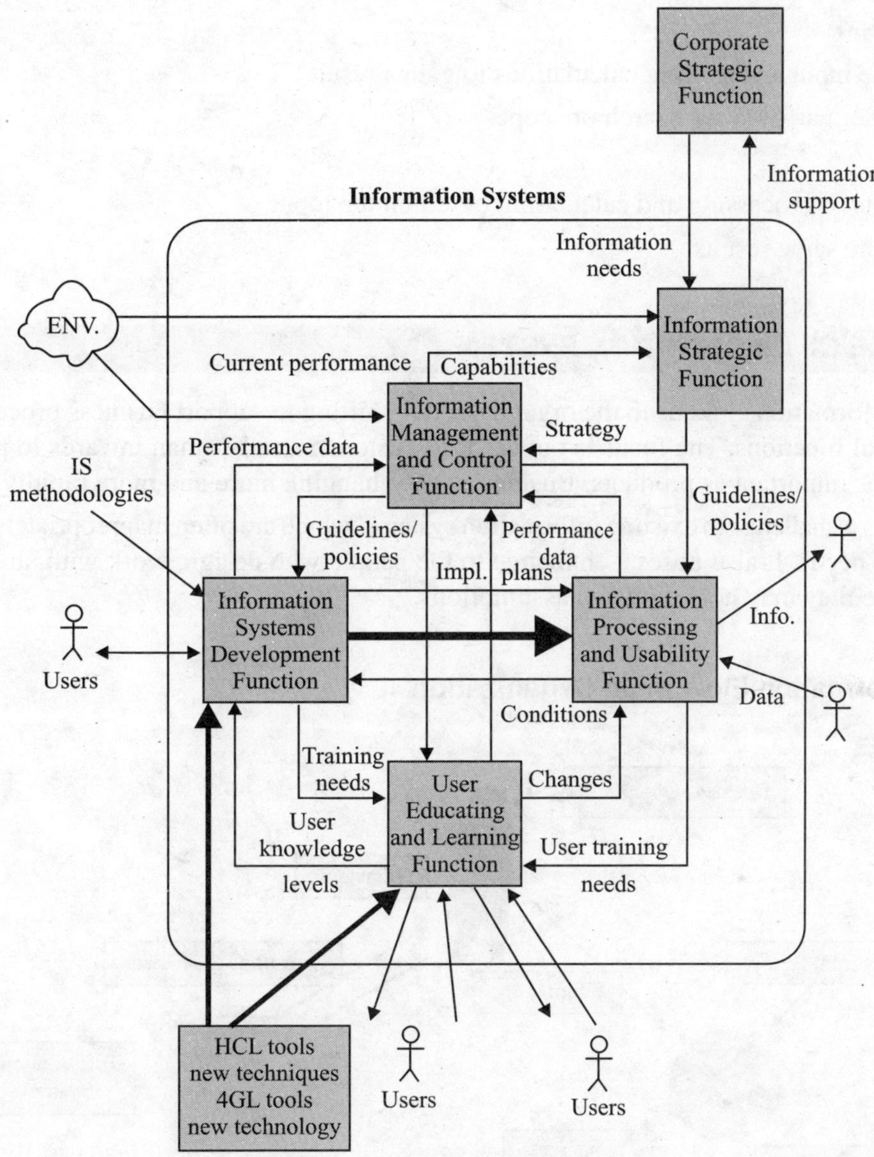

Figure 1.9

1.23 EXAMPLES OF INFORMATION SYSTEMS, INPUTS, OUTPUTS, AND PROCESSING

Input

Data entry

Import from a file that you received via email or FTP

Processing

Taking the input and making calculations to gain a result or to further narrow your search or scope.

Output

The results of processing and calculating based on the input.

Printing the same results.

1.24 ROLE OF INFORMATION SYSTEM

The role of information systems in the organization is shifting to support business processes rather than individual functions. The focus is outwards to customers, rather than inwards to procedures. Services are as important as products. Businesses are changing more and more rapidly.

This poses a challenge to existing information systems, which are often inappropriately structured to meet these needs. It also poses a challenge to the people who design, work with, and use these systems, since they may hold outdated assumptions.

1.24.1 Information Flow in an Organization

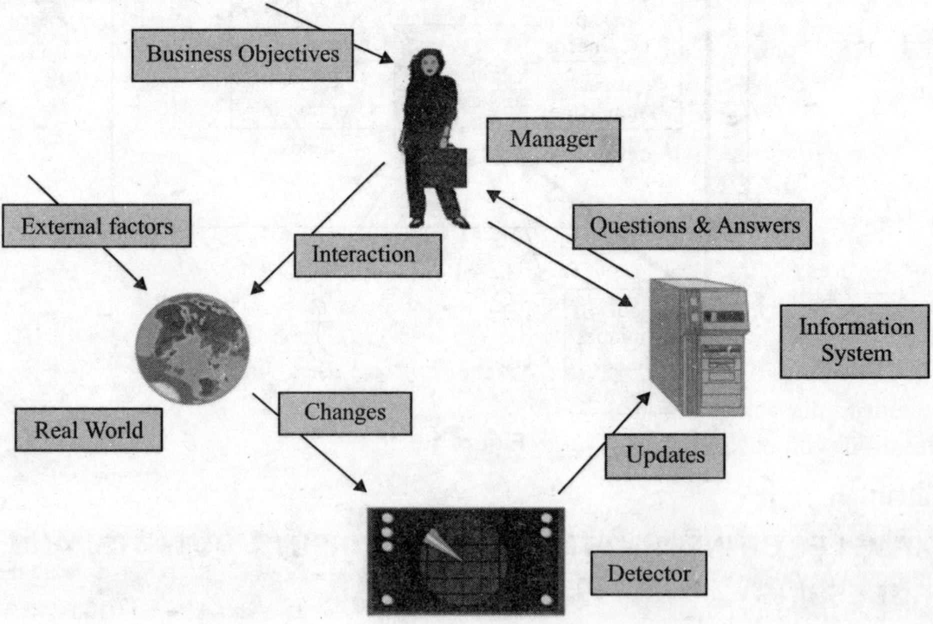

Figure 1.10

1.25 PATTERN OF PROCESSING

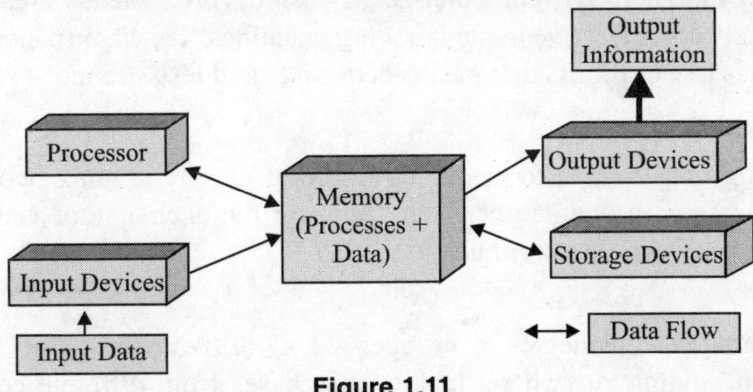

Figure 1.11

1.26 WHERE INFORMATION SYSTEM IS USED

For most businesses, there are a variety of requirements for information. Senior managers need information to help with their business planning. Middle management need more detailed information to help them monitor and control business activities. Employees with operational roles need information to help them carry out their duties.

As a result, businesses tend to have several "information systems" operating at the same time. This revision note highlights the main categories of information system and provides some examples to help you distinguish between them.

1.27 SOME OF THE ADVANTAGES OF INFORMATION SYSTEM (IMPORTANT)

Globalization

IT has not only brought the world closer together, but it has allowed the world's economy to become a single interdependent system. This means that we can not only share information quickly and efficiently, but we can also bring down barriers of linguistic and geographic boundaries. The world has developed into a global village due to the help of information technology allowing countries like Chile and Japan who are not only separated by distance but also by language to shares ideas and information with each other.

Communication

With the help of information technology, communication has also become cheaper, quicker, and more efficient. We can now communicate with anyone around the globe by simply text messaging them or sending them an email for an almost instantaneous response. The internet has also opened up face to face direct communication from different parts of the world thanks to the helps of video conferencing.

Cost effectiveness

Information technology has helped to computerize the business process thus streamlining businesses to make them extremely cost effective money making machines. This in turn increases productivity which ultimately gives rise to profits that means better pay and less strenuous working conditions.

Bridging the Cultural Gap

Information technology has helped to bridge the cultural gap by helping people from different cultures to communicate with one another, and allow for the exchange of views and ideas, thus increasing awareness and reducing prejudice.

More Time

IT has made it possible for businesses to be open 24 x7 all over the globe. This means that a business can be open anytime anywhere, making purchases from different countries easier and more convenient. It also means that you can have your goods delivered right to your doorstep with having to move a single muscle.

Creation of New Jobs

Probably the best advantage of information technology is the creation of new and interesting jobs. Computer programmers, Systems analyzers, Hardware and Software developers and Web designers are just some of the many new employment opportunities created with the help of IT.

1.28 SOME DISADVANTAGES OF INFORMATION SYSTEM (VERY IMPORTANT)

Unemployment

While information technology may have streamlined the business process it has also created job redundancies, downsizing and outsourcing. This means that a lot of lower and middle level jobs have been done away with causing more people to become unemployed.

Privacy

Though information technology may have made communication quicker, easier and more convenient, it has also bought along privacy issues. From cell phone signal interceptions to email hacking, people are now worried about their once private information becoming public knowledge.

Lack of Job Security

Industry experts believe that the internet has made job security a big issue as since technology keeps on changing with each day. This means that one has to be in a constant learning mode, if he or she wishes for their job to be secure.

Dominant Culture

While information technology may have made the world a global village, it has also contributed to one culture dominating another weaker one. For example it is now argued that US influences how most young teenagers all over the world now act, dress and behave. Languages too have become overshadowed, with English becoming the primary mode of communication for business and everything else.

1.29 REASON TO USE INFORMATION SYSTEMS IN BUSINESS TODAY

(UPTU-2010)

Six reasons why information systems are so important for business today include:

1. Operational excellence

2. New products, services, and business models

3. Customer and supplier intimacy

4. Improved decision making

5. Competitive advantage

6. Survival

The emergence of a global economy, transformation of industrial economies, transformation of the business enterprise, and the emergence of digital firm make information systems essential in business today. Information system is a foundation for conducting business today. In many businesses, survival and the ability to achieve strategic business goals is difficult without extensive use of information technology. There are six reasons or objectives why businesses use information system:

1. Operational excellence: Business improve the efficiency of their operations in order to achieve higher profitability. Information systems are important tools available to managers for achieving higher levels of efficiency and productivity in business operations.

Example: Wal-Mart that uses a Retail Link system , which digitally links its suppliers to every one of Wal-Mart's stores. as soon as a customer purchase an item , the supplier is monitoring the item , knows to ship a replacement to the shelf.

2. New products, services, and business models: Information system is a major tool for firms to create new products and services, and also an entirely new business models. A business model describe how a company produces, delivers, and sells a product or service to create wealth.

Example: Apple inc transformed an old business model based on its iPod technology platform that included iPod, the iTunes music service, and the iPhone.

3. Customer/supplier intimacy: When a business serves its customers well, the customers generally respond by returning and purchasing more. this raises revenue and profits. The more a business engage its suppliers, the better the suppliers can provide vital inputs. This lower costs.

Example: The Mandarin Oriental in Manhattan and other high-end hotels exemplify the use of information systems and technology to achieve customer intimacy. they use computers to keep track of guests' preferences, such as their preferred room temperature, check-in time, television programs.

4. Improved decision making: Many managers operate in an information bank, never having the right information at the right time to make an informed decision. These poor outcomes raise costs and lose customers. Information system made it possible for the managers to use real time data from the marketplace when making decision.

Example: Verizon Corporation uses a Web-based digital dashboard to provide managers with precise real -time information on customer complains, network performance.. Using this information managers can immediately allocate repair resources to affected areas, inform customers of repair efforts and restore service fast.

5. Competitive advantage: When firms achieve one or more of these business objectives(operational excellence, new products, services, and business models, customer/supplier intimacy, and improved decision making) chances are they have already achieved a competitive advantage. Doing things better than your competitors, charging less for superior products, and responding to customers and suppliers in real time all add up to higher sales, and higher profits.

Example: Toyota Production System focuses on organizing work to eliminate waste, making continues improvements, TPS is based on what customers have actually ordered.

6. Day to day survival: Business firms invest in information system and technology because they are necessities of doing business. This necessities are driven by industry level changes.

Example: Citibank introduced the first automatic teller machine to attract customers through higher service levels, and its competitors rushed to provide ATM's to their customers to keep up with Citibank. providing ATMs services to retail banking customers is simply a requirement of being in and surviving in the retail banking business. Firm turn to information system and technology to provide the capability to respond to these.

1.30 INFORMATION SYSTEMS FOUNDATION FOR CONDUCTING BUSINESS

Information systems are the foundation for conducting business today. In many industries, survival and even existence without extensive use of IT is inconceivable, and IT plays a critical role in increasing productivity. Although information technology has become more of a commodity, when coupled with complementary changes in organization and management, it can provide the foundation for new products, services, and ways of conducting business that provide firms with a strategic advantage

The business sector produces products and services for profit. Information technology describes any technology used to create, process and disseminate information that is critical to business performance. Information technology is important to the business sector as a management tool to optimize the processing of information to produce goods and services for profit.

1.30.1 Process Improvement

Information technology (IT) includes the management information systems (computers, hardware, software, networks) used to automate and support business tasks and decision-making. IT is used to automate simple, routine tasks such as word processing and advanced processes such as production, scheduling and logistics. In this manner, information technology enables businesses to operate efficiently and profitably.

1.30.2 Cost Reduction

Automation improvements achieved by deploying information technology usually decrease the number of personnel required. Economies of scale gained through the deployment of information technology reduce the overall cost for businesses to produce products and services. This has an overwhelmingly positive effect on the financial goals of a business.

1.30.3 Quality Assurance

Quality assurance entails systematic testing to ensure that a business is producing quality goods and services for its customers. Rigorous quality standards help business outputs meet the required specifications. Quality assurance can be used within processes such as marketing, customer support and accounting, as well as product testing. The effective and efficient processing of information related to achieving quality assurance goals is key to the delivery of quality goods and services to business customers.

1.30.4 Communications

The business sector must communicate internally with its workers and externally with its suppliers and customers on an efficient basis. Information technologies including word processing, publishing software, email, internal computer networks, and the Internet facilitate these communications. Mobile devices including PDAs and Internet-based social media networks are evolving as contemporary information technology platforms for business communications and becoming strategic to the business sector.

1.30.5 Competitive Intelligence

Strategic, competitive advantage plays a fundamental role in the success of a given business within its sector. Information technology has become fundamental to acquiring competitive advantage. The combination of process improvements, cost reductions, communications and quality assurance all contribute to the competitive advantage of a business unit. However, the constant identification and analysis of new risks and opportunities are critical to the ongoing success of a business. Evolving Internet aggregation technologies, including social networks, blogs and subscription databases, are becoming important tools needed to achieve and maintain advantages within the business sector.

1.31 BUSINESS ENVIRONMENT IN IS

There are some points which elaborate the role of IS in business which are as follow:

Support business process and operations: IS helps manager to conduct their daily activities and functions properly. e.g. in bank different activities like account creating, withdrawal of money, statement generation etc take place. IS help mangers to conduct such activities accurately and timely manner with the help of software.

Support decision making for employees and managers: IS can simply be defined as input -> process -> information.

IS takes data as input and processes them and generate information. Managers can use these information for the betterment of their organizations. e.g. IS can analyze existing historical data about customers in bank and generate information's like good customers, bad customers etc. Managers can use this information while deciding to provide loan for new customers.

Support in making strategic decision for competitive advantages: IS can give information like which items to launch in which location by analyzing data collected from different sources such that company can have advantage by using these information over their competitors. IS also can help business houses in conducting their business process differently than their competitors. strategic role is also helpful for the planning of the organisation because through strategic role the future will be planned.

1.32 DISTRIBUTED INFORMATION SYSTEM (UPTU-2010–11)

A distributed system consists of multiple autonomous computers that communicate through a computer network. The computers interact with each other in order to achieve a common goal. A computer program that runs in a distributed system is called a distributed program, and distributed programming is the process of writing such programs.

Distributed computing also refers to the use of distributed systems to solve computational problems. In distributed computing, a problem is divided into many tasks, each of which is solved by one computer.

Distributed does not considers location as an important part. It means that it is stored everywhere. Distributed information system means that for getting any type of information, geographic location is not considered an important part, but what is important is information only and which can be obtained from anywhere and everywhere. Best example is of goggle documents and such like many more. Other examples can be closed- computing which can be used for software as a service.

D/S aims at increasing enterprise productivity reducing IS development cost and enlarging the number of human competencies and skills, which allows not only to share experiences in different cultural environment but also to extend enterprise strategy to the global market.

1.33 NEED OF DISTRIBUTED INFORMATION SYSTEM

Distributed computing is a field of computer science that studies distributed systems. A **distributed system** consists of multiple autonomous computers that communicate through a computer network. The computers interact with each other in order to achieve a common goal. A computer program that runs in a distributed system is called a **distributed program**, and **distributed programming** is the process of writing such programs.

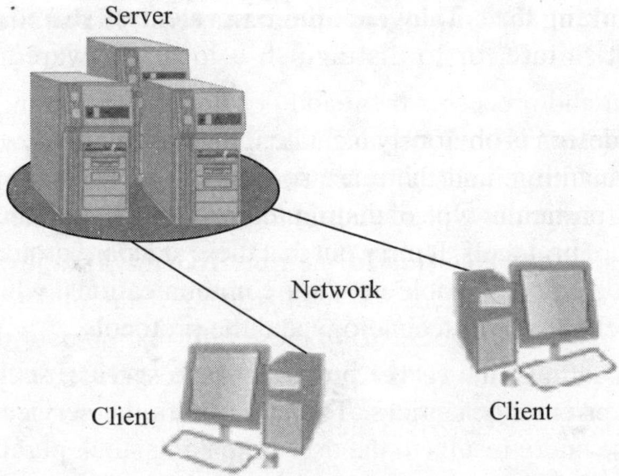

Figure 1.12

Distributed computing also refers to the use of distributed systems to solve computational problems. In distributed computing, a problem is divided into many tasks, each of which is solved by one computer. it is is an application that executes a collection of protocols to coordinate the actions of multiple processes on a network, such that all components cooperate together to perform a single or small set of related tasks.

To be truly reliable, a distributed system must have the following characteristics:

- **Fault-Tolerant:** It can recover from component failures without performing incorrect actions.
- **Highly Available:** It can restore operations, permitting it to resume providing services even when some components have failed.
- **Recoverable:** Failed components can restart themselves and rejoin the system, after the cause of failure has been repaired.
- **Consistent:** The system can coordinate actions by multiple components often in the presence of concurrency and failure. This underlies the ability of a distributed system to act like a non-distributed system.
- **Scalable:** It can operate correctly even as some aspect of the system is scaled to a larger size. For example, we might increase the size of the network on which the system is running. This increases the frequency of network outages and could degrade a "non-scalable" system. Similarly, we might increase the number of users or servers, or overall load on the system. In a scalable system, this should not have a significant effect.
- **Predictable Performance:** The ability to provide desired responsiveness in a timely manner.
- **Secure:** The system authenticates access to data and services

How Is It Done: Building a reliable system that runs over an unreliable communications network seems like an impossible goal. We are forced to deal with uncertainty. A process knows its own state, and it knows what state other processes were in recently. But the processes have no way of knowing each other's current state. They lack the equivalent of shared memory. They also lack accurate ways to detect failure, or to distinguish a local software/hardware failure from a communication failure.

Distributed systems design is obviously a challenging endeavor. How do we do it when we are not allowed to assume anything, and there are so many complexities? We start by limiting the scope. We will focus on a particular type of distributed systems design, one that uses a client-server model with mostly standard protocols. It turns out that these standard protocols provide considerable help with the low-level details of reliable network communications, which makes our job easier. Let's start by reviewing client-server technology and the protocols.

In client-server applications, the *server* provides some service, such as processing database queries or sending out current stock prices. The *client* uses the service provided by the server, either displaying database query results to the user or making stock purchase recommendations to an investor. The communication that occurs between the client and the server must be reliable. That is, no data can be dropped and it must arrive on the client side in the same order in which the server sent it.

There are many types of servers we encounter in a distributed system. For example, *file servers* manage disk storage units on which file systems reside. *Database servers* house databases and make them available to clients. *Network name servers* implement a mapping between a symbolic name or a service description and a value such as an IP address and port number for a process that provides the service.

In distributed systems, there can be many servers of a particular type, e.g., multiple file servers or multiple network name servers. The term *service* is used to denote a set of servers of a particular type. We say that a *binding* occurs when a process that needs to access a service becomes associated with a particular server which provides the service. There are many binding policies that define how a particular server is chosen. For example, the policy could be based on locality (a Unix NIS client starts by looking first for a server on its own machine); or it could be based on load balance (a CICS client is bound in such a way that uniform responsiveness for all clients is attempted).

A distributed service may employ *data replication*, where a service maintains multiple copies of data to permit local access at multiple locations, or to increase availability when a server process may have crashed. *Caching* is a related concept and very common in distributed systems. We say a process has cached data if it maintains a copy of the data locally, for quick access if it is needed again. A *cache hit* is when a request is satisfied from cached data, rather than from the primary service. For example, browsers use document caching to speed up access to frequently used documents.

Caching is similar to replication, but cached data can become stale. Thus, there may need to be a policy for validating a cached data item before using it. If a cache is actively refreshed by the primary service, caching is identical to replication.

As mentioned earlier, the communication between client and server needs to be reliable. You have probably heard of *TCP/IP* before. The Internet Protocol (IP) suite is the set of communication protocols that allow for communication on the Internet and most commercial networks. The Transmission Control Protocol (TCP) is one of the core protocols of this suite. Using TCP, clients and servers can create connections to one another, over which they can exchange data in packets. The protocol guarantees reliable and in-order delivery of data from sender to receiver.

The IP suite can be viewed as a set of layers, each layer having the property that it only uses the functions of the layer below, and only exports functionality to the layer above. A system that implements protocol behavior consisting of layers is known as a *protocol stack*. Protocol stacks can be implemented either in hardware or software, or a mixture of both. Typically, only the lower layers are implemented in hardware, with the higher layers being implemented in software.

There are four layers in the IP suite:

1. **Application Layer:** The application layer is used by most programs that require network communication. Data is passed down from the program in an application-specific format to the next layer, then encapsulated into a transport layer protocol. Examples of applications are HTTP, FTP or Telnet.
2. **Transport Layer :** The transport layer's responsibilities include end-to-end message transfer independent of the underlying network, along with error control, fragmentation and flow control. End-to-end message transmission at the transport layer can be categorized as either *connection-oriented* (TCP) or *connectionless* (UDP). TCP is the more sophisticated of the two protocols, providing reliable delivery. First, TCP ensures that the receiving computer is ready to accept data. It uses a three-packet handshake in which both the sender and receiver agree that they are ready to communicate. Second, TCP makes sure that data gets to its destination. If the receiver doesn't acknowledge a particular packet, TCP automatically retransmits the packet typically three times. If necessary, TCP can also split large packets into smaller ones so that data can travel reliably between source and destination. TCP drops duplicate packets and rearranges packets that arrive out of sequence.

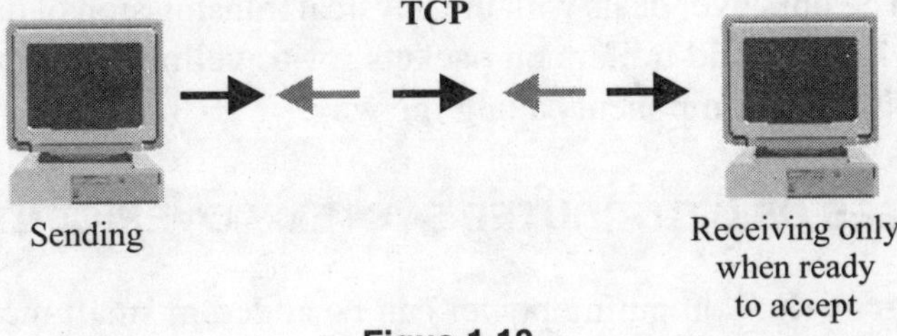

Figue 1.13

UDP is similar to TCP in that it is a protocol for sending and receiving packets across a network, but with two major differences. First, it is connectionless. This means that one program can send off a load of packets to another, but that's the end of their relationship. The second might send some back to the first and the first might send some more, but there's never a solid connection. UDP is also different from TCP in that it doesn't provide any sort of guarantee that the receiver will receive the packets that are sent in the right order. All that is guaranteed is the packet's contents. This means it's a lot faster, because there's no extra overhead for error-checking above the packet level. For this reason, games often use this protocol. In a game, if one packet for updating a screen position goes missing, the player will just jerk a little. The other packets will simply update the position, and the missing packet - although making the movement a little rougher - won't change anything.

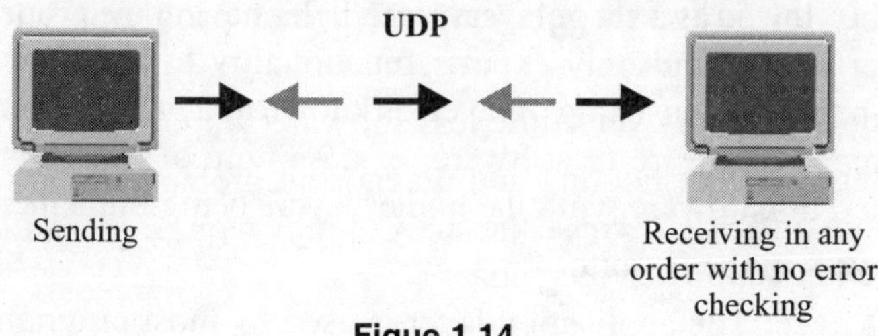

Figue 1.14

Although TCP is more reliable than UDP, the protocol is still at risk of failing in many ways. TCP uses acknowledgements and retransmission to detect and repair loss. But it cannot overcome longer communication outages that disconnect the sender and receiver for long enough to defeat the retransmission strategy. The normal maximum disconnection time is between 30 and 90 seconds. TCP could signal a failure and give up when both end-points are fine. This is just one example of how TCP can fail, even though it does provide some mitigating strategies.

3. **Network Layer:** As originally defined, the Network layer solves the problem of getting packets across a single network. With the advent of the concept of internetworking, additional functionality was added to this layer, namely getting data from a source network to a destination network. This generally involves routing the packet across a network of networks, example the Internet. IP performs the basic task of getting packets of data from source to destination.
4. **Link Layer :** The link layer deals with the physical transmission of data, and usually involves placing frame headers and trailers on packets for travelling over the physical network and dealing with physical components along the way.

1.34 ADVANTAGES OF DISTRIBUTED SYSTEMS OVER CENTRALIZED ONES

1. **Incremental growth:** Computing power can be added in small increments
2. **Reliability:** If one machine crashes, the system as a whole can still survive
3. **Speed:** A distributed system may have more total computing power than mainframe
4. **Open system:** This is the most important point and the most characteristic point of a distributed system. Since it is an open system it is always ready to communicate with other systems. an open system that scales has an advantage over a perfectly closed and self-contained system.
5. **Economic:** Microprocessors offer a better price/performance than mainframes

1.35 DISADVANTAGES OF DISTRIBUTED SYSTEMS OVER CENTRALIZED ONES

1. Distributed systems will have an inherent security issue.
2. **Networking:** If the network gets saturated then problems with transmission will surface.
3. **Software:**There is currently very little less software support for Distributed system.
4. **Troubleshooting:** Troubleshooting and diagnosing problems in a distributed system can also become more difficult, because the analysis may require connecting to remote nodes or inspecting communication between nodes.

To design distribute system we would do the following:

1. Distributed users always pose a threat to be exposed by hackers. Therefore i will create groups of users and will provide them constrained access to data.
2. Authentication required by all users who use the system.
3. Encryption..that is for message protection,
4. The whole Domain is also to be protected via firewalls..so i would install good Firewalls.
5. Would install good anti viruses on my machines which are a part of the distributed system, as these systems are prone to the domino effect that is if one system gets effected the whole network will be susceptible to becoming effected.
6. **Design:** As far as possible we'll keep the design simple and as local as possible. will probably use a virtual private network. Will use machines that are compatible with each other. Will enforce secure access on all users.will probably save the most important, the database on another well equipped machine so that it has a system that is only dedicated to look after the database.

1.36 ROLE OF INTERNET AND WEB SERVICES (UPTU-2010–11)

1.36.1 What is Web

Web, is a system of interlinked hypertext documents accessed via the Internet. With a web browser, one can view web pages that may contain text, images, videos, and other multimedia and navigate between them by via hyperlinks.

1.36.2 Web Services

The term Web services describes a standardized way of integrating Web-based applications using the XML, SOAP, WSDL and UDDI open standards over an Internet protocol backbone. XML is used to tag the data, SOAP is used to transfer the data, WSDL is used for describing the services available and UDDI is used for listing what services are available. Used primarily as a means for businesses to communicate with each other and with clients, Web services allow organizations to communicate data without intimate knowledge of each other's IT systems behind the firewall.

Unlike traditional client/server models, such as a Web server/Web page system, Web services do not provide the user with a GUI. Web services instead share business logic, data and processes through a programmatic interface across a network. The applications interface, not the users. Developers can then add the Web service to a GUI (such as a Web page or an executable program) to offer specific functionality to users.

Web services allow different applications from different sources to communicate with each other without time-consuming custom coding, and because all communication is in XML, Web services are not tied to any one operating system or programming language. For example, Java can talk with Perl, Windows applications can talk with UNIX applications. Web services do not require the use of browsers or HTML. Web services are sometimes called application services.

1.36.3 Reason to Use Web Services

There are two main reasons to use web services, both remarkably straightforward: someone else has information you require, or you have information you wish to provide to others. When planning a new web service, remember that servers can either provide or accept information. Remember that web services can provide any level of security, from a completely open service open to all who request it, to a private service with transfers happening over SSL and client-side certificates to validate identities.

1.36.4 Convincing the Boss

Here are a few more tidbits that should help convince the boss (or you) that web services are a route to look into:

- Web services make use of technology you already have deployed you already have a web server, you already have a database, and so on. Why not provide another way to access the data?
- Web services fit into the security scheme you are already employing. Careful deployment will keep security concerns in line with regular web access.
- Technically savvy users will find a way to access the information they desire. Without web services they will need to resort to methods like screen scraping, which is more difficult to control and can be unreliable (and providing unreliable access to your information is worse than providing none at all).
- Web services can help manage costs; easy integration with companies (like FedEx) that offer services to you can result in lower variable costs for your transactions.
- Web services will allow your business to scale; allowing clients to integrate their systems with yours will help encourage continued relationships, and avoid devoting resources to creating systems for specific clients.

1.36.5 Role of Internet

With the use of internet, it is possible to transmit/receive information containing images, graphics, sound and videos. ISP industry can offer services as:

- Linking consumers and businesses via internet.
- Monitoring/maintaining customer's Web sites.
- Network management/systems integration.
- Backbone access services for other ISP's.
- Managing online purchase and payment systems.

The internet is designed to be indefinitely extendible and the reliability of internet primarily depends on the quality of the service providers' equipments.

1.36.5.1 Benefits of Internet

- Doing fast business.
- Trying out new ideas.
- Gathering opinions.
- Allowing the business to appear alongside other established businesses.
- Improving the standards of customer service/support resource.
- Supporting managerial functions.

1.36.5.2 Limitations

- Security
- Privacy

Threats: Hackers, viruses etc.

1.37 INFORMATION SYSTEM THREATS AND ATTACKS DEFINED

(UPTU-2010)

Modern computer systems, linked by national and global networks, face a variety of threats and attacks that can result in significant financial and information losses. These threats vary considerably, from threats to data integrity resulting from accidental, unintentional errors and omissions to threats from malicious hackers attempting to crash a system. (See Figure 1.15)

1.37.1 Threats

Threats can be seen as potential violations of security and exist because of vulnerabilities, i.e. weaknesses, in a system. Computer systems are vulnerable to many threats, which can inflict various types of damage resulting in significant losses. There are two basic types of threats: accidental threats that result in either an exposure of confidential information or cause an illegal system state to occur and attacks that are intentional threats.

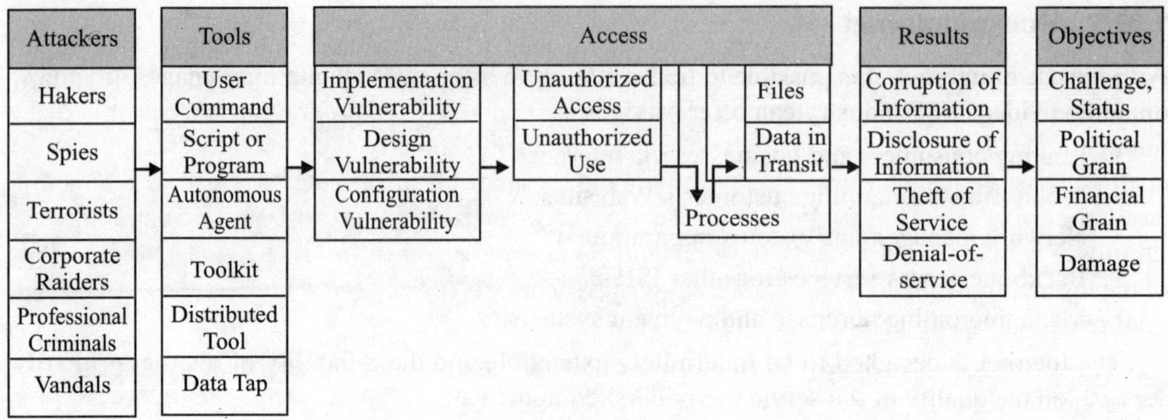

Figue 1.15

The most serious virus threat in terms of mobile security would be a self-replicating virus - a worm. Such malicious code is able to infect a large number of systems extremely quickly, disrupting the functioning of mobile networks or transforming a mobile network into a widely distributed network controlled by a malicious user.

We currently know of two worms (without including modifications) modified variants into account for mobile phones: Worm.SymbOS.Cabir, where the propagation algorithm exploits Bluetooth technology, and Worm.SymbOS.Comwar, which replicates via both Bluetooth and MMS. A detailed analysis of these worms can be found in the Virus Encyclopaedia, but here we will confine ourselves to an examination of their self-replication mechanisms.

Bluetooth is a technology used for wireless transmission of data, which was developed in 1998. It is currently widely used to exchange data between a wide range of devices - telephones and telephone accessories, PDAs and desktops and other hardware. Bluetooth connections normally function within a range of 10 to 20 meters, can be transmitted through physical objects, such as walls, and offer a theoretical transmission speed of up to 721 Kbytes a second.

Worm.SymbOS.Cabir uses Bluetooth technology as it is meant to be used i.e. it does not exploit any vulnerability. When launched, it starts to scan the surrounding area, searching for other Bluetooth devices which are in discoverable mode, and then transmit data - in this case a copy of the worm - in the form of an SIS archive. Regardless of which operating system is installed on the telephone under attack, the screen will show notification of an incoming file and asks if the file should be accepted. If the user answers yes, the file will be saved in memory and automatically launched for execution. The system for installing SIS files will ask the user to confirm that installation should be carried out, and the worm will be installed to the system only once this confirmation has been received. The worm then starts a new cycle of scanning and infecting nearby devices. Users of Windows Mobile can download this file, but it represents no threat as the worm functions only under Symbian. There is also no threat to cars' on-board computers which run Symbian OS: research has been conducted which shows it is impossible to infect these systems with a Bluetooth worm.

1.37.2 Accidental Threats

Accidental threats to security can be generated by system malfunctions, bugs in software or operational mistakes. Users, data entry clerks, system operators, and programmers frequently make unintentional errors, which contribute to security problems, directly and indirectly. Sometimes the error (such as a data entry error or a programming error) results in a system to crash while in other cases, the errors create vulnerabilities. These exposures can emerge from both hardware and software failures as well as from user and operational mistakes, and result in a violation of the confidentiality of the information or resource. For e.g., a threat to security could occur if a confidential or important mail reaches a wrong person unintentionally.

Threats by the ways of errors can occur in all phases of the system life cycle. Programming and development errors, often called bugs, range in severity from benign to catastrophic. Installation and maintenance errors can also cause security problems. These errors and omissions are important threats to data integrity. In the past decade, software quality has improved reducing this threat, yet there are instances when even the most sophisticated programs and software have failed.

Another instance of accidental loss can be the loss of supporting infrastructure that includes power failures, loss of communications, water outages and leaks, sewer problems, fire, flood, civil unrest, strikes, and so forth. These losses include events such as World Trade Center attacks and the Chicago tunnel flood along with other common events such as a broken water pipe. A loss of infrastructure often results in system downtime and loss of information and resources.

1.37.3 Type of Attacks

An attack is an intentional threat and is an action performed by an entity with the intention to violate security. Examples of attacks are destruction, modification, fabrication, interruption or interception of data. An attack is a violation of data integrity and often results in disclosure of information, a violation of the confidentiality of the information, or in modification of the data. An attacker can gain access to sensitive information by attacking in several steps, where each step involves an illegal access to the system. An intentional threat can be caused by an insider or outsider, can be a spy, hacker, corporate raider, or a disgruntled employee.

Any attack on the security of a system can be a direct and indirect attack. A direct attack aims directly at the desired part of the data or resources. Several components in a system may be attacked before the intended (final) information can be accessed. In an indirect attack, information is received from or about the desired data/resource without directly attacking that resource. Indirect attacks are often troublesome in database systems where it is possible to derive confidential information by posing indirect questions to the database. Such an indirect attack is often called inference.

1.37.4 Passive Attacks

Passive attacks are made by monitoring a system performing its tasks and collecting information. In general, it is very hard to detect passive attacks since they do not interact or disturb normal system functions. Monitoring network traffic, CPU and disk usage, etc are examples of passive attacks. Encryption of network traffic can only partly solve the problem since even the presence of traffic on a network may reveal some information. Traffic analysis such as measuring the length, time and frequency of transmissions can be very valuable to detect unusual activities.

1.37.5 Active Attack

An active attack changes the system behavior in some way. Examples of an active attack can be to insert new data, to modify, duplicate or delete existing data in a database, to deliberately abuse system software causing it to fail and to steal magnetic tapes, etc. A simple operation such as the modification of a negative acknowledgment (NACK) from a database server into a positive acknowledgment (ACK) could result in great confusion and/or damage. Active attacks are easier to detect if proper precautions are taken.

1.37.6 Covert Channels

A Covert channel is a simple and an effective mechanism for sending and receiving information data between machines without alerting any firewalls and IDS's on the network. It is an unprotected channel that can be used to send confidential information to unauthorized entities and thereby violate security. In general, it is very hard to identify covert channels in a system since they can be of many different types:

- Message length variations during transmissions
- Time and length of transmissions
- Presence and size of files
- Creation time for objects
- Modulation of disk usage
- CPU time usage, etc.

This technique derives its stealthy nature from the fact that it sends traffic through ports that most firewalls permit through. In addition, it can bypass an IDS by appearing to be an innocuous packet carrying ordinary information (when in fact it is concealing its actual data in one of the several control fields in the TCP and IP headers). Mandatory encryption of communication does not prevent the use of a covert channel by any entity to send information to another entity. Covert channels can further be classified as timing channels and storage channels. Timing channels are those covert channels that modulate a resource in time, while storage channels are those channels where actions like creation of objects reveal information to other entities.

It is very hard to completely eliminate covert channels in a system. A covert channel with a high bandwidth constitutes a higher threat than a covert channel with a low bandwidth; so most security mechanisms try to reduce the bandwidth of these channels as much as possible. Even a covert channel with a bandwidth as low as 100 baud is in some environments considered to be dangerous. However, actions to limit covert channel bandwidths always limit system performance.

For example, in order to avoid the length of messages from being used as an information carrier, all messages can be forced to be of equal length. The problem with this method is that it reduces the available bandwidth of the network as well.

1.37.7 Dealing with Attacks

To deal with any sort of threat or attack on the security of computers, there must be proper security mechanisms in place. Security mechanisms are method, tool, or procedure used to implement the rules stated in the security policy. By specifying "secure" and "non-secure" actions in the security policies, these security mechanisms can help in preventing, detecting and recovering from any attack. The strategies may be used together or separately. Security mechanisms can be classified as: prevention, detection and recovery mechanisms. Within each group, there are many security mechanisms available, where each mechanism focuses on a specific kind of threat and deals with a specific form and aspect of security.

A security prevention mechanism is one that enforces security during the operation of a system by preventing a security violation from occurring. For example restricting physical access to servers, machines or the use of access control mechanisms based on encryption to prevent unauthorized users from accessing objects, etc. Usually prevention involves implementation of mechanisms that users cannot override and that are trusted to be implemented in a correct, unalterable way, so that the attacker cannot defeat the mechanism by changing it. Preventative mechanisms are often very cumbersome and interfere with system use to the point that they hinder normal use of the system. However, some simple prevention mechanisms, such as passwords (to prevent unauthorized users from accessing the system), have become widely accepted.

A detection mechanism is used to detect both attempts to violate security and successful security violations, when or after they have occurred in a system. The goal of the detection mechanism is to determine that an attack is underway, or has occurred, and report it. Alarms can be used to detect unauthorized physical accesses and audit trails can be used to detect unusual system activities after they have occurred. Typical detection mechanisms monitor various aspects of the system, looking for actions or information indicating an attack. A good example of such a mechanism is one that gives a warning when a user enters an incorrect password three times. The login may continue, but an error messages in a system log reports the unusually high number of mistyped passwords. The resources protected by the detection mechanism must be monitored continuously or periodically.

A recovery mechanism is for restoring the system to a pre-security violation state and is normally used after a security violation has been detected. For example if the attacker deletes a file, a recovery mechanism could be to restore the file from backup tapes. Practically, recovery is far more complex due to the unique nature of each attack. Moreover, the attacker may return, so recovery involves identification and fixing of the vulnerabilities used by the attacker to enter the system. In some cases, retaliation (by attacking the attacker's system or taking legal action) is part of recovery.

It is also possible to make mechanisms that belong to several of these categories. A program registering all unusual system activities and thus working as a detection mechanism, may also prevent security breaches from occurring simply because it exists. In a system with a total lack of vulnerabilities and where the security prevention mechanisms fully implement all rules stated in the security policy, there would be no need for detection and recovery mechanisms.

Below are few techniques or tools that will help in implementing these security mechanisms.

1.37.8 Physical Access Security

The first line of defense locally to protect network equipment such as servers, switches, and routers is to keep them in a locked, climate controlled, and fire protected environment. If equipment is not physically accessible to unauthorized personnel, there is less chance of accidental or intentional tampering. It is important that access to critical system components such as the server is restricted to a small number of individuals (usually the administrator and his backup). The server should be located in a locked room to which access is restricted. Other considerations should include protection of equipment against theft, fire, and electrical hazards.

1.37.9 Login / Password Security

One of the main computer security elements is login names and passwords. Every system uses some form of password authentication and therefore must store a representation of the password in order to check whether a logon attempt is valid. Login and password security policy require that any user accessing a workstation or server have a valid login ID and password. Windows NT, Windows 2000, Windows XP, Novell Netware, and UNIX all have specific requirements for creating and changing passwords. The system administrator can also require that passwords be changed periodically. Setting screen savers that time out and activate the workstation lock are additional measures that enhance login security. If hardware manufactures supports, one can also set a NetBios password. This password is hardware dependent, less trivial to bypass than other passwords and comes up before an interloper has access to anything.

It has been common knowledge for quite some time that login names and password authentication schemes are inherently weak. Users usually choose bad passwords (i.e., ones that can easily be guessed), write passwords down, and mail passwords to co-workers or share passwords freely by telephone. For this reason, high security environments do not rely on password authentication alone, but combine password security with smart cards or biometrical authentication systems (finger, voice or eye iris scan).

1.37.10 Anti-Virus Software

In last few years, with the extensive use of the Internet, networks, and email, computers have become more vulnerable to virus attacks and threats. A virus can spread any time files are shared on a local system or the Internet and can do tremendous damage to individual PCs and network servers. Therefore, an early detection and prevention mechanism is very important for the security of the computer. Using antivirus software is a good way to detect viruses and it is advisable to use antivirus software on network operating systems and workstations for adequate protection.

Antivirus software is a program that searches the computer systems for any known or potential viruses. Antivirus programs are intended to prevent and detect viruses. Antivirus software may work differently and ranges from large security packages to small programs designed to handle a specific virus. While some software are designed to scan hard disks and floppy disks for infected programs, others check for any changes in files and alert the user if there are changes, which might indicate an infection. Antiviruses are very helpful in detecting viruses that are already in a system or that are attempting to enter a system and alerting the user to take action. Anti-viral software can be set up to run automatically each time a computer boots or run an executable. And antivirus software can be executed manually in case of a virus attack or threat.

1.37.11 Remote Access Security

Remote access means using any of the resources of a network (file server, printers, workstations) from a remote location-that is, a location not directly attached to the network. Remote access presents particular security risks of unauthorized system access. In remote access, the remote computer takes over a computer connected to the network and operates that computer remotely. Actual data traffic remains on the network between the PC that is being controlled and the rest of the network. Only screen images, keystrokes, and mouse motion are sent across the remote link. In a remote access, as the remote user is invisible, any formal or informal security measures operating at the workplace is not effective. The remote user has access not only to network resources, but also to local resources on the controlled workstation.

Simple password protection is not at all reliable for remote access systems. Over the modem all users are equally unknown. And also remote access typically occurs during off hours when the intruder has plenty of time to experiment, try multiple passwords and avenues of access, all unnoticed. Some systems erect extensive barriers to penetration, including modem access to a limited set of programs and files. A system with external access is, however, never fully secure against smart intruders. External access can be restricted by means of automatic callback systems. With such systems users must provide the system with pre-authorized telephone numbers from which they can call the system. Under this mechanism when a user calls and identifies him to the system, the system calls him back at one of the pre-authorized numbers before the access is allowed.

1.38 INFORMATION SYSTEM SECURITY (UPTU 2010–11)

Every time a home PC or small home/office network goes online, it connects to thousands of unknown networks and millions of their users. Connecting to Internet provides the opportunities to communicate and share information with others. But it also gives opportunities to Internet users that are involved in malicious activities. Its often believed by many that they don't possess anything that would be of any interest to intruders. But in most of the computer attacks, these computers are used as launching pads to spread viruses, worms and other attacks. They just serve as one link in a chain of multiple compromised systems.

Security concerns of a home network or SOHO are similar to those of big corporate networks. Faster Internet connections are becoming popular and as they are "always on"; the computer networks are becoming more vulnerable to attacks. Possible attacks on SOHO and home networks include a Denial of Service (DOS) attack, a Distributed Denial of Service (DDOS) attack using SOHO networks, accessing and destroying confidential information on the system, etc. The only way to secure a computer from online intruders is to turn it off or by disconnecting it from the Internet. According to the experts, use of firewalls is the best way of securing a computer network from online intrusion. Firewalls are the first line of defense in protecting computers. A firewall filters the network traffic on the basis of certain pre set rules, hence protecting one network from another. However, there are other tools that can be used to protect the networks like antivirus software, anti hacker tools, etc. Protecting personal computers using PC monitoring tools, file protection tools and password security tools further enhances the security mechanism of the small networks.

1.39 CLASSIFICATION OF SECURITY THREATS AND ACCESSING DAMAGES

Classification of threats has always been a major security decision issue when a person walks through a security portal.

In order for one to produce a secure system, it is important to classify threats. The classification of threats could be:

1. Physical threats
2. Accidental error
3. Unauthorized access
4. Malicious misuse.

1.39.1 Physical Threat

Physical threat to a computer system could be as a result of loss of the whole computer system, damage of hardware, damage to the computer software, theft of the computer system, vandalism, natural disaster such as flood, fire, war, earthquakes etc. Acts of terrorism such as the attack on the world trade centre is also one of the major threats to computer which can be classified as physical threat.

Another good example of a physical threat to computer system is the flooding of the city of New Orleans (Hurricane Katrina) during which valuable information was lost and billions of computer data were destroyed.

1.39.2 Accidental Error

This is also an important security issue which computer security experts should always put into consideration when designing security measures for a system. Accidental errors could occur at any time in a computer system but having proper checks in place should be the major concern of the designer. Accidental error includes corruption of data caused by programming error, user or operator error.

1.39.3 Unauthorized Access

Dada stored on the computer system has to be accessed for it to be translated into useful information. This also poses a great security threats to the computer system due to unauthorized person's having access to the system. Not only this, information can be accessed via a remote system in the process of being transmitted from one point to the other via network media which includes wired and wireless media. Considering an example of an organization in which a member of staff at a particular level of hierarchy within the establishment is only allowed access to specific area according to the policy of the organization. If this employee by other means not set in the organization policy gain access to the restricted data area on the computer, this can be termed an un authorized access.

1.39.4 Malicious Misuse

Any form of tampering of the computer system which includes penetration, Trojan horses' viruses and any form of illegal alteration of the computer system which also includes the generation of illegal codes to alter the standard codes within the system can be termed as malicious misuse. This could also lead to a great financial loss and should be prevented in all cases.

1.40 ACCESSING DAMAGES

As organizations adopt increasingly sophisticated information systems, the challenge of protecting those systems becomes enormous. Accordingly, the single critical decision security managers have to make is the amount an organization is willing to spend on security measures to protect assets of the organization. To arrive at this decision, security mangers need to know explicitly about the assets of their organizations, the vulnerability of their information systems to different threats, and their potential damages. Each threat and vulnerability must be related to one or more of the assets requiring protection. This means that prior to assessing damages we need to identify assets. Logical and physical assets can be grouped into five categories:

1. **Information:** Documented (paper or electronic) data or intellectual property used to meet the mission of an organization.
2. **Software:** Software applications and services that process, store, or transmit information.
3. **Hardware:** Information technology physical devices considering their replacement cost.
4. **People:** The people in an organization who posses skills, knowledge, and experience that are difficult to replace.
5. **Systems:** Information systems that process and store information (systems being a combination of information, software, and hardware assets and any host, client, or server being considered a system).

Various units of value or metrics for valuation of assets may be used. The common metric is monetary, which is generally used for data that represent money where the threat is direct financial theft or fraud. Some assets are difficult to measure in absolute terms but can be measured in relative ways, for example information. The value of information can be measured as a fraction or percentage of total budget, assets, or worth of a business in relative fashion. Assets may also be ranked by sensitivity or importance to an organization in relative ways. The authors believe that

1. Destruction of information and/or other resources,
2. Corruption or modification of information,
3. Theft, removal or loss of information and/or other resources,
4. Disclosure of information; and
5. Interruption of services; are major categories of threats to the information systems.

The impact of information security incidents may well be financial, in forms of immediate costs and losses of assets. For example, the cost of downtime per hour caused by a denial of service attack can be computed by measuring the loss of:

Productivity: (Number of employees impacted), (hours out), (burdened hourly rate)

Revenue: Direct loss, lost future revenues

Financial Performance: Credit rating, stock price

Other Expenses: Equipment rental, overtime costs, extra shipping costs, travel expenses, etc.

But, much more serious are the hidden costs. Consider the example of denial of service attack, where the damaged reputation of the company can have negative impact on the relationship of the company with its customers, suppliers, financial markets, banks, and business partners. These hidden costs are extremely difficult to quantify and to measure. Others suggest qualitative or quantitative approaches for these kinds of evaluations. However, qualitative or quantitative risk analysis in information security has its pros and cons.

We overview the existing classifications of the threats to the information systems and some of their shortcomings. We also present a more comprehensive classification of the threats and some security measures to confront them. In this classification, threats are considered from two points of view:

1. Threat agent, and
2. Threat technique.

Threat agent could be environmental factors, authorized users, unauthorized users and threat (penetration) technique could be personnel, physical, hardware, software, or procedural. We believe that the cost of an information system security incident on a company has to be measured in terms of the impact on its business; hence identical incidents in two different companies could have different costs. To evaluate these costs and measure the impact of a security incident on a company, we need a systematic approach and a comprehensive risk management system. Such a comprehensive security risk evaluation system is currently under development at the College of Computing, Georgia Institute of Technology. This system with five stages is aimed at helping managers to identify the vulnerabilities of their companies and to select the countermeasures and it includes:

1. Resource and application value analysis
2. Vulnerability and risk analysis
3. Computation of losses due to threats and benefits of countermeasures
4. Selection of countermeasures and
5. Evaluation of implementation alternatives

We provide a model of classification of security threats and develop a three-axis view of the threat space and a scheme for probabilistic evaluation of impact of the security threats. We present an analysis of five incidents. The agents and threats are classified and related to the damages within each organization.

1.41 BRIEF REVIEW OF INTERNET PROTOCOLS-TCP/IP, IPV4, IPV6

In networking, the communication language used by computer devices is called the protocol.

Imagine the number of people communicating in the world, the number of different languages they use, the number of different machines they use, the number of ways in which they transmit data and the different software they use. We would never be able to communicate worldwide if there were no 'standards' governing the way we communicate and the way our machines treat data. These standards are sets of rules.

There are rules governing how data is transferred over networks, how they are compressed, how they are presented on the screen and so on. These set of rules are called protocols. There are many protocols, each one governing the way a certain technology works. For example, the IP protocol defines a set of rules governing the way computers use IP packets to send data over the Internet or any other IP-based network. It also defines addressing in IP. Likewise, we have other protocols like:

Internet Protocols

The Internet Protocol family contains a set of related (and among the most widely used network protocols. Besides Internet Protocol (IP) itself, higher-level protocols like TCP, UDP, HTTP, and FTP all integrate with IP to provide additional capabilities. Similarly, lower-level Internet Protocols like ARP and ICMP also co-exist with IP. These higher level protocols interact more closely with applications like Web browsers while lower-level protocols interact with network adapters and other computer hardware. IP (Internet Protocol) is the primary network protocol used on the Internet, developed in the 1970s. On the Internet and many other networks, IP is often used together with the Transport Control Protocol (TCP) and referred to interchangeably as TCP/IP.

IP supports unique addressing for computers on a network. Most networks use the Internet Protocol version 4 (IPv4) standard that features IP addresses four bytes (32 bits) in length. The newer Internet Protocol version 6 (IPv6) standard features addresses 16 bytes (128 bits) in length.

Data on an Internet Protocol network is organized into packets. Each IP packet includes both a header (that specifies source, destination, and other information about the data) and the message data itself.

TCP/IP - Transmission Control Protocol / Internet Protocol

Transmission Control Protocol (TCP) and Internet Protocol (IP) are two distinct network protocols, technically speaking. TCP and IP are so commonly used together, however, that TCP/IP has become standard terminology to refer to either or both of the protocols.

IP corresponds to the Network layer (Layer 3) in the OSI model, whereas TCP corresponds to the Transport layer (Layer 4) in OSI. In other words, the term TCP/IP refers to network communications where the TCP transport is used to deliver data across IP networks.

The average person on the Internet works in a predominately TCP/IP environment. Web browsers, for example, use TCP/IP to communicate with Web servers.

1.42 FUNCTIONS OF VARIOUS NETWORKING COMPONENTS-ROUTERS, BRIDGES, SWITCHES, HUB, GATEWAY AND MODULATION TECHNIQUE (UPTU-2010)

Routers

A router is a networking device that forwards packets between networks using information in protocol headers and forwarding tables to determine the best next router for each packet. Routers work at the Network Layer of the OSI model and the Internet Layer of TCP/IP.

Bridges

A network bridge connects multiple network segments at the data link layer (layer 2) of the OSI model. Bridges do not promiscuously copy traffic to all ports, as hubs do, but learn which MAC addresses are reachable through specific ports. Once the bridge associates a port and an address, it will send traffic for that address only to that port. Bridges do send broadcasts to all ports except the one on which the broadcast was received.

Bridges learn the association of ports and addresses by examining the source address of frames that it sees on various ports. Once a frame arrives through a port, its source address is stored and the bridge assumes that MAC address is associated with that port. The first time that a previously unknown destination address is seen, the bridge will forward the frame to all ports other than the one on which the frame arrived.

Bridges come in three basic types:

1. **Local bridges:** Directly connect local area networks (LANs)
2. **Remote bridges:** Can be used to create a wide area network (WAN) link between LANs.

Remote bridges, where the connecting link is slower than the end networks, largely have been replaced with routers.

3. **Wireless bridges:** Can be used to join LANs or connect remote stations to LANs

Switches

A network switch is a device that forwards and filters OSI layer 2 datagrams (chunk of data communication) between ports (connected cables) based on the MAC addresses in the packets.[6] This is distinct from a hub in that it only forwards the packets to the ports involved in the communications rather than all ports connected. Strictly speaking, a switch is not capable of routing traffic based on IP address (OSI Layer 3) which is necessary for communicating between network segments or within a large or complex LAN. Some switches are capable of routing based on IP addresses but are still called switches as a marketing term. A switch normally has numerous ports, with the intention being that most or all of the network is connected directly to the switch, or another switch that is in turn connected to a switch.

Switch is a marketing term that encompasses routers and bridges, as well as devices that may distribute traffic on load or by application content (e.g., a Web URL identifier). Switches may operate at one or more OSI model layers, including physical, data link, network, or transport (i.e., end-to-end). A device that operates simultaneously at more than one of these layers is called a multilayer switch.

Overemphasizing the ill-defined term "switch" often leads to confusion when first trying to understand networking. Many experienced network designers and operators recommend starting with the logic of devices dealing with only one protocol level, not all of which are covered by OSI. Multilayer device selection is an advanced topic that may lead to selecting particular implementations, but multilayer switching is simply not a real-world design concept.

Hubs

A network hub contains multiple ports. When a packet arrives at one port, it is copied unmodified to all ports of the hub for transmission. The destination address in the frame is not changed to a broadcast address.

Gateway

In telecommunications, the term gateway has the following meaning:

- In a communications network, a network node equipped for interfacing with another network that uses different protocols.
  - — A gateway may contain devices such as protocol translators, impedance matching devices, rate converters, fault isolators, or signal translators as necessary to provide system interoperability. It also requires the establishment of mutually acceptable administrative procedures between both networks.

— A protocol translation/mapping gateway interconnects networks with different network protocol technologies by performing the required protocol conversions.

- Loosely, a computer configured to perform the tasks of a gateway. For a specific case, see default gateway.

Routers exemplify special cases of gateways.

Gateways, also called protocol converters, can operate at network layer and above. The job of a gateway is much more complex than that of a router or switch. Typically, a gateway must convert one protocol stack into another.

Modulation Technique

The basics of modulation is to take a message bearing signal like an audio signal and superimpose it upon a carrier signal for transmission. For ease of transmission such carrier signals use generally high frequencies:

- For easy propagation as electromagnetic waves with low loss and low dispersion
- Simultaneous transmission without interference from other signals
- Enables the construction of small antennas (a fraction, usually a quarter of the wavelength)
- Enables the multiplexing (combining) multiple signals for transmission at the same time over the same carrier

In general the four different modulation schemes amplitude, frequency, phase and code modulation are possible. Well known examples of high frequency carrier signals are:

- AM radio is 550-1600 KHz
- FM radio is 88 MHz-108 MHz
- TV is 52-88 MHz (channels 1-6), 174-216 MHz (channels 7-12) and 470-900 MHz (UHF)
- microwave and satellite signals are of the order of several GHz
- infra red fiber optic signals are of the order of 200-300 THz.

The selection of the modulation scheme is done according to power and bandwidth efficiency and the channel capacity. The power efficiency is a measure of how much signal power should be increased to achieve a particular BER (Bit Error Rate) for a given modulation scheme. Bandwidth efficiency is the ability to accommodate data within a limited bandwidth of a channel. Its also a tradeoff between data rate and pulse width.

SUMMARY

An information system (IS) is any combination of information technology and people's activities using that technology to support operations, management, and decision-making. In a very broad sense, the term information system is frequently used to refer to the interaction between people, algorithmic processes, data and technology. In this sense, the term is used to refer not only to the information and communication technology (ICT) an organization uses, but also to the way in which people interact with this technology in support of business processes. In another words an information system is a system that collects and stores data and a system is a group of interdependent items that interact regularly to perform a task. Information system deals with data of the organizations. The purposes of Information system are to process input, maintain data, produce reports, handle queries, handle on line transactions, generate reports, and other output. These maintain huge databases, handle hundreds of queries etc. The transformation of data into information is primary function of information system.

Information Systems (IS) is an academic/professional discipline concerned with the strategic, managerial and operational activities involved in the gathering, processing, storing, distributing and use of information, and its associated technologies, in society and organizations. As an area of study, IS bridges the multidisciplinary business field and the interdisciplinary computer science field that is evolving toward a new scientific discipline.

EXERCISES

1. What do you understand by information system.
2. Explain the history of IS.
3. What are importance of IS. Discuss it with its types.
4. What are various threats to IS.
5. Why we need to study distributed information system.
6. What is web? Explain it with its services.
7. Describe various issues in security in mobile and wireless computing.
8. What are attack? Explain it with its different types.
9. What is the rate of internet.
10. What are different types of IS.

CHAPTER 2

What is Security

2.1 INTRODUCTION

Security is a branch of computer technology known as information security as applied to computers and networks. The objective of computer security includes protection of information and property from theft, corruption, or natural disaster, while allowing the information and property to remain accessible and productive to its intended users. The term computer system security means the collective processes and mechanisms by which sensitive and valuable information and services are protected from publication, tampering or collapse by unauthorized activities or untrustworthy individuals and unplanned events respectively. The strategies and methodologies of computer security often differ from most other computer technologies because of its somewhat elusive objective of preventing unwanted computer behavior instead of enabling wanted computer behavior.

2.1.1 Security Architecture (UPTU-2010–11)

Security Architecture can be defined as the design artifacts that describe how the security controls (security countermeasures) are positioned, and how they relate to the overall information technology architecture. These controls serve the purpose to maintain the system's quality attributes, among them confidentiality, integrity, availability, accountability and assurance."

Confidentiality is an ethical principle associated with several professions (e.g., medicine, law, religion, professional psychology, and journalism). In ethics, and (in some places) in law and alternative forms of legal dispute resolution such as mediation, some types of communication between a person and one of these professionals are "privileged" and may not be discussed or divulged to third parties. In those jurisdictions in which the law makes provision for such confidentiality, there are usually penalties for its violation. It means "ensuring that information is accessible only to those authorized to have access" and is one of the cornerstones of information security. Confidentiality is one of the design goals for many cryptosystems, made possible in practice by the techniques of modern cryptography.

Integrity is a concept of consistency of actions, values, methods, measures, principles, expectations and outcomes. In ethics, integrity is regarded as the quality of having an intuitive sense of honesty and truthfulness in regard to the motivations for one's actions. Integrity can be regarded as the opposite of hypocrisy in that it regards internal consistency as a virtue, and suggests that parties holding apparently conflicting values should account for the discrepancy or alter their beliefs.

The word "integrity" stems from the Latin adjective *integer* (whole, complete).In this context, integrity is the inner sense of "wholeness" deriving from qualities such as honesty and consistency of character. As such, one may judge that others "have integrity" to the extent that one judges whether they behave according to the values, beliefs and principles they claim to hold.

Availability. In telecommunications and reliability theory, the term **availability** has the following meanings:

- The degree to which a system, subsystem, or equipment is in a specified operable and committable state at the start of a mission, when the mission is called for at an unknown, *i.e.,* a random, time. Simply put, availability is the proportion of time a system is in a functioning condition. This is often described as a **mission capable rate**. Mathematically, this is expressed as 1 minus unavailability.
- The ratio of (a) the total time a functional unit is capable of being used during a given interval to (b) the length of the interval.

Accountability and insurance is a concept in ethics and governance with several meanings. It is often used synonymously with such concepts as responsibility, answerability, blameworthiness, liability, and other terms associated with the expectation of account-giving. As an aspect of governance, it has been central to discussions related to problems in the public sector, nonprofit and private (corporate) worlds. In leadership roles, accountability is the acknowledgment and assumption of responsibility for actions, products, decisions, and policies including the administration, governance, and implementation within the scope of the role or employment position and encompassing the obligation to report, explain and be answerable for resulting consequences.

2.2 WIRELESS SECURITY

Wireless security is the prevention of unauthorized access or damage to computers using wireless networks.

Wireless networks are very common, both for organizations and individuals. Many laptop computers have wireless cards pre-installed. The ability to enter a network while mobile has great benefits. However, wireless networking has many security issues. Hackers have found wireless networks relatively easy to break into, and even use wireless technology to crack into wired networks. As a result, it's very important that enterprises define effective wireless security policies that guard against unauthorized access to important resources. Wireless Intrusion Prevention Systems are commonly used to enforce wireless security policies.

In telecommunications, **wireless communication** is the transfer of information without the use of wires. The distances involved may be short (a few meters as in television remote control) or long (thousands or millions of kilometers for radio communications). The term is often shortened to "wireless". It encompasses various types of fixed, mobile, and portable two-way radios, cellular telephones, personal digital assistants (PDAs), and wireless networking.

The term "wireless" has become a generic and all-encompassing word used to describe communications in which electromagnetic waves or RF (rather than some form of wire) carry a signal over part or the entire communication path. Common examples of wireless equipment in use today include:

- Professional LMR (Land Mobile Radio) and SMR (Specialized Mobile Radio) typically used by business, industrial and Public Safety entities.
- Consumer Two way radio including FRS Family Radio Service, GMRS (General Mobile Radio Service) and Citizens band ("CB") radios.
- The Amateur Radio Service (Ham radio).
- Consumer and professional Marine VHF radios.
- **Cellular telephones and pagers:** provide connectivity for portable and mobile applications, both personal and business.
- **Global Positioning System (GPS):** allows drivers of cars and trucks, captains of boats and ships, and pilots of aircraft to ascertain their location anywhere on earth.
- **Cordless computer peripherals:** the cordless mouse is a common example; keyboards and printers can also be linked to a computer via wireless.
- **Cordless telephone sets:** these are limited-range devices, not to be confused with cell phones.
- **Satellite television:** allows viewers in almost any location to select from hundreds of channels.
- **Wireless gaming:** new gaming consoles allow players to interact and play in the same game regardless of whether they are playing on different consoles. Players can chat, send text messages as well as record sound and send it to their friends. Controllers also use wireless technology. They do not have any cords but they can send the information from what is being pressed on the controller to the main console which then processes this information and makes it happen in the game. All of these steps are completed in milliseconds.

2.3 SECURITY GOALS TECHNICALLY DEFINED

Confidentiality

1. Data transmitted or stored should only be revealed to an intended audience
2. Confidentiality of entities is also referred to as anonymity

Data Integrity

1. It should be possible to detect any modification of data
2. This requires to be able to identify the creator of some data

Accountability

It should be possible to identify the entity responsible for any communication event

Availability

Services should be available and function correctly

Controlled Access

Only authorized entities should be able to access certain services or information

2.4 SECURITY SERVICES – OVERVIEW (IMPORTANT)

2.4.1 Authentication

The most fundamental security service which ensures, that an entity has in fact the identity it claims to have

2.4.2 Integrity

In some kind, the "small brother" of the authentication service, as it ensures, that data created by specific entities may not be modified without detection

2.4.3 Confidentiality

The most popular security service, ensuring the secrecy of protected data

2.4.4 Access Control

Controls that each identity accesses only those services and information it is entitled to.

2.4.5 Non Repudiation

Protects against that entities participating in a communication exchange can later falsely deny that the exchange occurred

2.4.6 Wireless communication

Wireless communication is the transfer of information over a distance without the use of electrical conductors or "wires." The distances involved may be short (a few meters as in television remote control using infrared light) or long (thousands or millions of kilometers for radio communications).

Wireless networks, handheld devices and mobile applications are changing the way the government does business, making it more flexible, accessible and affordable than ever before. Our wireless capabilities include:

- 802.11a/b/g multipoint logical/physical design and implementation
- Unlicensed and licensed point-to-point backhaul design and implementation

- Interference mitigation via antenna selection, RF propagation, channel selection, polarization, and more
- In-building distribution solutions
- Traffic monitoring, reporting and analysis
- Security management and billing software
- Acquisition support
- Seamless roaming between different carrier networks and technologies (wireless ISP or public hotspots, private corporate wireless networks and cellular or PCS networks for nationwide coverage)
- Public hotspot design and implementation
- Support for dynamic end-user provisioning and real-time billing integration

2.5 INFORMATION SECURITY RISKS

1. Social Networking: Sites such as Facebook, Bebo and MySpace offer cybercriminals a vast new world in which to target unsuspecting users. Malware can be cleverly disguised and can be distributed quickly and on a massive scale. The high levels of trust users place in social networking sites means they are an ideal target for the fraudsters, with a greatly likelihood they will succumb to an attack.

2. Malware attacks: Cyber criminals are using more creative means to package and deliver malware (viruses, worms, Trojans etc.). Increasingly, email is being used as the delivery mechanism containing seemingly innocent URL links shortened to disguise malicious site addresses, videos and pictures are all used to disguise and conceal malware. When activated, these software programs are designed to wreak havoc on a computer system and move on to infect more systems. The speed at which malware spreads and the damage caused continue to make malware rank highly as a security risk.

3. Scareware: Attackers and fraudsters use online pop-ups designed to look like messages from the operating system warning of a problem or virus infection to coerce users to download a program to "correct" the problem. In the worst cases, the program will itself be malicious and may damage the system or leave it vulnerable to attack/abuse. Ransomware enters a system through a security hole and encrypts personal files, making them inaccessible. The user is prompted to either buy a piece of decryption software or enter a code which can only be obtained by sending payment to the attacker.

4. Microsoft: Windows 7 is expected to be widely adopted by Microsoft users worldwide. This massive user base is a prime target for the opportunistic hacker looking to attack a new, unfamiliar operating system.

5. The Insider Threat: Information is stored in files and folders, accessible remotely by large numbers of users. Keeping it secure and safe from an internal breach, while allowing it to remain accessible to the majority of non-malicious employees, is an ongoing challenge. If employees feel their employment is under threat they may see sensitive data as a valuable commodity that can be used for their own gain – always to the detriment of their employer.

6. Localised attacks: Often attempts to deceive victims fail because they are clearly fraudulent, text used is grammatically incorrect, spelling errors raise red flags and graphics are poor replicas. However, attacks are becoming more refined, not only in appearance, but in relevance to the target. Attackers are researching more to use local references including culture; sports, events to appear more authentic and better their chances of defrauding their targets.

7. Smartphones: The convergence of telecommunications and computing is creating a new target for hackers. Smartphones are as likely to be attacked as traditional computers. The risk to personal and corporate data is greater as the availability of security applications for these devices is low. As the number of users and volume of data transmitted increases and more financial transactions are done using these devices they become a more attractive and lucrative target for attack.

8. Mac OS X: There is a widespread misconception that relative to PCs, Macs are resistant to attack. This results in users deploying far fewer security measures and not updating systems with security patches. Hackers will continue to target the OS X platform and Apple continues to respond with regular security updates.

9. Embedded Computing: As society relies increasingly on Information and Communications Technology (ICT) across all aspects of life, national critical information infrastructures – such as energy, transport and telecommunications- will become more and more connected to and reliant on the Internet. As beneficial as this is to the provision of services and communications it also exposes critical devices to the same risks and threats that exist online.

10. Virtualisation and Cloud Computing: Lower budgets and improvements in distributed computing and high-speed internet access, are making Cloud Computing and Virtualization appealing alternatives to costly and complex conventional computing methods. Cloud computing offers capacity and functionality over the Internet that is scalable, subscription-based and fully managed by the provider. Virtualization has lower power and space requirements and simplifies management. However, businesses need to consider the regulatory and legal issues associated with managing data and the new kinds of security challenges that these alternatives bring. How and where the data is stored and who has access to it? The issues are more complex if the data includes payment card information, as PCI-DSS requirements come into play.

2.6 SECURITY IN MOBILE AND WIRELESS COMPUTING (UPTU-2010–11)

Modern technologies are becoming ever more integrated with each other. Mobile phones are becoming increasing intelligent, and handsets are growing ever more like computers in functionality. And smart devices, such as PDAs, on-board car computers, and new generation household appliances are now equipped with communications functions. We are entering a new era the age of smart houses, global networks which encompass a wide range of devices, all of them exchanging data with each other via as cyberpunk authors say air saturated with bits and bytes. Such trends clearly open new horizons to malicious users, and the potential threats are self evident.

This wired world is still evolving. We should be grateful for the fact that it still requires a bit more than a laptop and a wireless connection to gain control over someone else's car. However, security for mobile devices is already an issue; and the first indication of trouble came, not surprisingly, in the form of a virus.

At first glance, the problem of malicious code appears only to be a part of the broader information security picture. However, malicious programs inevitably mutate from innocent amusements created by bored programmers and students who wish to show off their skills to professional solutions created expressly for financial gain. Today the boundary which previously existed between virus research on the one hand, and network security, program vulnerabilities, advertising software and criminal structures on the other, has effectively been eliminated. Therefore researching the techniques used by the authors of malicious code cannot be overestimated as an essential part of ensuring digital security.

Mobile devices have made securing organizations more challenging than ever. Computer networks are no longer confined to the office, even at small and medium-sized businesses (SMBs). However, SMBs can prevent and protect against mobile security vulnerabilities, even without a dedicated information security team. Existing IT and network staffs can follow these easy guidelines without increasing their workloads. The best practices listed below involve tweaks to systems and monitoring of networks, which you may already be doing. If not, add them to your daily routine and you'll be on your way to securing and protecting your mobile devices.

2.7 SECURITY ASPECTS OF MOBILE COMMUNICATION

The Security Aspects of Mobile Communication are as given below:

Mobile communication faces all threats that does its' fixed counterpart:

Masquerade, eavesdropping, authorization violation, loss or modification of transmitted information, repudiation of communication acts, forgery of information, sabotage, Thus, similar measures like in fixed networks have to be taken.

However, there are some specific issues arising out of mobility of users and / or devices:

Some already existing threats get more dangerous:

- Wireless communications is more accessible for eavesdropping
- The lack of a physical connection makes it easier to access services

Some new difficulties for realizing security services:

- Authentication has to be re-established when the mobile device moves
- Key management gets harder as peer identities can not be predetermined

One completely new threat:

- The location of a device / user becomes a more important information that is worthwhile to eavesdrop on and thus to protect

2.8 SECURING CHALLENGES IN MOBILE DEVICES

2.8.1 Mobile Devices

Mobile devices have become a plague for information security professionals. There are worms and other malware that specifically target these devices such as the iPhone worm that would steal banking data and enlist these devices in a botnet. Theft is still a major cause of data breaches as mobile devices, especially laptops, are the main culprits. Tens of thousands of laptops are stolen each year and often these have sensitive data that require public disclosure as a data breach.

Intelligent mobile devices are revolutionizing the way remote users connect to their business, and thus are presenting unique security opportunities for solution providers. Blackberrys, iPhones, and the emerging category of promising Mobile Internet Devices (MIDs) are exploding in popularity, fueled by the availability of easy-to-use application interfaces to access information (both business and personal) in non-traditional ways.

Solution providers would be wise to monetize their networking infrastructure experience by helping customers secure their mobile devices. Security Software as a Service (SaaS) opportunities exist for small and medium business markets that need to secure the professional use of personal devices. Ideas for security-related revenue include innovative approaches to configuration administration, secure remote access, compliance auditing and application delivery

There are different steps to take when securing mobile devices, depending on the type of device you have. USB keys and wireless access points (WAPs) are two very different creatures. What works for one may not work for the other.

1. **Choose Device Carefully:** Not all devices are created equally when it comes to security. For example, iPods are built for general consumers not as concerned by security and is therefore less inherently secure than a BlackBerry device designed for enterprise users.

   "The degree to which IT managers can control security on mobile devices is highly dependent upon the vendor that they select. You should try to get mobile devices that have the best possible control and security on them and then use those mechanisms and it will go a long way to locking down those mobile devices.

2. **Turn On Encryption:** Once you choose devices with stronger security controls, use those controls! Many organizations do not enforce or even set policies mandating the use of device encryption on mobile devices.

   "Many people don't go through the bother of doing the encryption. You always want to be careful and you always want to have a level of paranoia about what happens to your sensitive information. Mainstream enterprises need to lock it down and take it seriously like they do with a laptop and be really consistent with their policies and enforce them.

3. **Require Authentication:** A survey released by Credent Technologies in September 2008 found that in just a six month period more than 31,000 New Yorkers left behind mobile devices in a taxicab. The fact of the matter is that these devices are just too easy to lose to go without proper authentication. And yet, most enterprise users don't use the password function on their devices.

"So imagine, you lose your phone in a cab and the next passenger gets in opens it up and then they immediate access to your device because you didn't put any authentication in there.

It is critical that users be required to turn on device authentication so that lost devices can not be easily accessed by any person that finds or steals a device.

4. **Utilize Remote Wipe Capabilities:** Give IT staff the ability to remotely access and disable devices in the event of loss or theft. This could be very handy in a situation where, say, an executive loses his or her device at a conference along with yearly sales projections and strategies stored within. With the remote capability all it would take is a quick call to IT and they'll take care of it.

5. **Set Up a Lost Phone Hotline:** It is not good enough simply to have remote wipe capabilities. Organizations also need to have a procedure set for users who have lost their devices. Make it easy for them to call IT to alert staff that a device has been lost by setting up a direct line and publicize the procedure for IT notification in such an event.

   "If you're concerned about losing data, make sure your users have a contact point where they can get a hold of you so you can initiate that process to wipe them over the network and make sure that data isn't lost. They'll have an incentive to get a hold of you if they want another phone, but it's useful if they know who to call and that you can immediately start that process.

6. **Control Third-Party Apps:** Smart phones are so dangerous because they are essentially miniature computing platforms that can accept any nature of third-party applications. Cross recommends limiting the installation of unsigned third-party applications to prevent the bad guys from requisitioning control of your devices.

   "It makes sense to limit people's ability to install arbitrary third-party applications because that is exactly the how some of these Trojans will allow a bad guy to connect form the internet and get back out into your corporate VPN," Cross says. "That's how they work, they go out and say 'Here's this cool video game for your Blackberry! Install this, it's a lot of fun.' And people will install it and it will say 'This isn't signed,' and they'll say, 'That's OK.' And then their phone is now a gateway."

7. **Set Unique Firewall Policies:** Enterprises should set up unique firewall policies specifically for traffic coming from smartphones. The way Cross sees it, smart phone users don't necessarily need access to every bit of data on the network, so it makes sense to limit exposure by only offering access to the types of data they need.

   "There's stuff that they need access to, but they probably don't need access to your financial database. It probably doesn't work very well from a phone browser anyway," he says. "Stuff like that that has nothing to do with what people are doing from the phone, so you should firewall it off and traffic coming from the phone should only go to stuff that people would reasonably want to use."

8. **Use Intrusion Prevention Software:** As smart phones become more and more powerful, they're likely to become another weapon in the hacker toolbox. As a result, it makes sense to have your intrusion prevention software examining traffic coming through mobile devices.

   "It's possible that you could see attacks come in from phones; they're very sophisticated devices," Cross says. "I mean, you can run Metasploit on an iPhone. So that's something you need to think about."

9. **Keep an Open Mind About AV:** Cross says that he doesn't necessarily suggest enterprises go out today and buy host-based antivirus software for their smart phones, but he does believe they should be paying attention to advances in mobile device AV. He believes that it may be necessary in the coming years.

   "I don't know what the numbers are , but we've obviously seen a tremendous explosion in the sophistication of these devices and the number of these devices that are out there and i think that that's going to continue," he says. "It's my sort of futurist vision that in at some time maybe five or ten years from now there were actually be more smart phones on the Internet as client devices than there are PCs."

10. **Shore Up Bluetooth:** Bluetooth capabilities on today's smart phones may make it easy to talk on a hands-free headset, but they're also a target for hackers, who can take advantage of its default always-on, always-discoverable settings to launch attacks. In order to limit your exposure, US CERT recommends that users disable Bluetooth when it is not actively transmitting information. It also suggests switching Bluetooth devices to hidden mode. Organizations can limit exposure by making this company policy.

2.9 CHARACTERISTICS OF MOBILE DEVICES (VERY IMPORTANT)

A wide array of personal electronics are classified as mobile devices, from phones to barcode and RFID readers, and with so much technology branded as mobile, consumers can find it difficult to determine just what the characteristics of mobile devices are. In most cases, a mobile device can be defined by three distinct characteristics that set it apart from devices that may appear similar, but lack some characteristics of true mobile devices.

2.9.1 Portability

Mobile devices are defined by their ability to be moved frequently. Any mobile device should function and operate consistently while on the move, regardless of proximity to a power source or physical Internet connection. To aid in portability, mobile devices typically contain rechargeable batteries that allow several hours or more of operation without access to an external charger or power source.

2.9.2 Small Size

Mobile devices are also known as handhelds, palmtops and smartphones due to their roughly phone-like dimensions. A typical mobile device will fit in the average adult's hand or pocket. Some mobile devices may fold or slide from a compact, portable mode to a slightly larger size, revealing built-in keyboards or larger screens. Mobile devices make use of touch screens and small keypads to receive input, maintaining their small size and independence from external interface devices. The standard form of a mobile device allows the user to operate it with one hand, holding the device in the palm or fingers while executing its functions with the thumb.

Notebooks and small tablet computers are sometimes mistaken for true mobile devices, based on their similarity in form and function, but if the device's size prohibits one-handed operation or hinders portability, then it cannot be considered a true mobile device.

2.9.3 Wireless Communication

Mobile devices are typically capable of communication with other similar devices, with stationary computers and systems, with networks and portable phones. Base mobile devices are capable of accessing the Internet through Bluetooth or Wi-Fi networks, and many models are equipped to access cell phone and wireless data networks as well. Email and texting are standard ways of communicating with mobile devices, although many are also capable of telephony, and some specialized mobile devices, such as RFID and barcode readers, communicate directly with a central device.

2.9.4 Mobile Device Vulnerabilities

Smart mobile devices are still in their infancy, and consequently very vulnerable, both from a technical and a sociological point of view. On the one hand, their technical stability will improve only under arms race conditions, with a ceaseless stream of attacks and constant counter measures from the other side. This baptism of fire has only just begun for PDAs and smartphones, and consequently security for such devices is, as yet, almost totally undeveloped.

On the other hand, information security theory demonstrates that the human factor can negate all technical measures taken to secure systems. Usually, technical solutions to security issues will have little effect initially, due to lack of awareness among users. Rank and file computer users took years after the first virus epidemics to use antivirus utilities as standard, and months after the epidemics caused by email worms to learn not to launch unknown attachments which arrived via email.

- The worm does not exploit any vulnerability; for a smartphone to become infected, the user has to twice confirm that an unknown file should be uploaded and launched.
- There are several antivirus solutions for mobile devices available from a range of vendors
- The media hype which was raised around the appearance of the first worm for mobile devices should have reached the ears of even those mobile phone users who have no interest in technology.
- Information about Cabir was published on all sites about viruses and antivirus solutions.

All these facts taken together lead us to the conclusion that it is only appropriate human behavior which can guarantee the security of mobile devices at the moment.

We can estimate the technical level of smartphone security by how easy they are to destabilize and this, in the worst case, may make it necessary to install new firmware on Symbian devices. The table above shows that the functionality of the majority of known mobile viruses simply exploits the peculiarities of the operating system: the fact that it is possible to rewrite any file, including system files, and the extreme instability of the system when it meets files which are unexpected (i.e. those which are corrupted, or non-standard for the current distributive).

Another example: the majority of vendors who produce Bluetooth technologies ensure that the function will be enabled by default. Taking into account the antipathy of the average user to documentation, the user may not even suspect that his mobile phone is visible to all Bluetooth owners within a range of 10-20 metres, and potentially open for data transmission and information exchange.

This situation is undoubtedly frightening, particularly if we take into account the fact that mobile devices are attractive to all types of virus writers. Mobile malware is more potentially profitable than that for computers for the following reasons:

- Improved quality in the contact between devices: mobile devices are, after all, called mobile devices, as they constantly maintain contact with the outside world (with mobile networks, the Internet, with computers and with each other). Given this, they have a great number of technologies for transmitting data, ranging from traditional mobile technologies (such as SMS and MMS) to Bluetooth and wireless technologies.
- Increased volume of contact between devices, as users normally carry their mobiles everywhere. When being carried, they establish Bluetooth contact with each other, making data transmission between devices possible. This means that a mobile which is carried around by the user will come into contact with thousands of other telephones in a matter of hours, and in highly populated or crowded areas this creates a powerful network for data exchange.
- Mobile technologies integrated with computer technologies are extremely fertile soil for mass mailings and for political, industrial and other types of espionage.
- Wireless data transmission technologies currently offer malicious users close to complete anonymity.

Points one and two create the necessary conditions for an instant and global epidemic, if a significantly powerful Bluetooth worm were to appear. Points three and four will attract professional virus writers working in conjunction with criminal groups to the area of mobile malware.

2.10 MOBILE APPLICATION (VERY IMPORTANT)

Also called mobile apps, it is a term used to describe Internet applications that run on smartphones and other mobile devices. Mobile applications usually help users by connecting them to Internet services more commonly accessed on desktop or notebook computers, or help them by making it easier to use the Internet on their portable devices. A mobile app may be a mobile Web site bookmarking utility, a mobile-based instant messaging client, Gmail for mobile, and many other applications. There are some application of mobile as listed below:

The full list is as follows:

1. **Money Transfer:** This refers to people sending money via SMS messages. Like mobile payments, this service has more appeal in developing markets for now. However, there may come a time when even using your debit card seems passé, while paying for something with actual cash seems downright ancient.
2. **Location-Based Services:** As mentioned above, there are still far too many services to choose from when it comes to location-based social networking, fragmenting the market. Your friends on Loopt are often different than those on Brightkite and that list is different than those on Foursquare. But LBS extends to more than social networks - it includes any application that taps into your phone's GPS capabilities to offer up location-based services of any kind, whether that's local business reviews or directions to the nearest Starbucks. Gartner says this will be one of the most disruptive technologies in the future, with a user base growing from *96 million in 2009* to *526 million in 2012.*
3. **Mobile Search:** No, mobile search isn't new, but on the mobile platform, it may get shaken up a bit. Gartner predicts that consumers won't necessarily be sticking with the search services they know and use on the Web (think Google, Bing, Yahoo) and instead experiment with using a few different search providers that have "unique technologies" for mobile search. While that statement is a little vague, it sounds like good news for services like Taptu who have entered this field with search offerings designed from the ground-up for mobile devices.
4. **Mobile Browsing:** Saying that mobile browsing technologies will be heavily used in the future sounds a little bit like stating the obvious. But as Gartner notes, mobile browsing capabilities currently exist only on 60%+ of handsets today. By 2013, that number will climb to 80%, meaning that those who are still using the app-less,more basic feature phones will still be joining the mobile web in mass numbers over the coming years. That's also good news for web developers who can build mobile web applications to cater to this bunch as opposed to focusing all their efforts into building apps for the numerous mobile platforms like the iPhone, Android, RIM, and others.
5. **Mobile Health Monitoring:** Another technology whose impact will be felt more heavily in developing markets, mobile health monitoring is still at an early stage of maturity and implementation says Gartner. Project rollouts have been limited to pilot projects for now, but in the coming years the industry will begin to monetize these efforts by offering mobile healthcare monitoring products, services, and solutions to various care delivery organizations.
6. **Mobile Payments:** Like mobile transfers, mobile payments are more common in developing markets at the moment, but that is quickly changing. Yet even as this type of service grows, Gartner admits there will be challenges. Mobile payments will be a "highly fragmented market" where there will not be "standard practices of deployment," notes the report.

That makes it sound like this is one technology that will still need some work, even when 2012 rolls around.

7. **Near Field Communications (NFC):** More popular in some European and Asian markets than in the U.S., NFC still isn't a standard feature on many of today's phones. That may be about to change, too. In late 2010, Gartner says that NFC-enabled phones will begin to ship in volume, with Asia leading deployments, followed by Europe and North America.
8. **Mobile Advertising:** Also not new but growing fast, mobile advertising is one of the most important ways to monetize mobile content. Total spending on *mobile advertising in 2008 was $530.2 million* and it will grow to *$7.5 billion in 2012.* And mobile advertising will also be used by companies alongside their other campaigns including TV, radio, print, and outdoors.
9. **Mobile Instant Messaging:** Gartner says that latent user demand and market conditions are conductive to mobile IM's future adoption. It will appeal to developing markets where mobile phones are often the only connectivity device a user owns. But will it be a major app by 2012? It seems that SMS is still the service to beat, especially in the developing world. We'll have to wait and see on this one.
10. **Mobile Music:** Sure, you have the iPhone, but what about your other options? What about mobile music services - especially those for non-iPhone devices? We're still waiting on Spotify in the U.S., for example, and their competition too. Gartner says that we're beginning to see new innovative models in this area that will include both device (think "Comes with Music") and service bundles

2.10.1 RFID **(UPTU 2010-11)**

Radio frequency identification technology is likely to be incorporated into mobile phones in the near future. In several parts of the world, consumers are already testing mobile phones equipped with radio frequency identification devices and experience the ease of making payments for things like transit fares and fast food purchases. They are also getting a first taste of mobile advertising on their RFID-enabled mobile phones because the phones come equipped with RFID-readers.

The reader can be used to scan advertising and other information from nearby RFID tagged items in consumers' environments, such as "smart" advertising posters placed in transit terminals to obtain information about nearby restaurants or promotional materials about new products and services.

Mobile RFID (M-RFID) can be defined as services that provide information on objects equipped with an RFID tag over a telecommunication network. The reader is installed in a mobile device such as a mobile phone or PDA. This completely new approach is different from current implementations of ordinary RFID: Now the readers are mobile and the tags are fixed, instead the other way around. M-RFID has some major and obvious advantages over RFID: No wires to fixed readers are needed anymore and several mobile readers are enough to cover a whole area, instead of dozens of fixed readers.

New mobile phones have been designed to include delivery of mobile advertising and other useful location-based services, but have they also been designed to protect consumers' privacy, One of the key enabling technologies for these new types of phones and new mobile services is Radio Frequency Identification (RFID), a wireless communication technology that enables the unique identification of tagged objects. In the case of RFID enabled mobile phones, the personal nature of the devices makes it very likely that, by locating a phone, businesses will also be able to locate its owner. Consumers are currently testing new RFID-enabled phones around the globe, but the phones are not yet in general use by consumers in the United States and Europe. The incorporation of RFID into cell phones in order to deliver mobile advertising and other location-based services raises a host of important privacy questions that urgently need to be addressed before the phones become widely available.

Analyzing the risks to consumer privacy in this new context, this offers a comparative law analysis of the applicable regulatory frameworks and recent policy developments in the European Union and the United States and concludes that there are many privacy concerns not presently addressed by E.U. and U.S. laws. This article also offers specific ideas to protect consumers' ./ privacy through applications of fair information practices and privacy-enhancing technologies. When mobile phones are RFID-equipped, consumers will need new privacy protections in order to understand the risks and make knowledgeable decisions about their privacy.

No longer simply mobile telephones, mobile phones can deliver new communication and information services for consumers that are made possible by location-aware technologies.

1. Location-based services (LBS) for mobile phones empower subscribers to use their phones to find information about nearby businesses or services, such as movie theaters, banks or cafés.
2. They can also use their phones for navigation. For example, one user can receive directions from one location to another, locate another person's mobile phone, and receive updates or alerts about bus delays, traffic jams, or sales at nearby businesses. Mobile phones designed to receive location-based services will enable users to receive mobile advertising and other useful mobile services that are customized to them based on their geographic locations.
3. One of the enabling technologies for new location-based services is Radio Frequency Identification (RFID), which is "a wireless communication technology that is used to uniquely identify tagged objects or people."
4. In this case, the "tag" is a small computer chip with its own antenna that is attached to or embedded in a consumer product. It is designed to store digital information such as a unique number to identify an individual consumer product. For example, it can be used to distinguish one can of soda from another, even though the products are identical in all other respects.
5. The tag's antenna is able to broadcast that number and does not need to have its own power source because it operates by using energy received from nearby radio frequency identification readers that scan the tag.
6. Tags can be read by readers even when they are not in the line of sight of the reader and without human intervention.

The advent of location-based services, including mobile advertising, and the incorporation of RFID into cell phones for the purpose of delivering these services raises a host of important privacy questions that urgently need to be addressed while there is still time to protect consumers' privacy through privacy-enhancing design decisions and/or legislative action. The privacy issues relating to the provision of location- based services and mobile advertising include the need to protect location and other personal data that is collected and used. Other privacy concerns relate to the possibility of exposing consumers to more spam and the enhanced risk of unauthorized persons gaining access to personal information stored on mobile phones. Privacy questions also arise from RFID applications that enable marketers to automatically track and profile consumers in order to deliver time and location-specific

advertising to them on their mobile phones. These privacy and data protection concerns are grounded in emerging scholarship about the vision of an ambient intelligence (AmI) era that includes discussion of the Internet of Things, the dissemination of RFIDs, ubiquitous computing, smart objects and surveillance devices.

2.11 INFORMATION SYSTEMS SECURITY AND CONTROL

2.11.1 Information Systems Security

Information systems security is responsible for the integrity and safety of system resources and activities. Most organizations in developed countries are dependent on the secure operation of their information systems. In fact, the very fabric of societies often depends on this security. Information systems are at the heart of intensive-care units and air-traffic-control systems. Financial institutions could not survive a total failure of their information systems for longer than a day or two. Electronic funds transfer systems (EFTS) handle immense amounts of money that exist only as electronic signals.

2.11.2 Computer Crime and Abuse

Computer crime **cybercrime,** also called computer crime, the use of a computer as an instrument to further illegal ends, such as committing fraud, trafficking in child pornography and intellectual property, stealing identities, or violating privacy. Cybercrime, especially through the Internet, has grown in importance as the computer has become central to commerce, entertainment, and government.

Because of the early and widespread adoption of computers and the Internet in the United States, most of the earliest victims and villains of cybercrime were Americans.

Illegal acts in which computers are the primary tool costs the world economies many billions of dollars annually. Computer abuse does not rise to the level of crime, yet it involves some unethical use of a computer. Some of the more widespread security threats related to computer crime or abuse include impersonation, Trojan horse attack, logic bombs, and computer viruses and worms.

Impersonation, as the name implies, involves gaining access to a system by impersonating a legitimate user a feat that usually requires knowing or guessing a legitimate user's password.

2.11.3 Securing Information

Controlling access to information systems became profoundly more difficult with the spread of wide area networks (WANs) and the Internet. Users, as well as interlopers, may access systems from any unattended computer within an organization or from virtually anywhere over the Internet. One security measure is to require some form of physical authentication, such as an object (a key or a smart card) or a personal characteristic (fingerprint, retinal pattern, hand geometry, or signature). Another common security measure is to assign a unique password to each legitimate user.

2.11.4 Organizational Impacts of Information Systems

Information systems bring new options to the way companies interact, the way organizations are structured, and the way workplaces are designed. In general, use of network-based information systems can significantly lower the costs of communication among workers and firms and enhance coordination on collaborative projects. This has led many organizations to concentrate on their core competencies and to outsource other parts of their value chain to specialized companies.

2.12 AUTHENTICATION SERVICE SECURITY

Authentication is the verification of the identity of a party who generated some data, and of the integrity of the data. A principal is the party whose identity is verified. The *verifier* is the party who demands assurance of the principal's identity. Data integrity is the assurance that the data received is the same as generated. Authentication mechanisms differ in the assurances they provide: some indicate that data was generated by the principal at some point in the past, a few indicate that the principal was present when the data was sent, and others indicate that the data received was freshly generated by the principal. Mechanisms also differ in the number of verifiers: some support a single verifier per message, while others support multiple verifiers. A third difference is whether the mechanism supports non-repudiation, the ability of the verifier to prove to a third party that the message originated with the principal.

Because these differences affect performance, it is important to understand the requirements of an application when choosing a method. For example, authentication for electronic mail may require support for multiple recipients and non-repudiation, but can tolerate greater latency. In contrast, poor performance would cause problems for authentication to a server responding to frequent queries.

Other security services include confidentiality and authorization. Confidentiality is the protection of information from disclosure to those not intended to receive it. Most strong authentication methods optionally provide confidentiality. Authorization is the process by which one determines whether a principal is allowed to perform an operation. Authorization is usually performed after the principal has been authenticated, and may be based on information local to the verifier, or based on authenticated statements by others.

2.13 SECURITY LEVELS OF MOBILE COMMUNICATIONS

The mobile networks protect users and their privacy using some security methods. Each mobile device has an ID placed inside SIM card. This ID uniquely identifies every user. The user can protect the SIM card using a personal identity number (PIN) with at least four digits.

Even though the user identity has a basic level of protection, there is need to secure the mobile communications during wireless sessions. The security level of the mobile communications depends on the security methods implemented by the mobile network. In this section we give a brief overview of three basic security levels of mobile communications and their generic implementations with PKI infrastructure. Level 1 security is implemented by passcode identification . The user sends a passcode to the mobile network. Then, the passcode is compared with the one in the device database.

Level 2 security is implemented by symmetric key schemes as presented in Figure 2.1. The main feature is that the client is able to authenticate the identity of the gateway. Currently, WTLS session is established between the WAP client and the gateway. Future versions of WAP will allow a WTLS session to terminate beyond the gateway. In this way the routing is via gateway, but communication is not transparent to the gateway.

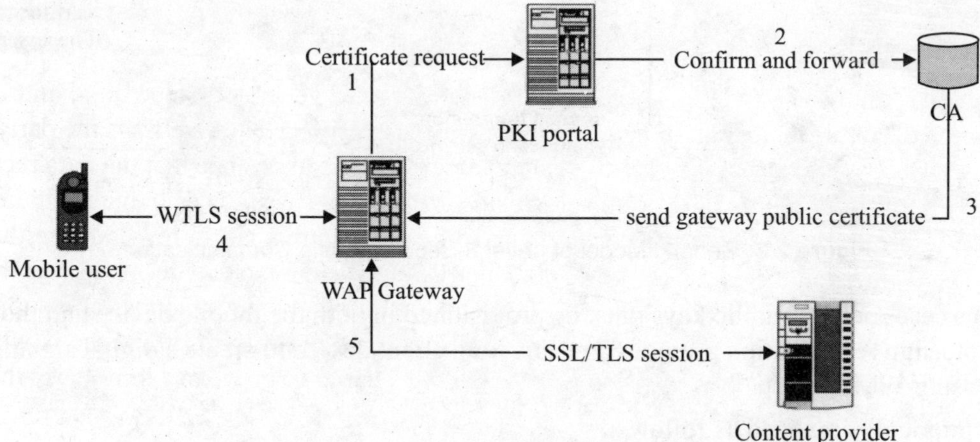

Figure 2.1: Generic Model of Level 2 Secure Mobile Communication

The mobile device possesses partial or complete CA root public key information. The WAP gateway generates a key pair: public key and private key.

The protocol continues as follows:

1. Gateway sends certificate request to PKI portal.
2. PKI portal confirms the gateway ID and forwards the request to CA.
3. CA sends gateway public certificate to client.
4. WTLS session is established between the mobile device and the gateway.
5. SSL or TLS connection is established between the gateway and the content provider server.

Level 3 security is implemented by asymmetric key schemes. The client is able to authenticate gateway's identity. Equally, the gateway can ask the user to prove the possession of the private keys with the same ID. The gateway sends some data to the user. The user signs with his private keys and sends back to the server, which verifies the user's signature, as presented in Figure 2.2.

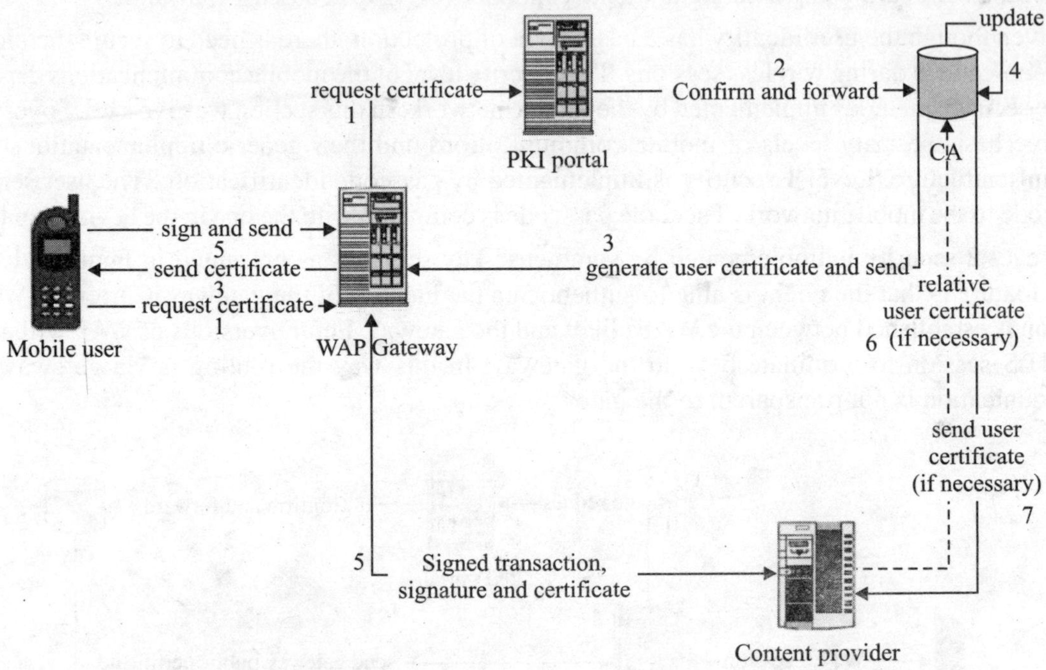

Figure 2.2: Generic Model of Level 3 Secure Mobile Communication

In this case root CA public keys must be provisioned in both the mobile device and the server. The Crypto.signText function provides a means for a client device to create a digital signature and sends it using WMLScript.

The protocol is realized as follows:

1. The client requests a certificate from PKI portal via gateway.
2. PKI portal confirms the user ID and forwards the request to the CA.
3. CA generates user certificate and sends certificate URL to the client. CA may choose to send the complete client certificate to the device. Then, for example, it can be stored on the SIM/WIM card.
4. If necessary, CA updates the database with user public key certificate.
5. The client signs the transaction and sends the transaction, signature and certificate URL to the content provider via gateway. The server may be possess the client's certificate.

   If the server is not in the possession of the client's certificate then:
6. The server uses Certificate URL to retrieve user certificate from CA database.

7. CA sends the user certificate to the server. The gateway may choose to challenge a client to sign some data with his private key when the user requests a certificate from the PKI portal. In this way the client gives proof about possession of the private key associated to ID.

2.14 IMPLEMENTING SECURE MOBILE COMMUNICATIONS

Implementation of the security levels of mobile communications requires that the mobile devices and the mobile network support certain technologies and standards.

The implementation of security level 1 mobile communications is straightforward. The client can send the passcode by SMS or WAP and after verification of the passcode the user is granted to access the information services.

The implementation of security level 2 mobile communications depends on the capability of storing private keys. If the client is not capable to store private keys, than the private key must be stored either in the mobile device (for example, JAVA enabled phones), which is not a tamper resistant device, or entered by the user. If the client is able to store the key in the mobile device, than it is possible to develop applications (which are phone specific) that provide the same functionality as WTLS. However, this is very expensive, narrow and unlikely solution.

It is also possible to develop WMLScript functions that will encrypt and send sensitive information to the gateway. The user will enter the private key in some input box and only the sensitive information will be encrypted and sent to the gateway as part of some WAP application. This is presented in figure 2.3. The gateway knows the client's public key and the client knows the password.

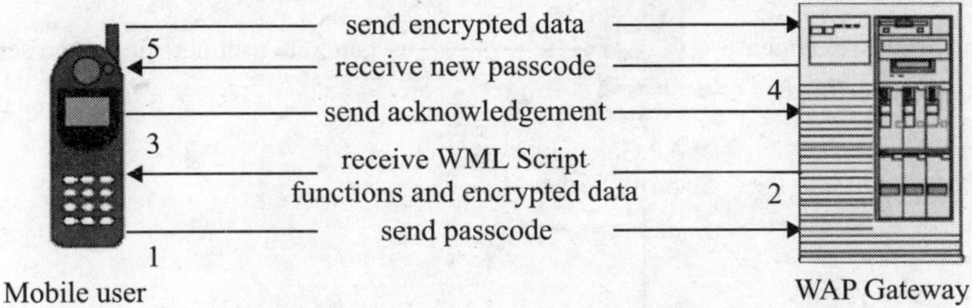

Figure 2.3: Implementing security level 2 of mobile communications on application level

1. The user sends the passcode to the gateway.
2. The gateway verifies the passcode in the database and encrypts the sensitive information using the client's public key. Afterwards it sends the encrypted information to the user and the needed WMLScript functions.
3. The client decrypts the received data and sends acknowledgement.
4. The gateway sends new passcode to the client. The old passcode is no longer valid.
5. The client sends the encrypted data to the gateway. The gateway receives the secure data and the protocol continues as in the Figure 2.1, step 2.

Note that the gateway is treated as part of trusted environment. It holds the private and the public keys of client so that it can establish a secure session with the client. Only the sensitive data is protected.

The passcode can be intercepted if it is not sent through secure channels. However, the passcode is used for one session only and afterwards the client receives new passcode and the old one is invalidated. The private key is never sent over the air and thus is protected from eavesdroppers. The downfall of this model is that the client must find a way to memorize the passcode and the private key outside the mobile device. Thus, the client must enter the passcode and the private key during every secure session.

The implementation of security level 3 depends both on the capability of the client to store private keys and the ability to generate digital signatures. If the client is not capable to store private keys than level 2 secure mobile communications can be implemented as previously described.

If the client is not able to generate digital signatures than we use delegated PKI signing, which means that, the security server signs a contract on behalf of the mobile device presented in figure 2.4.

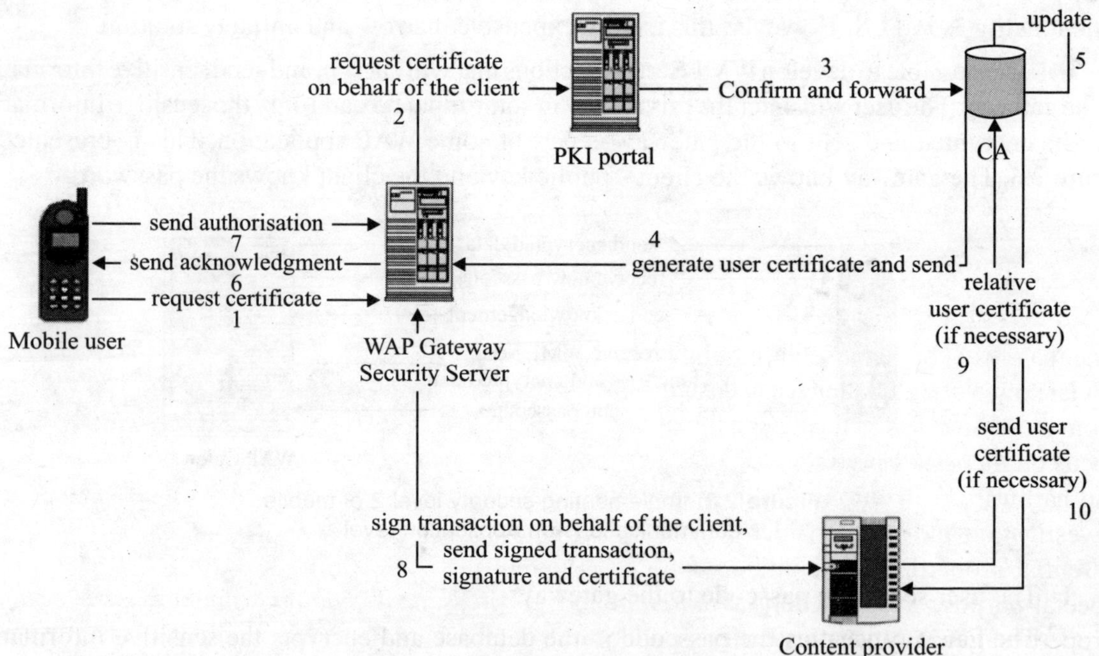

Figure 2.4: Implementing security level 3 of mobile communications on application level using delegated signing

Note that the gateway and the security server are implemented as one server, since the security server acts as the part of mobile device that generates signatures. If the phone is not capable to store private keys then the secure connection between the mobile device and the gateway is established as in Figure 2.3.

1. The client requests a certificate from PKI portal via gateway.
2. The gateway receives the request and the security server sends request for certificate on client's behalf.
3. PKI portal confirms the user ID and forwards the request to CA.
4. CA generates user certificate and sends certificate URL to the security server. CA may choose to send the complete client certificate to the security. For example, it can be stored/updated in the security server database.
5. If necessary, CA updates the database with user public key certificate.
6. The security server send acknowledgement that the public key certificate has been generated (via gateway).
7. The client sends authorization to the security server to sign the contract on his behalf.
8. The security server signs the transaction on behalf of the client and sends the transaction, signature and certificate URL to the content provider via gateway. The content provider server may possess the client's certificate. If the server is not in the possession of the client's certificate then:
9. The server uses Certificate URL to retrieve user certificate from CA database.
10. CA sends the user certificate to the server. If the client is not capable to store private keys then the secure connection can be implemented on application level as presented on figure 2.3.

2.15 TECHNICAL AND OTHER CHALLENGES AND LIMITATIONS OF MOBILE COMPUTING

The technical challenges that mobile computing must surmount to achieve its potential are hardly trivial. Some of the challenges in designing software for mobile computing systems are quite different from those involved in the design of software for today's stationary networked systems. The authors focus on the issues pertinent to software designers without delving into the lower level details of the hardware realization of mobile computers. They look at some promising approaches under investigation and also consider their limitations. The many issues to be dealt with stem from three essential properties of mobile computing: communication, mobility, and portability. Of course, special-purpose systems may avoid some design pressures by doing without certain desirable properties. For instance portability would be less of a concern for mobile computers installed in the dashboards of cars than with hand-held mobile computers. However, the authors concentrate on the goal of large-scale, hand-held mobile computing as a way to reveal a wide assortment of issues

2.15.1 Insufficient Bandwidth

Mobile Internet access is generally slower than direct cable connections, using technologies such as GPRS and EDGE, and more recently HSDPA and HSUPA 3G networks. These networks are usually available within range of commercial cell phone towers. Higher speed wireless LANs are inexpensive, but have very limited range.

2.15.2 Security Standards

When working mobile one is dependent on public networks, requiring careful use of VPNs.

2.15.3 Power Consumption

When a power outlet or portable generator is not available, mobile computers must rely entirely on battery power. Combined with the compact size of many mobile devices, this often means unusually expensive batteries must be used to obtain the necessary battery life.

2.15.4 Transmission Interferences

Weather, terrain, and the range from the nearest signal point can all interfere with signal reception. Reception in tunnels, some buildings, and rural areas is often poor.

2.15.5 Potential Health Hazards

More car accidents are related to drivers who were talking through a mobile device. Cell phones may interfere with sensitive medical devices. There are allegations that cell phone signals may cause health problems.

2.15.6 Human Interface with Device

Screens and keyboards tend to be small, which may make them harder to use. Alternate input methods such as speech or handwriting recognition require training.

2.16 SECURITY IMPLICATION FOR ORGANIZATION (VERY IMPORTANT)

So what Layered Security is, and how it can help us tighten the security in our organization. This model gives us is a better understanding of how should we approach, in order to have real security. There are many schemes and pictures about it, but the essentials are as simple as the picture below:

The first layer should always be security policy, approved for implementation in your organization. The policy should be discussed carefully, implemented and then strictly followed. I know Symantec from many years and I can say that they have a product for every single layer of that security model. If you look at the portfolio, you can really get lost there, because there is a product for every single branch of IT security industry. To prove that, let me show you which Symantec products applies perfectly for Layered Security model.

Web Filtering

One thing that I like here (and not many vendors have it) is that we can choose from two solutions: software and hardware.

If you have a dedicated box or you have a virtual infrastructure you'll probably go for the software solution – Message Labs Web Security, which is working with Symantec AV engine. If you like the reliability of a dedicated hardware box, you can go for Symantec Web Gateway – a powerful combination of software and hardware optimized for best performance.

E-Mail Filtering

Same applies here, hardware and software solutions are available for implementation. One thing that I want to mention here is Symantec Mail Security for Exchange. I have some experience with it and I definitely can say that this is the fastest mail filtering solution developed . It totallyJfor Exchange servers (and we know how slow actually Exchange is beats by functionality and speed Mail Marshal (Marshal) or Group Shield (McAfee) for Exchange. Let's go further and look at

Anti-Virus and Firewall for PC and Servers

We all know how great is Symantec Endpoint Protection 11. To be honest, I wasn't a big fan of the previous version - Symantec AV Enterprise Edition 10 and there are many reasons behind it. But my first experience with SEP 11 was really good. I was amazed form the Intrusion Prevention module as well as the Firewall. Most of the big vendors in IT Security, for some reason, does not have firewall for Windows based servers (which is quite odd), but Symantec has it! Reporting features are also good organized, and now I monitor my hosts with 5 reports, generated every week.

Anti-Virus for Mobile Devices

We don't know a modern company without Windows Mobile or Symbian devices. And many of you may ask this question – Why we need security for my mobile or PDA? Because you are using Internet to communicate with your HQ or family. If cyber criminals want to steal data from your organization, they will not test only your HQ computers for vulnerabilities, but every single device which has connection with your company. And BOOM! We have unsecured Windows Mobile device. It's an easy one!

We want to open brackets here and add another layer – Encryption. Encryption has become more and more popular and especially products that encrypts whole disk drive. Let's give an example with the SFO laptop that was stolen a year ago from San Francisco International Airport. This laptop was containing unencrypted personal information about 30 000+ passengers and I really do not believe that this was by accident. It could happen to you, and you can lose your business if you data is not encrypted. Symantec Endpoint Encryption has capabilities to encrypt the whole HDD of your mobile computers and you can protect your sensitive data even your.

Backup and Archiving:

When we talk about Backup and archiving I cannot miss "The Big Four" Net Backup, Backup Exec, Storage Foundation and of course Enterprise Vault. I have experience with most of them (except Storage Foundation) and I cannot find a better portfolio in this branch. Some people will say – Ok, they are good but this is group for security articles. Yes it is, but if a hardware failure or disaster occurs in your organization and you don't have backup of your data, your business is as good as dead. That's why I consider backups as part of my security policy implemented in our organization.

The last thing that I want to mention with regards to security that, we should look every day after it, in order to have adequate response on today's threats. Information has become business and cyber criminals would not hesitate to steal it from poorly secured networks. I've seen companies losing their business in days, just because they didn't have security policy in place. Symantec helps us to achieve Layered Security, with their one-stop security solutions, so we no more need to know 5 different products from 5 different vendors and at the end we still don't have fully implemented security policy. So act proactively and build your networks with security in mind.

2.17 LAPTOPS SECURITY AND BASIC PRINCIPLES OF INFORMATION SECURITY

For over twenty years, information security has held confidentiality, integrity and availability (known as the CIA triad) to be the core principles of information security.

There is continuous debate about extending this classic trio. Other principles such as Accountability have sometimes been proposed for addition - it has been pointed out that issues such as Non-Repudiation do not fit well within the three core concepts, and as regulation of computer systems has increased (particularly amongst the Western nations) Legality is becoming a key consideration for practical security installations.

2.17.1 Confidentiality

Confidentiality is the term used to prevent the disclosure of information to unauthorized individuals or systems. For example, a credit card transaction on the Internet requires the credit card number to be transmitted from the buyer to the merchant and from the merchant to a transaction processing network. The system attempts to enforce confidentiality by encrypting the card number during transmission, by limiting the places where it might appear (in databases, log files, backups, printed receipts, and so on), and by restricting access to the places where it is stored. If an unauthorized party obtains the card number in any way, a breach of confidentiality has occurred.

Breaches of confidentiality take many forms. Permitting someone to look over your shoulder at your computer screen while you have confidential data displayed on it could be a breach of confidentiality. If a laptop computer containing sensitive information about a company's employees is stolen or sold, it could result in a breach of confidentiality. Giving out confidential information over the telephone is a breach of confidentiality if the caller is not authorized to have the information.

Confidentiality is necessary (but not sufficient) for maintaining the privacy of the people whose personal information a system holds.

2.17.2 Integrity

In information security, integrity means that data cannot be modified undetectably. This is not the same thing as referential integrity in databases, although it can be viewed as a special case of Consistency as understood in the classic ACID model of transaction processing. Integrity is violated when a message is actively modified in transit. Most cipher systems provide message integrity along with privacy as part of the encryption process. Messages that have been tampered with in flight will not decrypt successfully.

2.17.3 Availability

For any information system to serve its purpose, the information must be available when it is needed. This means that the computing systems used to store and process the information, the security controls used to protect it, and the communication channels used to access it must be functioning correctly. High availability systems aim to remain available at all times, preventing service disruptions due to power outages, hardware failures, and system upgrades. Ensuring availability also involves preventing denial-of-service attacks.

2.17.4 Authenticity

In computing, e-Business and information security it is necessary to ensure that the data, transactions, communications or documents (electronic or physical) are genuine. It is also important for authenticity to validate that both parties involved are who they claim they are.

2.17.5 Non-repudiation

In law, non-repudiation implies one's intention to fulfill their obligations to a contract. It also implies that one party of a transaction cannot deny having received a transaction nor can the other party deny having sent a transaction.

Electronic commerce uses technology such as digital signatures and encryption to establish authenticity and non-repudiation

2.18 INFORMATION CLASSIFICATION AND THEIR ROLES

2.18.1 Security Classification for Information

An important aspect of information security and risk management is recognizing the value of information and defining appropriate procedures and protection requirements for the information. Not all information is equal and so not all information requires the same degree of protection. This requires information to be assigned a security classification.

The first step in information classification is to identify a member of senior management as the owner of the particular information to be classified. Next, develop a classification policy. The policy should describe the different classification labels, define the criteria for information to be assigned a particular label, and list the required security controls for each classification.

Some factors that influence which classification information should be assigned include how much value that information has to the organization, how old the information is and whether or not the information has become obsolete. Laws and other regulatory requirements are also important considerations when classifying information.

The type of information security classification labels selected and used will depend on the nature of the organization, with examples being:

- In the business sector, labels such as: **Public, Sensitive, Private, Confidential**.
- In the government sector, labels such as: **Unclassified**, **Sensitive But Unclassified**, **Restricted**, **Confidential**, **Secret**, **Top Secret** and their non-English equivalents.
- In cross-sectoral formations, the Traffic Light Protocol, which consists of: **White, Green, Amber** and **Red**.

All employees in the organization, as well as business partners, must be trained on the classification schema and understand the required security controls and handling procedures for each classification. The classification a particular information asset has been assigned should be reviewed periodically to ensure the classification is still appropriate for the information and to ensure the security controls required by the classification are in place.

2.19 SECURITY CHALLENGES IN THE FUTURE MOBILE INTERNET

The last decade showed a trend from the closed telephone network provided by a few operators towards open networks provided by many companies. With ad hoc networks, we even see a trend towards networks without any ownership by ISPs or other commercial providers and without any centralized infrastructure. Furthermore, the technologies to access these networks are developing rapidly and will be very heterogeneous. In the upcoming personal area networks (PAN), people will wear a couple of devices around themselves and install them in a self-configurable manner in the personal LAN of their flats.

Research in the area of security for (1) privacy, (2) authentication, (3) accounting and billing, (4) availability, and (5) reliability is to be conducted to make mobile communication trustworthy and successful. The key objectives are to analyse the security problems, to develop appropriate secure solutions related to all layers, to implement sample prototype solutions and finally to stimulate the standardization process. To make this integrated secure system approach a reality in the future secure Internet, at least the following problems have to be solved, and protocols as well as data formats have to be standardized.

In the last couple of years we have witnessed a silent revolution in computing and in our daily lifestyle. Computing and electronics have gone mobile without us changing our security approach. Moreover, thanks to the new communication standards, mostly wireless, each piece of equipment is usually able to communicate with each other device. So how can we balance security with mobile communicating, sometimes even embedded, devices.

Mobile applications share most of the security issues of traditional networked applications. These include authentication of devices and users, hiding information from prying eyes using encryption, viruses, and access control. However, the mobile world adds some unique issues to the already complex security arena. Mobile devices are easily misplaced or stolen, so physical security is important. Information that is usually confined behind a corporate firewall is now winging its way through the air, possibly spending some time on hosted servers or wireless gateways. If your solution uses a wireless LAN (WLAN) for connectivity, there are a host of WLAN-specific security issues that are currently making consultants a lot of money. Although in its infancy, the hacking of mobile devices (even cell phones!) has begun.

SUMMARY

Security is a branch of computer technology known as information security as applied to computers and networks. The objective of computer security includes protection of information and property from theft, corruption, or natural disaster, while allowing the information and property to remain accessible and productive to its intended users. The term computer system security means the collective processes and mechanisms by which sensitive and valuable information and services are protected from publication, tampering or collapse by unauthorized activities or untrustworthy individuals and unplanned events respectively. The strategies and methodologies of computer security often differ from most other computer technologies because of its somewhat elusive objective of preventing unwanted computer behavior instead of enabling wanted computer behavior. Wireless security is the prevention of unauthorized access or damage to computers using wireless networks.

Wireless networks are very common, both for organizations and individuals. Many laptop computers have wireless cards pre-installed. The ability to enter a network while mobile has great benefits. However, wireless networking has many security issues. Hackers have found wireless networks relatively easy to break into, and even use wireless technology to crack into wired networks. As a result, it's very important that enterprises define effective wireless security policies that guard against unauthorized access to important resources. Wireless Intrusion Prevention Systems are commonly used to enforce wireless security policies.

Modern technologies are becoming ever more integrated with each other. Mobile phones are becoming increasing intelligent, and handsets are growing ever more like computers in functionality. And smart devices, such as PDAs, on-board car computers, and new generation household appliances are now equipped with communications functions. We are entering a new era - the age of smart houses, global networks which encompass a wide range of devices, all of them exchanging data with each other via - as cyberpunk authors say - air saturated with bits and bytes Such trends clearly open new horizons to malicious users, and the potential threats are self evident.

This wired world is still evolving. We should be grateful for the fact that it still requires a bit more than a laptop and a wireless connection to gain control over someone else's car. However, security for mobile devices is already an issue; and the first indication of trouble came, not surprisingly, in the form of a virus.

Mobile devices have become a plague for information security professionals. There are worms and other malware that specifically target these devices such as the iPhone worm that would steal banking data and enlist these devices in a botnet. Theft is still a major cause of data breaches as mobile devices, especially laptops, are the main culprits. Tens of thousands of laptops are stolen each year and often these have sensitive data that require public disclosure as a data breach.

Information systems security is responsible for the integrity and safety of system resources and activities. Most organizations in developed countries are dependent on the secure operation of their information systems. In fact, the very fabric of societies often depends on this security. Information systems are at the heart of intensive-care units and air-traffic-control systems. Financial institutions could not survive a total failure of their information systems for longer than a day or two. Electronic funds transfer systems (EFTS) handle immense amounts of money that exist only as electronic signals.

The mobile networks protect users and their privacy using some security methods. Each mobile device has an ID placed inside SIM card. This ID uniquely identifies every user. The user can protect the SIM card using a personal identity number (PIN) with at least four digits.

Even though the user identity has a basic level of protection, there is need to secure the mobile communications during wireless sessions. The security level of the mobile communications depends on the security methods implemented by the mobile network. In this section we give a brief overview of three basic security levels of mobile communications and their generic implementations with PKI infrastructure. An important aspect of information security and risk management is recognizing the value of information and defining appropriate procedures and protection requirements for the information. Not all information is equal and so not all information requires the same degree of protection. This requires information to be assigned a security classification.

EXERCISES

1. Why information is so important for an individual or an organisation.
2. Explain the role of information system for computer service.
3. Why confidentiality is important to corporate information.
4. What is the difference security and threat.
5. Explain how confidentiality can be achieved.
6. Explain in what is web security.
7. What is access control. Discuss its types.
8. What is security? Explain it with proper example.
9. What are security challenges in mobile devices.
10. What are various mobile devices.
11. What is wireless computing.
12. What are the issues in security in mobile and wireless computing.
13. What are the security implication for organization.
14. Discuss laptops security.
15. Explain the concept of confidentiality, integrity, availability in information security.
16. What is information classification and their roles.
17. Explain the basic principles of information security.

UNIT – 2

CHAPTER 3

What is E-commerce

3.1 INTRODUCTION

Ecommerce (e-commerce) or electronic **commerce**, a subset of ebusiness, is the purchasing, selling, and exchanging of goods and services over computer networks (such as the Internet) through which transactions or terms of sale are performed electronically. Contrary to popular belief, ecommerce is not just on the Web. In fact, ecommerce was alive and well in business to business transactions before the Web back in the 70s via EDI (Electronic Data Interchange) through VANs (Value-Added Networks). Ecommerce can be broken into four main categories: B2B, B2C, C2B, and C2C.

E-Commerce refers to the exchange of goods and services over the Internet. All major retail brands have an online presence, and many brands have no associated bricks and mortar presence. However, e-Commerce also applies to business to business transactions, for example, between manufacturers and suppliers or distributors.

In the online retail space, there are a number of models that retailers can adopt. Traditionally, the Web presence has been kept distinct from the bricks and mortar presence, so transactions were limited to buying online and delivering the goods or services. The online presence is also important for researching a product that a customer can purchase later in the store. Recently, there has been a trend towards multi-channel retail, allowing new models such as purchasing online and picking up in store.

E-Commerce systems are also relevant for the services industry. For example, online banking and brokerage services allow customers to retrieve bank statements online, transfer funds, pay credit card bills, apply for and receive approval for a new mortgage, buy and sell securities, and get financial guidance and information.

E-commerce, a prime driver of the global economy, has changed business processes worldwide, increasing logistical efficiencies and facilitating the buying, selling, and marketing of goods. Similarly, e-commerce has benefited millions of consumers through decreased prices, increased competition, and faster order and delivery times.

Large and small companies across multiple industries depend on e-commerce applications to survive and compete in local, national, and global economies. These companies use e-mail to communicate with customers and suppliers and the Internet to handle marketing and electronic transaction processing and settlement. They rely on myriad hardware and software solutions to manage large databases and carry out sophisticated analysis of complex business operations, support back office automation, assist document sharing, and facilitate communication with clients, customers and colleagues.

While e-commerce has advanced most rapidly in developed countries, companies in developing countries increasingly use e-commerce to strengthen their core business practices and spin off new businesses.

E-commerce can be divided into:

- E-tailing or "virtual storefronts" on Web sites with online catalogs, sometimes gathered into a "virtual mall"
- The gathering and use of demographic data through Web contacts
- Electronic Data Interchange (EDI), the business-to-business exchange of data
- E-mail and fax and their use as media for reaching prospects and established customers (for example, with newsletters)
- Business-to-business buying and selling
- The security of business transactions

3.1.1 Type of E-commerce

E-commerce is the use of Internet and the web to transact business but when we focus on digitally enabled commercial transactions between and among organizations and individuals involving information systems under the control of the firm it takes the form of e-business. Nowadays, 'e' is gaining momentum and most of the things if not everything is getting digitally enabled. Thus, it becomes very important to clearly draw the line between different types of commerce or business integrated with the 'e' factor.

There are mainly five types of e-commerce models:

1. **Business to Consumer (B2C):** As the name suggests, it is the model involving businesses and consumers. This is the most common e-commerce segment. In this model, online businesses sell to individual consumers. When B2C started, it had a small share in the market but after 1995 its growth was exponential. The basic concept behind this type is that the online retailers and marketers can sell their products to the online consumer by using crystal clear data which is made available via various online marketing tools. E.g. An online pharmacy giving free medical consultation and selling medicines to patients is following B2C model.
2. **Business to Business (B2B):** It is the largest form of e-commerce involving business of trillions of dollars. In this form, the buyers and sellers are both business entities and do not involve an individual consumer. It is like the manufacturer supplying goods to the retailer or

wholesaler. E.g. Dell sells computers and other related accessories online but it is does not manufacture all those products. So, in order to sell those products, it first purchases them from different businesses i.e. the manufacturers of those products.

3. **Consumer to Consumer (C2C):** It facilitates the online transaction of goods or services between two people. Though there is no visible intermediary involved but the parties cannot carry out the transactions without the platform which is provided by the online market maker such as eBay.
4. **Peer to Peer (P2P):** Though it is an e-commerce model but it is more than that. It is a technology in itself which helps people to directly share computer files and computer resources without having to go through a central web server. To use this, both sides need to install the required software so that they can communicate on the common platform. This type of e-commerce has quite low revenue generation as from the beginning it has been inclined to the free usage due to which it sometimes got entangled in cyber laws.
5. **m-Commerce:** It refers to the use of mobile devices for conducting the transactions. The mobile device holders can contact each other and can conduct the business. Even the web design and development companies optimize the websites to be viewed correctly on mobile devices.

There are other types of e-commerce business models too like Business to Employee (B2E), Government to Business (G2B) and Government to Citizen (G2C) but in essence they are similar to the above mentioned types. Moreover, it is not necessary that these models are dedicatedly followed in all the online business types. It may be the case that a business is using all the models or only one of them or some of them as per its needs.

3.1.2 How E-commerce Works

E-commerce allows people to create completely new business models. Unless you have been living under a rock for the last few years, you have probably heard about e-commerce. And you have heard about it from several different angles. You may have: heard about all of the companies that offer e-commerce.

Our secure shopping cart allows your customers to purchase their products online without worry. The orders placed by your customers online will appear in your Control Panel as invoices, where you can print and process them the way you do all your regular orders. Also, and email copy of the invoice is automatically sent to the customer and to an email address you have chosen for your own information.

There is no need for you to have a Merchant Account (an account which allows you to actually capture credit card dollars online in real-time)...but if you decide you want one, a special area within your Control Panel will show you step by step how to set one up with just a few clicks.

Unless you have been living under a rock for the last few years, you have probably heard about e-commerce. And you have heard about it from several different angles. You may have:

- heard about all of the companies that offer e-commerce because you have been bombarded by their TV and radio ads

- read all of the news stories about the shift to e-commerce and the hype that has developed around e-commerce companies
- seen the huge valuations that Web companies get in the stock market, even when they don't make a profit
- purchased something on the Web, so you have direct personal experience with e-commerce
- Still, you may feel like you don't understand e-commerce at all. What is all the hype about? Why the huge valuations? And most importantly, is there a way for you to participate? If you have an e-commerce idea, how might you get started implementing it? If you have had questions like these, then this article will help out by exposing you to the entire e-commerce space.

3.2 E-COMMERCE TECHNOLOGY (EXPECTED)

E Commerce is one of the most important facets of the Internet to have emerged in the recent times. Ecommerce or electronic commerce involves carrying out business over the Internet with the assistance of computers, which are linked to each other forming a network. To be specific ecommerce would be buying and selling of goods and services and transfer of funds through digital communications.

3.2.1 The Benefits of E-commerce

- Ecommerce allows people to carry out businesses without the barriers of time or distance. One can log on to the Internet at any point of time, be it day or night and purchase or sell anything one desires at a single click of the mouse.
- The direct cost-of-sale for an order taken from a web site is lower than through traditional means (retail, paper based), as there is no human interaction during the on-line electronic purchase order process. Also, electronic selling virtually eliminates processing errors, as well as being faster and more convenient for the visitor.
- Ecommerce is ideal for niche products. Customers for such products are usually few. But in the vast market place i.e. the Internet, even niche products could generate viable volumes.

Figure 3.1: Benefits of E-commerce

- Another important benefit of Ecommerce is that it is the cheapest means of doing business.
- The day-to-day pressures of the marketplace have played their part in reducing the opportunities for companies to invest in improving their competitive position. A mature market, increased competitions have all reduced the amount of money available to invest. If the selling price cannot be increased and the manufactured cost cannot be decreased then the difference can be in the way the business is carried out. Ecommerce has provided the solution by decimating the costs, which are incurred.

- From the buyer's perspective also ecommerce offers a lot of tangible advantages.
    1. Reduction in buyer's sorting out time.
    2. Better buyer descisions
    3. Less time is spent in resolving invoice and order discrepancies.
    4. Increased opportunities for buying alternative products.
- The strategic benefit of making a business 'ecommerce enabled', is that it helps reduce the delivery time, labour cost and the cost incurred in the following areas:
    1. Document preparation
    2. Error detection and correction
    3. Reconciliation
    4. Mail preparation
    5. Telephone calling
    6. Data entry
    7. Overtime
    8. Supervision expenses
- Operational benefits of e commerce include reducing both the time and personnel required to complete business processes, and reducing strain on other resources. It's because of all these advantages that one can harness the power of ecommerce and convert a business to ebusiness by using powerful turnkey ecommerce solutions made available by ebusiness solution providers.

3.2.2 Ecommerce Security Issues

Most ecommerce merchants leave the mechanics to their hosting company or IT staff, but it helps to understand the basic principles. Any system has to meet four requirements:

- **privacy:** information must be kept from unauthorized parties.
- **integrity:** message must not be altered or tampered with.
- **authentication:** sender and recipient must prove their identities to each other.
- **non-repudiation:** proof is needed that the message was indeed received.
- Privacy is handled by encryption. In PKI (public key infrastructure) a message is encrypted by a public key, and decrypted by a private key. The public key is widely distributed, but only the recipient has the private key. For authentication (proving the identity of the sender, since only the sender has the particular key) the encrypted message is encrypted again, but this time with a private key. Such procedures form the basis of RSA (used by banks and governments) and PGP (Pretty Good Privacy, used to encrypt emails).
- Unfortunately, PKI is not an efficient way of sending large amounts of information, and is often used only as a first step - to allow two parties to agree upon a key for symmetric secret key encryption. Here sender and recipient use keys that are generated for the

particular message by a third body: a key distribution center. The keys are not identical, but each is shared with the key distribution center, which allows the message to be read. Then the symmetric keys are encrypted in the RSA manner, and rules set under various protocols. Naturally, the private keys have to be kept secret, and most security lapses indeed arise here.

3.2.3 Digital Signatures and Certificates

Digital signatures meet the need for authentication and integrity. To vastly simplify matters (as throughout this page), a plain text message is run through a hash function and so given a value: the message digest. This digest, the hash function and the plain text encrypted with the recipient's public key is sent to the recipient. The recipient decodes the message with their private key, and runs the message through the supplied hash function to that the message digest value remains unchanged (message has not been tampered with). Very often, the message is also time stamped by a third party agency, which provides non-repudiation.

What about authentication? How does a customer know that the website receiving sensitive information is not set up by some other party posing as the e-merchant? They check the digital certificate. This is a digital document issued by the CA (certification authority: Verisign, Thawte, etc.) that uniquely identifies the merchant. Digital certificates are sold for emails, e-merchants and web-servers.

3.2.4 Secure Socket Layers

Information sent over the Internet commonly uses the set of rules called TCP/IP (Transmission Control Protocol / Internet Protocol). The information is broken into packets, numbered sequentially, and an error control attached. Individual packets are sent by different routes. TCP/IP reassembles them in order and resubmits any packet showing errors. SSL uses PKI and digital certificates to ensure privacy and authentication. The procedure is something like this: the client sends a message to the server, which replies with a digital certificate. Using PKI, server and client negotiate to create session keys, which are symmetrical secret keys specially created for that particular transmission. Once the session keys are agreed, communication continues with these session keys and the digital certificates.

3.2.5 PCI, SET, Firewalls and Kerberos

Credit card details can be safely sent with SSL, but once stored on the server they are vulnerable to outsiders hacking into the server and accompanying network. A PCI (peripheral component interconnect: hardware) card is often added for protection, therefore, or another approach altogether is adopted: SET (Secure Electronic Transaction). Developed by Visa and Mastercard, SET uses PKI for privacy, and digital certificates to authenticate the three parties: merchant, customer and bank. More importantly, sensitive information is not seen by the merchant, and is not kept on the merchant's server.

Firewalls (software or hardware) protect a server, a network and an individual PC from attack by viruses and hackers. Equally important is protection from malice or carelessness within the system, and many companies use the Kerberos protocol, which uses symmetric secret key cryptography to restrict access to authorized employees.

3.2.6 Transactions

Sensitive information has to be protected through at least three transactions:

- credit card details supplied by the customer, either to the merchant or payment gateway. Handled by the server's SSL and the merchant/server's digital certificates.
- credit card details passed to the bank for processing. Handled by the complex security measures of the payment gateway.
- order and customer details supplied to the merchant, either directly or from the payment gateway/credit card processing company. Handled by SSL, server security, digital certificates (and payment gateway sometimes).

3.2.7 Practical Consequences

1. The merchant is always responsible for security of the Internet-connected PC where customer details are handled. Virus protection and a firewall are the minimum requirement. To be absolutely safe, store sensitive information and customer details on zip-disks, a physically separate PC or with a commercial file storage service. Always keep multiple back-ups of essential information, and ensure they are stored safely off-site.
2. Where customers order by email, information should be encrypted with PGP or similar software. Or payment should be made by specially encrypted checks and ordering software.
3. Where credit cards are taken online and processed later, it's the merchant's responsibility to check the security of the hosting company's webserver. Use a reputable company and demand detailed replies to your queries.
4. Where credit cards are taken online and processed in real time, four situations arise:
   (i) You use a service bureau. Sensitive information is handled entirely by the service bureau, which is responsible for its security. Other customer and order details are your responsibility as in 3. above.
   (ii) You possess an ecommerce merchant account but use the digital certificate supplied by the hosting company. A cheap option acceptable for smallish transactions with SMEs. Check out the hosting company, and the terms and conditions applying to the digital certificate.
   (iii) You possess an ecommerce merchant account and obtain your own digital certificate (costing some hundreds of dollars). Check out the hosting company, and enter into a dialogue with the certification authority: they will certainly probe your credentials.

(iv) You possess a merchant account, and run the business from your own server. You need trained IT staff to maintain all aspects of security firewalls, Kerberos, SSL, and a digital certificate for the server (costing thousands or tens of thousands of dollars).

Security is a vexing, costly and complicated business, but a single lapse can be expensive in lost funds, records and reputation. Don't wait for disaster to strike, but stay proactive, employing a security expert where necessary.

3.3 SECURITY ISSUES IN ELECTRONIC COMMERCE ON WEB

(Very Important)

Most businesses that have made the move towards an online presence have experienced some kind of security threat to their business. Since the Internet is a public system in which every transaction can be tracked, logged, monitored and stored in many locations, it is important for businesses to understand possible security threats to their business.

There are many threats to e-commerce that may come from sources within an organization or through some external channel. The following are the top corporate security threats categorized by internal and external threats.

- Unauthorized internal users who accesses confidential information by using a stolen passwords for the purpose of committing fraud or theft.
- Former employees of an organization that maintain access to information resources directly by creating alternative passwords, "back doors" into the computer system, or indirectly through former co-workers.
- Weak access points in information infrastructure and security that can expose company information and trade secrets.
- Management that undermines security is maybe the greatest risk to e-commerce as there Contractors, partners, consultants, and temps who take advantage of even limited access to important systems.
- Peoples mentality on Internet security is changing this is evident through the increase in sales of antivirus software and subscriptions to email virus protection.
- Businesses may take Visa's lead of requiring its service providers and merchants to have firewalls, encryption, as well as testing and access policies as a condition of doing business with them. They feel that the security of their B2B partner is as important as their creditworthiness.

3.3.1 Security Risks in eBusiness

Security risks can include theft of data (credit card numbers from your database), distortion of data (changes to payment files or invoices so that people appear to owe you more or less than they do), destruction of data, or broadcasting of data (showing visitors" real names instead of their nicknames in a chat room or forum). All of these cost your business money in terms of data recovery and goodwill recovery.

3.3.2 Criminal vs. Civil Laws

One of the points that this white paper really brings home is that most problems businesses experience with hackers have to be resolved in a civil court, not a criminal court. The difference is that when a law that's broken is civil, the company being harmed must collect its own evidence of the crime and take the perpetrator to court on its own dime. With criminal laws, you can call and ask police or the FBI for assistance. This distinction matters immensely for planning purposes. If a business doesn't have a plan in place, with resources readily available, vital forensic evidence can be lost in the time it does take to find the appropriate resources. Usually the evidence is all digital and smart crackers know how to erase their tracks before you have a chance to get a copy of the server log or other files with which they've been tinkering. Without evidence you have no case. Companies need to have a culture of security to prevent abuse of computer systems by insiders and to be on the lookout for attempted hacking. According to the report, most companies will find evidence of attempted hacking in their server logs, if they look for it. One problem is that companies don't do anything about attempted hacking until it becomes effective hacking. The report suggests that any hacking attempts be prosecuted as vigorously as successful hacking to discourage it and to make clear that they're not easy pickings.

Annual employee training should include security training and cybercrime awareness so that all employees know that your company doesn't take it lightly. They should also be aware of what suspicious activities on their own and network computers looks like, so they can report it when they see it. Finally, your company should have clear procedures in place so that when someone reports unusual activity on a computer, a database, or a server, that person doesn't inadvertently destroy the forensic evidence, the IT team knows how to proceed, and management is both informed and involved in following through with the investigation.

3.3.3 Privacy and Security Issues in E-Commerce

As mentioned, security is also a major concern for e-commerce sites and consumers alike. Consumers fear the loss of their financial data, and e-commerce sites fear the financial losses associated with break-ins and any resulting bad publicity. Not only must e-commerce sites and consumers judge security vulnerabilities and assess potential technical solutions, they must also assess, evaluate, and resolve the risks involved. We cover each in turn.

3.3.4 Security Vulnerabilities in Electronic Commerce

There are many points of failure, or vulnerabilities, in an e-commerce environment. Even in a simplified e-commerce scenario a single user contacts a single web site, and then gives his credit card and address information for shipping a purchase many potential security vulnerabilities exist. Indeed, even in this simple scenario, there are a number of systems and networks involved. Each has security issues:

A user must use a web site and at some point identify, or authenticate, himself to the site. Typically, authentication begins on the user's home computer and its browser. Unfortunately, security problems in home computers offer hackers other ways to steal ecommerce data and identification data from users. Some current examples include a popular home-banking system that stores a user's account number in a Web "cookie" which hostile web-sites can crack ineffective encryption or lack of encryption for home wireless networks and, mail-borne viruses that can steal the user's financial data from the local disk .While these specific security problems will be fixed by some software developers and web-site administrators, similar problems will continue to occur. Alternatives to the home computer include Point-of- Sale (POS) terminals in brick-and-mortar stores, as well as a variety of mobile and handheld devices.

The user's web browser connects to the merchant front-end. When a consumer makes an online purchase, the merchant's web-server usually caches the order's personal information in an archive of recent orders. This archive contains everything necessary for credit-card fraud. Further, such archives often hold 90 days' worth of customers' orders.

The merchant back-end and database. A site's servers can weaken the company's internal network. This not easily remedied, because the web servers need administrative connections to the internal network, but web server software tends to have buggy security. Here, the cost of failure is very high, with potential theft of customers' identities or corporate data. Additionally, the back-end may connect with third party fulfillment centers and other processing agents. Arguably, the risk of stolen product is the merchant's least-important security concern, because most merchants' traditional operations already have careful controls to track payments and deliveries. However, these third parties can release valuable data through their own vulnerabilities.

In summary, privacy and security are still ongoing research problems. There have been some interesting and significant findings, however, in the last five years that bear important consequences for e-commerce sites and consumers. Privacy is now understood, by many, to be social construction with expectations the largest consideration. Yet, privacy is also considered a public issue by regulators, who have nonetheless largely allowed technology to unfold to date. Security is now understood to be largely imperfect, the continual cat-and-mouse game of security expert and hacker. Important technical developments have been deployed in the last five years; however, it is clear that organizational policies may play as an important a role in site security. Finally, detailed economics- and sociologically- based analyses are beginning to find their way into the published literature, and we expect that these studies will bring greater clarity and proficiency to admittedly murky areas.

3.4 SECURITY TECHNOLOGIES

There are many relevant technologies, including cryptographic technologies that can mitigate the above vulnerabilities. However, none is comprehensive or airtight by itself. Accordingly, we next present a brief overview of the major technologies, also considering the advantages and disadvantages of each.

3.4.1 Economic Issues

Again, an understanding of security would be incomplete without an analysis of the underlying economic issues. The above presented security either as a technical imperative or as a set of social and organizational issues; however, it must be stressed that security for both consumer and site requires an analysis with the proper weighing of potential risk. More importantly, as Anderson points out, security engineering is a matter of control and power as well as access. Security mechanisms can be used to govern compatibility and attempt to control network effects governing the adoption of new or potentially replacing technologies . Indeed, Anderson argues that security technologies are often deployed as much for risk reassignment as risk reduction.

3.4.2 e-Commerce Security: Attacks and Preventive Strategies

Web Sphere Commerce is business middleware that accelerates the development of any business transaction-oriented application, from the smallest online retailer to B2B portals, to supply chain management applications. For many of our clients, Web Sphere Commerce provides an integrated platform that runs both their customer facing online shopping sites, and their internal distributor or supplier portals as shown in Figure 3.2.

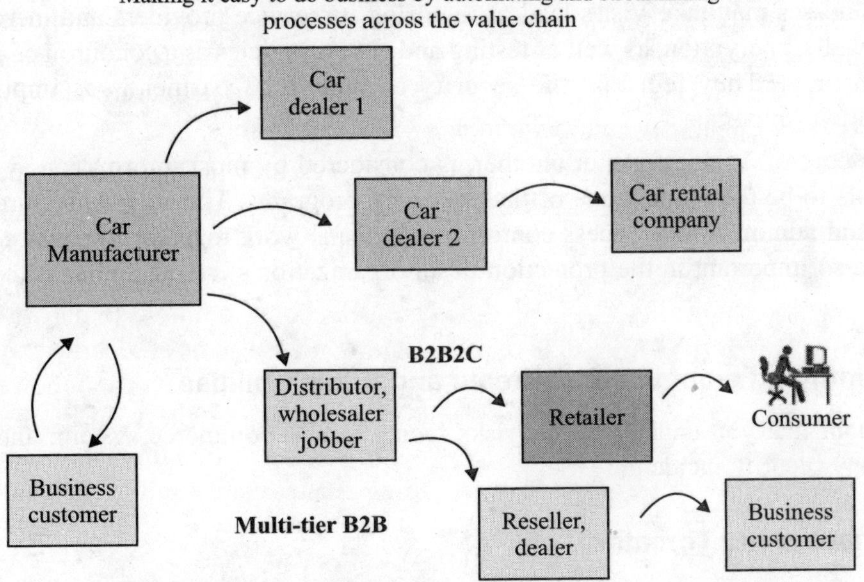

Figure 3.2: Common WebSphere Commerce Business Model

3.5 SECURITY THREATS TO ELECTRONIC COMMERCE (IMPORTANT)

Most businesses that have made the move towards an online presence have experienced some kind of security threat to their business. Since the Internet is a public system in which every transaction can be tracked, logged, monitored and stored in many locations, it is important for businesses to understand possible security threats to their business.

There are many threats to e-commerce that may come from sources within an organization or through some external channel. The following are the top corporate security threats categorized by internal and external threats.

1. Unauthorized internal users who accesses confidential information by using a stolen passwords for the purpose of committing fraud or theft.
2. Former employees of an organization that maintain access to information resources directly by creating alternative passwords, "back doors" into the computer system, or indirectly through former co-workers.
3. Weak access points in information infrastructure and security that can expose company information and trade secrets.
4. Management that undermines security is maybe the greatest risk to e-commerce as there Contractors, partners, consultants, and temps who take advantage of even limited access to important systems.
5. Peoples mentality on Internet security is changing this is evident through the increase in sales of antivirus software and subscriptions to email virus protection.
6. Businesses may take Visa's lead of requiring its service providers and merchants to have firewalls, encryption, as well as testing and access policies as a condition of doing business with them. They feel that the security of their B2B partner is as important as their creditworthiness.

Access control, in one form or another, is considered by most information systems security professionals to be the cornerstone of their security programs. The various features of physical, technical, and administrative access control mechanisms work together to construct the security architecture so important in the protection of an organization's critical and sensitive information assets.

3.5.1 Identifying e-commerce Threats and Vulnerabilities

It is important that you understand the risks facing your e-commerce system, and the potential impact of any security incident.

3.5.2 What are the Threats

Threats to e-commerce systems can be either malicious or accidental. The procedures and controls you put in place to protect your site should help minimize both.

Malicious threats could include:

- hackers attempting to penetrate a system to read or alter sensitive data
- burglars stealing a server or laptop that has unprotected sensitive data on its disk
- imposters posing as legitimate users and even creating a website similar to yours

- authorized users downloading a webpage or receiving an email with hidden active content that attacks your systems or sends sensitive information to unauthorized people

You should consider potential threats to sensitive information from three angles:

- Where (or who) are the potential sources of threats?
- What level of expertise is the hacker likely to possess? How much effort are they likely to expend in attempting to breach your security?
- What facilities and tools are available to them?

The real threat may not be the most obvious one. Attacks from authorized users (such as a disaffected employee or partner) are far more common than attacks by hackers.

3.5.3 E-commerce Systems Risk Assessment

A risk assessment can be carried out to provide an organization with a clear understanding of the risks facing its e-commerce system and associated business processes, and the potential impact if a security incident arises.

A key part of a risk assessment is defining the business' information access requirements. This will cover the rules of access for different groups of users. For example, different rules may apply for employees, consultants, managed service providers, suppliers, customers, auditors and government agencies.

Any analysis should also take account of how electronic transactions are verified. How do you know that an order has actually come from a known customer? Where contracts are exchanged electronically, who can sign them and how can it be proved which is the signed version?

3.6 E-COMMERCE SECURITY ISSUES (IMPORTANT)

E-commerce systems are based upon internet use, which provides open and easy communications on a global basis. However, because the internet is unregulated, unmanaged and uncontrolled, it poses a wide range of risks and threats to the systems operating on it.

The use of the internet means that your internal IT and e-commerce systems are potentially accessible by anyone, irrespective of their location.

3.6.1 Threats from Hackers and the Risks to Business

Some of the more common threats that hackers pose to e-commerce systems include:

- carrying out denial-of-service (DoS) attacks that stop access to authorized users of a website, so that the site is forced to offer a reduced level of service or, in some cases, ceases operation completely
- gaining access to sensitive data - such as price lists, catalogues and valuable intellectual property, and altering, destroying or copying it

- altering your website, thereby damaging your image or directing your customers to another site
- gaining access to financial information about your business or your customers, with a view to perpetrating fraud
- using viruses to corrupt your business data

3.6.2 Impact of a Security Incident on the Business

If your website is hacked into, it can have a significant impact upon a business running an e-commerce service. The potential business implications of a security incident include the following:

- direct financial loss as a consequence of fraud or litigation
- subsequent loss as a result of unwelcome publicity
- criminal charges if you are found to be in breach of the Data Protection or Computer Misuse Acts, or other regulation on e-commerce
- loss of market share if customer confidence is affected by a DoS attack

The image presented by your business, together with the brands under which you trade, are valuable assets. It is important to recognize that the use of e-commerce creates new ways for both image and brands to be attacked.

3.7 SECURITY OVERVIEW (VERY IMPORTANT)

A secure system accomplishes its task with no unintended side effects. Using the analogy of a house to represent the system, you decide to carve out a piece of your front door to give your pets' easy access to the outdoors. However, the hole is too large, giving access to burglars. You have created an unintended implication and therefore, an insecure system.

In the software industry, security has two different perspectives. In the software development community, it describes the security features of a system. Common security features are ensuring passwords that are at least six characters long and encryption of sensitive data. For software consumers, it is protection against attacks rather than specific features of the system. Your house may have the latest alarm system and windows with bars, but if you leave your doors unlocked, despite the number of security features your system has, it is still insecure. Hence, security is not a number of features, but a system process. The weakest link in the chain determines the security of the system. In this article, we focus on possible attack scenarios in an e-Commerce system and provide preventive strategies, including security features, that you can implement.

Security has three main concepts: confidentiality, integrity, and availability. Confidentiality allows only authorized parties to read protected information. For example, if the postman reads your mail, this is a breach of your privacy. Integrity ensures data remains as is from the sender to the receiver. If someone added an extra bill to the envelope, which contained your credit card bill, he has violated the integrity of the mail. Availability ensures you have access and are authorized to resources. If the post office destroys your mail or the postman takes one year to deliver your mail, he has impacted the availability of your mail.

3.7.1 The Players

In a typical e-Commerce experience, a shopper proceeds to a Web site to browse a catalog and make a purchase. This simple activity illustrates the four major players in e-Commerce security. One player is the shopper who uses his browser to locate the site. The site is usually operated by a merchant, also a player, whose business is to sell merchandise to make a profit. As the merchant business is selling goods and services, not building software, he usually purchases most of the software to run his site from third-party software vendors. The software vendor is the last of the three legit imate players. The attacker is the player whose goal is to exploit the other three players for illegitimate gains. Figure 3.3 illustrates the players in a shopping experience.

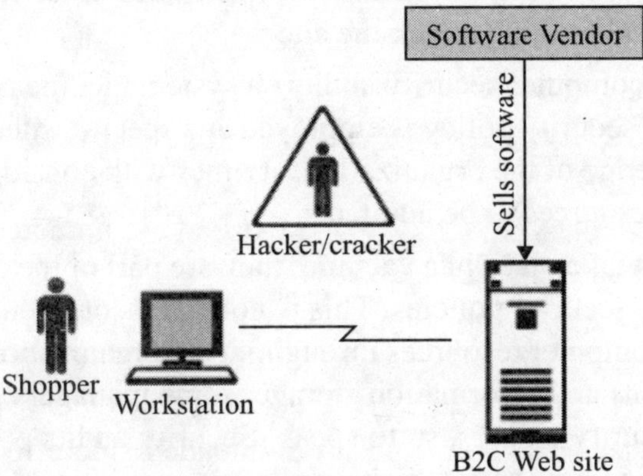

Figure 3.3: The players

The attacker can besiege the players and their resources with various damaging or benign schemes that result in system exploitation. Threats and vulnerabilities are classified under confidentiality, integrity, and availability. A threat is a possible attack against a system. It does not necessarily mean that the system is vulnerable to the attack. An attacker can threaten to throw eggs against your brick house, but it is harmless. A vulnerability is a weakness in the system, but it is not necessarily known by the attacker. For example, only you know that you have left your front door unlocked. Vulnerabilities exist at entry and exit points in the system. In a house, the vulnerable points are the doors and windows. When the burglar threatens to break into your house and finds the vulnerability of the unlocked door, he is exploiting the assets in the house.

3.7.2 Security Audits **(UPTU 2010-11)**

The word "audit" can send shivers down the spine of the most battle-hardened executive. It means that an outside organization is going to conduct a formal written examination of one or more crucial components of the organization. Financial audits are the most common examinations a business manager encounters. This is a familiar area for most executives: they know that financial auditors are going to examine the financial records and how those records are used. They may even be familiar with physical security audits. However, they are unlikely to be acquainted with information security audits; that is, an audit of how the confidentiality, availability and integrity of an organization's information is assured. They should be. An information security audit is one of the best ways to determine the security of an organization's information without incurring the cost and other associated damages of a security incident.

What is a Security Audit

You may see the phrase "penetration test" used interchangeably with the phrase "computer security audit". They are not the same thing. A penetration test (also known as a pen-test) is a very narrowly focused attempt to look for security holes in a critical resource, such as a firewall or Web server. Penetration testers may only be looking at one service on a network resource. They usually operate from outside the firewall with minimal inside information in order to more realistically simulate the means by which a hacker would attack the site.

On the other hand, a computer security audit is a systematic, measurable technical assessment of how the organization's security policy is employed at a specific site. Computer security auditors work with the full knowledge of the organization, at times with considerable inside information, in order to understand the resources to be audited.

Security audits do not take place in a vacuum; they are part of the on-going process of defining and maintaining effective security policies. This is not just a conference room activity. It involves everyone who uses any computer resources throughout the organization. Given the dynamic nature of computer configurations and information storage, some managers may wonder if there is truly any way to check the security ledgers, so to speak. Security audits provide such a tool, a fair and measurable way to examine how secure a site really is.

Computer security auditors perform their work though personal interviews, vulnerability scans, examination of operating system settings, analyses of network shares, and historical data. They are concerned primarily with how **security policies** - the foundation of any effective organizational security strategy - are actually used. There are a number of key questions that security audits should attempt to answer:

- Are passwords difficult to crack?
- Are there access control lists (ACLs) in place on network devices to control who has access to shared data?
- Are there audit logs to record who accesses data?
- Are the audit logs reviewed?
- Are the security settings for operating systems in accordance with accepted industry security practices?
- Have all unnecessary applications and computer services been eliminated for each system?
- Are these operating systems and commercial applications patched to current levels?
- How is backup media stored? Who has access to it? Is it up-to-date?

- Is there a disaster recovery plan? Have the participants and stakeholders ever rehearsed the disaster recovery plan?
- Are there adequate cryptographic tools in place to govern data encryption, and have these tools been properly configured?
- Have custom-built applications been written with security in mind?
- How have these custom applications been tested for security flaws?
- How are configuration and code changes documented at every level? How are these records reviewed and who conducts the review?

These are just a few of the kind of questions that can and should be assessed in a security audit. In answering these questions honestly and rigorously, an organization can realistically assess how secure its vital information is.

Security Policy Defined

As stated, a security audit is essentially an assessment of how effectively the organization's security policy is being implemented. Of course, this assumes that the organization has a security policiy in place which, unfortunately, is not always the case. Even today, it is possible to find a number of organizations where a written security policy does not exist. Security policies are a means of standardizing security practices by having them codified (in writing) and agreed to by employees who read them and sign off on them. When security practices are unwritten or informal, they may not be generally understood and practiced by all employees in the organization. Furthermore, until all employees have read and signed off on the security policy, compliance of the policy cannot be enforced. Written security policies are not about questioning the integrity and competency of employees; rather, they ensure that everyone at every level understands how to protect company data and agrees to fulfill their obligations in order to do so.

Natural tensions frequently exist between workplace culture and security policy. Even with the best of intentions, employees often choose convenience over security. For example, users may know that they should choose difficult-to-guess passwords, but they may also want those passwords to be close at hand. So every fledgling auditor knows to check for sticky notes on the monitor and to pick up the keyboard and look under it for passwords. IT staff may know that every local administrator account should have a password; yet, in the haste to build a system, they may just bypass that step, intending to set the password later, and therefore place an insecure system on the network.

The security audit should seek to measure security policy compliance and recommend solutions to deficiencies in compliance. The policy should also be subject to scrutiny. Is it a living document, accurately reflecting how the organization protects IT assets on a daily basis? Does the policy reflect industry standards for the type of IT resources in use throughout the organization

3.8 SECURITY FEATURES

While security features do not guarantee a secure system, they are necessary to build a secure system. Security features have four categories:

- **Authentication:** Verifies who you say you are. It enforces that you are the only one allowed to logon to your Internet banking account.
- **Authorization:** Allows only you to manipulate your resources in specific ways. This prevents you from increasing the balance of your account or deleting a bill.
- **Encryption:** Deals with information hiding. It ensures you cannot spy on others during Internet banking transactions.
- **Auditing:** Keeps a record of operations. Merchants use auditing to prove that you bought a specific merchandise.

3.8.1 The Criminal Incentive

Attacks against e-Commerce Web sites are so alarming, they follow right after violent crimes in the news. Practically every month, there is an announcement of an attack on a major Web site where sensitive information is obtained. Why is e-Commerce vulnerable? Is e-Commerce software more insecure compared to other software? Did the number of criminals in the world increase? The developers producing e-Commerce software are pulled from the same pool of developers as those who work on other software. In fact, this relatively new field is an attraction for top talent. Therefore, the quality of software being produced is relatively the same compared to other products. The criminal population did not undergo a sudden explosion, but the incentives of an e-Commerce exploit are a bargain compared to other illegal opportunities.

Compared to robbing a bank, the tools necessary to perform an attack on the Internet is fairly cheap. The criminal only needs access to a computer and an Internet connection. On the other hand, a bank robbery may require firearms, a getaway car, and tools to crack a safe, but these may still not be enough. Hence, the low cost of entry to an e-Commerce site attracts the broader criminal population.

The payoff of a successful attack is unimaginable. If you were to take a penny from every account at any one of the major banks, it easily amounts to several million dollars. The local bank robber optimistically expects a windfall in the tens of thousands of dollars. Bank branches do not keep a lot of cash on hand. The majority is represented in bits and bytes sitting on a hard disk or zipping through a network.

While the local bank robber is restricted to the several branches in his region, his online counterpart can choose from the thousands of banks with an online operation. The online bank robber can rob a bank in another country, taking advantage of non-existent extradition rules between the country where the attack originated, and the country where the attack is destined.

An attack on a bank branch requires careful planning and precautions to ensure that the criminal does not leave a trail. He ensures the getaway car is not easily identifiable after the robbery. He cannot leave fingerprints or have his face captured on the surveillance cameras. If he performs his actions on the Internet, he can easily make himself anonymous and the source of the attack untraceable.

The local bank robber obtains detailed building maps and city maps of his target. His online counterpart easily and freely finds information on hacking and cracking. He uses different sets of tools and techniques everyday to target an online bank.

3.8.2 Points the Attacker Can Target

As mentioned, the vulnerability of a system exists at the entry and exit points within the system. Figure 3.4 shows an e-Commerce system with several points that the attacker can target:

- Shopper
- Shopper' computer
- Network connection between shopper and Web site's server
- Web site's server
- Software vendor

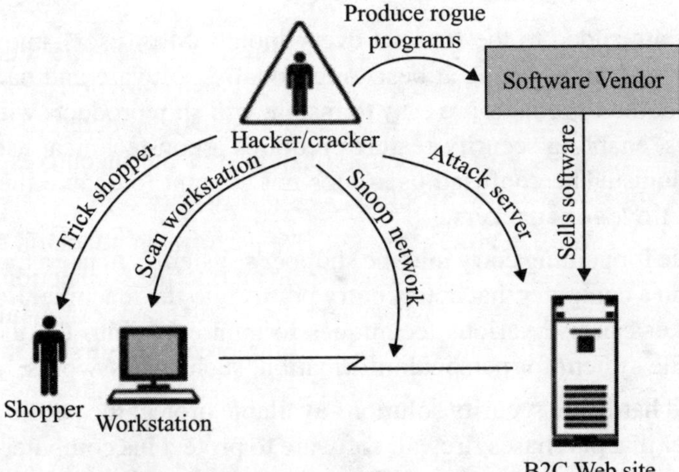

Figure 3.4: Points the attacker can target

These target points and their exploits are explored later in this article.

3.9 ATTACKS

This section describes potential security attack methods from an attacker or hacker.

3.9.1 Tricking the Shopper

Some of the easiest and most profitable attacks are based on tricking the shopper, also known as social engineering techniques. These attacks involve surveillance of the shopper's behavior, gathering information to use against the shopper. For example, a mother's maiden name is a common challenge question used by numerous sites. If one of these sites is tricked into giving away a password once the challenge question is provided, then not only has this site been compromised, but it is also likely that the shopper used the same logon ID and password on other sites.

A common scenario is that the attacker calls the shopper, pretending to be a representative from a site visited, and extracts information. The attacker then calls a customer service representative at the site, posing as the shopper and providing personal information. The attacker then asks for the password to be reset to a specific value.

Another common form of social engineering attacks are phishing schemes. Typo pirates play on the names of famous sites to collect authentication and registration information. For example, http://www.ibm.com/shop is registered by the attacker as www.ibn.com/shop. A shopper mistypes and enters the illegitimate site and provides confidential information. Alternatively, the attacker sends emails spoofed to look like they came from legitimate sites. The link inside the email maps to a rogue site that collects the information.

3.9.2 Snooping the Shopper's Computer

Millions of computers are added to the Internet every month. Most users' knowledge of security vulnerabilities of their systems is vague at best. Additionally, software and hardware vendors, in their quest to ensure that their products are easy to install, will ship products with security features disabled. In most cases, enabling security features requires a non-technical user to read manuals written for the technologist. The confused user does not attempt to enable the security features. This creates a treasure trove for attackers.

A popular technique for gaining entry into the shopper's system is to use a tool, such as SATAN, to perform port scans on a computer that detect entry points into the machine. Based on the opened ports found, the attacker can use various techniques to gain entry into the user's system. Upon entry, they scan your file system for personal information, such as passwords.

While software and hardware security solutions available protect the public's systems, they are not silver bullets. A user that purchases firewall software to protect his computer may find there are conflicts with other software on his system. To resolve the conflict, the user disables enough capabilities to render the firewall software useless.

3.9.3 Sniffing the Network

In this scheme, the attacker monitors the data between the shopper's computer and the server. He collects data about the shopper or steals personal information, such as credit card numbers.

There are points in the network where this attack is more practical than others. If the attacker sits in the middle of the network, then within the scope of the Internet, this attack becomes impractical. A request from the client to the server computer is broken up into small pieces known as packets as it leaves the client's computer and is reconstructed at the server. The packets of a request is sent through different routes. The attacker cannot access all the packets of a request and cannot decipher what message was sent.

Take the example of a shopper in Toronto purchasing goods from a store in Los Angeles. Some packets for a request are routed through New York, where others are routed through Chicago. A more practical location for this attack is near the shopper's computer or the server. Wireless hubs make attacks on the shopper's computer network the better choice because most wireless hubs are shipped with security features disabled. This allows an attacker to easily scan unencrypted traffic from the user's computer.

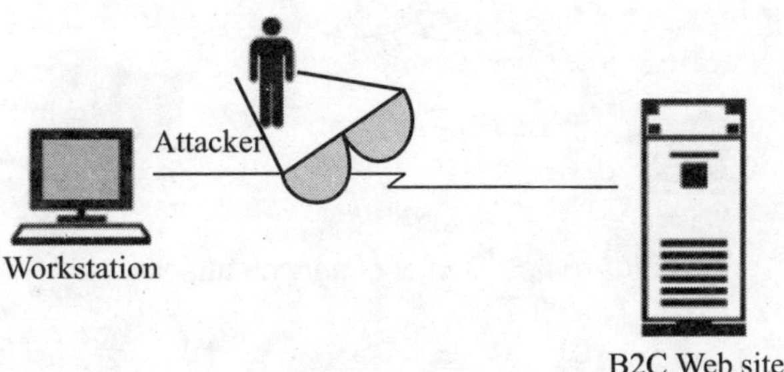

Figure 3.5: Attacker sniffing the network between client and server

3.9.4 Guessing Passwords

Another common attack is to guess a user's password. This style of attack is manual or automated. Manual attacks are laborious, and only successful if the attacker knows something about the shopper. For example, if the shopper uses their child's name as the password. Automated attacks have a higher likelihood of success, because the probability of guessing a user ID/password becomes more significant as the number of tries increases. Tools exist that use all the words in the dictionary to test user ID/password combinations, or that attack popular user ID/password combinations. The attacker can automate to go against multiple sites at one time.

3.9.5 Using Denial of Service Attacks

The denial of service attack is one of the best examples of impacting site availability. It involves getting the server to perform a large number of mundane tasks, exceeding the capacity of the server to cope with any other task. For example, if everyone in a large meeting asks you your name all at once, and every time you answer, they ask you again. You have experienced a personal denial of service attack. To ask a computer its name, you use ping. You can use ping to build an effective DoS attack. The smart hacker gets the server to use more computational resources in processing the request than the adversary does in generating the request.

Distributed DoS is a type of attack used on popular sites, such as Yahoo!®. In this type of attack, the hacker infects computers on the Internet via a virus or other means. The infected computer becomes slaves to the hacker. The hacker controls them at a predetermined time to bombard the target server with useless, but intensive resource consuming requests. This attack not only causes the target site to experience problems, but also the entire Internet as the number of packets is routed via many different paths to the target.

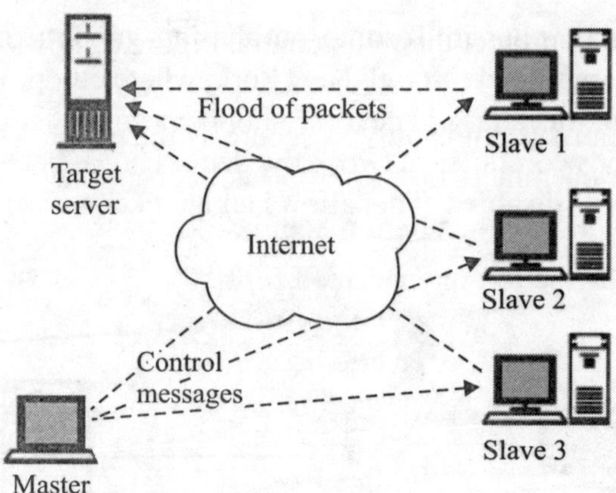

Figure 3.6: Denial of service attacks

3.9.6 Using known Server Bugs

The attacker analyzes the site to find what types of software are used on the site. He then proceeds to find what patches were issued for the software. Additionally, he searches on how to exploit a system without the patch. He proceeds to try each of the exploits. The sophisticated attacker finds a weakness in a similar type of software, and tries to use that to exploit the system. This is a simple, but effective attack. With millions of servers online, what is the probability that a system administrator forgot to apply a patch?

3.9.7 Using Server Root Exploits

Root exploits refer to techniques that gain super user access to the server. This is the most coveted type of exploit because the possibilities are limitless. When you attack a shopper or his computer, you can only affect one individual. With a root exploit, you gain control of the merchants and all the shoppers' information on the site. There are two main types of root exploits: buffer overflow attacks and executing scripts against a server.

In a buffer overflow attack, the hacker takes advantage of specific type of computer program bug that involves the allocation of storage during program execution. The technique involves tricking the server into execute code written by the attacker.

The other technique uses knowledge of scripts that are executed by the server. This is easily and freely found in the programming guides for the server. The attacker tries to construct scripts in the URL of his browser to retrieve information from his server. This technique is frequently used when the attacker is trying to retrieve data from the server's database.

3.9.8 Defenses

Despite the existence of hackers and crackers, e-Commerce remains a safe and secure activity. The resources available to large companies involved in e-Commerce are enormous. These companies will pursue every legal route to protect their customers. Figure 6 shows a high-level illustration of defenses available against attacks.

At the end of the day, your system is only as secure as the people who use it. Education is the best way to ensure that your customers take appropriate precautions:

- Install personal firewalls for the client machines.
- Store confidential information in encrypted form.

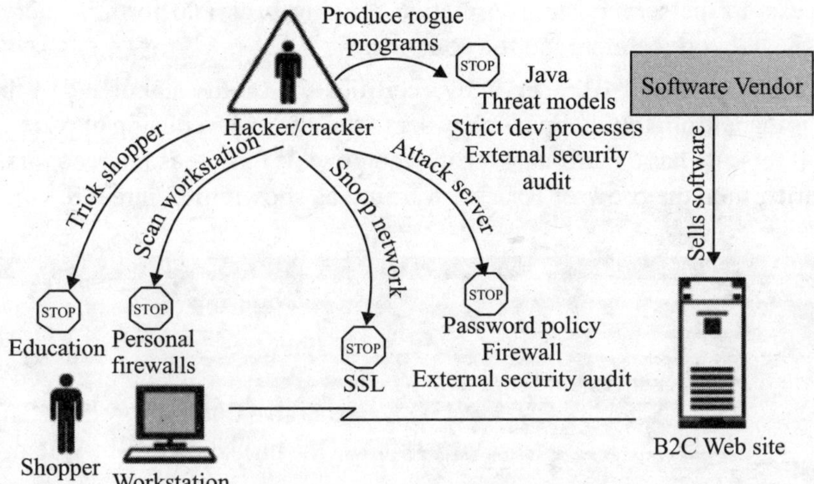

Figure 3.7: Attacks and their defenses

- Encrypt the stream using the Secure Socket Layer (SSL) protocol to protect information flowing between the client and the e-Commerce Web site.
- Use appropriate password policies, firewalls, and routine external security audits.
- Use threat model analysis, strict development policies, and external security audits to protect ISV software running the Web site.

3.9.9 Education

Your system is only as secure as the people who use it. If a shopper chooses a weak password, or does not keep their password confidential, then an attacker can pose as that user. This is significant if the compromised password belongs to an administrator of the system. In this case, there is likely physical security involved because the administrator client may not be exposed outside the firewall. Users need to use good judgement when giving out information, and be educated about possible phishing schemes and other social engineering attacks.

3.9.10 Personal Firewalls

When connecting your computer to a network, it becomes vulnerable to attack. A personal firewall helps protect your computer by limiting the types of traffic initiated by and directed to your computer. The intruder can also scan the hard drive to detect any stored passwords.

3.9.11 Secure Socket Layer (SSL)

Secure Socket Layer (SSL) is a protocol that encrypts data between the shopper's computer and the site's server. When an SSL-protected page is requested, the browser identifies the server as a trusted entity and initiates a handshake to pass encryption key information back and forth. Now, on subsequent requests to the server, the information flowing back and forth is encrypted so that a hacker sniffing the network cannot read the contents.

The SSL certificate is issued to the server by a certificate authority authorized by the government. When a request is made from the shopper's browser to the site's server using https://..., the shopper's browser checks if this site has a certificate it can recognize. If the site is not recognized by a trusted certificate authority, then the browser issues a warning as shown in Figure 3.8.

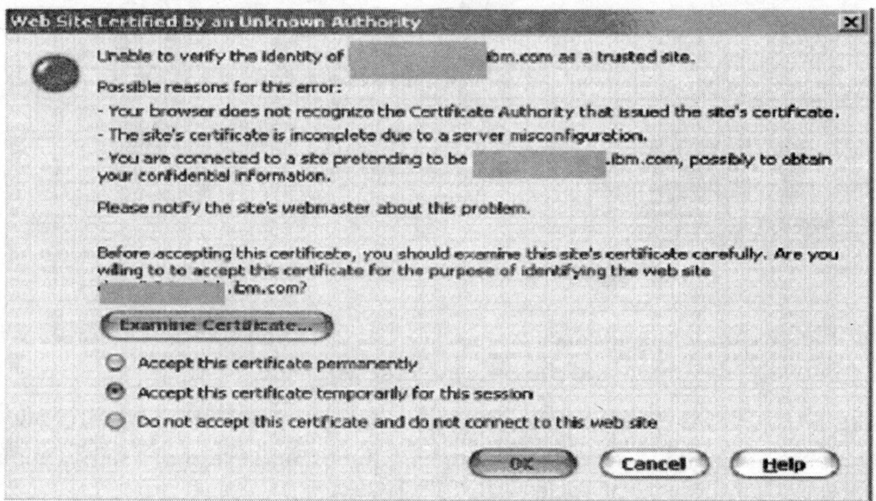

Figure 3.8: Warning to user

As an end-user, you can determine if you are in SSL by checking your browser. For example, in Mozilla® Firefox, the secure icon is at the top in the URL entry field as shown in Figure 3.9.

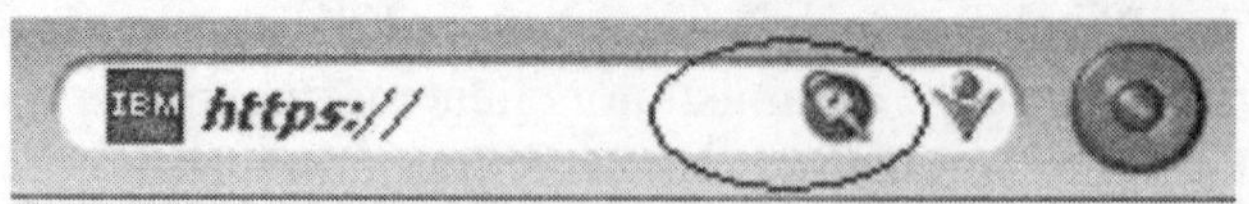

Figure 3.9: Secure icon in Mozilla Firefox

In Microsoft® Internet Explorer, the secure icon is at the bottom right of the browser as shown in Figure 3.10.

Figure 3.10: Secure icon in Microsoft Internet

3.9.12 Server Firewalls

A firewall is like the moat surrounding a castle. It ensures that requests can only enter the system from specified ports, and in some cases, ensures that all accesses are only from certain physical machines.

A common technique is to setup a demilitarized zone (DMZ) using two firewalls. The outer firewall has ports open that allow ingoing and outgoing HTTP requests. This allows the client browser to communicate with the server. A second firewall sits behind the e-Commerce servers. This firewall is heavily fortified, and only requests from trusted servers on specific ports are allowed through. Both firewalls use intrusion detection software to detect any unauthorized access attempts.

Another common technique used in conjunction with a DMZ is a honey pot server. A honey pot is a resource (for example, a fake payment server) placed in the DMZ to fool the hacker into thinking he has penetrated the inner wall. These servers are closely monitored, and any access by an attacker is detected.

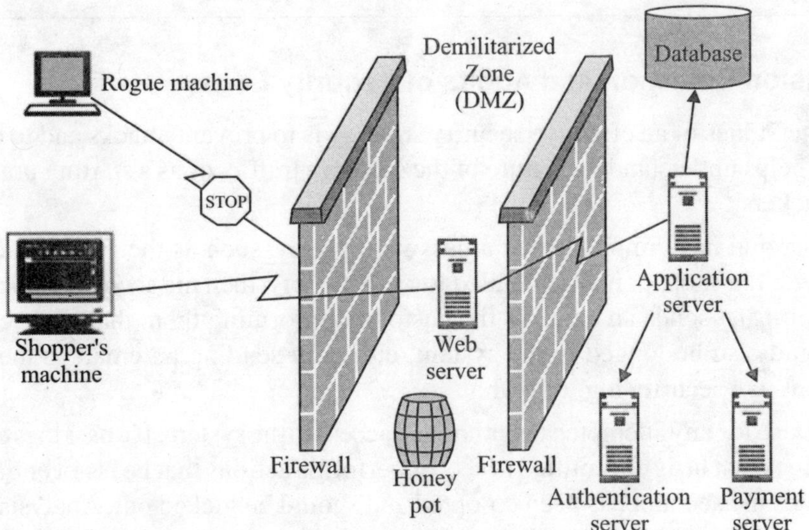

Figure 3.11: Firewalls and honey pots

3.9.13 Password Policies

Ensure that password policies are enforced for shoppers and internal users. A sample password policy, defined as part of the Federal Information Processing Standard (FIPS), is shown in the table given on next page.

You may choose to have different policies for shoppers versus your internal users. For example, you may choose to lockout an administrator after 3 failed login attempts instead of 6. These password policies protect against attacks that attempt to guess the user's password. They ensure that passwords are sufficiently strong enough so that they cannot be easily guessed. The account lockout capability ensures that an automated scheme cannot make more than a few guesses before the account is locked.

Table 3.1

Policy	Value
Account lockout threshold	6 attempts
Consecutive unsuccessful login delay	10 seconds
Matching user ID and password	N (no, they cannot match)
Maximum occurrence of consecutive characters	3 characters
Maximum instances of any character	4 instances
Maximum lifetime of passwords	180 days
Minimum number of alphabetic characters	1 alphabetic character
Minimum number of numeric characters	1 numeric character
Minimum length of password	6 characters
Reuse user's previous password	N (no, cannot be reused)

3.9.14 Intrusion Detection and Audits of Security Logs

One of the cornerstones of an effective security strategy is to prevent attacks and to detect potential attackers. This helps understand the nature of the system's traffic, or as a starting point for litigation against the attackers.

Suppose that you have implemented a password policy, such as the FIPS policy described in the section above. If a shopper makes 6 failed logon attempts, then his account is locked out. In this scenario, the company sends an email to the customer, informing them that his account is locked. This event should also be logged in the system, either by sending an email to the administrator, writing the event to a security log, or both.

You should also log any attempted unauthorized access to the system. If a user logs on, and attempts to access resources that he is not entitled to see, or performs actions that he is not entitled to perform, then this indicates the account has been co-opted and should be locked out. Analysis of the security logs can detect patterns of suspicious behavior, allowing the administrator to take action.

In addition to security logs, use business auditing to monitor activities such as payment processing. You can monitor and review these logs to detect patterns of inappropriate interaction at the business process level.

The infrastructure for business auditing and security logging is complex, and most likely will come as part of any middleware platform selected to host your site. Web Sphere Commerce, for example, has extensive capabilities in this area.

3.10 SECURITY POLICIES AND STANDARDS

There are many established policies and standards for avoiding security issues. However, they are not required by law. Some basic rules include:

- Never store a user's password in plain text or encrypted text on the system. Instead, use a one-way hashing algorithm to prevent password extraction.
- Employ external security consultants (ethical hackers) to analyze your system.
- Standards, such as the Federal Information Processing Standard (FIPS), describe guidelines for implementing features. For example, FIPS makes recommendations on password policies.
- Ensure that a sufficiently robust encryption algorithm, such as triple DES or AES, is used to encrypt all confidential information stored on the system.
- When developing third-party software for e-Commerce applications, use external auditors to verify that appropriate processes and techniques are being followed.
- Recently, there has been an effort to consolidate these best practices as the Common Criteria for IT Security Evaluation (CC). CC seems to be gaining attraction. It is directly applicable to the development of specific e-Commerce sites and to the development of third party software used as an infrastructure in e-Commerce sites.

Security best practices remain largely an art rather than a science, but there are some good guidelines and standards that all developers of e-Commerce software should follow.

3.10.1 Using Cookies

One of the issues faced by Web site designers is maintaining a secure session with a client over subsequent requests. Because HTTP is stateless, unless some kind of session token is passed back and forth on every request, the server has no way to link together requests made by the same person. Cookies are a popular mechanism for this. An identifier for the user or session is stored in a cookie and read on every request. You can use cookies to store user preference information, such as language and currency. This simplifies Web page development because you do not have to be concerned about passing this information back to the server.

The primary use of cookies is to store authentication and session information, your information, and your preferences. A secondary and controversial usage of cookies is to track the activities of users.

Different types of cookies are:

- **Temporary cookies:** These cookies are valid only for the lifetime of your current session, and are deleted when you close your browser. These are usually the good type. They are mostly used to keep your session information.

- **Permanent cookies:** These are for a time period, specified by the site, on the shopper's computer. They recall your previous session information.
- **Server-only cookies:** These cookies are usually harmless, and are only used by the server that issued them.
- **Third-party cookies:** These are usually used for tracking purposes by a site other than the one you are visiting. Your browser or a P3P policy can filter these cookies.

If you do not want to store cookies, here are other alternatives:

- Send user ID/password on every request: This was popular 5-10 years ago, but now recognized as an insecure technique. The user ID/password flowing under non-SSL is susceptible to attacks. This alternative is not practical for a high volume site. Pages that run under SSL would slow down site performance.
- SSL client side authentication: This is the most secure, but it is cumbersome for shoppers to install on their browsers. You have to pay for a company to verify who you are and to issue a certificate. The popularity of this technique for client-side authentication has decreased in recent years. It remains very popular on server sites.
- URL rewriting: This is a popular alternative to cookies. Each HTTP link on the page is specially encoded, but it is expensive for the site to implement. It interferes with the performance of the site because the pages cannot be cached and reused for different users. This alternative is susceptible to attack if it is not used under SSL.

Cookies marked as secure (storing encrypted data and passing to the user only under SSL) remain the most popular method of providing a secure online experience.

3.10.2 Using Threat Models to Prevent Exploits

When architecting and developing a system, it is important to use threat models to identify all possible security threats on the server. Think of the server like your house. It has doors and windows to allow for entry and exit. These are the points that a burglar will attack. A threat model seeks to identify these points in the server and to develop possible attacks.

Threat models are particularly important when relying on a third party vendor for all or part of the site's infrastructure. This ensures that the suite of threat models is complete and up-to-date.

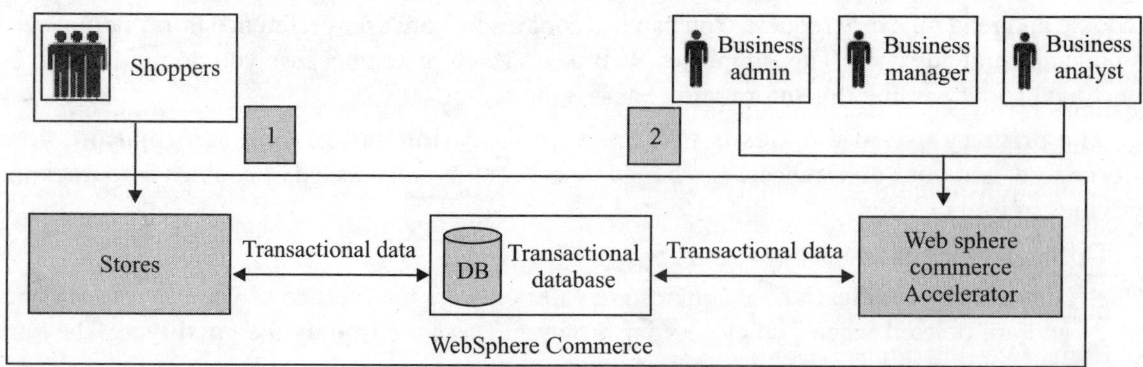

Figure 3.12: Threat models

3.10.3 Responding to Security Issues

An effective overall security strategy is to be prepared when vulnerabilities are detected. This also means ensuring that software vendors selected for all or part of the site's infrastructure have proactive and reactive policies for handling security issues.

In the case of Web Sphere Commerce, we can quickly form a SWAT team with key developers, testers, and support personnel. This becomes the highest priority for all involved parties. An assessment is made immediately, usually within the first few hours, to determine the vulnerability of the merchant's sites. A workaround or permanent solution is developed for the affected sites within a day. Then a "flash" issued to all customers to notify them of the problem, the solution, and how to check if they have been exploited. For critical issues, no one leaves until there is a solution.

3.10.4 Using an Online Security Checklist

Use this security checklist to protect yourself as a shopper:

- Whenever you logon, register, or enter private information, such as credit card data, ensure your browser is communicating with the server using SSL.
- Do not shop at a site when the browser does not recognize the server's SSL certificate. This check is done by your browser the first time your URL becomes HTTPS for the site. If the certificate is not recognized, then your browser presents a pop-up message to inform you.
- Use a password of at least 6 characters, and ensure that it contains some numeric and special characters (for example, c0113g3).
- Avoid reusing the same user ID and password at multiple Web sites.
- If you are authenticated (logged on) to a site, always logoff after you finish.
- Use a credit card for online purchases. Most credit card companies will help you with non-existent or damaged products.
- A bricks and mortar store with an online brand is most likely a legitimate site. However, the site may still have vulnerabilities

So here they are, the top five application-security risks.

1. Injection Attack: All web applications that collect and transmit data (using forms, for example) are susceptible to injection attacks. By sending specific commands through your application's forms, hackers can modify various elements of the code. In extreme cases, injection attacks could allow attackers to penetrate a firewalled environment, such as a network or database.

SQL injections like the ones that compromised Symantec and NASA this year dominate this attack category, but there are many additional varieties to which you could fall prey.

Some of the best protective measures for injection attacks include:

- Input Validation. Cleanse your input data.
- Human Verification.

- Restrictive Privileges. When connecting applications to databases and other proprietary systems.
- Vague Error Messages. Gives attackers little detail to go on and can help defray an onslaught

2. Cross-site Attack: Cross-site scripting (XSS) attacks steal private information like cookies or session tokens that unsuspecting users have associated with a particular website. XSS exploits can also redirect victims to familiar-looking web content that has been devised by the attacker to steal personally identifiable information or install malware.

Hackers deliver the malicious XSS-laden content that makes these exploits possible in the form of JavaScript, HTML, Flash or any executable code format for that matter. Any web application that compiles user-generated content without validating or encoding it first could fall prey to an XSS exploit. Social media hubs and blogs that allow users to post un-moderated comments are extremely susceptible to malicious XSS exploits (as was the case with Reddit's stored XSS attack earlier this year). This can include customer reviews and comments.

Reflected XSS exploits can be combined with phishing techniques to invade private information systems like email. Lancc James and his team of experts reveal how easily they exploited an XSS vulnerability to win Strong Webmail's $10,000 challenge in a quick two weeks.

Developers can help prevent XSS Attacks by deploying code that:

- Validates user input.
- Does not give a site or page "full trust" simply because HTTPS is present.
- Is heavily tested. Test, test, test, and then test again before launching or introducing website enhancements.

3. Cross-site Request Forgery: Cross-site request forgery (CSRF) exploits force unknowing users to carry out any number of malicious activities as long as the action is allowable within their permission set during an authenticated user session. If a web application administrator's credentials are compromised for example, CSRF could overtake the entire website.

Here's a short list of some common (and catastrophic) CSRF capabilities:

- Force a user to post an insulting comment or malicious link on a blog, forum, or product review.
- Change passwords, emails, and login credentials, effectively terminating access.
- Submit a user's email address and sign up for a newsletter.
- Make a purchase and use the hacker's shipping address.

CSRF capabilities are so powerful, you can understand why banks, financial brokers, bill pay services, and basically any institution that ties user credentials to money would need to approach each day with extreme caution and oversight. In a blog post this year, SECCOM Labs demonstrated how easily a CSRF banking scheme could be carried out.

Prohibiting users from submitting HTML code is one way help prevent CSRF. In many cases; however, that's not feasible because sites containing blogs, product reviews, and social media rely heavily on user-generated content. If your application has social web components like product reviews or comments, be aware that extremely effective, proprietary tools capable of disarming security features of even the most popular social vehicles like Twitter and Facebook do exist.

Protect applications from CSRF vulnerabilities by:

- Only accepting POST transactions.
- Create unique token values for each request.
- Re-authenticate based on the unique token or a password.

4. Insecure Direct Object References: Insecure direct object reference flaws allow attackers access to private directories, for example, by manipulating the URL to gain access. The primary risks with insecure direct object references include data leakage and identity theft. Adobe Flash Player fell victim to this type of flaw last year, and the company has since addressed and patched the vulnerability.

Developers with expertise in securing applications can help prevent insecure direct object references by:

- Creating a schema to protect and identify each object accessible by users.
- Using indirect reference maps in code when referring to file names, URLs and database keys.
- Ensuring the session is authenticated to view the requested information or files and only grant access for that specific request when direct references are required.

5. Broken Authentication and Session Management: Because all web applications have (at least) an administrator account, every website is susceptible to authentication and session management flaws. All too often, fingers point toward typical website functions like logout, forgotten password retrieval, and account update procedures when problems with authentication and session management arise.

Custom applications have increased risk. In fact, many instances of authentication and session management flaws occur when the code includes custom methods for validating user names and passwords and/or homegrown techniques for handling cookies or session tokens. Session hijacking is a good example of the trouble that can crop up when authentication and session management flaws reside within your application.

Using widely accepted mechanisms for user authentication and session management is a good, preventative start. Additionally, you can take these steps to protect your application from these vulnerabilities.

- Use https:// encryption on every page with form fields and store credentials in encrypted format and limit browser caching so hitting the back button doesn't grant unwanted parties access or visibility.
- Make sure users can logout from every page within the application and set short visitor sessions and force visitors to time out more often.
- Limit unsuccessful login attempts and require users to verify old password credentials when establishing new ones.

3.11 WEB SERVICES INTRODUCTION

Web Services can convert your applications into Web-applications. Web Services are published, found, and used through the Web.

- Web services are application components
- Web services communicate using open protocols
- Web services are self-contained and self-describing
- Web services can be discovered using UDDI
- Web services can be used by other applications
- XML is the basis for Web services

3.11.1 Why Web Services

Interoperability has Highest Priority

When all major platforms could access the Web using Web browsers, different platforms could interact. For these platforms to work together, Web-applications were developed.

Web-applications are simple applications that run on the web. These are built around the Web browser standards and can be used by any browser on any platform.

Web Services have Two Types of Uses

Reusable application-components. There are things applications need very often. So why make these over and over again?

Web services can offer application-components like: currency conversion, weather reports, or even language translation as services.

Connect existing software

Web services can help to solve the interoperability problem by giving different applications a way to link their data. With Web services you can exchange data between different applications and different platforms.

3.12 TOP FIVE SECURITY ISSUES (EXPECTED)

Small and medium-sized businesses use the Internet and networked applications to reach new customers and serve their existing ones more effectively. At the same time, new security threats and legislation puts increased pressure on business networks to be reliable and secure. Cisco® delivers comprehensive, affordable, integrated security solutions tailored for small and medium-sized businesses that help ensure business continuity, maintain customer privacy, and reduce operating costs. Businesses can confidently spend more time growing their business, and less time focusing on network security issues.

3.12.1 Business Challenges

Today's globally competitive business environment has small and medium-sized businesses focused on expanding their business and improving customer satisfaction while simultaneously controlling costs. Fortunately, the Internet and networked applications have leveled the playing field. Small and medium-sized businesses use their networks to extend their market reach and communicate with their customers and partners quickly and cost-effectively. But swift and agile e-business is a double-edged sword-access can also open up businesses to costly security breaches. It is more important than ever to have a reliable, secure, and available network.

3.12.2 Security Issues

According to recent studies, security is the biggest challenge facing small and medium-sized businesses. Ever-changing security threats from both inside and outside the business network can wreak havoc on business operations, affecting profitability and customer satisfaction. Small and medium-sized businesses must also comply with new regulations and laws created to protect consumer privacy and secure electronic information.

Security issues 1-worms and viruses

Computer worms and viruses remain the most common security threat, with 75 percent of small and medium businesses affected by at least one virus in the last year [Maritz Research, 2005]. Worms and viruses can have a devastating effect on business continuity and the bottom line. Smarter, more destructive strains are spreading faster than ever, infecting an entire office in seconds. Cleaning the infected computers takes much longer. The catastrophic results are lost orders, corrupted databases, and angry customers. As businesses struggle to update their computers with the latest operating system patches and antivirus software, new viruses can penetrate their defenses any day of the week. Meanwhile, employees spread viruses and spyware by unwittingly accessing malicious Websites, downloading untrustworthy material, or opening malicious e-mail attachments. These attacks are unintentionally invited into the organization, but still cause significant financial losses. Security systems must detect and repel worms, viruses, and spyware at all points in the network.

Security issue 2-information theft

Information theft is big business today. Malevolent hackers break into business networks to steal credit card or social security numbers for profit. Small and medium-sized businesses are at risk because they are seen as an easier mark than large corporations. Protecting the perimeter of the network is a good start, but it isn't enough, since many information thefts have help from a trusted insider, such as an employee or contractor.

Information theft can be costly to small and medium-sized businesses, since they rely on satisfied customers and a good reputation to help grow their business. Businesses that don't adequately protect their information could face negative publicity, government fines, or even lawsuits. For example, new consumer laws enacted in California require any business that suspects customer information has been viewed by unauthorized people must notify all their customers. Any security strategy must prevent theft of sensitive electronic information from both inside and outside the business.

3.13 FEATURES OF SECURITY IN TERMS OF INFORMATION SYSTEM

There are some feature of security as given below:

Authorization Manager. Authorization Manager gives application developers a flexible framework for integrating role-based access control into their applications, and it lets administrators who use those applications provide access in a natural, intuitive way: through assigned user roles relating to job function.

Stored user names and passwords. This utility provides secure storage for user names and credentials that are needed to access network or Internet resources.

Software restriction policies. This new security policy enables administrators to prevent software applications from running based on a hash algorithm of the software, the software's associated file path, the software publisher's certificate, or the Internet zone that hosts the software. Changes to existing technologies.

Certification authoritities. Numerous improvements and added features are included for certification authorities.

Constrained delegation. With this new security feature, you can specify what services you want to trust for delegation for a server.

Effective permissions tool. This tool calculates the permissions that are granted to a specified user or group.

Encrypting File System (EFS) no longer requires a recovery agent. Everyone membership. The built-in Everyone group includes Authenticated Users and Guests, but no longer includes members of the Anonymous group.

Operation-based auditing. Operation based auditing offers more descriptive auditing events and provides you with the opportunity to choose what operations you want to audit when auditing object accesses.

Reapplying security defaults. This procedure enables you to easily reapply the default security settings for the Windows Server 2003 family.

Every business, including yours, has valuable IT assets such as computers, networks, and data. And protecting those assets, requires that companies big and small conduct their own IT security audits in order to get a clear picture of the security risks they face and how to best deal with those threats.

3.13.1 What is the Security Perimeter

The security perimeter is both a conceptual and physical boundary within which your security audit will focus, and outside of which your audit will ignore. You ultimately decide for yourself what your security perimeter is, but a general rule of thumb is that the security perimeter should be the smallest boundary that contains the assets that you own and/or need to control for your own company's security.

3.14 VIRTUAL OGRANIZATIONS (UPTU-2010–11)

A virtual organization or company is one whose members are geographically apart, usually working by computer e-mail and groupware while appearing to others to be a single, unified organization with a real physical location.

The aim of this chapter is to explain the concept 'virtual organization' (VO) in a more detailed manner (in order to realise what security challenges a VO has to cope with). Below we will present definitions of VO, give some examples of VOs, and describe main characteristics of VOs. We will also list the benefits and the security challenges associated with VOs.

VO is a relatively new concept that has emerged in the beginning of 1990s. There is no single clear-cut definition of what a VO is. Different sources define it somewhat differently. For example, in VO is defined as a "dynamic collection of individuals and institutions which are required to share resources to achieve certain goals".

VO as "a temporary or permanent coalition of geographically dispersed individuals, groups, organizational units or entire organizations that pool resources, capabilities and information to achieve common objectives".

Jet in a concept IT infrastructure, namely network, is introduced: "VO refers to both the members of a switch able interorganizational electronic network and to the network itself that delivers non-standard products".

3.14.1 Reasons Behind a VO

The first two definitions speak about "certain goals" or "common objectives" while the third opens up what these goals/objectives can be, i.e. non-standard products.

Indeed, the incentive behind the creation of VOs is a collaborative delivery or creation of a customer-specified product or service. The reasons why organizations cannot provide such products/ services on their own and why they need virtual amalgamation are technical complexity of demanded products and constantly changing customer and market requirements. In addition development, production and support of modern products is highly complex. Often provision of such products would involve great risks for organizations unless they unite virtually, share resources, capabilities, and experience, utilize common facilities all to meet a specific customer demand.

3.14.2 What Does "virtuality" Imply

It is not a novelty in the organizational history to unite in order to grab a good market opportunity. In the case of virtual organizations the "virtual" part of the concept cannot be ignored. As pointed out in the related terms "virtual", "virtually" and "virtuality" imply that something exists having a potential effect but this something is not tangible. In classical organizations the boundaries are clearly defined, while VOs are characterized by fuzzy boundaries, flexible structure and the ability to include new partners as the need arises. All this became possible with the rise of Internet, networking, distributed computing and sophisticated web services. So, according to our point of view, in the definition of VO the IT infrastructure can not be ignored. Therefore in this thesis we define a VO as follows:

VO is a temporary or permanent coalition of geographically dispersed individuals, groups, organizational units or entire organizations that pool resources, capabilities and information to achieve common objectives, while decisively relying on information technology (IT).

3.14.3 Characteristics of a VO

VOs can be large or small, long- or short-lived. Other characteristics of VOs are:

- VO exists for a specific purpose, e.g. to implement a long-term marketing strategy, to launch a new groundbreaking product or to achieve some scientific goal. Non-standard product is the end-goal of a VO. VOs quickly deliver products/services that are innovative and customized.
- Membership and structure of a VO evolve over time.
- Switching: VO members can switch from one project to another.
- Dynamic VOs have a capability to unite quickly.
- Usually members of a VO have shared responsibilities, shared control, shared leadership, shared access to computing resources and services and shared loyalty.
- Resources, services and people that comprise a VO can be single- or multi-institutional, homogenous or heterogeneous.
- Principle of synergy (many-to-one): VO exhibits a unifying property because it is constituted from different organizational entities that create an effect of a single organization.
- Principle of divergence (one-to-many): a single organization can exhibit multiplication property by participating in many VOs at the same time.
- Virtualness is a matter of degree rather than a categorical property of an organization. Organization can choose to virtualizes its different parts, like production core, front end or back end.
- The presence of IT infrastructure is a necessary but not sufficient condition for a VO formation. Examples of IT that can be used are email, electronic file transfer, telephone, fax, screen sharing applications, videoconferencing, groupware tools, project management applications etc.
- VO is dependent on electronic linking, lies on the electronic space and is characterized by loose coupling.
- Spatial dispersion: VOs can be formed across country borders throughout the world.

3.14.4 VO Lifecycle

Some examples

Let's look briefly at some examples of what a VO may look like. This will illustrate the usefulness of VOs.

Example 1: A small software company wants to bid for a new contract, which is beyond its scope of the resources. This company forms a VO with other similar small companies and by doing that it is suddenly able to compete with larger corporations to gain the contract.

Example 2: A business traveller comes to a foreign country and wants to do something in the evening. He/she goes to a WLAN-equipped café and requests a multi-media city guide to be shown using his personal computer and the café's facilities. This service can only be provided if the café, content providers, the user's home service provider, and other network operators have previously formed a VO.

Example 3: EC (Electronics Company) has been producing equipment for broadband networks. EC develops 1) software control modules for broadband networks and 2) new strategic products. Control modules for broadband networks are the most critical products of EC. They are very complex too. EC found out that it is more efficient and cost-effective to entrust the programming of the machinery to external parties. So, EC has engaged itself in a VO relationship with multiple software vendors. EC runs several projects at a time and each project involves more than one vendor. External software vendors are small software shops situated either in the neighbourhood or far away. The business process goes typically in the following manner. A customer orders a network control unit from EC. EC assembles a project team responsible for this request. Project engineers design the product. A part of this product - the computer-driver machinery for producing the boards- needs to be reprogrammed, and new code needs to be developed. Engineers determine the software specification. Software vendors are selected and the contracts with them signed electronically. Software specification is then sent to the vendors and after a while (typically several days) the vendor delivers the code electronically. Engineers download the code and continue developing their prototype for the customer.

To develop new strategic products EC collaborates with similar companies located at other continents. These are long-term projects that aim to move broadband network technology forward.

3.14.5 Benefits and Challenges of VOs

To summon up our discussion on VOs we would like to list the benefits of engaging into a VO and the security risks associated with this process.

Benefits

- VOs make it possible to satisfy constantly changing customer and market requirements in a competitive manner. The access to market increases.
- It becomes possible to provide services precisely tailored to a specific customer need.
- An ability to participate in VOs increases the total service range a company can offer to its customers.
- Participation in VOs increases the total number of end-customers a company can reach indirectly via its partners.

- A particular organization can both "multiply itself" virtually by participating in several VOs and initiate a VO that will be constituted from different parties. This creates the possibility for coexistence of the opposites in one organization.
- By participation in a VO the concept-to-cash time is reduced.

Security Risks in VO

The most challenging part of VOs is the establishment and maintenance of trust. needs to be established at several levels: authentication, policy based management, business rules. In it is claimed that trust is a cognitive phenomenon rather than an affective one, meaning that it is based on rational calculations. The main challenges related to the trust establishment are:

- Each party has its own policies on access control and conditions of use.
- The allocation of resources is often dynamic since the structure of Vos may change dynamically. This implies that the Vo initiator may not know until part way through the job that additional resource X is required.
- Vo parties need to establish trust between them on a peer-to-peer basis.
- Trust needs to be established "on the fly", which means that some mechanism needs to negotiate conditions of use, through the delegation of trust from one party to another.
- Parties may be located in different countries under different jurisdictions and, as a consequence, adhere to different legal and business requirements.
- Since Vos rely on IT, exposure to fraud or misuse of technology is a major concern.
- Security systems of Vo partners must be mutually trusted. This brings up the challenge to come up with an effective and flexible security system.
- Contract management needs to be effective in order to be able to quickly reconfigure in Vos. Services for management of electronic contracts must be trusted.
- SLA monitoring is important to ensure that parties perform according to contracts.
- Confidentiality, privacy, integrity availability and accountability at a Vo level have to be assured. At the same time parties have to provide access to their services and resources, as specified in agreements.
- It is a challenging task to choose between different potential vendors/parties. Sometimes options are closed and only few players are available on the market. In these cases a Vo initiator is to choose whoever is available.
- It can be difficult to anchor an IT infrastructure in a Vo. People may experience as being forced to use it rather than as having it for assistance.
- It may happen that dispersed project members are incapable of communicating in a professional domain. For example, one may prefer open standard technologies, while the other proprietary ones.

Trust is established by the means of digital identities, certification, access control mechanisms, authentication, secure connection, reputation and inspection of the parties. Electronic commerce is generally considered to be the sales aspect of e-business.

3.15 BUSINESS TRANSACTION ON WEB (IMPORTANT)

A Business Transaction is a consistent change in the state of the business that is driven by a well-defined business function.

A business transaction is driven by well-defined business tasks and events that directly or indirectly contribute to generating economic value, such as processing and paying an insurance claim, and has also an associated number of parameters that represent security and timing requirements. Business transactions always either succeed or fail with respect to the business tasks (functions) that initiated them and govern them throughout their execution. If a business transaction completes successfully then each participant will have made consistent state changes, which, in aggregate, reflect the desired outcome of the multi-party business interaction.

At structural level, a business transaction is made up of a requesting (initiating) business activity performed by an initiating partner (party) and a responding business activity performed by the responding business partner. The initiating business activity sends a business document to a responding business activity that may return a business signal (signifying the completion of an activity) and possibly a business document as the last responding message. A transaction is associated with an SLA that describes the agreed upon QoS requirements and usually outlines what each party can do in the event the intended actions are not carried out (e.g., promised services not rendered, services rendered but payment not issued). A series of collaborative activities that explicitly enforces the achievement of an agreed-upon business objective in end-to-end processes. This objective is subject to service-level agreements that govern the choreographed/orchestrated behavior, non-functional and timing requirements, correlated exchange of information, and control flow of composed services.

It also consists of the exchange of data to facilitate the financing and payment aspect of the business transaction. It is similar to buying and selling of products and services on the web.

Some of the advantages of doing business transaction on the web are:

1. **Global reach:** Goods and service can be sold to customers world wide.
2. **Personalization:** Companies can customize products and reduce inventory.
3. **Interactivity:** Customers and suppliers can negotiate prices online.
4. **Right time and integrated marketing:** Online retailers provide products when and where customers want them and promotions can be direct to individual customers.
5. **Cast reducing:** E-business can reduce cost.

3.15.1 Examples of Business Transactions

Choose your favorite five:

- A sale of merchandise or services.
- A purchase of supplies or raw material.
- Receipt of a payment for an Accounts Receivable.

- Payment of a bill in Accounts Payable.
- Receipt of loan proceeds.
- Repayment of a loan.
- Issuance of a paycheck.
- Payment of employer taxes.
- Payment of income taxes.
- Purchase of a Fixed Asset.

A business transaction may be as short as a phone call to the bank for an account balance or as long as a mortgage (from the initial mortgage application to final satisfaction being sent after the last payment) and perhaps even as long as the lifelong relationship with a bank (covering multiple accounts used for different purposes). Business transactions may have hierarchical relationships (such as the relationships between the business transaction represented by a check to the business transaction represented by a bank account).

Each type of business transaction may have multiple states before it is completed. At each stage in its lifecycle it may generate various measurements (financial or otherwise) that may be used by management/stockholders/regulators to monitor and/or control the business.

3.15.2 General Requirements

Long Running Transactions

The business transactions that I described above are not the traditional transactions that are handled by TP monitors such as CICS. They have a long lifetime (may even be days or years) and multiple interactions with users over their lifetime. The traditional transactions only cover a small part of the life of these transactions and multiple traditional transactions are often required in order to complete a single business transaction. Often, the traditional transactions execute in different environments and it becomes difficult to connect all of the pieces back to the original customer need that started the whole process.

I believe that a traditional transaction has approximately the same relationship to a business transaction that a method has to an object. Just as a method may transition an object from one valid state to another, a traditional transaction may transition a business transaction from one valid state to another.

Work Flow

A BTPS should have the ability to process work flows. Each state of the business transaction can be represented by a step in the work flow. Each step in the work flow may be composed of the following phases:

1. **Work Planning:** The periodic process of planning for future work. This often involves review of historical work levels and/or the results of Work Plans from "upstream" processing areas that generate work for this processing area.

2. **Work Receiving and Arrival Reporting:** The process of receiving and getting control over newly arrived work. This often includes notifications to processors of work awaiting processing.
3. **Work Monitoring:** Review all available work, prioritization and scheduling the work to be done.
4. **Work Processing and Recording:** Doing the work and recording the results of the work.
5. **Work Routing:** Based on the change in state to the work, pass the work along to the next stage in the processing.
6. **Work Evaluation:** On a periodic basis, analyze the work. The information from this step is often the input to the Work Planning phase (step 1 above).

The work flow component of the system should allow the rules that define sequence of steps (dependencies) and the rules that define the processing to be performed at each step to be easily modified by the users. (This process should also be a work flow.)

Accounting

Accounting information is only one type of information to be collected by the work flow processing. Since internal and external financial reporting is often used to monitor and control a business, collecting this information is important. However, there are many business transactions that are not directly recorded in the financial reporting systems (i.e. the number of calls to the "banking by phone" unit that did not get through to a bank employee) that may generate useful information for internal reporting purposes.

Authorization

Just as accounting records what happened after the transaction is processed, a large part of business transactions involves authorizing each transaction before the real processing is done. In my experience, these rules are changed on a fairly frequent basis as the business changes it policies. However, once the authorization step(s) is (are) completed the underlying work often does not change.

Queue Management

In order to decouple the work flow steps from one another it is usually necessary to add queues between steps. A good work flow engine should allow the users (and managers) to monitor queues in order to shift processing resources as necessary. (Mostly in Work Receiving and Arrival Reporting or Work Monitoring phases defined above.)

Difficult Problems

The work flow engine should be responsible for doing all of steps defined above except for Work Processing and Recording (phase 4 above) which is unique to each step in each business transaction. It is even possible to reuse Work Processing programs associated with authorization in multiple business transactions. However, there are three functions that look like responsibilities of the work flow engine that often require detailed knowledge of the business transactions. This breaks the encapsulation of the business transactions.

Authorization Rule Dependence on Business Transaction Data

The authorization rules often vary based on the current state (the values of some fields) of the business transaction. It is difficult to write a generic authorization processor without detailed knowledge of each business transaction.

Routing

It is often possible to route a business transaction to one of many steps depending on the results of the Work Processing in this step. The routing rules often vary based on the current state of the business transaction. It is difficult to write a generic routing engine without detailed knowledge of each business transaction.

Work Monitoring

When human beings are the business transaction processors at some point in the Work Processing they often need the ability to select work based on varying criteria (i.e. I normally want to process work in the order it was received except when I am near the end of day - when I want the "big" transactions first).

3.16 E GOVERNANCE AND EDI (VERY IMPORTANT)

e-Government (from electronic government, also known as e-gov, digital government, online government or in a certain context transformational government) refers to government's use of information technology to exchange information and services with citizens, businesses, and other arms of government. e-Government may be applied by the legislature, judiciary, or administration, in order to improve internal efficiency, the delivery of public services, or processes of democratic governance. It also refers to the citizen to government interaction including the feed back of policies. The primary delivery models are Government-to-Citizen or Government-to-Customer (G2C), Government-to-Business (G2B) and Government-to-Government (G2G) & Government-to-Employees (G2E). The most important anticipated benefits of e-government include improved efficiency, convenience, and better accessibility of public services.

3.16.1 What is E-Governance

It is the use of a range of modern Information and Communication Technologies such as Internet, Local Area Networks, mobiles etc. by Government to improve the effectiveness, efficiency, service delivery and to promote democracy

Governance : An Information perspective

- Representative democracy relies on supposition that best way to make a decision is wider participation for all its citizens having access to relevant information.
- Government is by nature an information intensive organization.
- Information is power and information management is political .

Governance : In IT framework

- Expansion of Internet and electronic commerce, is redefining relationships among various stake holders in the process of Governance.
- A new model of governance would be based upon the transactions in virtual space, digital economy and dealing with knowledge oriented societies.
- Electronic Governance is an emerging trend to re-invent the way the Government works.

E-Governance: Focus

- Greater attention to improve service delivery mechanism
- Enhancing the efficiency of production
- Emphasis upon the wider access of information

E-Governance vs. E-Government

- Government's foremost job is to focus society on achieving the public interest."
- Governance is a way of describing the links between government and its broader environment - political, social and administrative."

Table 3.2

Government	Governance
superstructure	functionality
decisions	processes
rules	goals
rules	performance
implementation	coordination
outputs	outcomes
e-Government	e-Governance
electronic service delivery	electronic consultation
electronic workflow	electronic controllership
electronic voting	electronic engagement
electronic productivity	networked societal guidance

3.16.2 Why introduced EGovernances

EGovernment can transform citizen service, provide access to information to empower citizens, enable their participation in government and enhance citizen economic and social opportunities, so that they can make better lives, for themselves and for the next generation.

3.17 ELECTRONIC DATA INTERCHANGE (EDI)

Electronic Data Interchange is the computer-to-computer exchange of routine business data between trading partners in standard data formats. This definition contains 3 key concepts about EDI:

1. **Computer-to-computer:** EDI in its most efficient form flows directly out of a sender's computer system directly into a receiver's computer system without any human intervention; however, it is not always possible for EDI to flow in this most efficient manner.
2. **Routing business data:** EDI is used for routine business documents like Purchase Orders and Invoices. It is not used for non-routine business documents like complicated contracts or information meant for humans to read and analyze.
3. **Standard data formats:** A standard definition of the location and structure of the data is provided. Unstructured text is not EDI.

The diagram above illustrates how much slower the conventional paper process than the EDI process. Additionally, the conventional paper process includes substantially more human intervention to move business information from one company to another.

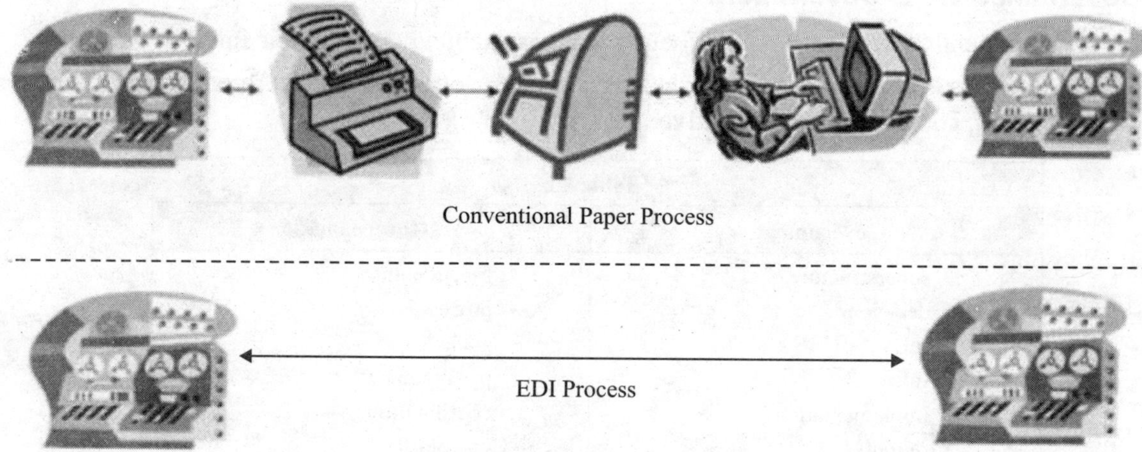

Figure 3.12

The conventional process requires someone to handle a printed computer generated form and mail it. Then, the recipient re-keys the data back into another computer for their internal processing. (It is estimated that 80% of the data that is keyed into computers is output from other computers!) The EDI process is a computer transmitting the information directly to another computer, eliminating the paperwork and human intervention.

Electronic Data Interchange, or EDI, is not a new technology and in fact has been around since the late 1960s. While EDI has benefited enormously from advances in technology, eg the introduction of the internet, EDI is not technology dependant. There are preferred ways to implement EDI in a company, but there are many approaches to choose from. The approach chosen should be driven by a company's business needs, not a particular implementation or technology.

In its simplest form, EDI is the computer to computer exchange, between two companies, of standard business documents in electronic format. There are two key elements in basic EDI. First, electronic documents replace paper based ones. Second, the exchange of documents takes place in a standardized format. Using these two basic concepts, any business can enter the world of EDI and begin taking advantage of the speed and economy of electronic commerce, or e-Commerce.

Figure 3.13

In today's fast-paced business world, your business may already be moving in this direction, customers or suppliers may already be approaching you to begin trading information electronically. For the newcomer to EDI, it may seem a very confusing subject area.

So what is a document? A document is any form of communication, usually paper based, sent between two companies, examples include:

- Purchase Orders
- Invoices
- Shipping Notices
- Export / Import Notices
- Carrier to carrier waybills
- Funds transfer
- Design specifications
- Health insurance claims

EDI is essentially a data processing concept which is independent of communication protocols or transmission media. EDI is a logical outgrowth of the standard computerization going on within companies over the last few decades. With EDI, the type of electronic communication between departments within a company can now easily be extended to reach out to other companies or trading partners.

EDI replaces human readable, paper or electronic based documents with machine readable, electronically coded documents. With EDI, the sending computer creates the message and the receiving computer interprets the message without any human involvement at all.

Before learning about what makes up an EDI system and how to implement one, it is important to look at an example that highlights some of the key differences between traditional paper document transactions and EDI. One of the first places where many companies implement EDI is in the exchange of a purchase order, (PO). In the traditional method of processing a purchase order, a buyer or purchasing agent will go through a fairly standard procedure to create a purchase order, consisting of the following steps:

- A buyer reviews data from an inventory or planning system
- The buyer enters data into a screen in the purchasing system to create a PO
- The buyer waits for the PO to be printed, usually on a special form
- After the PO is printed, the buyer mails it to the vendor
- The vendor receives the PO and posts it in their order entry system
- The buyer calls the vendor periodically to determine if the PO has been received and processed

When you add up the internal processing time required by the sender and receiver, and then add a couple of days in the mail, this process normally takes between three and five days. This assumes first that both the sender and receiver handled the PO quickly and that at every point along the way there were no errors in transcribing data from a form to a system.

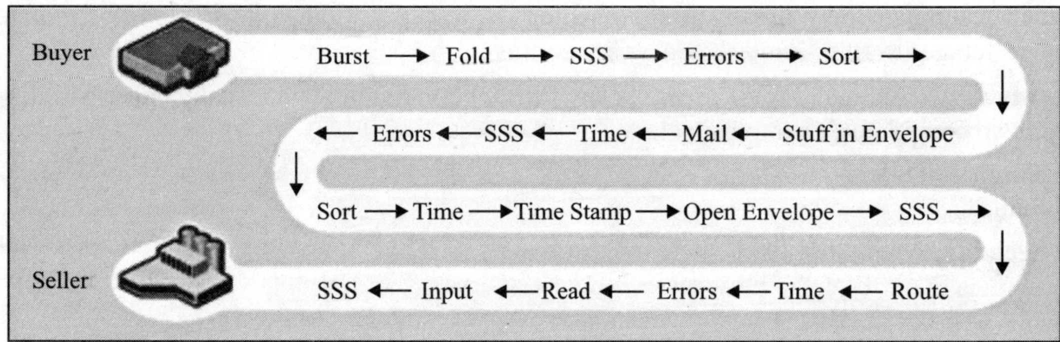

Figure 3.14

Now consider the same document exchange when a company places its purchase orders electronically using EDI:

- The buyer reviews the data and creates the PO, but does not print it
- EDI software creates an electronic version of the PO and transmits it automatically to the sender within minutes
- The vendor's order entry system receives the PO and updates the system immediately upon receipt

What took up to five days with paper and the postal system has just taken less than one hour. By eliminating the paper handling from most of the stages of the process, EDI has the potential to transform a traditional paper based process to look like this:

The major benefits of implementing EDI within your business are discussed in more detail in the 'Benefits of EDI' section of this Micro site but in summary EDI can help improve speed and accuracy of transactions, reduce costs and it provides improved flexibility when interacting on a daily basis with your trading partners or customers.

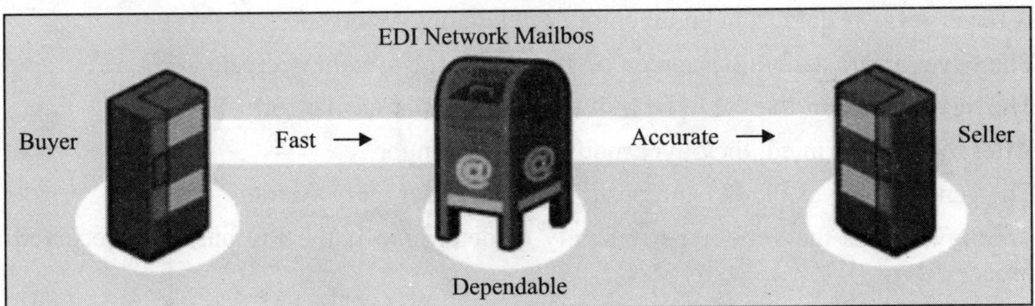

Figure 3.15

3.17.1 Benefits of EDI

- **Speed:** Data can move directly out of one computer system and into another with little to no delay.
- **Accuracy:** Errors are reduced because data is not being re-keyed. Error rates from entering data are between .5 - 3%. On large volumes of transactions, the possibility for the introduction of errors is enormous.
- **Simplicity:** EDI standards specify how data will be formatted and where it can be found.
- **Security:** Much less likely to lose information transmitted through EDI than information sent via mail. EDI can be accessed only by authorized users, and then there are audit trails and archives of data. EDI data cannot be easily changed by unauthorized users. It is also not subject to viruses.

These 4 benefits produce the following results:

- Faster buy-sell cycle time
- Faster cash flow
- Reduced order lead time
- Reduced inventories
- Ability to conduct just-in-time manufacturing
- Improved trading partner relationships

3.17.2 How does the EDI Process Work in the Retail Environment?

The retailer will initiate the process with an electronic transmission of an electronic Purchase Order (850). The supplier will receive the order, case it and print UCC-128 labels. Then, the order is packed and the UCC-128 labels are placed on the cartons. The cartons are then shipped to the retailer and the supplier electronically transmits an Advanced Ship Notice (856). After the shipment has been sent, the supplier transmits an electronic Invoice (810) for the goods. These electronic documents are sent in a standard Electronic Data Interchange (EDI) format.

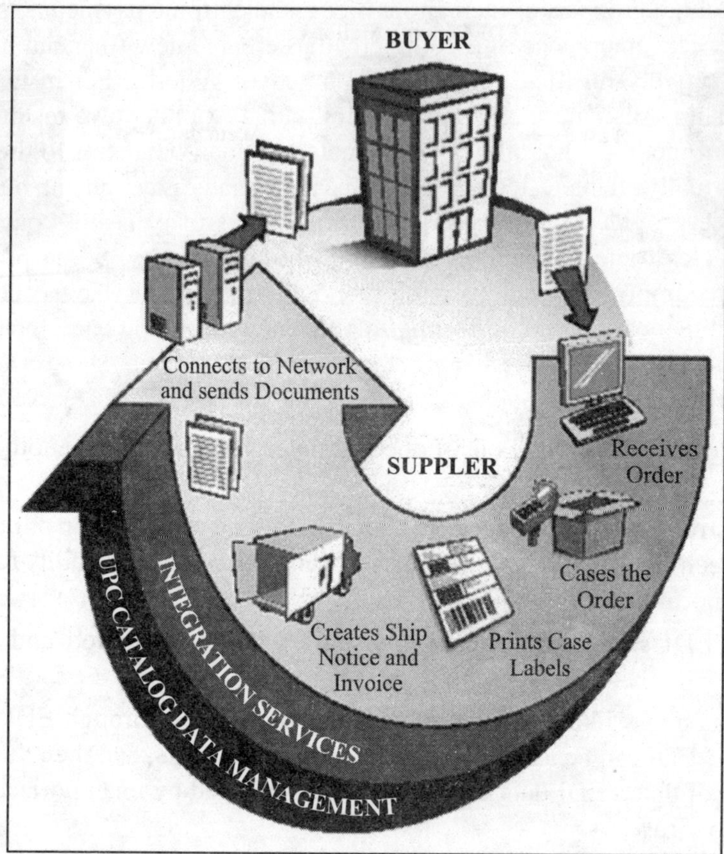

Figure 3.16

3.18 ELECTRONIC PAYMENT (UPTU-2010–11)

The emergence of e-commerce has created new financial needs that in many cases cannot be effectively fulfilled by the traditional payment systems. Recognizing this, virtually all interested parties are exploring various types of electronic payment system and issues surrounding electronic payment system and digital currency. Broadly electronic payment systems can be classified into four categories: Online Credit Card Payment System, Online Electronic Cash System, Electronic Cheque System and Smart Cards based Electronic Payment System. Each payment system has its advantages and disadvantages for the customers and merchants. These payment systems have numbers of requirements: e.g. security, acceptability, convenience, cost, anonymity, control, and traceability. Therefore, instead of focusing on the technological specifications of various electronic payment systems, the researcher have distinguished electronic payment systems based on what is being transmitted over the network; and analyze the difference of each electronic payment system by evaluating their requirements, characteristics and assess the applicability of each system.

As payment is an integral part of mercantile process, electronic payment system is an integral part of e-commerce. The emergence of e-commerce has created new financial needs that in many cases cannot be effectively fulfilled by traditional payment systems. For instance, new types of purchasing relationships-such as auction between individuals online-have resulted in the need for peer-to-peer payment methods that allows individuals to e-mail payments to the other individual. Recognizing this, virtually all interested parties (i.e. academicians, government, business community and financial service providers) are exploring various types of electronic payment system and issues surrounding electronic payment system and digital currency. Some proposed electronic payment systems are simply electronic version of existing payment systems such as cheques and credit cards, while, others are based on the digital currency technology and have the potential for definitive impact on today's financial and monetary system. While popular developers of electronic payment system predict fundamental changes in the financial sector because of the innovations in electronic payment system, Therefore, electronic payment systems and in particular, methods of payment being developed to support electronic commerce cannot be studied in an isolation. A failure to take place these developments into the proper context is likely to result in undue focus on the various experimental initiatives to develop electronic forms of payment without a proper reflection on the broader implications for the existing payment system.

3.18.1 Concept and Size of Electronic Payment

Payment systems that use electronic distribution networks constitute a frequent practice in the banking and business sector since 1960s, especially for the transfer of big amounts of money. In the four decades that have passed since their appearance, important technological developments have taken place, which on the one hand have expanded the possibilities of electronic payment systems and on the other hand they have created new business and social practice, which make the use of these systems necessary. These changes, naturally, have affected the definition of electronic payments, which is evolving depending on the needs of each period. In its, most general form, the term electronic payment includes any payment to businesses, bank or public services from citizens or businesses, which are executed through a telecommunications or electronic networks using modern technology. It is obvious that based on this definition, the electronic payments that will be the objects of present result, are the payment that are executed by the payer himself, whether the latter is a consumer or a business, without the intervention of the another natural person. Furthermore, the payment is made from distance, without the physical presence of the payer and naturally it does not include cash. By providing such definition for the electronic payment system, researcher include the transfer of information concerning the accounts of the parties involved in the e-commerce transactions, as well as the technological means of distribution channels through which the transactions is executed.

3.18.2 Size of Electronic Payments

Electronic payment system is conducted in different e-commerce categories such as Business-to-Business (B2B), Business-to-Consumer (B2C), Consumer-to-Business (C2B) and Consumer-to-

Consumer (C2C). Each of which has special characteristics that depend on the value of order. Danial, (2002) classified electronic payment systems as follows:

Micro Payment (less than $ 10) that is mainly conducted in C2C and B2C e-commerce.

Consumer Payment that has a value between $ 10 and $ 500. It is conducted mainly in B2C transactions.

Business Payment that has the value more than $ 500. it is conducted mainly in B2B e-commerce. B2B transactions account about 95% of e-commerce transactions, while others account about 5% (Turban et al, 2004). P2P, which is related to the C2C category transactions, is relatively small due to its stiff usability. Further, Cavarretta and de Silva (1995), identify three classes of typical electronic transactions:

Tiny value transactions: below $1.

Medium value transactions: between $ 1 and $ 1,000

Large value transactions: above $ 1,000.

Systems that can support tiny value transactions have to trade-off between conveniences of transactions (the major part of a cost in an extremely cheap transaction) vs. the security or durability of transactions. On the other side of the amount range, large value transactions will require highly secure protocols whose implementations are costly: be on-line and/or carry traceability information. Finally, nearly all the system can perform medium value transactions.

3.18.3 Conventional vs. Electronic Payment System (UPTU-2010)

To get into the depth of electronic payment process, it is better to understand the processing of conventional or traditional payment system. A conventional process of payment and settlement involves a buyer-to-seller transfer of cash or payment information (i.e., cheque and credit cards). The actual settlement of payment takes place in the financial processing network. A cash payment requires a buyer's withdrawals form his/her bank account, a transfer of cash to the seller, and the sellers deposit of payment to his/her account. Non-cash payment mechanisms are settled by adjusting i.e. crediting and debiting the appropriate accounts between banks based on payment information conveyed via cheque or credit cards.

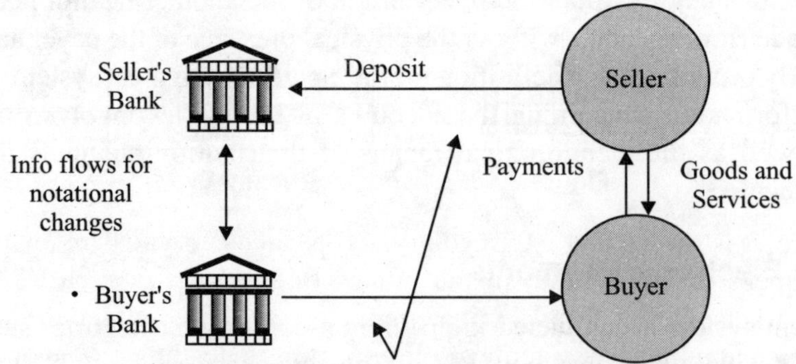

Figure 3.17: Conventional/Traditional Payment System

Figure 3.17 is simplified diagram for both cash and non-cash transactions. Cash moves from the buyers? bank to sellers? bank through face-to-face exchange in the market. If a buyer uses a non-cash method of payment, payment information instead of cash flows from the buyer to the seller, and ultimate payments are settled between affected banks, who notation ally adjust accounts based on payment information.

3.18.4 Process of Electronic Payment System **(Important)**

Electronic payment systems have been in operations since 1960s and have been expanding rapidly as well as growing in complexity. After the development of conventional payment system, EFT (Electronic Fund Transfer) based payment system came into existence. It was first electronic based payment system, which does not depend on a central processing intermediary. An electronic fund transfer is a financial application of EDI (Electronic Data Interchange), which sends credit card numbers or electronic cheques via secured private networks between banks and major corporations. To use EFT to clear payments and settle accounts, an online payment service will need to add capabilities to process orders, accounts and receipts. But a landmark came in this direction with the development of digital currency. The nature of digital currency or electronic money mirrors that of paper money as a means of payment. As such, digital currency payment systems have the same advantages as paper currency payment, namely anonymity and convenience. As in other electronic payment systems (i.e. EFT based and intermediary based) here too security during the transaction and storage is a concern, although from the different perspective, for digital currency systems double spending, counterfeiting, and storage become critical issues whereas eavesdropping and the issue of liability (when charges are made without authorizations) is important for the notational funds transfer. Figure 3.13 shows digital currency based payment system.

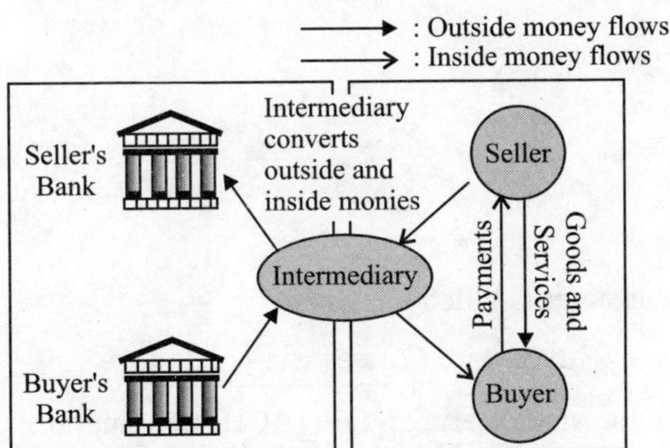

Figure 3.18: Electronic Payment System

In this figure, it is shown that intermediary acts as an electronic bank, which converts outside money (e.g. Rupees or US $), into inside money (e.g. tokens or e-cash), which is circulated within online markets. However, as a private monetary system, digital currency has wide ranging impact on money and monetary system with implications extending far beyond more transactional efficiency.

3.18.5 Payment Instructions **(UPTU-2010-11)**

A payment instruction is the instance of a payment method with the details necessary to perform payment actions. For example, if a payment method name is Visa, then the payment instruction consists of Visa, the payment amount, cardholder's name, billing address, account number, and expiration date.

A shopper adds a payment instruction during the checkout flow. When the payment instruction is added, the PIAdd command runs and persists payment information to the payment tables. A payment instruction is created in the EDPPAYINST and PPCPAYINST tables. The protocol data is stored in the PPCEXTDATA table.

Payment Methods

Payment methods are the means by which payments are made. Payment methods include credit card brands, electronic checks, gift certificates, and manufacturers' coupons. The shopper selects the payment method on the Order Summary page.

Payment methods have the following properties: payment method name, priority, ability to be edited (whether the amount can be changed by an administrator, or by the system), and amount limits. The payment policy is specified in the POLICY and POLICYDESC database tables. The properties are defined in the PaymentMethodConfigurations.xml file.

A shopper can use more than one payment method to pay for an order. The priority determines which payment method should be used first. For example, if a gift certificate has a high priority and a credit card has a medium priority, the gift certificate is used first.

By default, the following payment methods are available:

Credit cards

- AMEX
- MasterCard
- VISA

BillMeLater

Offline transaction, customer is billed

Check

Electronic check or automated clearing house (ACH) transaction

COD

Cash on delivery

LOC

Line of credit

3.19 TYPES OF ELECTRONIC PAYMENT SYSTEMS (EXPECTED)

With the growing complexities in the e-commerce transactions, different electronic payment systems have appeared in the last few years. At least dozens of electronic payment systems proposed or already in practice are found (Murthy, 2002). The grouping can be made on the basis of what information is being transferred online. Murthy explained six types of electronic payment systems: (1) PC-Banking (2) Credit Cards (3) Electronic Cheques (i-cheques) (4) Micro payment (5) Smart Cards and (6) E-Cash. Kalakota and Whinston (1996) identified three types of electronic payment systems: (1) Digital Token based electronic payment systems, (2) Smart Card based electronic payment system and (3) Credit based electronic payment systems. Dennis (2001) classified electronic payment system into two categories: (1) Electronic Cash and (2) Electronic Debit-Credit Card Systems. Thus, electronic payment system can be broadly divided into four general types (Anderson, 1998):

- Online Credit Card Payment System
- Electronic Cheque System
- Electronic Cash System and
- Smart Card based Electronic Payment System

3.20 ONLINE CREDIT CARD PAYMENT SYSTEM (VERY IMPORTANT)

Credit card is made of plastic whose holder has been granted a revolving credit lines. This enables the holder to make purchase and/ or cash advances upto a pre arranged limits. The credit granted can be settled in full by the end of a specific period or in part, with the balance taken as extended credit. Interest may be charged on the transaction amounts from the date of each transaction or only the extended credit where the credit granted has not been settled in full.

The card normally contains the cardholders name and account number and many other information encoded on the magnetic strip. Some credit cards may be used in ATM. Credit cards began in the late 40's when banks began giving out paper certificates that could be used like cash in local stores. Frankline National Bank of New York used the first real credit card in 1951.

It seeks to extend the functionality of existing credit cards for use as online shopping payment tools. This payment system has been widely accepted by consumers and merchants throughout the world, and by far the most popular methods of payments especially in the retail markets (Laudon and Traver, 2002). This form of payment system has several advantages, which were never available through the traditional modes of payment. Some of the most important are: privacy, integrity, compatibility, good transaction efficiency, acceptability, convenience, mobility, low financial risk and anonymity. Added to all these, to avoid the complexity associated with the digital cash or electronic-cheques, consumers and vendors are also looking at credit card payments on the internet as one of possible time-tested alternative. But, this payment system has raised several problems before the consumers and merchants. Online credit card payment seeks to address several limitations of online credit card payments for merchant including lack of authentication, repudiation of charges and credit card frauds. It also seeks to address consumer fears about using credit card such as having to reveal credit information at multiple sites and repeatedly having to communicate sensitive information over the Internet. Basic process of Online Credit Card Payment System is very simple. If consumers want to purchase a product or service, they simply send their credit card details to the service provider involved and the credit card organization will handle this payment like any other. This can be understood very easily with the format (Figure 3.19) of Credit Card Payment Form.

Credit Card Type: Fraud Protection Guaranteed Click Here AMERICAN EXPRESS
O VISA
O MASTERCARD O DISCOVER
O AMERICAN EXPRESS

Expiration date: ....
Card number: ....
Card holder's name (on card): ....
....
Full billing address of credit card :.
....
Your email address: ....
Comment/Description: ....

In the comment field please enter the service you are ordering, the domain or username this information should be applied to, or further information to help up speed and assist your order.

Figure 3.19: Credit card payment form (Sample)

3.21 ELECTRONIC CHEQUE PAYMENT SYSTEM (IMPORTANT)

Electronic cheque also known as e-cheque and I-cheque are used to make electronic payment between two parties through an intermediary and not very much different from the traditional or current cheque processing system. Electronic cheques are generated and exchanged online. The intermediary will debit the customer account and credit the merchant account. Electronic cheque is different from the electronic fund transfer (EFT) in several ways. For electronic chequing, electronic versions of cheques are issued, received and processed. So, the payee issues an electronic cheque for each payment. For EFT, automatic withdrawals are made for monthly bills or other fixed payments; no charges are issues. Thus, a complete electronic cheque transaction may consist of several basic steps and these steps are executed in three distinct and optionally separate phases. In the first phase, the consumer makes a purchase; in the second phase, the merchant sends the electronic cheques to its bank for the redemption. In the third phase, the merchant's bank approaches the clearinghouse or consumer's bank to cash the electronic cheques.

Electronic cheques address the electronic needs of millions of businesses, which today exchange traditional paper cheques with the other vendors, consumers and government. The e-cheque method was deliberately created to work in much the same way as conventional paper cheque. An account holder will issue an electronic document that contains the name of the financial institution, the payer's account number, the name of payee and amount of cheque. Most of the information is in uncoded form. Like a paper cheques e-cheques also bear the digital equivalent of signature: a computed number that authenticates the cheque from the owner of the account. Digital chequing payment system seeks to extend the functionality of existing chequing accounts for use as online shopping payment tools. Electronic cheque system has many advantages: (1) they do not require consumers to reveal account information to other individuals when setting an auction (2) they do not require consumers to continually send sensitive financial information over the web (3) they are less expensive than credit cards and (4) they are much faster than paper based traditional cheque. But, this system of payment also has several disadvantages. The disadvantage of electronic cheque system includes their relatively high fixed costs, their limited use only in virtual world and the fact that they can protect the users' anonymity. Therefore, it is not very suitable for the retail transactions by consumers, although useful for the government and B2B operations because the latter transactions do not require anonymity, and the amount of transactions is generally large enough to cover fixed processing cost. The process of electronic chequing system can be described using (Figure 4) the following steps.

Step 1: a purchaser fills a purchase order form, attaches a payment advice (electronic cheque), signs it with his private key (using his signature hardware), attaches his public key certificate, encrypts it using his private key and sends it to the vendor.

Step 2: the vendor decrypts the information using his private key, checks the purchaser's certificates, signature and cheque, attaches his deposit slip, and endorses the deposit attaching his public key certificates. This is encrypted and sent to his bank.

Step 3: the vendor's bank checks the signatures and certificates and sends the cheque for clearance. The banks and clearing houses normally have a private secure data network.

Step 4: when the cheque is cleared, the amount is credited to the vendor?s account and a credit advice is sent to him.

Step 5: the purchaser gets a consolidated debit advice periodically.

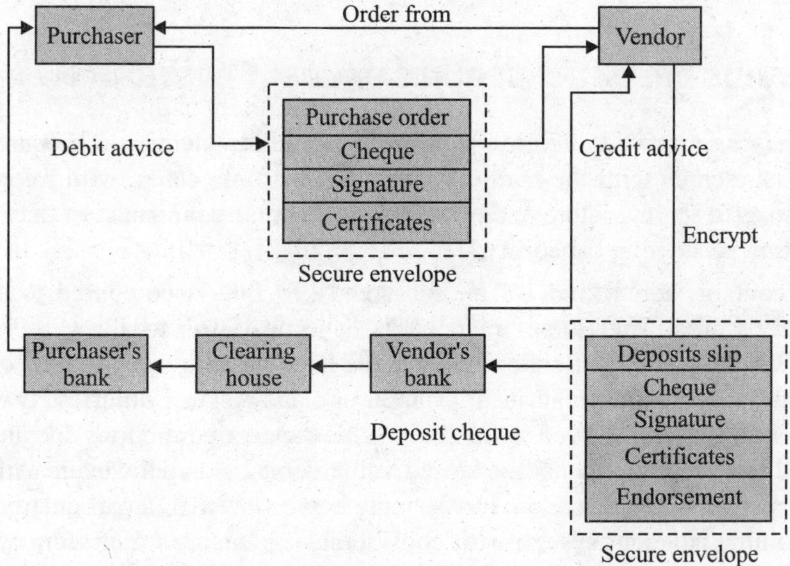

Figure 3.20: Clearing Cheque Payment Electronically

E-cheque provide a security rich Internet payment option for businesses and offer an easy entry into electronic commerce without a significant investment in new technologies or legal systems.

3.22 ELECTRONIC CASH PAYMENT SYSTEM (IMPORTANT)

E-cash portability means that it must be freely transferable between any two parties in all forms of e-commerce transactions. In contrast, credit cards do not possess this property of portability or transferability between every combination of two parties. In credit card transactions, the credit card payment recipient must already have a merchant account established with a bank- a condition that is not required with electronic cash.

Electronic cash (e-cash) is a new concept in online payment system because it combines computerized convenience with security and privacy that improve on paper cash. Its versatility opens up a host of new markets and applications. E-cash is an electronic or digital form of value storage and value exchange that have limited convertibility into other forms of value and require intermediaries to convert. E-cash presents some characteristics like monetary value, storability and irretrievability, interoperability and security. All these characteristics make it more attractive payment system over the Internet. Added to these, this payment system offers numerous advantages like authority, privacy, good acceptability, low transactions cost, convenience and good anonymity.

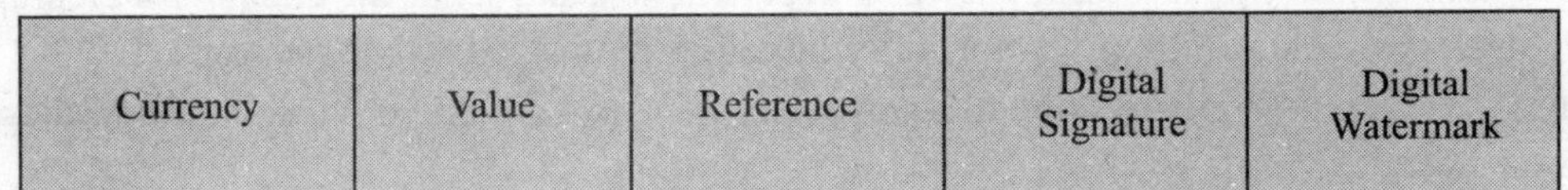

Figure 3.21: E-cash Structure

3.23 SMART CARDS BASED ELECTRONIC PAYMENT SYSTEM (IMPORTANT)

Smart cards are receiving renewed attention as a mode of online payment. They are essentially credit card sized plastic cards with the memory chips and in some cases, with microprocessors embedded in them so as to serve as storage devices for much greater information than credit cards with inbuilt transaction processing capability.

This card also contains some kinds of an encrypted key that is compared to a secret key contained on the user's processor. Some smart cards have provision to allow users to enter a personal identification number (PIN) code. Smart cards have been in use for well over the two decades now and have been widespread mostly in Europe and Asian Countries. Owing to their considerable flexibility, they have been used for a wide range of functions like highway toll payment, as prepaid telephone cards and as stored value debit cards. However, with the recent emergence of e-commerce, these devices are increasingly being viewed as a particularly appropriate method to execute online payment system with considerably greater level of security than credit cards.

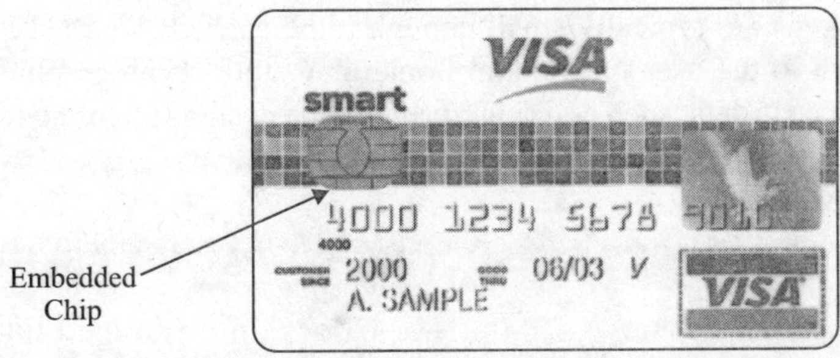

Figure 3.22: Smart Card Image

Table 3.3: Electronic payment in India

E-Commerce Payment Systems	Percentage	Rank
Credit Card	35	1
Debit Card (Smart Card)	26.5	2
Cash on Delivery	23.5	3
Bank Transfer	9	4
Money Transfer	5	5
Postal Transfer	1	6
Prepaid Card	0	0
Payment Through Convenience Store	0	0
Total	**100**	**0**

3.24 MAGNETIC STRIP AND DIGITAL TOKEN

A consumer first had to establish an account at a bank that was using e-cash system. Once the account is established, the consumer then downloaded the e-wallet software onto his/her computer's hard drive. Then consumer could request a transfer of digital cash. Once the digital wallet had cash, the consumer could spend that cash at merchants who were willing to accept it. The software would deduct the cash from digital wallet and transfer it to the merchant. The merchant could then transfer the cash back to the bank to confirm that it had not been double spent. The bank would cancel the e-coins or credit the merchant account at bank. Credit cards store a single charge account number in the magnetic strip on the back, smart cards can hold 100 times more data, including multiple credit card numbers and information regarding health insurance, transportation, personal identification, bank accounts and loyalty programs, such as frequent flyer accounts. This capacity makes them attractive alternatives to carrying a dozen or so credit and ID cards in a physical wallet.

A Digital token (or sometimes a hardware token, authentication token or cryptographic token) may be a physical device that an authorized user of computer services is given to aid in authentication. The term may also refer to software tokens.

Hardware tokens are typically small enough to be carried in a pocket or purse and often are designed to attach to the user's keychain. Some may store cryptographic keys, such as a digital signature, or biometric data, such as a fingerprint. Some designs feature tamper resistant packaging, other may include small keypads to allow entry of a PIN.

3.25 SUCCESS FACTORS OF E-COMMERCE PAYMENT SYSTEM

(Very Important)

The factors which are critical for the success of e-commerce payment systems are multifaceted. These include integrity, non-repudiation, authentication, authorization, confidentiality and reliability, which are discussed below:

Integrity: transaction data are transmitted and received unchanged and as intended.

Non-repudiation: transactions have the quality of non deniable proof or receipts.

Authentication: identities and attributes of parties engaged in commerce are established at some tolerable level of risk.

Authorization: individuals are established and recognized as entitled to receive, send or view transactions.

Confidentiality: transactions can be protected from view except by those who are authorized.

Reliability: probability of failure in the transaction-send, receive, acknowledge-is low.

3.26 COMPARISON OF ELECTRONIC PAYMENT SYSTEMS

The electronic payment system- the ability to pay electronically for goods and services purchased online- are an integral part of e-commerce and an essential infrastructure for e-commerce models. One of the major reasons for the widespread of e-commerce transactions is perhaps the rapid development and growth of various electronic payment systems. In the developed countries, credit cards have been used even before the advent of Internet. The present part of the study revealed many electronic payment systems and broadly these electronic payment system can be grouped or classified into four categories:

1. Online Credit Card Payment System
2. Online Electronic Cash System
3. Electronic Cheque System and
4. Smart Cards based Electronic Payment System.

These payment systems have numbers of requirements: e.g. security, acceptability, convenience, cost, anonymity, control, and traceability. Therefore, instead of focusing on the technological specifications of various electronic payment systems, the researcher have distinguished electronic payment systems based on what is being transmitted over the network; and analyze the difference of each electronic payment system by evaluating their requirements, characteristics and assess the applicability of each system.

Table 3.4: Comparison of electronic payment systems				
Features	**Online Credit Card Payment**	**Electronic Cash**	**Electronic Cheque**	**Smart Cards**
Actual payment time	**Paid later**	**Prepaid**	**Paid later**	**Prepaid**
Transaction information transfer	The store and bank checks the status of the credit card	Free transfer. No need to leave the name of involved	Electronic checks or payment indication must be endorsed	The smart card of both parties make the transfer
Online and offline transactions	Online transactions	Online transactions	Offline transfers are allowed	Offline transfers are allowed
Bank account involvement	Credit card account makes the payment	No involvement	The bank account makes the payment	The samrt card account makes the payment
Usres	Any legitimate credit card users	Anyone	Anyone with a bank account	Anyone with a bank or credit card account
Party to which payment is made out	Distributing Bank	Store	Store	Store
Consumer's transaction risk	Most of the risk is borne by the distributing bank, consumers only have to bear part of the risk	Consumer is at risk of the electronic cash getting stolen, lost, or misused	Consumer bearns most of the risk, but the consumer can stop check payments at any time	Consumer is at risk of the smart card getting stolen, lost or misused
Current degree of popularity	Credit card organizations check for certification then total the purchases. Therefore, it can be used internationally, and is the most popular payment type	Unable to meet financial internet standards in the areas of expansion potential and internationalis m.	Can not meet international standards, therefore its not very popular	Credit card organizations check for certification then total the purchases. Therefore, it can be used internationally, and is becoming more widely used.
Anonymity	Partially or entirely anonymous	Entirely anonymous	No anonymity	Entirely anonymous, but if needed, the central processing agency can ask stores to provide information about a consumer

Small payments	Transaction costs are high. Not suitable for small payments	Transaction costs are low, suitable for small payments	Allows stores to accumulate debts unitl it reaches a limit before paying for it. Suitable for small payments	Transaction costs are low. Allows stores to accumulate debts unitl it reaches a limit before paying for it. Therefore, it is suitable for small payments.
Database safeguarding	Safeguards regular credit card account	Needs to safeguard a large database and maintain records of the serial numbers of used electronic cash.	Safeguards regular account information	Safeguards regular account information
Transaction information face value	Can be signed and issued freely in compliance with the limit	Face value is often set, and cannot be changed	Can be signed and issued freely in compliance with the limit	Can be deducted freely in compliance with the limit.
Real/Virutal world	Can be partially used in real world	Can only be used in the virtual world	Limited to virtual world, but can share a checking account in the real world.	Can be used in real or virtual worlds.
Limit on transfer	Depends on the limit of the credit card	Depends on how much is prepaid	No limit	Depends on how much money is saved.
Mobility	Yes	No	No	Yes

After analysis and comparison of various modes of electronic payment systems, it is revealed that it is quite difficult, if not impossible, to suggest that which payment system is best. Some systems are quite similar, and differ only in some minor details. Further, all these systems have ability or potential to displace cash. Added to this, widely different technical specifications makes it difficult to choose an appropriate payment system. On the basis of above analysis it is concluded that, smart cards based electronic payment system is best. It has numerous advantages over the other electronic payment systems. Therefore, establishing a standard smart card based system, or making different system interoperable with one another is critical success factor for the smart cards based payment system. Smart card organizations around the world must establish a smart card interface standard and a conformance testing organization to make all smart card system compatible; otherwise smart card related products will not develop fully.

Technology has inarguably made our lives easier. It has cut across distance, space and even time. One of the technological innovations in banking, finance and commerce is the Electronic Payments. Electronic Payments (e-payments) refers to the technological breakthrough that enables us to perform financial transactions electronically, thus avoiding long lines and other hassles. Electronic Payments provides greater freedom to individuals in paying their taxes, licenses, fees, fines and purchases at unconventional locations and at whichever time of the day, 365 days of the year. On the basis of present study, first remark is that despite the existence of variety of e-commerce payment systems, credit cards are the most dominant payment system. This is consequences of advantageous characteristics, most importantly the long established networks and very wide users? base. Second, alternative e-commerce payment systems are some countries are debit cards. In fact, like many other studies, present study also reveals that the smart card based e-commerce payment system is best and it is expected that in the future smart cards will eventually replace the other electronic payment systems. Third, given the limited users bases, e-cash is not a feasible payment option. Thus, there are number of factors which affect the usage of e-commerce payment systems. Among all these user base is most important.

Added to this, success of e-commerce payment systems also depends on consumer preferences, ease of use, cost, industry agreement, authorization, security, authentication, non-refutability, accessibility and reliability and anonymity and public policy.

SUMMARY

E-Commerce refers to the exchange of goods and services over the Internet. All major retail brands have an online presence, and many brands have no associated bricks and mortar presence. However, e-Commerce also applies to business to business transactions, for example, between manufacturers and suppliers or distributors.

Most businesses that have made the move towards an online presence have experienced some kind of security threat to their business. Since the Internet is a public system in which every transaction can be tracked, logged, monitored and stored in many locations, it is important for businesses to understand possible security threats to their business. There are many threats to e-commerce that may come from sources within an organization or through some external channel. The following are the top corporate security threats categorized by internal and external threats.

A virtual organization or company is one whose members are geographically apart, usually working by computer e-mail and groupware while appearing to others to be a single, unified organization with a real physical location. A Business Transaction is a consistent change in the state of the business that is driven by a well-defined business function.

A business transaction is driven by well-defined business tasks and events that directly or indirectly contribute to generating economic value, such as processing and paying an insurance claim, and has also an associated number of parameters that represent security and timing requirements. Business transactions always either succeed or fail with respect to the business tasks (functions) that initiated them and govern them throughout their execution. If a business transaction completes successfully then each participant will have made consistent state changes, which, in aggregate, reflect the desired outcome of the multi-party business interaction.

e-Government (from electronic government, also known as e-gov, digital government, online government or in a certain context transformational government) refers to government's use of information technology to exchange information and services with citizens, businesses, and other arms of government. e-Government may be applied by the legislature, judiciary, or administration, in order to improve internal efficiency, the delivery of public services, or processes of democratic governance. It also refers to the citizen to government interaction including the feed back of policies.

Electronic Data Interchange is the **computer-to-computer** exchange of **routine business data** between trading partners in **standard data formats**.

The emergence of e-commerce has created new financial needs that in many cases cannot be effectively fulfilled by the traditional payment systems. Recognizing this, virtually all interested parties are exploring various types of electronic payment system and issues surrounding electronic payment system and digital currency. Broadly electronic payment systems can be classified into four categories: Online Credit Card Payment System, Online Electronic Cash System, Electronic Cheque System and Smart Cards based Electronic Payment System. Each payment system has its advantages and disadvantages for the customers and merchants. These payment systems have numbers of requirements: e.g. security, acceptability, convenience, cost, anonymity, control, and traceability. Therefore, instead of focusing on the technological specifications of various electronic payment systems, the researcher have distinguished electronic payment systems based on what is being transmitted over the network; and analyze the difference of each electronic payment system by evaluating their requirements, characteristics and assess the applicability of each system.

Payments. Electronic Payments (e-payments) refers to the technological breakthrough that enables us to perform financial transactions electronically, thus avoiding long lines and other hassles. Electronic Payments provides greater freedom to individuals in paying their taxes, licenses, fees, fines and purchases at unconventional locations and at whichever time of the day, 365 days of the year. On the basis of present study, first remark is that despite the existence of variety of e-commerce payment systems, credit cards are the most dominant payment system. This is consequences of advantageous characteristics, most importantly the long established networks and very wide users? base. Second, alternative e-commerce payment systems are some countries are debit cards. In fact, like many other studies, present study also reveals that the smart card based e-commerce payment system is best and it is expected that in the future smart cards will eventually replace the other electronic payment systems. Third, given the limited users bases, e-cash is not a feasible payment option. Thus, there are number of factors which affect the usage of e-commerce payment systems. Among all these user base is most important.

EXERCISES

1. Explain the concept of electronic commerce.
2. What is security threat in E-commerce.
3. What are virtual organization.
4. Write down the advantages of virtual organization.
5. Discuss EDI.
6. Explain electronic payment system.
7. Explain the concept of E-cash.
8. What are credit/debit card.
9. Explain the comparison of different payment system.

CHAPTER 4

Physical Security

4.1 INTRODUCTION

Physical security describes both measures that prevent or deter attackers from accessing a facility, resource, or information stored on physical media, and guidance on how to design structures to resist various hostile acts. It can be as simple as a locked door or as elaborate as multiple layers of armed security guards and guardhouse placement.

Physical security is not a modern phenomenon. Physical security exists in order to deter persons from entering a physical facility. Historical examples of physical security include city walls, moats, etc.

Physical security is the protection of personnel, hardware, programs, networks, and data from physical circumstances and events that could cause serious losses or damage to an enterprise, agency, or institution. This includes protection from fire, natural disasters, burglary, theft, vandalism, and terrorism.

Physical security is often overlooked (and its importance underestimated) in favor of more technical and dramatic issues such as hacking, viruses, Trojans, and spyware. However, breaches of physical security can be carried out with little or no technical knowledge on the part of an attacker. Moreover, accidents and natural disasters are a part of everyday life, and in the long term, are inevitable.

There are three main components to physical security. First, obstacles can be placed in the way of potential attackers and sites can be hardened against accidents and environmental disasters. Such measures can include multiple locks, fencing, walls, fireproof safes, and water sprinklers. Second, surveillance and notification systems can be put in place, such as lighting, heat sensors, smoke detectors, intrusion detectors, alarms, and cameras. Third, methods can be implemented to apprehend attackers (preferably before any damage has been done) and to recover quickly from accidents, fires, or natural disasters.

4.2 PHYSICAL SECURITY PLAN COMPONENTS

Those responsible for security must address such issues as computer security, perimeter control, asset protection, business continuity, and risk management. Consider these suggestions when determining your credit union's physical security plan:

- Control access to all building entrances. In the rush to focus on IT security, many organizations have discounted controlling access to physical facilities in evaluating threat scenarios.
- Enhance perimeter security by placing alarm systems in high-value storage areas and monitoring important pieces of equipment electronically.

  Replace surveillance cameras relying on video tape with digital video. This allows for more efficient archival monitoring, as well as the integration of video input into broader digital security databases.
- Hard-wire generators to building systems using automatic transfer switches so employees won't need to operate equipment manually. As Hurricane Katrina disaster recovery demonstrated, electrical generators operating on diesel, propane, or natural gas are essential as electric power may be offline for extended periods during a major disruptive event. Gasoline-powered generators are less valuable due to limited storage capacity and gasoline's relatively short shelf life.
- Store emergency medical supplies, food, water, and communications gear onsite to support an extended stay by staff during a major emergency. Keep on hand generic unisex clothing such as jumpsuit coveralls and sturdy footwear to guard against leaking water and injury-causing debris. Make available portable stoves, sealed drums of potable water, and sufficient numbers of chemical toilets. Train employees how to use this equipment before disaster strikes.
- Review how to implement security/safety measures incrementally over the next five years during routine building renovations and redesigns. The ability to integrate security measures into facility upgrades reduces costs and shortens payback periods. In addition, taking such steps will reassure staff that management is doing everything necessary for their protection and well-being in case disaster strikes.

4.3 DISASTER AND CONTROL (VERY IMPORTANT)

4.3.1 Natural Disaster

A **natural disaster** is the effect of a natural hazard (e.g., flood, tornado, hurricane, volcanic eruption, earthquake, or landslide) that affects the environment, and leads to financial, environmental and/or human losses. The resulting loss depends on the capacity of the population to support or resist the disaster, and their resilience. This understanding is concentrated in the formulation: "disasters occur when hazards meet vulnerability. A natural hazard will hence never result in a natural disaster in areas without vulnerability, e.g. strong earthquakes in uninhabited areas. The term natural has consequently been disputed because the events simply are not hazards or disasters without human involvement.Natural disasters which occur the movement of plate tectonics are earthquakes, volcanoes, geyser eruptions and tsunami.

4.3.2 Earthquakes

An earthquake is a shaking of the ground caused by the sudden dislocation of material within the earth's outer layer, or crust. When forces pushing on a mass of rock overcome the friction holding the rock in place and blocks of rock slip against each other a earthquake may occur. Some earthquakes are so slight, and some occur in such remote areas, that they are barely felt. Others are so violent that they cause extensive damage.

4.3.3 Lahars

A lahar is a volcanic mudflow or landslide. The 1953 Tangiwai disaster was caused by a lahar, as was the 1985 Armero tragedy in which the town of Armero was buried and an estimated 23,000 people were killed.

4.3.4 Hurricanes

Hurricanes are one of natures many destructive forces. The word comes from West Indian; huracan ("big wind"). Hurricanes are seasonal storms and are most prevalent in August and September. They develop from easterly waves, which can later develop into a tropical depression with winds up to 31 miles per hour. Later, it might develop into a tropical storm with winds up to 73 miles per hour, and eventually a hurricane. Thunderstorms often form with hurricanes and then produce waterspouts.

Hurricanes are huge tropical cyclones that originate over oceans near the equator, such as the Caribbean Sea and the Gulf of Mexico. Usually they follow a parabola shaped path and sometimes do not reach any land at all. However, if they do reach land, destruction of property is imminent. Winds whirl in a counter clockwise direction in the northern hemisphere and clockwise in the southern hemisphere. Wind speeds of a hurricane range from seventy to one hundred fifty miles per hour. These winds blow circularly around a low-pressure center known as the eye of the storm. Hurricanes cause numerous deaths in addition to the millions of dollars of property damage each year due to the intense winds and huge tidal surges.

4.3.5 Tsunami

"Tsunami" is the Japanese word meaning tidal wave. A tidal wave is a large sea wave caused by a submarine earthquake or volcanic explosion. When the ocean floor is tilted or offset during an earthquake, a set of waves is created. These waves are similar to the concentric waves generated by an object dropped into the water.

Usually tsunamis move entirely across an ocean to the shore. A tsunami can have wavelengths of 60 to 120 mi and may reach speeds of 800 km/h. When the wave enters shallow waters, the wave, which may have been half a meter high out at sea, grows rapidly. When the wave reaches the shore, it may be 50 ft. high or more. Tsunamis have incredible energy because of the great volume of water affected. They bring waves of destruction capable of killing thousands of residents along the coast. Towering walls of water have struck populated coastlines with such fury that entire towns have been destroyed. In 1896 a population of 20,000 in Sanriku, Japan were wiped out. Tsunamis have resulted in waves as high as 135 ft. above normal sea level.

When a tsunami strikes the shore, it creates a number of waves with troughs that are lower than normal sea level. Each following wave is higher than the one before it. The period between waves is 10 to 30 minutes. This usually gives people ample time to escape to high ground after the first wave.

4.3.6 Tornadoes

Tornadoes are one of weathers most deadly and fascinating forces. Even though they are often limited by size (not being more than one kilometer wide at most) they leave vast areas of destruction and death behind them. They are also called twisters or cyclones.

Tornadoes are characterized by violent winds that swirl in a counter clockwise direction north of the equator and clockwise south of the equator. Most people recognize them as a towering black funnel extending downward from the base of a large cumulonimbus cloud. It rotates at speeds up to three hundred miles per hour (480 kpm) or in some rare cases, even faster. In the center of the tornado, the air pressure is very low in comparison to surrounding air pressure.

4.3.7 Volcano

A Volcano is a vent in the earth through which hot gases and molten rock rise to the surface. A coneshaped mountain of erupted material around such a vent is also called a volcano. The name is taken from Vulcano, an island north of Sicily in the Mediterranean Sea. The island was given its name by the ancient Romans because it spewed smoke like vapor, and was thought to be the home of Vulcan, their god of fire.

A Volcano consists of a fissure in the earth's crust, above which a cone of volcanic material has accumulated. At the top of the cone is a bowl-shaped vent called a crater. The cone is formed by the deposition of molten or solid matter that flows or is ejected through the vent from the interior of the earth. The study of volcanoes and volcanic phenomena is called volcanology.

4.3.8 Drought

Drought is a period or condition of unusually dry weather within a geographic area where rainfall is normally present. During a drought there is a lack of precipitation. Droughts occur in all climatic zones. However, its characteristics vary significantly from one region to another.

Drought usually results in a water shortage that seriously interferes with human activity. Water-supply reservoirs empty, wells dry up, and crop damage ensues. Its seriousness depends on the degree of the water shortage, size of area affected, and the duration and warmth of the dry period.

In many underdeveloped countries, such as India, people place a great demand on water supply. During a drought period there is a lack of water, and thus many of the poor die.

Most precipitation depends on water vapor carried by winds from an ocean or other source of moisture. If these moisture-carrying winds are replaced by winds from a dry region, or if they are modified by downward motion, as in the center of an anticyclone, the weather is abnormally dry and often persistently cloudless. If the drought period is short, it is known as a dry spell. A dry spell is usually more than 14 days without precipitation, whereas a severe drought may last for years.

A goal of business recovery planning is to ensure the safety of personnel and assets during and following a disaster, a critical aspect of the risk analysis process is to identify the preparedness and preventive measures in place at any point in time. Once the potential areas of high exposure to the organization are identified, additional preventative measures can be considered for implementation.

Disaster prevention and preparedness begins at the top of an organization. The attitude of senior management toward security and prevention should permeate the entire organization. Therefore, management's support of disaster planning can focus attention on good security and prevention techniques and better prepare the organization for the unwelcome and unwanted.

Disaster prevention techniques include two categories: procedural prevention and physical prevention.

Procedural prevention relates to activities performed on a day-to-day, month-to-month, or annual basis, relating to security and recovery. Procedural prevention begins with assigning responsibility for overall security of the organization to an individual with adequate competence and authority to meet the challenges. The objective of procedural prevention is to define activities necessary to prevent various types of disasters and ensure that these activities are performed regularly.

Physical prevention and preparedness for disaster begins when a site is constructed. It includes special requirements for building construction, as well as fire protection for various equipment components. Special considerations include: computer area, fire detection and extinguishing systems, record(s) protection, air conditioning, heating and ventilation, electrical supply and UPS systems, emergency procedures, vault storage area(s), archival systems.

Security and controls refer to all the measures adopted within an organization to safeguard assets, ensure the accuracy and reliability of records, and encourage operational efficiency and adherence to prescribed procedures. The system of internal controls also includes the measures adopted to safeguard the computer system.

The nature of internal controls is such that certain control procedures are necessary for a proper execution of other control procedures. This interdependence of control procedures may be significant because certain control objectives that appear to have been achieved may, in fact, not have been achieved because of weaknesses in other control procedures upon which they depend.

Concern over this interdependence of control procedures may be greater with a computerized system than with a manual system because computer operations often have a greater concentration of functions, and certain manual control procedures may depend on automated control procedures, even though that dependence is not readily apparent. Adequate computer internal controls are a vital aspect of an automated system.

Security is an increasing concern because computer systems are increasingly complex. Particular security concerns result from the proliferation of PCs, local area networking, and on-line systems that allow more access to the mainframe and departmental computers. Modern technology provides computer thieves with powerful new electronic safecracking tools.

Computer internal controls are especially important because computer processing can circumvent traditional security and control techniques. There are two types of computer control techniques: (1) general controls that affect all computer systems, and (2) application controls that are unique to specific applications.

Important areas of concern related to general computer internal controls include: organization controls, systems development and maintenance controls, documentation controls, access controls, data and procedural controls, physical security, password security systems, communications security.

Application controls are security techniques that are unique to a specific computer application system. Application controls are classified as: input controls, processing controls, output controls.

4.4 BASIC TENETS OF PHYSICAL SECURITY

Physical security is the one area with which you are most likely to be familiar. It deals with such things as personnel, the environment, the facility and its power supply(ies), fire protection, physical access, and even the protection of software, hardware, and data files. Your command must provide physical security for your AIS facility. The degree of physical security at your installation or command depends on its physical characteristics, its vulnerability within the AIS environment, and the type of data processed. Minimum physical security requirements include four basic areas that your command must address: physical security protection, physical access controls, data file protection, and natural disaster protection.

Physical security protection: Physical security protection takes on two forms. The first is physical barriers, such as solid walls, caged-in areas, bulletproof glass, locked doors, and even continual surveillance of the controlled area. The second involves people and the procedures that you must follow, such as looking up names on the access list to determine who is authorized in a given space or area. There are also escort procedures you must follow to be sure that your party gets to the right place and/or person.

Physical access controls: Physical access controls are implemented to prevent unauthorized entry to your computer facility or remote terminal areas. Physical access controls can be accomplished in several ways: conventional key and lock set, electronic key system, mechanical combination lock, or electronic combination lock. Regardless of the type of system installed at your command, it is important to remember that keys belong on your key-ring or chain, electronic keys or cards should be in your possession at all times , and combinations should be memorized, not written down somewhere for everyone to see.

Data file protection: Physical access to data files and media libraries (magnetic disks, tape files, microforms, and so on) is authorized only to those personnel requiring access to perform their job.

Natural disaster protection. The effects of you, and never hesitate to challenge or question someone or something that you feel is wrong or out of character.

Environmental Security: Temperature and humidity can affect the operation of your- computer facility. Whenever possible, computer equipment is operated within the manufacturer's optimum temperature and humidity range specification. Fluctuations in temperature and/or humidity over an extended period of time can cause serious damage to the equipment. So, with that in mind, you are probably asking yourself, "What are the acceptable levels for computer operation?" Normally, you can find this information in the command's standard operating procedures (SOPs), or you can check with your supervisor. If neither are available, a safe rule of thumb is a temperature of 72° Fahrenheit, ±2°, and a humidity of 55%, ±5%. To maintain a constant temperature and humidity to the computer facility or remote terminal areas, keep all doors and windows closed. Because temperature and humidity are vitally important to computer performance, it is essential that only designated personnel be allowed to regulate these types of environmental controls. If your workspace has a recording instrument to monitor the temperature and humidity, by all means check it periodically to be sure it is within the prescribed limits. If you notice a significant fluctuation (up or down), notify your supervisor. Some devices have built-in warning signals (a light, audible sound, or both) to warn you of near-limit conditions for temperature and/or humidity. Lighting You are responsible for ensuring that adequate lighting is maintained. Be particularly attentive to emergency lights. If they are not functioning properly,report the problem to your supervisor as soon as possible. Emergency lights are installed for your protection and safety, not for the safety of the equipment. They are there to ensure a quick exit if you must evacuate in a hurry.

4.4.1 Seven Elements of Highly Effective Security Policies

With cybercrime on the rise, protecting your corporate information and assets is vital. Your bible should be a security policy document that outlines what you plan to protect and how you plan to do so. You can prepare a security policy document in-house, or outsource the project to security consultants.

The first step in any project to prepare a security policy document is to determine what elements to include in your policy. Be sure to consider all the key elements your IT staff manages. I recommend you cover each of the areas listed below in a section within your document. I have room here to cover just the basics, but I hope to explore each topic in greater depth in the upcoming months.

- **Security accountability:** Stipulate the security roles and responsibilities of general users, key staff, and management. Creating accountability in these three employee categories helps your organization understand and manage expectations and provides a foundation for enforcing all other ancillary policies and procedures. This section should also define various classes of data, such as internal, external, general, and confidential. By classifying the data, you can then make stipulations as to what types of employees are responsible for, and allowed to modify or distribute, particular classes of data. For example, you can send out memos that say, "No confidential data may be circulated outside the company without management sign-off."

- **Network service policies:** Generate policies for secure remote access, IP address management and configuration, router and switch security procedures, and access list (ACL) stipulations. Indicate which key staff need to review which change procedures before they are implemented. For example, your security team should review all proposed ACL changes before your network administrators implement the changes. Define your remote network access policies and your network intrusion detection systems in this section.
- **System policies:** Define the host security configuration for all mission-critical operating systems and servers. Include which services should be running on which networks, account management policies, password management policies, messaging, database, anti-virus, host-based intrusion detection, and firewall policies.
- **Physical security:** Define how buildings and card-key readers should be secured, where internal cameras should be installed, how visitors should be handled, and what inventory rules and regulations your shipping and receiving folks should follow. Though this might seem a bit afield of a discussion of IT security, remember that no organization is secure from attack unless it's physically secure too.
- **Incident handling and response:** Specify what procedures to follow in the event of a security breach or incident. Include policies such as how to evaluate a security incident, how the incident should be reported, how the problem should be eradicated, and what key personnel your organization should engage in the process.
- **Behavior and acceptable use policies:** Stipulate what type of behavior is expected of employees and your management team, and what forms and documents need to be read, reviewed, filled out, and followed. Employees should be required to read and sign the acceptable use policy so that management has the option to take disciplinary action in the event that the policy is violated.
- **Security training:** Define a security training plan for key staff who manage day-to-day security operations in order to sustain your security policy and keep your security staff current with the latest techniques.

Once you've established policies that suit your organization, you should draft procedures that outline how to comply with the policies. Define how you secure operating systems, what files to edit and configure, what ports should be open and closed on the firewall, how databases should be secured, and what updates need to be applied on what timeframe. Include what jobs should be run and when.

4.5 PHYSICAL ENTRY CONTROL

Physical entry controls restrict the entry and exit of personal from an area, such as an office building, suite, data center are room comparing a LAN server. Physical entry control should address not only the area containing system hardware, but also locations of wiring used to connect elements of the system, the electric power service, the air conditioning the heating plant, telephone and data lines, backup media and source documents and any other elements required system's operation. This means that all the areas in the building that contain system elements must be identified. It is also important to review the effectiveness of physical access controls in each area, both during normal business hours, and at other timers particularly when an area may be unoccupied.

Effectiveness depends on both the characteristics of the control devices used (e.g. keyboard-controlled doors) and the implementation and operation.

Statements to the effect that "only authorized" persons may enter this area are not particularly effective, organisations should determine whether intruders can easily defeat the controls, the extent to which strangers are challenged and the effectiveness of other control procedures.

4.6 ACCESS CONTROL OVERVIEW

With NTFS access permissions, the foundation of the security for your Web server, you can define the level of file and directory access granted to Windows users and groups. For example, if a business decided to publish its catalog on your Web server, you would need to create a Windows user account for that business and then configure permissions for the specific Web site, directory, or file.

4.6.1 Certificates Overview

Certificates are digital identification documents that allow both servers and clients to authenticate each other. They are required for both the server and the browser belonging to the client to set up an SSL connection over which encrypted information can be sent. The certificate-based SSL features in IIS consist of a server certificate, a client certificate, and various digital keys. You can create these certificates with Microsoft Certificate Services or obtain them from a mutually trusted, third-party organization called a certification authority (CA). For more information about setting up certificates and keys, see "Setting Up SSL on Your Server" in the IIS 5.0 Documentation.

4.6.2 Server Certificates

Server certificates provide a way for users to confirm the identity of your Web site. A server certificate contains detailed identification information, such as the name of the organization affiliated with the server content, the name of the organization that issued the certificate, and a public key used in establishing an encrypted connection. This information helps to assure users of the authenticity of Web server content and the integrity of the secure HTTP connection.

4.6.3 Client Certificates

With SSL, your Web server also has the option of authenticating users by checking the contents of their client certificates. A typical client certificate contains detailed identification information about a user and the organization that issued the certificate and a public key. You can use client certificate authentication, along with SSL encryption, to implement a highly secure method for verifying the identity of your users.

4.6.4 Encryption Overview

You can enable users to exchange private information with your server, such as credit card numbers or phone numbers, in a secure way by using encryption. Encryption "scrambles" the information before it is sent, and decryption "unscrambles" it after it is received. The foundation for this encryption in IIS is the SSL 3.0 protocol, which provides a secure way of establishing an encrypted communication link with users. SSL confirms the authenticity of your Web site and, optionally, the identity of users accessing restricted Web sites.

Certificates include keys used in establishing an SSL secure connection. A key is a unique value used to authenticate the server and the client in establishing an SSL connection. A public key and a private key form an SSL key pair. Your Web server uses the key pair to negotiate a secure connection with the Web browser to determine the level of encryption required for securing communications.

For this type of connection, both your Web server and the Web browser must be equipped with compatible encryption and decryption capabilities. During the exchange an encryption, or session, key is created. Both your server and the Web browser use the session key to encrypt and decrypt transmitted information. The degree of encryption, or strength, of a session key is measured in bits. The greater the number of bits comprising the session key, the greater the level of encryption and security. Although these greater encryption key strengths offer greater security, they also require more server resources to implement. The session key of your Web server is typically 40 bits long, but can be 128 bits long depending upon the level of security you require.

4.7 ACCESS CONTROL (VERY IMPORTANT)

Access control, in one form or another, is considered by most information systems security professionals to be the cornerstone of their security programs. The various features of physical, technical, and administrative access control mechanisms work together to construct the security architecture so important in the protection of an organization's critical and sensitive information assets.

4.7.1 What are Biometrics

"Biometric" come from the Greek words "bio" (life) and "metric" (to measure). Biometrics are technologies used for measuring and analyzing a person's unique characteristics. There are two types of biometrics: behavioral and physical. Behavioral biometrics are generally used for verification while physical biometrics can be used for either identification or verification.

4.7.1.1 Modules of a Biometric System

Any biometric system is basically made of the following components:

1. **Portal:** Its purpose is to protect some assets. An example of a portal is the gate at an entrance of a building. If the user has been successfully authenticated and is authorised to access an object then access is granted.

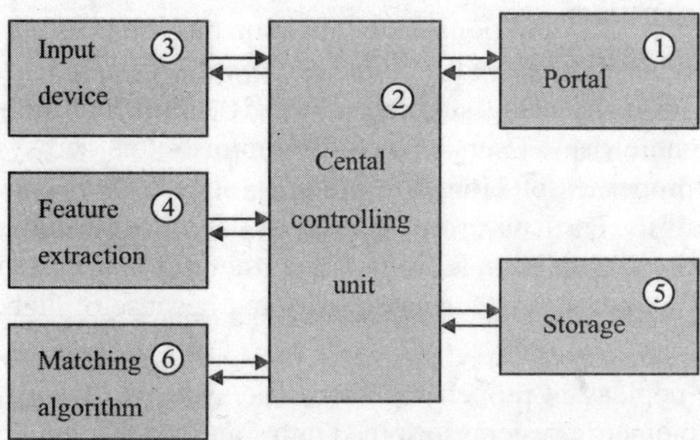

Figure 4.1: The model of a biometric system

2. **Central controlling unit:** Its receives the authentication request, controls the biometric authentication process and returns the result of user authentication.
3. **Input device:** The aim of the input device is biometric data acquisition. During the acquisition process user's liveness and quality of the sample may be verified.
4. **Feature extraction module:** Its processes the biometric data. The output of the module is a set of extracted features suitable for the matching algorithm. During the feature extraction process the module may also evaluate quality of the input biometric data.
5. **Storage of biometric templates:** This will typically be some kind of a database. Biometric templates can also be stored on a user-held medium (e.g., smartcard). In that case a link between the user and her biometric template must exist (e.g., in the form of an attribute certificate).
6. **The biometric matching algorithm:** Its compares the current biometric features with the stored template. The desired security threshold level may be a parameter of the matching process. In this case the result of the matching will be a yes/no answer. Otherwise a score representing the similarity between the template and the current biometric sample is returned. The central unit then makes the yes/no decision.

Where not to use biometrics

Although good for user authentication, biometrics cannot be used to authenticate computers or messages. Biometric characteristics are not secret and therefore they cannot be used to sign messages or encrypt documents. If my fingerprint is not secret there is no sense in adding it to documents we have written. Anyone else could do the same. Cryptographic keys derived from biometric data are nonsense, too.

Remote biometric authentication is not trivial at all. The assumption that anyone who can provide my fingerprint can also use my bank account in the homebanking application is not a good idea. Remote biometric authentication requires a trusted biometric sensor. Will a bank trust your home biometric sensor to be sufficiently tamper resistant and provide trustworthy liveness test. Although remote biometric authentication may work in the theory, few (if any) current devices are trustworthy enough to be used for remote biometric authentication.

While using biometrics as an additional authentication method does not weaken the security of the whole system (if users do not rely on the biometric component so much to ignore the traditional authentication method, e.g., by using simple passwords), replacing an existing system with a biometric one may be more risky. Users as well as administrators and system engineers tend to overestimate security properties of biometric systems; such a decision must be based on and confirmed by a risk analysis. Particularly, reviewing the process of the biometric data capture and transfer is very important. Sometimes biometric authentication systems replace traditional authentication systems not because of higher security but because of higher comfort and ease of use.

False rejects – the unpleasant property of biometric systems causing authorised users to be rejected - may prevent biometric systems to spread into some specific applications, where inability of a user to authenticate herself (and run an action) may imply serious problems.

Few basic conclusions at the very end:

- Different biometric samples of the same person will never be same.
- Biometric systems make errors.
- Biometric data are not secret.
- The role of the input device is crucial, and this device must be trusted or well secured.
- The biometric system should check user's liveness.
- Biometrics are good for user authentication. They cannot be used to authenticate data or computers.

4.7.1.2 Characteristics of Biometric *(UPTU 2010-11)*

Biometrics comprises methods for uniquely recognizing humans based upon one or more intrinsic physical or behavioral traits. In computer science, in particular, biometrics is used as a form of identity access management and access control. It is also used to identify individuals in groups that are under surveillance.

Biometric characteristics can be divided in two main classes:

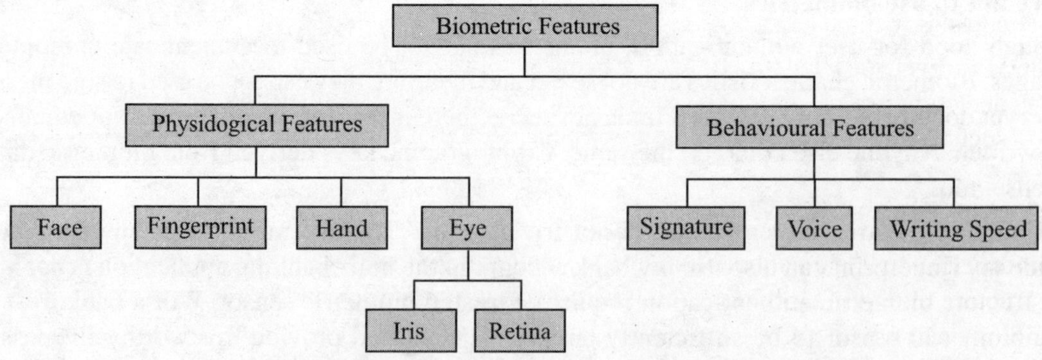

Figure 4.2: Biometric features classification

- Physiological are related to the shape of the body. Examples include, but are not limited to fingerprint, face recognition, DNA, Palm print, hand geometry, iris recognition, which has largely replaced retina, and odour/scent.
- Behavioral are related to the behavior of a person. Examples include, but are not limited to typing rhythm, gait, and voice. Some researchers[1] have coined the term behaviometrics for this class of biometrics.

Strictly speaking, voice is also a physiological trait because every person has a different vocal tract, but voice recognition is mainly based on the study of the way a person speaks, commonly classified as behavioral.

List and briefly describe the principle physical characteristics used for biometric identification:

1. **Facial characteristics:** Facial characteristics are the most common means of human-to-human identification; thus it is natural to consider them for identification by computer.
2. **Fingerprints:** Fingerprints have been used as means of identification for centuries, and the process has been systematized and automated particularly for law enforcement purposes.
3. **Hand geometry:** Hand geometry systems identify features of the hand, including shape, and lengths and widths of fingers.
4. **Retinal pattern:** The pattern formed by veins beneath the retinal surface is unique and therefore suitable for identification.
5. **Iris:** Another unique physical characteristic is the detailed structure of the iris.
6. **Signature:** Each individual has a unique style of handwriting and this is reflected especially in the signature, which is typically a frequently written sequence.
7. **Voice:** Whereas the signature style of an individual reflects not only unique physical attributes of writer but also the writing habit has developed voice patterns are more closely tied to the physical and anatomical characteristics of he speaker. This method is composed by several stages, starting with the acquisition/record of the voice, extract some features (characteristics), such as spectral analysis, tone, speed, and energy density, among others. This data can be storage on a card, such as a magnetic card or a chip card, which can be carried by the user.
8. **Handwriting:** This method is a behavioral approach based on user handwriting. Sensors detect the speed, direction, and pressure of individual handwriting for a predefined pattern, such as the individual's signature. The accuracy of this method can vary.

4.7.2 How Biometrics Works

In this article, you'll learn about biometric systems that use handwriting, hand geometry, voiceprints, iris structure and vein structure. You'll also learn why more businesses and governments use the technology and whether Q's fake contact lenses, recorded voice and silicone hand could really get James Bond into the lab (and let him save the world).

You take basic security precautions every day -- you use a key to get into your house and log on to your computer with a username and password. You've probably also experienced the panic that comes with misplaced keys and forgotten passwords. It isn't just that you can't get what you need -- if you lose your keys or jot your password on a piece of paper, someone else can find them and use them as though they were you.

Instead of using something you have (like a key) or something you know (like a password), biometrics uses **who you are** to identify you. Biometrics can use **physical characteristics**, like your face, fingerprints, irises or veins, or **behavioral characteristics** like your voice, handwriting or typing rhythm. Unlike keys and passwords, your personal traits are extremely difficult to lose or forget. They can also be very difficult to copy. For this reason, many people consider them to be safer and more secure than keys or passwords.

Biometric systems can seem complicated, but they all use the same three steps:

- **Enrollment:** The first time you use a biometric system, it records basic information about you, like your name or an identification number. It then captures an image or recording of your specific trait.
- **Storage:** Contrary to what you may see in movies, most systems don't store the complete image or recording. They instead analyze your trait and translate it into a code or graph. Some systems also record this data onto a smart card that you carry with you.
- **Comparison:** The next time you use the system, it compares the trait you present to the information on file. Then, it either accepts or rejects that you are who you claim to be.

Systems also use the same three components:

- A sensor that detects the characteristic being used for identification
- A computer that reads and stores the information
- Software that analyzes the characteristic, translates it into a graph or code and performs the actual comparisons

4.7.3 What are Biometric Systems used for? (UPTU-2010-11)

Biometrics are used for identification and verification:

Identification is determining who a person is. It involves trying to find a match for a person's biometric data in a database containing records of people and that characteristic. This method requires time and a large amount of processing power, especially if the database is very large.

Verification is determining if a person is who they say they are. It involves comparing a user's biometric data to the previously recorded data for that person to ensure that this is the same person. This method requires less processing power and time, and is used for access control (to buildings or data).

4.7.4 Principles of Fingerprint Biometrics

A fingerprint is made of a number of ridges and valleys on the surface of the finger. Ridges are the upper skin layer segments of the finger and valleys are the lower segments. The ridges form so-called minutia points: ridge endings (where a ridge end) and ridge bifurcations (where a ridge splits in two). Many types of minutiae exist, including dots (very small ridges), islands (ridges slightly longer than dots, occupying a middle space between two temporarily divergent ridges), ponds or lakes (empty spaces between two temporarily divergent ridges), spurs (a notch protruding from a ridge), bridges (small ridges joining two longer adjacent ridges), and crossovers (two ridges which cross each other).

The uniqueness of a fingerprint can be determined by the pattern of ridges and furrows as well as the minutiae points. There are five basic fingerprint patterns: arch, tented arch, left loop, right loop and whorl. Loops make up 60% of all fingerprints, whorls account for 30%, and arches for 10%.

Fingerprints are usually considered to be unique, with no two fingers having the exact same dermal ridge characteristics.

4.7.5 How does Fingerprint Biometrics Work

The main technologies used to capture the fingerprint image with sufficient detail are optical, silicon, and ultrasound.

There are two main algorithm families to recognize fingerprints:

Minutia matching compares specific details within the fingerprint ridges. At registration (also called enrollment), the minutia points are located, together with their relative positions to each other and their directions. At the matching stage, the fingerprint image is processed to extract its minutia points, which are then compared with the registered template.

Pattern matching compares the overall characteristics of the fingerprints, not only individual points. Fingerprint characteristics can include sub-areas of certain interest including ridge thickness, curvature, or density. During enrollment, small sections of the fingerprint and their relative distances are extracted from the fingerprint. Areas of interest are the area around a minutia point, areas with low curvature radius, and areas with unusual combinations of ridges.

4.7.6 Iris

Principles of iris biometrics

The iris is the elastic, pigmented, connective tissue that controls the pupil. The iris is formed in early life in a process called morphogenesis. Once fully formed, the texture is stable throughout life. It is the only internal human organ visible from the outside and is protected by the cornea. The iris of the eye has a unique pattern, from eye to eye and person to person.

How does iris biometrics work

An iris scan will analyze over 200 points of the iris, such as rings, furrows, freckles, the corona and will compare it it a previously recorded template.

Glasses, contact lenses, and even eye surgery does not change the characteristics of the iris.

To prevent an image / photo of the iris from being used instead of a real "live" eye, iris scanning systems will vary the light and check that the pupil dilates or contracts.

4.7.7 Retina

Principles of retina biometrics

The blood vessels at the back of the eye have a unique pattern, from eye to eye and person to person.

How does retina biometrics work

Retina scans require that the person removes their glasses, place their eye close to the scanner, stare at a specific point, and remain still, and focus on a specified location for approximately 10 to 15 seconds while the scan is completed. A retinal scan involves the use of a low-intensity coherent light source, which is projected onto the retina to illuminate the blood vessels which are then photographed and analysed. A coupler is used to read the blood vessel patterns.

A retina scan cannot be faked as it is currently impossible to forge a human retina. Furthermore, the retina of a deceased person decays too rapidly to be used to deceive a retinal scan.

A retinal scan has an error rate of 1 in 10,000,000, compared to fingerprint identification error being sometimes as high as 1 in 500.

4.7.8 Hand

Principles of hand biometrics

An individual's hand does not significantly change after a certain age. Unlike fingerprints, the human hand isn't unique. Individual hand features are not descriptive enough for identification. However, hand biometric recognition systems are accurate for verification purposes when combining various individual features and measurements of fingers and hands.

How does hand biometrics work

Biometric hand recognition systems measure and analyze the overall structure, shape and porportions of the hand, e.g. length, width and thickness of hand, fingers and joints; characteristics of the skin surface such as creases and ridges. Some hand geometry biometrics systems measure up to 90 parameters.

As hand biometrics rely on hand and finger geometry, the system will also work with dirty hands. The only limitation is for people with severe arthristis who cannot spread their hands on the reader.

The user places the palm of his or her hand on the reader's surface and aligns his or her hand with the guidance pegs which indicate the proper location of the fingers. The device checks its database for verification of the user. The process normally only takes a few seconds.

To enroll, the users places his or her hand palm down on the reader's surface.

To prevent a mold or a cast of the hand from being used, some hand biometric systems will require the user to move their fingers. Also, hand thermography can be used to record the heat of the hand, or skin conductivity can be measured.

4.7.9 Palm vein

Principles of palm vein biometrics

The pattern of blood veins is unique to every individual, even among identical twins. Palms have a broad and complicated vascular pattern and thus contain a wealth of differentiating features for personal identification. Furthermore, it will not vary during the person's lifetime. It is a very secure method of authentication because this blood vein pattern lies under the skin. This makes it almost impossible for others to read or copy.

How does palm vein biometrics work

An individual's vein pattern image is captured by radiating his/her hand with near-infrared rays. The reflection method illuminates the palm using an infrared ray and captures the light given off by the region after diffusion through the palm. The deoxidized hemoglobin in the in the vein vessels absorbs the infrared ray, thereby reducing the reflection rate and causing the veins to appear as a black pattern. This vein pattern is then verified against a preregistered pattern to authenticate the individual.

As veins are internal in the body and have a wealth of differentiating features, attempts to forge an identity are extremely difficult, thereby enabling a high level of security. In addition, the sensor of the palm vein device can only recognize the pattern if the deoxidized hemoglobin is actively flowing within the individual's veins.

This system is not dangerous, a near infrared is a component of sunlight: there is no more exposure when scanning the hand than by walking outside in the sun.

4.7.10 Face

Principles of face biometrics

The dimensions, proportions and physical attributes of a person's face are unique.

How does face biometrics work

Biometric facial recognition systems will measure and analyze the overall structure, shape and porportions of the face: Distance between the eyes, nose, mouth, and jaw edges; upper outlines of the eye sockets, the sides of the mouth, the location of the nose and eyes, the area surrounding the cheekbones.

At enrolment, several pictures are taken of the user's face, with slightly different angles and facial expressions, to allow for more accurate matching. For verification and identification, the user stands in front of the camera for a few seconds, and the scan is compared with the template previously recorded.

To prevent an image / photo of the face or a mask from being used, face biometric systems will require the user to smile, blink, or nod their head. Also, facial thermograph can be used to record the heat of the face (which won't be affected by a mask).

The main facial recognition methods are: feature analysis, neural network, eigenfaces, and automatic face processing.

There are also a number of behavioral biometric technologies such as voice recognition (analyzing a speaker's vocal behavior), keystroke (measuring the time spacing of typed words), gait recognition (manner of walking), or signature (analyzing the way you sign).

Other biometric techniques, still in exploratory stages would include DNA biometrics, ear shape, finger nails or odor.

4.8 CRITERIA FOR SELECTION OF BIOMETRICS

The main biometrics systems on the market work by scanning an individual fingerprints, hands, face, iris, retina, voice patter, signature, or strokes on a keyboard. According to Hogan, finger scanning accounts for 34 percent of biometric system sales followed by hand scanning with 26 percent, face scanning with 15 percent, voice scanning and eye scanning with 11 percent each, and signature scanning with 3 percent. Retinal scanning which reads the blood vessels in the back of the eye and requires the used to be within six inches of the scanning device-is the most accurate system but also the least likely to enjoy widespread use because of people's natural protectiveness toward their eyes.

4.9 DESIGN ISSUES IN BIOMETRIC SYSTEMS

Innate characteristics can significantly affect a user's performance and influence the ability of the system to perform successfully. For instance, consider the impact of the following characteristics on the design of a biometric system:

- Age
- Gender
- Experience
- Ability

By designing with these characteristics in mind, developers of biometric systems can produce a system that is more effective and efficient. With a focus on users and the usability of biometric systems, design teams have the opportunity to improve image captures, increase throughput, and reduce errors.

Following is a partial list of design questions that project teams must consider in the creation of a biometric system. Please note, this list is not an exhaustive list of design considerations. Rather, it is intended to stimulate design teams to begin thinking about the needs of users and the potential impact of user's inherent qualities on the performance of a system.

Age

- How does an individual's age affect the quality of a sample?
- Does age affect user's abilities to learn and use a biometric system?
- Are younger users more successful in their attempts?
- Do older users take longer to present a sample?

Gender

- Does gender affect the quality of a sample?
- Does gender affect the accuracy of a sample?
- What role does gender play, if any, in the presentation and capture of a sample?

Experience and Ability

- What role does experience play in users abilities to present a sample?
- Are more experienced individuals more successful?
- Do first-time users struggle more than experienced users?
- How does past experience affect a user's interaction with a system?
- How do disabilities affect the user in submitting a biometric sample?
- Which disabilities impact success in presentation and capture?

In addition to these demographic characteristics, it is also important to consider other opportunities to enhance the usability of a biometric system through the use of user-centered instructions, greater awareness of anthropometrics, enhanced affordance and improved accessibility.

4.10 PROBLEMS OF INTEROPERABILITY

One of the largest hurdles facing the system is that of interoperability. 'Interoperability' is concerned with how the processes, devices and systems involved in the identification process interact with one another; how the process of (for example) a thumbprint being scanned at one end of the system translates into the correct data being found in a database and relayed back to the source for verification.

This problem is magnified if applied on a more worldwide scale, as would be the case with biometric passports - systems in every country in the world would need to be compatible to a pre-set international standard, despite presumably being designed and manufactured by different companies.

Also, it should be considered that different countries will take biometrics to a different scale, due to both financial and political reasons - a rich country like the US may be able to afford fingerprint or iris scanning on all of their passports. This has a knock-on effect throughout the system, as even if a poorer country simply incorporates facial recognition scanning in their passport photos, they still would need the technology at their airports to receive the more complex US passports.

4.10.1 The Cost of ID Cards

Worldwide interoperability leads into another concern many have raised about biometric identification - cost. Beyond the material cost of the technology and equipment, there's the logistical cost of organizing and registering the world's citizenry into this central database. The initial costs for the UK's system alone were officially stated to be £5.8 billion by the government, but a London School of Economics investigation in 2005 estimated that the true cost could run as high as £18 billion. This would put the cost to the individual citizen at around £300 each, significantly higher than the government's £93 estimate.

4.10.2 Legal Problems with ID Database

There are also problems within the legal system which would need to be addressed before a biometric identification system could be introduced. The current set of UK data protection laws were not designed with any kind of biometric ID card or database scheme in mind, and as such are lacking in specific legislation to protect the data. The law as it stands does allow for the implementation of an ID card scheme, but fresh legislation needs to bc drafted to ensure the safety of biometric data; questions also arise over how the data is to be used, and whether the subjects of the data have intellectual property rights over it.

It is clear that there are a host of practical problems, from the technological to the financial, which must be overcome before a fully biometric identity card system will be possible in the UK and beyond - and this is before public opposition is even taken into account. This suggests that it may be some time yet until the system is fully enacted.

4.11 ECONOMIC AND SOCIAL ASPECT OF BIOMETRICS (UPTU-2010-11)

The key sociocultural concerns associated with biometric fact into three main categories:

1. Informational privacy.
2. Physical privacy.
3. Religious objectives

Biometric application have the potential to further reduce anonymity. In addition, as with any technological innovation, some people will find certain aspects of biometric discomforting are unacceptable for a variety of sociocultural reasons. Additional purposes can be useful and valuable to society but ethical concerns arise when biometrics are used beyond their original purpose, without the informed and voluntary consent of the participants. These concerns include whether participants have the right to reassess their participation given the new purpose for the data, the implications of a decision not to cooperate in processing biometric data, and justification of the new purposes, given the program's original intent.

1. Informational Privacy: The must significant informational privacy concern relate to the threat of function creep and the tracking capabilities of biometrics. These concerns are addressed below:

(i) Function creep

(ii) Tracking

(iii) Misuse of data

2. Physical Privacy: The use of biometrics may raise physical concerns. These concerns are three fold:

The stigma associated with some biometrics, such as fingerprints, the possibility of actual harm to the participants by the technology itself and the concern that the devices used to obtain or "read" the biometric may be unhygienic.

(i) Stigmatization

(ii) Actual harm

(iii) Hygiene

3. Religious Objectives: Certain Christians interpret biometrics to be a "Mark of the Beast". The objection is based on language in revelation. In the case of biometric identification religious objections contributed, at least in part to be the failure of fingerprint program.

4.12 BIOMETRIC SYSTEMS OFFER MANY IMPORTANT BENEFITS

Biometrics is concerned with identifying a person based on his / her physiological or behavioral characteristics. Examples of biometrics systems include fingerprint, hand, face, eye (iris or retina), and speech recognition.

4.12.1 Why are Biometrics Secure

Unique: The various biometrics systems have been developed around unique characteristics of individuals. The probability of 2 people sharing the same biometric data is virtually nil. Cannot be shared: Because a biometric property is an intrinsic property of an individual, it is extremely difficult to duplicate or share (you cannot give a copy of your face or your hand to someone!).

Cannot be copied: Biometric characteristics are nearly impossible to forge or spoof, especially with new technologies ensuring that the biometric being identified is from a live person.

Cannot be lost: A biometric property of an individual can be lost only in case of serious accident.

4.12.2 What are the Advantages and Disadvantages of Biometric (UPTU 2010-11)

The primary advantage of biometric authentication methods over other methods of user authentication is that they really do what they should, i.e., they authenticate the user. These methods use real human physiological or behavioral characteristics to authenticate users. These biometric characteristics are (more or less) permanent and not changeable.

It is also not easy (although in some cases not principally impossible) to change one's fingerprint, iris or other biometric characteristics. Users cannot pass their biometric characteristics to other users as easily as they do with their cards or passwords. Biometric objects cannot be stolen as tokens, keys, cards or other objects used for the traditional user authentication, yet biometric characteristics can be stolen from computer systems and networks. Biometric characteristics are not secret and therefore the availability of a user's fingerprint or iris pattern does not break security the same way as availability of the user's password. Even the use of dead or artificial biometric characteristics should not let the attacker in.

Most biometric techniques are based on something that cannot be lost or forgotten. This is an advantage for users as well as for system administrators because the problems and costs associated with lost, reissued or temporarily issued tokens/cards/passwords can be avoided, thus saving some costs of the system management.

Another advantage of biometric authentication systems may be their speed. The authentication of a habituated user using an iris-based identification system may take 2 (or 3) seconds while finding your key ring, locating the right key and using it may take some 5 (or 10) seconds.

Disadvantages of Biometric Authentication

So why do not we use biometrics everywhere instead of passwords or Tokens. Nothing is perfect, and biometric authentication methods also have their own shortcomings. First of all the performance of biometric systems is not ideal. Biometric systems still need to be improved in the terms of accuracy and speed. Biometric systems with the false rejection rate under 1% (together with a reasonably low false acceptance rate) are still rare today. Although few biometric systems are fast and accurate (in terms of low false acceptance rate) enough to allow identification (automatically recognising the user identity), most of current systems are suitable for the verification only, as the false acceptance rate is too high.

The fail to enrol rate brings up another important problem. Not all users can use any given biometric system. People without hands cannot use fingerprint or hand-based systems. Visually impaired people have difficulties using iris or retina based techniques. As not all users are able to use a specific biometric system, the authentication system must be extended to handle users falling into the FTE category. This can make the resulting system more complicated, less secure or more expensive.

Even enrolled users can have difficulties using a biometric system. The FTE rate says how many of the input samples are of insufficient quality. Data acquisition must be repeated if the quality of input sample is not sufficient for further processing and this would be annoying for users.

Biometric data are not considered to be secret and security of a biometric system cannot be based on the secrecy of user's biometric characteristics. The server cannot authenticate the user just after receiving her correct biometric characteristics. The user authentication can be successful only when user's characteristics are fresh and have been collected from the user being authenticated. This implies that the biometric input device must be trusted. Its authenticity should be verified (unless the device and the link are physically secure) and user's liveness would be checked. The input device also should be under human supervision or tamper-resistant. The fact that biometric characteristics are not secret brings some issues that traditional authentication systems need not deal with. Many of the current biometric systems are not aware of this fact and therefore the security level they offer is limited.

Some biometric sensors (particularly those having contact with users) also have a limited lifetime. While a magnetic card reader may be used for years (or even decades), the optical fingerprint reader (if heavily used) must be regularly cleaned and even then the lifetime need not exceed one year.

Biometric systems may violate user's privacy. Biometric characteristics are sensitive data that may contain a lot of personal information. The DNA (being the typical example) contains (among others) the user's preposition to diseases. This may be a very interesting piece of information

for an insurance company. The body odour can provide information about user's recent activities. It is also told that people with asymmetric fingerprints are more likely to be homosexually oriented, etc. Use of biometric systems may also imply loss of anonymity. While one can have multiple identities when authentication methods are based on something the user knows or has, biometric systems can sometimes link all user actions to a single identity.

Biometric systems can potentially be quite troublesome for some users. These users find some biometric systems intrusive or personally invasive. Even if no biometric system is really dangerous, users are occasionally afraid of something they do not know much about. In some countries people do not like to touch something that has already been touched many times (e.g., biometric sensor), while in some countries people do not like to be photographed or their faces are completely covered.

Lack of standards (or ignorance of standards) may also posses a serious problem. Two similar biometric systems from two different vendors are not likely to interoperate at present.

4.13 FACTORS IN BIOMETRICS

In recent years, biometrics is being used more and more in security applications. This fact has led suppliers and researchers to analyze biometric algorithms powers and vulnerabilities, as to improve the feasibility of this technology. Nevertheless, as many authors claim, biometric performance also depends on other factors such as usability and/or user acceptance, which can influence significantly their performance. Only a few of these factors have already been studied, using specific approaches and only for certain biometric modalities, such us fingerprint and face. However, there is no general and independent methodology implemented to assess how these factors affect biometric system performance and to produce intercomparable results. Based on previous works and following procedures and requirements addressed in the International Standard ISO/IEC 19795-2 for scenario evaluations, these authors have developed a general methodology to analyze end-to-end system performance when some usability factors are modified. Such factors cover different ways of presenting biometric characteristics to the sensor and also the biometric characteristic variability caused by illness or climatic changes. A generic and controlled scenario has been modelled to carry on all sets of trials. Then, the methodology has been particularized defining specific protocols, methods, and considerations for each parameter to assess. Furthermore, details for analysing these parameters through different modalities have been defined. In addition, this methodology has been checked for one modality considering different usability aspects to obtain the feedback necessary to test its validity and viability and to detect points of interest for improvement.

4.14 CRITICAL FACTORS IN THE ASSESSMENT OF BIOMETRIC PRODUCTS

When selecting a biometric product for implementation, the following factors should be used for assessment of product performance:

4.14.1 Matching Accuracy

The fundamental measure of the effectiveness of a biometric system (i.e. a biometric capture device + encoding and matching algorithm) is how effectively it matches a person against the reference database. The key metrics here are:

- **False Match Rate ("FMR")** - How often a person is positively matched against the wrong record in the database. Also known as False Accept Rate ("FAR").
- **False Non-Match Rate ("FNMR")** - How often a person is not matched against their own record in the database. Also known as False Reject Rate ("FRR").
- **Failure-to-Encode Rate ("FTE Rate")** - How often presented biometric images cannot be converted into match-able templates.

Thresholds for Acceptability

Most biometric systems exhibit a tradeoff of FMR and FNMR depending on the match thresholds chosen, and the thresholds chosen may depend on whether the application is positive (e.g. for access control) or negative (e.g. a blacklist check). However, a biometric system should be able to exhibit a FMR of less than 1 x 10-6 (1 in 1 million) at a FNMR of less than 0.01 (1%). FTE Rate can be exchanged with FNMR, but the combined total of the two should be less than 1%. Note that if a variety of biometric capture products are used in a given deployment, captured biometric samples from these devices must be interoperable with each other such that the matching accuracy is not measurable degraded.

4.14.2 Failure-to-Acquire ("FTA") Rate

Failure-to-Acquire ("FTA") rate is a measure of what fraction of the time a person simply cannot use a biometric system. This is a critical and often overlooked measure of functionality. The FMR or FNMR on a system is irrelevant if a system cannot capture images from an individual. FTA rates can be measured in either a "raw" way, in which every try is considered an attempt, or in a "transactional" way, in which a person is allowed multiple tries to successfully capture. The latter way is a more accurate measure of real implementation, as people are nearly always offered multiple tries before giving up. The impact of multiple tries should be measured as an impact on overall throughput, as mentioned below.

Thresholds for Acceptability

Transactional FTA rates for a deployed biometric system should be less than 1%, as the net impact of an FTA is very much the same as a false non-match or an FTE. When measuring the FTA rates of a given system, proper sampling of a wide demographic, including variety in age, ethnicity, gender, and attire is critical to a true analysis for deployment.

4.14.3 System Throughput

System throughput is a measure of the average time needed to process individuals through a biometric system. This measure should take into account the following:

- The time required for a single capture attempt.
- Any time required for additional attempts if a FNM, FTE, or FTA is associated with the first attempt. This should include physical repositioning, such as replacing a finger on a fingerprint sensor platen, or walking back to place in an iris or face recognition system (if the individual has moved out of position before receiving a match result).

Thresholds for Acceptability

Required average capture times depend on the application at hand. For enrollment or blacklist checks, where accuracy is paramount, biometric samples should be captured in less than 5 seconds for each biometric. For identification checks, where enhanced throughput may be required, biometric samples should be captured in less than 2 seconds. These times do not include the time to transition from one capture subject to the next, which should be less than 2 seconds.

4.14.4 Ease-of-Use

While this factor is deeply intertwined with system throughput, matching accuracy, and FTA rate, it is worthy of consideration unto itself. Ease-of-use, or usability, is a critical factor for any real world biometric deployment, as it will determine the overall success of the biometric system - including system administrator, operator, and capture subject frustration or satisfaction. Simply put, the harder biometric systems are to use, the more costly they are to system operators and users alike, and the less likely they are to be used consistently over time.

Aside from an assessment of the three factors stated above, ease-of-use can be measured by answering a few key questions:

- How long does it take to explain how to use the biometric system?
- Can system usage be easily described to individuals who do not speak the same language and have no experience with similar technology?
- How often, and to what extent, do operators need to be involved to ensure proper functionality?

Thresholds for Acceptability

Usage instructions should take less than 5 seconds, and should not typically require further oversight or interaction from system operators. The instructions should be able to be conveyed to completely non-technical and non-acclimated subjects as well as subjects who do not even speak the same language.

4.14.5 Appropriate Concept of Operations

Concept of Operations (or "ConOps") is an industry term referring to how a biometric system is used when deployed. Ensuring appropriate ConOps is critical to effective system layout, operator oversight, and conveyance of results to capture subjects. The following questions should be asked when considering different concept of operations:

- Do the ConOps allow the proper level of control over the capture subject?
- Do the ConOps clearly delineate security boundaries?
- Do the ConOps support minimal intervention from operators?
- Do the ConOps support rapid, straightforward retries, in case of an FTA, FNM, or FTE?

Thresholds for Acceptability

The answers to all of the above questions should be in the affirmative to support a reliable biometric system deployment. The system ConOps should be such that they allow a proper level of control over the capture subject while requiring a minimum of intervention from system operators. Furthermore, the ConOps should support clearly delineated secure / non-secure boundaries, and they should support rapid and straightforward retries in the case of a failed biometric capture attempt.

4.15 BIOMETRIC AUTHENTICATION

Because of the cost and complexity of most biometric systems, use of biometric authentication is generally limited to ultra high security applications (e.g. the defense industry). Historically, biometric systems have been a mixed bag when it comes to availability, compatibility, and security. Training is a significant issue and logistics are perhaps more difficult than with any other two-factor solution.

Deployment involves collecting the biometric data to compare against, which can be a daunting task for users and IT departments. In addition, most biometric authentication solutions rely on fingerprint readers, retinal scanners, or other biometric devices, which are attached to the pc or laptop. The cost and IT resources required to purchase, deploy, and maintain biometric readers creates an often insurmountable challenge.

In addition to being expensive and time consuming to deploy and maintain, both the login credentials and the biometric data are being collected and transmitted through a single channel, making it vulnerable to emerging threats, such as man-in-the-middle attacks. As the sophistication of attacks continues to increase, Out-of-Band authentication, which utilizes a separate channel for the additional authentication factors, is becoming widely recognized as a best practice for multi-factor authentication.

Technology

- Typically across a single channel
- Limited integration points
- Cumbersome deployment process

User Adoption

- Prone to errors
- A biometric reader must be available on the user's pc or laptop

Cost

- Requires hardware, management software, and readers for end users
- User training is required

4.16 THE PROBLEM WITH BIOMETRIC SYSTEMS

4.16.1 Recognition Errors

There are two basic types of recognition errors: the false accept rate (FAR) and the false reject rate (FRR). A False Accept is when a non matching pair of biometric data is wrongly accepted as a match by the system. A False Reject is when a matching pair of biometric data is wrongly rejected by the system. The two errors are complementary: When you try to lower one of the errors by varying the threshold, the other error rate automatically increases. There is therefore a balance to be found, with a decision threshold that can be specified to either reduce the risk of FAR, or to reduce the risk of FRR.

In a biometric authentication system, the relative false accept and false reject rates can be set by choosing a particular operating point (i.e., a detection threshold). Very low (close to zero) error rates for both errors (FAR and FRR) at the same time are not possible. By setting a high threshold, the FAR error can be close to zero, and similarly by setting a significantly low threshold, the FRR rate can be close to zero. A meaningful operating point for the threshold is decided based on the application requirements, and the FAR versus FRR error rates at that operating point may be quite different. To provide high security, biometric systems operate at a low FAR instead of the commonly recommended equal error rate (EER) operating point where FAR = FRR.

4.16.2 Compromised Biometric Data

Paradoxically, the greatest strength of biometrics is at the same time its greatest liability. It is the fact that an individual's biometric data does not change over time: the pattern in your iris, retina or palm vein remain the same throughout your life. Unfortunately, this means that should a set of biometric data be compromised, it is compromised forever. The user only has a limited number of biometric features (one face, two hands, ten fingers, two eyes). For authentication systems based on physical tokens such as keys and badges, a compromised token can be easily canceled and the user can be assigned a new token. Similarly, user IDs and passwords can be changed as often as required. But if the biometric data are compromised, the user may quickly run out of biometric features to be used for authentication.

4.17 BIOMETRICS ISSUES (IMPORTANT)

At present, many applications of biometric technologies exist both in the private and public sector. Some of these are considered large-scale, for example the FBI fingerprint database in the US or the Malaysian multi purpose smart card. But so far no application comes close in scale to the proposed scheme for passports and visas. The widespread implementation of biometric applications in the public sector and their potential proliferation in the private sector will pose a series of challenges which policy-makers need to address. In the next sections we will discuss the social, economic, legal and technological implications of biometric technologies and we will make a short but important analysis of the medical implications. In each of these analyses, the issues of security, privacy, interoperability with other systems and costs are examined.

1. Security
2. Privacy
3. Interoperability
4. Costs
5. Social aspects
6. Economic aspects
7. Legal aspects
8. Technological aspects
9. Medical aspects

4.17.1 Security

Biometric systems are more secure than traditional identification systems. But they only represent a secure identification process in that they provide a strong link between physical persons with their identity data. This means that the integrity of the linking process must be high. This will depend on the secure operation of each one of the four stages of a biometric identification process (enrolment, storage, acquisition, matching). In addition it cannot rely on secrecy, since most biometric features are either self-evident or easily obtainable.

On the other hand, since biometrics are only a part of the system, it is not enough to secure the biometric system if the rest of the process remains open to circumvention. In the end, the notion of a biometric identifier being absolute proof of identity has to be discarded. Biometric identification systems are subject to errors and circumvention and thus are not perfect. It is important for whoever uses biometric identification systems to understand this principle.

4.17.2 Privacy

While the use of a biometric technology is not an invasion of privacy, in many cases the way the digital data is produced, stored, compared and possibly linked to other information about the individual, may raise a set of concerns. Although these are concerns the existing legal framework for Data protection can handle the widespread diffusion of biometrics into the commercial sphere may challenge the legal framework in ways that will have a negative impact on user acceptability. For example should the habit of sharing biometric data among private sector entities proliferate, then it is likely that users may find that the current data protection frame is unable to protect them adequately and thus become disenchanted with convenience application altogether.

Moreover, one would have to consider ethical consequence of large scale deployment. One could argue that the use of a part of oneself (the biometric feature that is being digitised, stored and compared) as one's identity is eliminating the space that we traditionally place between our physical selves and our identity. Currently, any individual has the option of changing identity if the need arises (e.g. witness protection programme). This becomes harder or even impossible when identity is tied up with the physical self.

4.17.3 Interoperability

For any emerging technology, interoperability across geographical borders and business sectors, across processes, devices and systems is beneficial to its diffusion. National interests in maintaining control and vendor resistance (aspiring to future market dominance due to lock-in effects) are natural barriers to interoperability. There is significant work being done at national and international levels to develop standards, which will be useful in promoting open systems development and interoperability.

Technical interoperability is likely to be achieved in the near future but interoperability of processes may be more challenging especially when biometrics become more widely diffused in society. When systems become more interoperable, the need for building safeguards against abuse grows as well. Moreover, since individuals have many different biometrics at their disposal, there is the possibility for different applications to make use of different biometrics, in the sense that limited interoperability may create barriers and thus protect against abuse. Such systems may still be compatible at the data transmission level and thus it may still be possible to cross-check information as to who was identified and where.

4.17.4 Costs

Costs vary between technologies and also between low-end and high-end equipment within any one technology. It is the purpose and scale of an application that determine costs. Thus costs will depend on the choice of open- or closed-system architecture, type of application, centralised or decentralised storage, whether encryption is used as a means of data protection, and the decision of where in the system matching takes place.

Moreover, enhanced market competition or market distortions will also impact on costs, as will regulatory decisions on interoperability, standards and intellectual property rights.

In addition, it must be noted that real costs include overall system security (at all biometric stages) as well as those of the fall-back system which is an indispensable element of any proper biometric application.

4.18 SOCIAL ASPECTS

Biometric technologies are just a tool, but their social implications may be far-reaching. Europe faces the challenge of better understanding the longer-term implications of large-scale deployment of biometrics so as to ensure their beneficial implementation. The following four themes have been identified as the main social issues:

4.18.1 Clarity of Purpose in Relation to Biometric Applications

"Function creep" is an important concern, i.e. that technology and processes introduced for one purpose will be extended to other purposes which were not discussed or agreed upon at the time of their implementation. Thus it is important to be clear about what the needs of the application are and how biometrics will be able to achieve them.

4.18.2 Interoperability and Equivalence of Performance and Process

This is not only a technical issue. Process equivalence (for instance backup procedures that are the same everywhere) is extremely important as it impacts on system performance, especially where biometrics are used in international situations (example, border control).

4.18.3 Human Factors, Usability and Social Exclusion

Human factors such as age, ethnicity, gender, diseases or disabilities (including natural ageing) ought to be studied on a case-by-case basis so as to minimise the possibility of social exclusion of a small but significant part of the population. More research is also needed on the usability and the user-friendliness of biometrics in real-life situations.

4.18.4 Impact upon the Trust Model Between Citizen and State

People may temporarily accept a loss of some of their personal freedom in exchange for a more secure world. But when government control is perceived as excessive, disproportionate and/or 'too efficient' this may lead to an erosion of trust which will be in the interest of neither governments nor citizens.

4.19 ECONOMIC ASPECTS (UPTU-2010–11)

Biometric technologies are strong identification technologies and as such influence the level of 'trust' in economic transactions. In other words they can help reduce fraud and thus help materialize the efficiency and equity gains of the Information Society. They help simplify things from the user's perspective and minimize the likelihood of error. At the same time their widespread deployment in the public sector will make identification over the network easier, more secure and may bring down costs per secure transaction. This in turn will help consumers make more efficient transactions. Standards and interoperability issues, however, determine widespread adoption and shape economic challenges. The following five themes summarise the economic implications of biometrics:

4.19.1 The Concept of Optimal Identity

The economic importance of identity is growing in a digital society, but the strongest identity protection is not necessarily the optimal one.

4.19.2 Negative Implications of Stronger Identification

Identity errors and abuse may become less frequent, but when they happen, they could potentially be more dangerous. For example identity theft may become less frequent but more severe and with wider social repercussions.

4.19.3 Interoperability is Vital for Market Operation

There is a serious danger that the biometrics identification market - and markets that depend on identity - may fragment into clusters that will not interoperate, thus becoming vulnerable to monopolisation or dominance by a few players.

4.19.4 Biometrics-related IPRs Threaten open Competition

The unregulated exploitation of intellectual property rights to aspects of biometrics can significantly reduce competition in biometrics and/or distort development, direction and speed of uptake.

4.19.5 Public Sector uptake will Shape the Market

The use of biometrics in eGovernment initiatives and associated large-scale public procurement could be key levers to ensure open and competitive markets, and rapid and socially-productive innovation.

4.20 LEGAL ASPECTS AND CHALLENGES (UPTU-2010–11)

Up to now biometric technologies have been operating in various closed environments; by contrast, their use in private transactions will be based on consent. The existing legal framework does not hinder public and private actors from implementing applications. The deployment of biometrics does not threaten procedural rights (i.e. rights in a court of law); their use is deemed intrusive but within reasonable limits and a few unresolved issues arising from the data protection framework have not hindered recent choices for biometrics in European passports. However, their widespread implementation and the fear of a 'surveillance' society that may follow from the so-called 'diffusion effect' may call for a rethink of the legal tools available. The following four points are briefly described so as to enable a better understanding of the legal implications of biometrics:

4.20.1 Enabling Legal Environment

The existing legal environment (privacy and data protection) is flexible in that it is an 'enabling' legislation legitimizing the de facto commercial use of personal data. Data protection rules regulate the use of biometrics but they lack normative content and raise no ethical debate.

4.20.2 Opacity/Transparency Rules Required

Data protection (transparency rules) does not specify what the limits of use and abuse of biometrics are. Opacity (privacy) rules may prohibit use in cases where there is the need to guarantee against outside steering or disproportionate power balances.

4.20.3 Wider Implementation Raises Fundamental Concerns

As biometrics are diffused in society some concerns are gaining in importance: concerns about power accumulation, about further use of existing data, about specific threats related to the use of biometrics by the public sector, about the failure to protect individuals from their inclination to trade their own privacy with what seems to be very low cost convenience.

4.20.4 Use of Biometrics in Law Enforcement

It is imperative that biometrics evidence be regulated when presented as evidence in courts of Law so as to protect suspects adequately (e.g. being heard, right to counter-expertise).

4.20.5 Technological Aspects

Biometric technologies are still largely undergoing development and are not yet mature enough for widespread use in society. Enrolment is the first and most important stage of any biometric application since the overall efficiency, accuracy and usability of a system depends on this stage. Re-enrolment during the life-cycle of an application is not only necessary because of natural and accidental changes to biometric features, but also to ensure that the acquisition of the sample patterns is performed using state-of-the-art sensor technology. However, not enough large-scale trials exist to help draw conclusions on enrolment procedures. Biometric sample or template storage and their protection are also very important issues. Storing can be done in centralised databases or on portable media such as smart cards. Next follow four technological concerns:

4.20.6 Performance/Accuracy

There will always be a compromise between the level of accuracy that can be obtained from a biometric system and the level of performance obtained in operating a live system with a threshold based on operator- or application-defined constraints.

4.20.7 Biometric Privacy

Biometrics could be used in the future to enhance privacy by using a biometric feature to encode a security key, for example a PIN code which allows access to a bank account. There are many advantages to this use of biometrics - primarily that keys thus produced are not linked to the original patterns, are not stored and can be revoked at will.

4.20.8 Interoperability

Technical interoperability and the availability of widely accepted standards and specifications are issues that are currently being researched. They are particularly important in border-control applications, in which different countries are inevitably involved but that will also be the case in the future with worldwide consumer applications (e.g. bank ATMs).

4.20.9 Multimodality

Combining several modalities, e.g. fingerprint and iris, in sequence results in the improvement of a system's overall efficiency, while combining them in parallel improves a system's flexibility by providing alternative modes for the verification/identification process. The choice of which modalities to combine is driven by the specific application design. This combination may be performed at different stages of the process, resulting in various benefits. Multimodality could also be viewed as a security enhancement, for example by having the system request alternative modalities to be tested at random in an effort to keep potential impostors at bay.

4.20.10 Medical Aspects

Direct medical implications include potential risks to human health from the use of biometrics as well as public concerns related to possible hazards. Indirect implications relate to the ethical risk of biometric data being used to reveal private medical information. The former are more a matter of public perception while the latter are more difficult to deal with. Developing this further:

4.20.11 Direct Medical Implications

Interaction with a biometric sensor holds two potential health risks. If the system uses a contact sensor there is a risk (real or perceived) of the sensor being contaminated. The real risk may be minimal, especially when compared to similar everyday actions (touching doorknobs, railings) but the perceived risk may have a negative impact on public acceptance. Regular cleaning (e.g. through periodic irradiation with UV light) can minimise concerns and improve sensor performance. The second risk relates to technologies that use radiation to assist acquisition (e.g. retinal scanning which use infrared light). There is a fear that this radiation could be damaging to the eyes. Retinal scanning could cause thermal injury on the back of the eye, but it is a biometric technique that is not currently in use. Data from iris recognition equipment manufacturers show no evidence that iris systems could pose a risk. It would be reasonable however to validate this claim in independent laboratories.

4.20.12 Indirect Medical Implications

These are more controversial as they refer to fears about the possibility of biometric data revealing sensitive health information, leading to ethical concerns. Iridologists allege that the iris exposes potential health problems, but these claims are scientifically unfounded and thus the only risk may be one of public fear. Retinal scanning could have serious implications as it may enable detection of a subject's vascular dysfunction. There are also concerns that in the future, face recognition may be used to detect expressions and thus emotional conditions. The ethical debate gets extremely heated when the use of DNA is considered, although the regions of DNA necessary for identification are 'non-coding'.

4.21 FEATURES OF BIOMETRIC IDENTIFICATION

Biometric identification is a statistical process. Variations in conditions between enrolment and acquisition as well as bodily changes (temporary or permanent) mean that there is never a 100% match. For a password or a PIN, the answer given is either exactly the same as the one that has been stored, or it is not - the smallest deviation is a reason for refusal; for a biometric, there is no clear line between a match and a non-match. Whether a match exists depends therefore not only on the two data sets to be compared, but also on what margin of error is deemed tolerable. A 90% probability of a match may or may not be considered acceptable, depending on the implementation of the biometric in question and the application security requirements.

As a consequence of this statistical nature, biometric systems are never 100% accurate. There are two kinds of possible errors: false matches, and false non-matches. A false match occurs when an acquired template is erroneously matched to a template stored from enrolment, although the two templates are from two different persons. A false non-match occurs when an acquired template is not judged to match the template stored from enrolment, although both are from the same person. These error rates vary from one biometric technology to another, and they depend very much on the setting of the threshold above which a "match" is calculated: a 99% threshold will have more false non-matches and fewer false matches than a 98% threshold, and so on.

Any biometric application must therefore provide a fallback procedure to deal with these errors. Fallback procedures are equally necessary to deal with people who have difficulties to provide a sample of any given biometric. This can be permanently, e.g. for sight-impaired people using an iris recognition system; or it may be temporarily, e.g. for an individual with a bandaged face using a face recognition system. The percentage of the population giving rise to a variety of such problems may be small but significant. Therefore, fallback procedures will need sufficiently flexible human involvement to handle the variety of potential problems.

A second point worth mentioning is that the biological data themselves, the so-called samples, need not actually be stored in the biometric identification systems. Iris pictures, fingerprints and faces are converted via mathematical algorithms and stored into fixed format files so-called templates. The use of biometric algorithms facilitates the statistically constant matching of the features extracted during acquisition. Whilst the algorithms are different for each technology, this procedure is usually non-reversible, i.e. it is not possible from a template to recreate the sample which was its source. Another advantage of the use of algorithms to create templates is that a new and different template can be produced if the previously produced template has been stolen and is abused by a third party, even though the biometric characteristics of the body themselves are not revocable - your fingerprint remains your fingerprint, even if someone else has obtained a copy of it.

4.21.1 The Seven Pillars

Biometric features include various subsets of body characteristics, but not all such subsets are suitable for identification purposes. For example, a photograph of one particular body part (the face) is sufficient for many purposes, while a photograph of other body parts (say, elbows or feet) is useless. The evaluation whether a particular body characteristic is suitable for biometric use can be done on the following seven criteria:

- **Universality:** All human beings are endowed with the same physical characteristics - such as fingers, iris, face, DNA - which can be used for identification
- **Distinctiveness:** For each person these characteristics are unique, and thus constitute a distinguishing feature
- **Permanence:** These characteristics remain largely unchanged throughout a person's life
- **Collectability:** A person's unique physical characteristics need to be collected in a reasonably easy fashion for quick identification
- **Performance:** The degree of accuracy of identification must be quite high before the system can be operational
- **Acceptability:** Applications will not be successful if the public offers strong and continuous resistance to biometrics
- **Resistance to Circumvention:** In order to provide added security, a system needs to be harder to circumvent than existing identity management systems

One must bear in mind that the degree to which each criterion must be fulfilled by a biometric depends clearly on the application for which it is used. A border control check must be done in a few seconds; a criminal investigation can take months. A convenience application, say highway tolls, may accept a significant error rate; a banking system will require a much lower one. It is therefore necessary to look at the purposes for which biometrics can be used.

4.21.2 Biometric Application Types

In functional terms the current uses of biometrics can be categorised under the following headings: verification, identification and screening. Another potential use of biometrics, though not yet in a mature state of development, is biometric encryption.

4.21.3 Verification (1-to-1 matching)

Verification is a test to ensure whether person X is really who he or she claims to be. Two types of verification can be envisaged: with centralised storage or distributed storage.

4.21.4 Verification with Centralised Storage

If a centralised database exists where all biometric data and the associated identities are stored, the biometric sample of the claimed identity is retrieved from the database. This is then compared to the live sample provided by person X, resulting in a match or a non-match. Two types of error are possible for verification: a false match and a false. The matching can be done locally on the device temporarily storing the acquired sample or remotely by the hardware that stores the sample acquired during enrolment. False rejects will cause unnecessary inconvenience to innocent individuals whereas false matches are more insidious as they allow a fraudulent individual to pass, but the mistake goes unnoticed by the system.

4.21.5 Verification with Distributed Storage

If the biometric data is stored in a memory device that is carried by the individual, for example a smart card or a chip integrated into an identity document, person X will provide a live biometric sample and this will be compared to the biometric data stored on the memory device. This can be done either by the verification system which retrieves person X's biometric data from the memory device and compares them to the live sample, or by the memory device itself, if it is sufficiently sophisticated to perform the verification. The identity details are either stored on the memory device or written on the accompanying documents e.g. in the case of a passport, identity information might be printed next to the chip. If the verification process succeeds, then person X is confirmed to be the valid bearer of the identification documents. As before, false acceptance and false rejection errors are possible. In addition, there is the possibility that the documentation or the memory device are fraudulent or have been tampered with.

4.21.6 Identification (1-to-many Matching)

Identification is used to discover the identity of an individual when the identity is unknown. Contrary to verification, for the process of identification a central database is necessary that holds records for all people known to the system; without a database of records, the process of identification is not possible. When person X comes to be identified, he provides a live biometric sample, e.g. a fingerprint is taken or the iris is scanned. The data is processed and the resulting biometric template is compared against all the entries in the database to find a match. The system then returns as a response either the match it has found, or that there is no match against the enrolled population. Identification may result in one of two types of error described previously: i.e. a false match or a false reject. Since the system checks against a database of enrolled templates or full images, the maintenance of the integrity of the database is essential in protecting individuals from identity theft.

4.22 LEGAL CHALLENGES (IMPORTANT)

Out of the many different social issues to be discussed when reflecting upon the implementation of biometrics, the following main themes will be touched upon:

1. Clarity of purpose in relation to technology implementation.
2. Interpretability and equivalence of performance and process.
3. Biometrics as an enabler for other aspirations.
4. Human factors, social inclusion and exclusion.
5. Impact upon the trust modal between citizen and state.

Biometric systems have a number of advantages, however, as with any other new technology, there is the potential for abase. Thus, there is legitimate public concern that biometric technology can be misused to invade or violate personal privacy or other civil liberties. Some of fears surrounding biometric information include that it will be gathered without permission, knowledge or clearly defined reason. It is used for a multitude of purposes other than the one for which it was initially gathered. There are also concerns about tracking, which is real time surveillance of an individual and profiling where a person's past activities are reconstructed both of these would display a person's anonymity and there are also concerns about identify fraud.

SUMMARY

Physical security describes both measures that prevent or deter attackers from accessing a facility, resource, or information stored on physical media, and guidance on how to design structures to resist various hostile acts.It can be as simple as a locked door or as elaborate as multiple layers of armed security guards and guardhouse placement.

Physical security is not a modern phenomenon. Physical security exists in order to deter persons from entering a physical facility. Historical examples of physical security include city walls, moats, etc.

Physical security is the protection of personnel, hardware, programs, networks, and data from physical circumstances and events that could cause serious losses or damage to an enterprise, agency, or institution. This includes protection from fire, natural disasters, burglary, theft, vandalism, and terrorism.

A **natural disaster** is the effect of a natural hazard (e.g., flood, tornado, hurricane, volcanic eruption, earthquake, or landslide) that affects the environment, and leads to financial, environmental and/or human losses. The resulting loss depends on the capacity of the population to support or resist the disaster, and their resilience. This understanding is concentrated in the formulation: "disasters occur when hazards meet vulnerability. A natural hazard will hence never result in a natural disaster in areas without vulnerability, e.g. strong earthquakes in uninhabited areas. The term natural has consequently been disputed because the events simply are not hazards or disasters without human involvement. Natural disasters which occur the movement of plate tectonics are earthquakes, volcanoes, geyser eruptions and tsunami.

Physical security is the one area with which you are most likely to be familiar. It deals with such things as personnel, the environment, the facility and its power supply(ies), fire protection, physical access, and even the protection of software, hardware, and data files. Your command must provide physical security for your AIS facility. The degree of physical security at your installation or command depends on its physical characteristics, its vulnerability within the AIS environment, and the type of data processed. Minimum physical security requirements include four basic areas that your command must address: physical security protection, physical access controls, data file protection, and natural disaster protection.

Access control, in one form or another, is considered by most information systems security professionals to be the cornerstone of their security programs. The various features of physical, technical, and administrative access control mechanisms work together to construct the security architecture so important in the protection of an organization's critical and sensitive information assets.

Biometrics are used for Identification and Verification

Identification is determining who a person is. It involves trying to find a match for a person's biometric data in a database containing records of people and that characteristic. This method requires time and a large amount of processing power, especially if the database is very large.

Verification is determining if a person is who they say they are. It involves comparing a user's biometric data to the previously recorded data for that person to ensure that this is the same person. This method requires less processing power and time, and is used for access control (to buildings or data).

EXERCISES

1. What is physical security.
2. What is disaster. Explain it with its different types.
3. What are basic tenets of physical security and physical entry control.
4. What do you mean by access control.
5. What is biometric and does it work.
6. Explain all the factors of biometric system.
7. What are the benefits and criteria for selection of biometric system.
8. What is interoperability issues.
9. What are the selection criteria for biometric system.
10. Explain the social, economic and legal issues of biometric system.

UNIT – 3

CHAPTER 5

Cryptography

5.1 INTRODUCTION

Cryptography is the science of using mathematics to encrypt and decrypt data. Cryptography enables you to store sensitive information or transmit it across insecure networks (like the Internet) so that it cannot be read by anyone except the intended recipient.

Cryptography is a study of how to scramble data so that:

1. Anyone who steals it will be unable to scramble it.
2. Your intended recipients will be able to unscramble it with ease.

5.1.1 Important Terms in Cryptography

The transformation of actual message into coded form (scrambling) is known as encryption or Enciphering and reverse of this (unscrambling) is known as Decryption or Deciphering. The message to be encrypted is known as Plaintext or Message text. The output of encryption Process is known as Cipher text or Cryptogram. The person who sends a message text is known as Sender and person who intends to receive the message text is known as Receiver. Sending a message in plaintext rather in cipher text to receiver is termed as sending in the Clear text. The person who intends to hack/steal the cipher text between sender and receiver is known as Intruder or Attacker. The set of data transformation used to do encryption or workhouse of cryptography is known as Cryptographic Algorithm or simply a Cipher, normally the transformation is parameterized by one or more s. The art of breaking ciphers is known as Cryptanalysis and the art of developing and breaking cipher is collectively known as Cryptology.

5.1.2 Types of Cryptography

There are two types of encryption techniques.

- Symmetric or Conventional encryption
- Asymmetric or Public key encryption

In the world where information and communication is the indispensable composition of human activities, where men and technology must communicate or share information in order to make decisions; it therefore behooves that this composite essence of humans should be protected and managed to ensure its sustainability, integrity, accuracy.

5.1.3 The Goal of Cryptography (UPTU 2010-11)

Cryptography is the science of protecting information, while cryptanalysis is the science of breaking protection, provided by cryptography. Cryptography and cryptanalysis together make cryptology.

The goal of cryptography is to protect information using a mathematical approach. Cryptography is often expected to provide for the following types of protection:

Nondisclosure: Cryptography allows for encryption of information and therefore protection of that information against disclosure to unauthorized individuals. For example, if Alice needs to send a secret message to Bob and no one else should be able to read this message, Alice can encrypt the message before sending it and Bob will decrypt the message to read it.

Signatures and data integrity: Cryptography can be used to add a signed integrity control structure to messages so that the recipient of a message can determine if the message is genuine or has been modified. If Alice needs to send a message to Bob and wants to make sure that no one else will be able modify the contents of the message, then she needs to sign the message to protect its integrity.

Signatures and non-repudiation: Cryptographic signatures can be used to determine whether a message has really been sent by a particular individual or is fake. If Alice enters into an agreement with Bob and digitally signs a contract, this certifies that Alice has agreed with all the requirements and benefits of that contract. The digital signature is proof of her identity and consent, similar to the signature on a piece of paper.

Identification and authentication: Cryptography can be used to determine the identity and to authenticate users and services. In fact, most authentication methods are based on some cryptographic transformations. If Bob needs to make sure that Alice is who she says she is, he can use cryptographic algorithms to validate her identity.

Timestamping: Cryptography can be used to add a timestamp to messages sent by a user or service. The timestamp is typically added by an independent party (a notary) to certify that a message has been sent at a certain time and date. If Alice sends a message to Bob at a specific date and time, a time notary service can add a signed timestamp to Alice's message to validate the time when the message was sent.

Cryptography achieves the above goals by two main cryptographic mechanisms: encryption and signing.

Protection provided by cryptography is not unbreakable. Cryptography is not impossible to overcome by a determined and skilful attacker that has unlimited time and resources at his disposal. Virtually every protection method is susceptible to compromise. The goal of cryptography is to make potential attacks computationally, and as a result financially and timewise infeasible. For example, information about patents is worth protecting for a limited period of time. Once the patent protection period has ended, information can be considered public. If breaking the protection of a document containing information about a patent will take 30 years, then it is not computationally feasible to try and break it. Furthermore,if protected information can be worth $100,000, and computing resources to break it will cost $500,000, then it is not financially acceptable to look at breaking the protection. In a similar fashion, if breaking the encryption of an encrypted user password will take two months, and a password policy forces users to change passwords every 14 days, then decrypting the password will not be worth the effort. Similarly, if a user account has access to information that may cost $10,000, and the resources needed to break the authentication mechanism are worth $50,000, then it is not cost effective to even attempt to break the protection

Threat Cryptography

If an attacker does not have a username and a password or other credentials, and is not able to authenticate to a system, he may try to bypass the authentication process. This can be accomplished in a number of ways, depending on the application, and the type of access that attackers have to the computer where the application is running.

If an application is running locally on a computer, and an attacker has physical access to this computer, then the attacker can potentially obtain administrative privileges, which may well be already available or may be obtained by privilege escalation. Once the attacker has administrative access, he can typically access all files and processes on the local computer, which allows him to debug running applications or swap files on the file system. The attacker can therefore debug an application that requires authentication, and potentially modify the application to replace the command or statement that compares the user password with commands that do nothing or return successful authentication. The user can then access the application. The modification can be performed for either code that is already in memory or for executable files on the file system, and take effect the next time the executable is launched. To protect against such attacks, the operating system can implement tools that detect and potentially alert the administrator or the user if they determine that the content of the file has been changed. This includes software that scans files on the file system and saves their hashes in a hash database, as well as signed executables.

The above authentication bypassing technique is more difficult to implement for network servers unless the server is vulnerable to some attack over the network, where techniques such as smashing the application stack can be used to launch arbitrary code, or obtain administrative or local access. However, there are other approaches for bypassing authentication to network servers. One common approach is authentication to Web resources. Very often, these resources are published with anonymous authentication. Later on, system administrators may decide that they want to protect resources. A simple login form may exist on the home page, and it may require the user to enter a username and password, which may be statically configured in the code behind HTML/HTTP, or reside in a user database. Once the user has authenticated to that Web page, he can access resources. This approach is easy to implement but apparently there are problems associated with it. One of them is that if a user knows (or manages to guess) the URL behind the authentication page, he may be able to access resources without authentication. To resolve this problem, one of the best possible methods is to have the Web server impersonate requests from users using their actual user accounts, and access resources on behalf of the user; at the same time, Web pages and other files should be protected with permissions for actual users or groups of users. In this case, even if an application login page is bypassed, when a user tries to access the actual resource (a file), the operating system will request user authentication for the user, and will not allow access to the file. If the user refuses or fails to authenticate, the operating system will return a failure result.

5.2 WHAT IS ENCRYPTION

Data that can be read and understood without any special measures is called plaintext or clear text. The method of disguising plaintext in such a way as to hide its substance is called encryption. Encrypting plaintext results in unreadable gibberish called cipher text. You use encryption to ensure that information is hidden from anyone for whom it is not intended, even those who can see the encrypted data. The process of reverting cipher text to its original plaintext is called decryption.

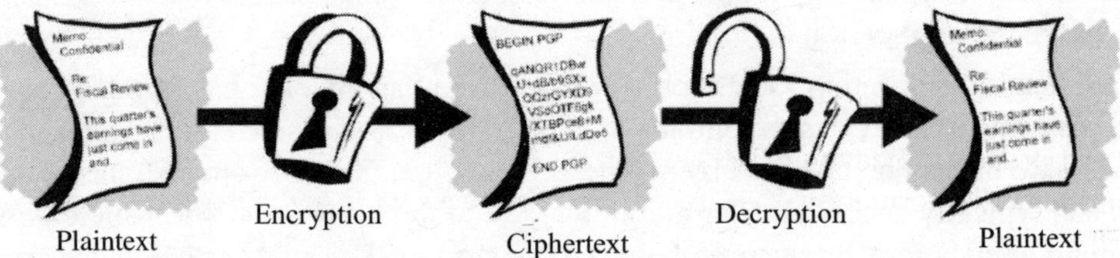

Figure 5.1: Encryption and Decryption

5.3 ENCRYPTION TECHNIQUES

Encryption techniques have become the immediate solution to protect information against third parties. These techniques required that data and information should be encrypted with some sort of mathematical algorithm where only the party that shares the information could possible decrypt to use the information. This phenomenon has long existed and is not fully reliable which pose danger to the information sharing. However, many method of encryption emerge to serve the need of the emergent trend of rapid technological advancement. These emergent techniques were more reliable and are fast in operation and performance wise.

However, as this new trend of fast and reliable cryptography emerged, there is a very big concern on that issue of using to hide proof of violent scheme as many government authorities see it as impending danger. Since Cryptography has become so powerful that messages scrambled with so-called strong cryptography are virtually undecipherable. Like many powerful technologies, this is a double-edged sword. For good, we know that Encryption can keep email and financial transactions over the Internet secure and private, but law enforcement officials worry those criminals and terrorists could use the same tools to conceal incriminating evidence and violent plots.

This concern has convoked many viewpoint and argument, which has alerted the formation of policies by some law enforcement agencies to regulate the encryption techniques.

In this view, we will be discussing popular encryption system, types of cryptography, issues of regulating Encryption technology, social and legal implication, computer ciphers and encryption and other cryptosystems, which will aid the understanding of Encryption Techniques and its advantages and challenges in the electronic age.

5.3.1 Definiton and Origin of Encryption Technique

Encryption, process of converting messages or data into a form that cannot be read without decrypting or deciphering it. The root of the word encryption crypt comes from the Greek word kryptos, meaning "hidden" or "secret."

The study and practice of encryption and decryption is called the science of cryptography.

Scientists who study different ways to protect and ensure the confidentiality, integrity, and authenticity of information are called cryptologists. Cryptologists also engage in cryptanalysis to find ways to break encryption methods.

For centuries before the age of electronic communication and computers, individuals, militaries, and other groups coded written information. As electronic forms of communication and information storage and processing have developed, the opportunities to intercept, modify, use, disclose, and read confidential information has grown, and the need for powerful encryption techniques has increased.

Government agencies, banks, and many corporations now routinely send a great deal of confidential information from one computer to another. Such data are usually transmitted via telephone lines or other non-private channels, such as the Internet. Continuing development of secure computer systems and networks will ensure that confidential information can be securely transferred across computer networks.

5.3.2 Basic Vocabulary of Classical Encryption

Plaintext: This is what you want to encrypt.

Ciphertext: The encrypted output.

Enciphering or encryption: The process by which plaintext is converted into ciphertext.

Encryption algorithm: The sequence of data processing steps that go into transforming plaintext into ciphertext. Various parameters used by an encryption algorithm are derived from a secret key. In classical cryptography for commercial and other civilian applications, the encryption algorithm is made public.

Secret key: A secret key is used to set some or all of the various parameters used by the encryption algorithm. The important thing to note is that the same secret key is used for encryption and decryption in classical cryptography. It is for this reason that classical cryptography is also referred to as symmetric key cryptography.

Deciphering or decryption: Recovering plaintext from ciphertext decryption algorithm: The sequence of data processing steps that go into transforming ciphertext back into plaintext. Various parameters used by a decryption algorithm are derived from the same secret key that was used in the encryption algorithm.

In classical cryptography for commercial and other civilian applications, the decryption algorithm is made public.

Cryptography: The many schemes available today for encryption cipher processes a block of input data at a time and produces a ciphertext block of the same size.

Stream cipher: A stream cipher encrypts data on the fly, usually one byte at a time.

Cryptanalysis: Means "breaking the code". Cryptanalysis relies on a knowledge of the encryption algorithm (that for civilian applications should be in the public domain) and some knowledge of the possible structure of the plaintext (such as the structure of a typical inter-bank financial transaction) for a partial or full reconstruction of the plaintext from ciphertext. Additionally, the goal is to also infer the key for decryption of future messages.

5.3.3 How Encryption Works

Encryption uses a systematic or step-by-step procedure called an algorithm to convert data or the text of an original message, known as plaintext, into ciphertext, its encrypted form.

Cryptographic algorithms normally require a string of characters called a key to encrypt or decrypt data. Those who possess the key and the algorithm can encrypt the plaintext into ciphertext and then decrypt the ciphertext back into plaintext.

Cryptologists engage in an unending competition to create stronger cryptographic techniques and to break them. Many recent cryptography techniques are nearly unbreakable even with the most powerful computers. These systems produce ciphertext that appears to be random characters. These systems resist most existing methods for deciphering back into plaintext.

The many different types of new cryptosystems use highly complex mathematical language and resist breaking even though cryptologists may know the techniques used in creating them.

5.3.4 Pretty Good Privacy(PGP)

Pretty Good Privacy (PGP) helps users of e-mail keep their communications private. In this two-key system, also known as the public key system, the computer sending an encrypted message uses a chosen private key that is never shared and so is known only to the sender.

All computers authorized to receive and decrypt the message are given the matching public key. This method also establishes who sent the message. If a sending computer first encrypts the message with the intended receiver's public key and again with the sender's secret, private key, then the receiving computer may decrypt the message, first using its secret key and then the sender's public key. Using this public-key cryptographic method, the sender and receiver are able to authenticate one another as well as protect the secrecy of the message. The use of the keys is done.

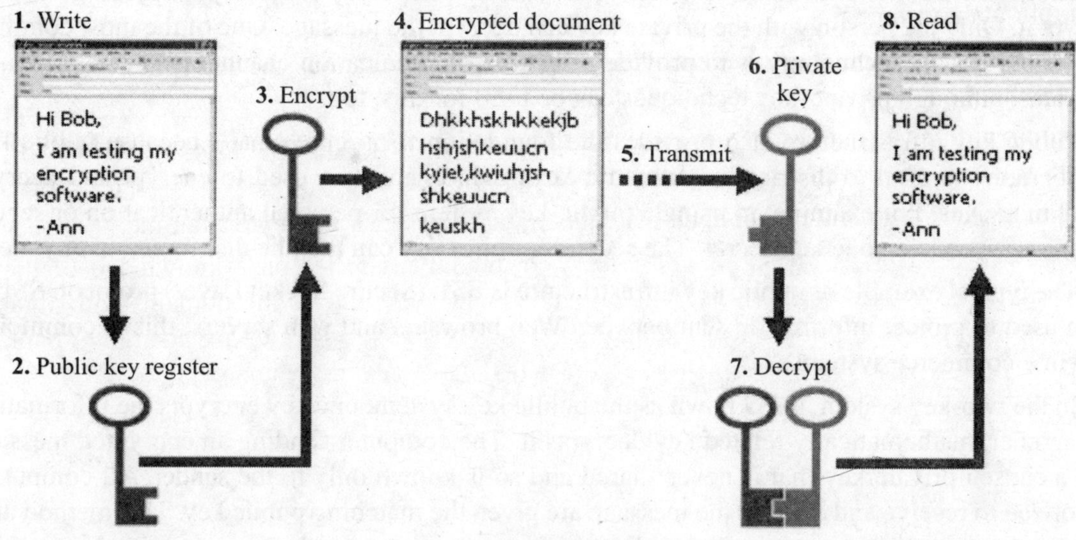

Figure 5.2

5.3.5 Popular Encryption Systems

Three of the most popular cryptography systems used are the Data Encryption Standard (DES), Pretty Good Privacy (PGP), and the Rivest, Shamir, Adleman (RSA) system. Most of this has been shortly describe above, however, We will elaborate it below.

DES uses a single key for both encrypting and decrypting. In private-key cryptography,. A secret key may be held by one person or exchanged between the sender and the receiver of a message. For example, if you encrypt data for storage on a hard drive, you remember the key and usually do not give it to another person. But if you want to send secure messages to a business partner using symmetric cryptography, you need to make sure your partner knows the key that will decrypt the messages The secret (or private) key in a public-key cryptographic system is never transmitted or shared. For example, when using this method for client-side authentication, the server sends some data to your client program. The client uses your private key to encrypt that data. Using your public key, the server will attempt to decrypt the returned data, and, if successful, know that it has established communication with you.

If private -key cryptography is used to send secret messages between two parties, both the sender and receiver must have a copy of the secret key. However, the key may be compromised during transit. If you know the party you are exchanging messages with, you can give them the key in advance. However, if you need to send an encrypted message to someone, you have never met; you will need to figure out a way to exchange keys in a secure way. One method is to send it via another secure channel.

The Rivest, Shamir, Adleman (RSA) algorithm is a popular encryption method that uses two keys. Unlike symmetric cryptography, the keys are mathematically related, yet it is computationally infeasible to deduce one from the other. Anyone with the public key can encrypt a message but not decrypt it. Only the person with the private key can decrypt the message. One of the most common uses of public-key technology is to provide a secure communication channel between computer programs, although private-key techniques can be used for this, too.

Public key infrastructure also provides the foundation for secure emails because public key cryptography is used to distribute symmetric keys, which are then used to encrypt and decrypt actual messages. For example, in using a public-key system for personal authentication or secure messaging, you keep one key secret. The second (public) key can then be distributed to anyone.

The typical example of public key infrastructure is SSL (Secure Socket Layer) protocol. SSL is often used to protect information sent between Web browsers and web servers; this is commonly used in e-commerce systems.

In the two-key system, also known as the public key system, one key encrypts the information and another, mathematically related key decrypts it. The computer sending an encrypted message uses a chosen private key that is never shared and so is known only to the sender. All computers authorized to receive and decrypt the message are given the matching public key. This method also establishes who sent the message. If a sending computer first encrypts the message with the intended receiver's public key and again with the sender's secret, private key, then the receiving computer may decrypt the message, first using its secret key and then the sender's public key. Using this public-key cryptographic method, the sender and receiver are able to authenticate one another as well as protect the secrecy of the message. Single key methods, in contrast, require great secrecy in conveying a key from sender to recipient.

5.3.6 Building Blocks of Classical Encryption Techniques

Two building blocks of all classical encryption techniques are substitution and transposition.

- Substitution means replacing an element of the plaintext with an element of ciphertext.
- Transposition means rearranging the order of appearance of the elements of the plaintext.
- Transposition is also referred to as permutation.

5.3.7 Caesar Cipher

- This is the earliest known example of a substitution cipher.
- Each character of a message is replaced by a character three position down in the alphabet.

  plaintext: are you ready

  ciphertext: DUH BRX UHDGB
- If we represent each letter of the alphabet by an integer that corresponds to its position in the alphabet, the formula for replacing each character 'p' of the plaintext with a character 'C' of the ciphertext can be expressed as

$$C = E(3, p) = (p + 3) \bmod 26$$

- A more general version of this cipher that allows for any degree of shift would be expressed by

$$C = E(k, p) = (p + k) \bmod 26$$

- The formula for decryption would be

$$p = D(k, C) = (C - k) \bmod 26$$

- In these formulas, 'k' would be the secret key. The symbols 'E' and 'D' represent encryption and decryption.

5.3.8 Problems of Encryption Techniques

Although, encryption mechanisms make information unreadable. Therefore, no third parties, including server administrators and others, have access to plain text version of transmitted information through public networks such as internet, but the following are the problems encountered or associated with encryption techniques.

5.4 SYMMETRIC ENCRYPTION

Symmetric or **Conventional** encryption is one of the very old encryption schemes used in very early days and also known as encryption. In this scheme both the sender and the receiver shares the same encryption and decryption secret key Obviously, this scheme uses old substitutions and permutations functions of mathematics to replace one character of plaintext with other to do encryption and decryption and that is why it given the name as symmetric encryption scheme. This scheme is shown in figure below

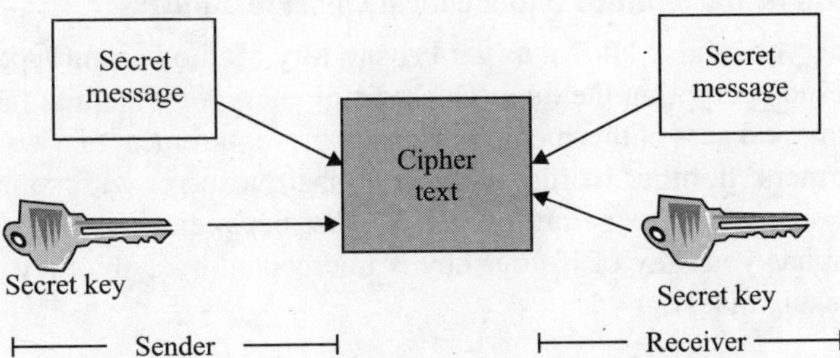

Figure 5.3: How symmetric encryption works

NET Framework provides us with the following secret key encryption algorithms:

- DES CryptoServiceProvider
- RC2 CryptoServiceProvider
- Rijndael Managed / AES (Advance encryption Standard)
- TripleDESCryptoServiceProvider

5.4.1 Block Cipher

Block Ciphers operates in a purely combinational fashion with a fixed transformation applied to a large block of plaintext on block by block basis the most common block size is eight bytes. Because each block is heavily processed, block ciphers provide a higher level of security. However, block cipher algorithms tend to execute more slowly.

Block ciphers use the same encryption algorithm for each block. Because of this, a block of plain text will always return the same cipher text when encrypted with the same key and algorithm. Because this behavior can be used to crack a cipher, cipher modes are introduced that modify the encryption process based on feedback from earlier block encryption. The resulting encryption provides a higher level of security than a simple block encryption

5.4.2 Block Cipher Modes

- **Cipher Block chaining** mode (CBC) introduces feedback. Before each plain text block is encrypted, it is combined with the cipher text of the previous block by a bitwise exclusive OR operation. This ensures that even if the plain text contains many identical blocks, they will each encrypt to a different cipher text block. The initialization vector is combined with the first plain text block by a bitwise exclusive OR operation before the block is encrypted.
- The **Cipher Feedback** (CFB) mode processes small increments of plain text into cipher text, instead of processing an entire block at a time. This mode uses a shift register that is one block in length and is divided into sections. For example, if the block size is eight bytes, with one byte processed at a time, the shift register is divided into eight sections.

The Electronic Codebook (ECB) mode encrypts each block individually. This means that any blocks of plain text that are identical and are in the same message, or in a different message encrypted with the same key will be transformed into identical cipher text blocks.

In symmetric encryption also known as the Private Key Method or encryption, a single key is used for encrypting and decrypting the data. This type of encryption is quite fast, but has a severe problem. The inherent weakness of this method is mostly the requirement of a key exchange between communications partners. In other words, in order to share a secret with someone, they have to know your key. This implies a very high level of trust between people sharing secrets, if an unscrupulous person has your key or if your key is intercepted by a spy they can decrypt all the messages you send using that key.

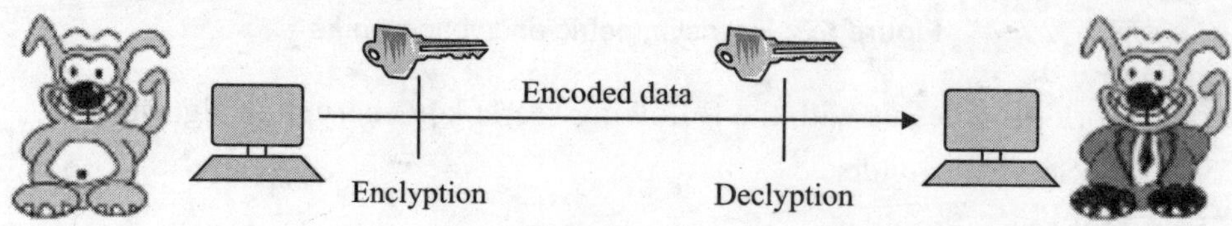

Figure 5.4

However, Asymmetric encryption solves the trust problem inherent in symmetric encryption by using two different keys: a public key for encrypting messages, and a private key for decrypting messages. This makes it possible to communicate in secrecy with people you don't fully trust. If an unscrupulous person has your public key, who cares? The public key is only good for encryption; it's useless for decryption. They can't decrypt any of your messages! However, asymmetric encryption is very slow. It's not recommended for use on more than roughly 1 kilobyte of data.

5.4.3 Key Management

One of the big challenges in using cryptography on a widespread basis especially public-key encryption--is the management of private and public keys. Key management deals with the secure generation, distribution, and storage of keys. Secure methods of key management are extremely important. Once a key is randomly generated, it must remain secret to avoid unfortunate mishaps. Most attacks on public-key systems will probably be aimed at the key management level, rather than at the cryptographic algorithm itself.

Users must be able to securely obtain a key pair suited to their efficiency and security needs. There must be a way to look up other people's public keys and to publicize one's own public key. Users must be able to legitimately obtain others' public keys; otherwise, an intruder can either change public keys listed in a directory, or impersonate another user.

If someone's private key is lost or compromised, others must be made aware of this, so they will no longer encrypt messages under the invalid public key nor accept messages signed with the invalid private key. Users must be able to store their private keys securely, so no intruder can obtain them, yet the keys must be readily accessible for legitimate user. Keys need to be valid only until a specified expiration date but the expiration date must be chosen properly and publicized in an authenticated channel.

5.4.4 Digital Certificates

A digital certificate is an attachment to an electronic message used for security purposes. It is commonly used to verify that a user is who he/she claims to be and to provide the receiver with the means to encode a reply.

When you obtain a certificate by applying to a certificate authority (CA). Once the CA verifies you are who you say you are, it creates a certificate--a digital document--for you.

The certificate contains:

- A name that is unique to you
- The length of time the certificate is valid
- Your public key
- Your key's purpose: to sign messages or to encrypt data

Certificates do the following for your system:

- Backed up and recoverable

- Protected against theft
- Matched with encrypted data
- Accessible from many systems
- Accessible only to the authorized user

In order for you to manage your certificate to be used with applications, you will need to do the followings:

- Production and maintenance of a very large standards-based directory
- Support for a highly distributed computing environment
- Methodologies supporting transparent access by applications
- Private and public key storage and access issues
- Incompatibility of browser vendors' certificate formats
- Issues that Certificate Authority deals with are as follows:
- Maintenance of a certificate repository
- Methodology for verifying individuals and departments
- Management of certificate revocation lists (CRLs)
- Renewal of key pairs and certificates
- Support for trust relationships with other certificate authorities
- Secure messaging is the principal driver for using personal certificates.

Other alternatives can be used to address security problems in online systems, including Web-based transaction systems. However, the technical, policy, and management issues mentioned previously must be resolved before any wide scale deployment of a public-key infrastructure is reasonable.

5.4.5 Data Encryption Standard

A commonly accepted definition of a good symmetric key algorithm, such as the DES, is that there exists no attack better than key exhaustion to read an encrypted message. Critics argued that the 56-bit DES key was too short for long-term security, and that expected increases in computer power would soon make a 56-bit key vulnerable to attack by exhaustion.

DES uses a sequence of operations, including several substitution and permutation primitives, to encrypt a data block. The DES algorithm is a block cipher that uses the same binary key both to encrypt and decrypt data blocks, and thus is called a symmetric key cipher. DES operates on 64-bit "plaintext" data blocks, processing them under the control of a 56-bit key to produce 64 bits of encrypted ciphertext. Similarly, the DES decryption process operates on a 64-bit ciphertext block using the same 56-bit key to produce the original 64-bit plaintext block.

5.4.6 DES Explanation

Data Encryption Standard (DES) is a widely-used method of data encryption using a private (secret) key that was judged so difficult to break by the U.S. government that it was restricted for exportation to other countries. There are 72,000,000,000,000,000 (72 quadrillion) or more possible encryption keys that can be used. For each given message, the key is chosen at random from among this enormous number of keys. Like other private key cryptographic methods, both the sender and the receiver must know and use the same private key.

It was developed in the 1970s by the National Bureau of Standards with the help of the National Security Agency. Its purpose is to provide a standard method for protecting sensitive commercial and unclassified data. IBM created the first draft of the algorithm, calling it LUCIFER. DES officially became a federal standard in November of 1976.

To understand this implementation, you'll first need to understand bit operations and read some more general explanations of DES.

In general, DES takes as input a 64 bit key, of which only 56 bits are used. From these 56 bits, 16 48 bit subkeys are created. The message is split into 64 bit chunks, and a complex series of steps enciphers the message using each subkey. As Javascript only supports 32 bit integers, all 48 or 64 bit integers are represented by two 32 bit integers in an array.

Creating the Keys - PC1

DES must first create the 16 subkeys. First, the 8 character string representing the key is turned into two integers which are passed to the des_createKeys function. The bits of these two integers are then reorganised according to PC1 (permuted choice 1). The bits end up in the following places:

57	49	41	33	25	17	9	1
58	50	42	34	26	18	10	2
59	51	43	35	27	19	11	3
60	52	44	36	0	0	0	0
63	55	47	39	31	23	15	7
62	54	46	38	30	22	14	6
61	53	45	37	29	21	13	5
28	20	12	4	0	0	0	0

This means that the first 57th bit of the original key becomes the first bit, etc. The permuting is done using a permutation sequence, which is a clever way of rotating and switching bits between 2 integers. For instance, temp = ((left >>> 4) ^ right) & 0x0f0f0f0f; right ^= temp; left ^= (temp << 4); rotates 4x4 blocks of bits:

33	34	35	36	1	2	3	4
41	42	43	44	9	10	11	12
49	50	51	52	17	18	19	20
57	58	59	60	25	26	27	28
37	38	39	40	5	6	7	8
45	46	47	48	13	14	15	16
53	54	55	56	21	22	23	24
61	62	63	64	29	30	31	32

5.4.7 Triple Encryption

In cryptography, **Triple DES** is the common name for the Triple Data Encryption Algorithm (TDEA) block cipher, which applies the Data Encryption Standard (DES) cipher algorithm three times to each data block. Because of the availability of increasing computational power, the key size of the original DES cipher was becoming subject to brute force attacks; Triple DES was designed to provide a relatively simple method of increasing the key size of DES to protect against such attacks, without designing a completely new block cipher algorithm.

5.4.8 Secret Key Encryption

Secret-key encryption uses one key, the secret key, to both encrypt and decrypt messages. This is also called symmetric encryption. The term "private key" is often used inappropriately to refer to the secret key. A private key is one of the keys in the public/private key pair for asymmetric cryptography. In this scheme, a user has two keys, one that is made public and one that is held privately.

In secret-key cryptography schemes, a single key is used to encrypt data. A secret key may be held by one person or exchanged between the sender and the receiver of a message. For example, if you encrypt data for storage on a hard drive, you remember the key and usually don't give it to someone else. But if you want to send secure messages to a business partner using symmetric cryptography, you need to make sure your partner knows the key that will decrypt the messages.

If secret-key cryptography is used to send secret messages between two parties, both the sender and receiver must have a copy of the secret key. However, the key may be compromised during transit. If you know the party you are exchanging messages with, you can give them the key in advance. However, if you need to send an encrypted message to someone you have never met, you'll need to figure out a way to exchange keys in a secure way. One method is to send it via another secure channel or even via overnight express, but this may be risky in some cases.

As mentioned, secret-key cryptography is often used to encrypt data on hard drives. The person encrypting the data holds the key privately and there is no problem with key distribution. Secret-key cryptography is also used for communication devices like bridges that encrypt all data that cross the link. A network administrator programs two devices with the same key, and then personally transports them to their physical locations.

5.5 ASYMMETRIC KEY ENCRYPTION

Asymmetric key encryption uses different keys for encryption and decryption. These two keys are mathematically related and they form a key pair. One of these two keys should be kept private, called private-key, and the other can be made public (it can even be sent in mail), called public-key. Hence this is also called Public Key Encryption.

A private key is typically used for encrypting the message-digest; in such an application private-key algorithm is called message-digest encryption algorithm. A public key is typically used for encrypting the secret-key; in such a application private-key algorithm is called key encryption algorithm.

Popular private-key algorithms are RSA (invented by Rivest, Shamir and Adlemen) and DSA (Digital Signature Algorithm). While for an ordinary use of RSA, a key size of 768 can be used, but for corporate use a key size of 1024 and for extremely valuable information a key size of 2048 should be used.

Asymmetric key encryption is much slower than symmetric key encryption and hence they are only used for key exchanges and digital signatures.

5.5.1 Asymmetric Encryption

Asymmetric encryption also known as the Public Key Method, it uses two different keys: the private key and public key. The public key is distributed freely and the private key is known only to the owner of a key. The two keys have a (mathematical) relationship. However, for obvious reasons, calculation of a private key on the basis of the public key must be impossible or at least not feasible.

Both keys have different functions depending on the application at hand. In the case of data encryption, data is encoded using the public key. The private key is required in order to decrypt the message. The private key can also be used to generate digital signatures, which can later be verified using the public key.

The disadvantage or problem of this method compared to symmetric encryption is the greater amount of processing time required for the calculation or a process. This is why usually the so-called hybrid technology, which is a mix of both asymmetric and symmetric encryption, is used when dealing with a greater amount of data. In this case, symmetric encryption is used to encode the data but the symmetric key is communicated on a previously determined frequency using asymmetric encryption.

5.5.2 Public Key vs. Secret Key Encryption

Definition: The purpose of a key in encryption systems is to ensure privacy by keeping information hidden from whom it is not intended. There are two types of encryption systems: secret-key and public-key systems.

Encryption is the transformation of data, the plaintext, into a form that is as close to impossible as possible to read, the ciphetext, without the appropriate knowledge (a key). Its purpose is to ensure privacy by keeping information hidden from anyone for whom it is not intended, even those who have access to the encrypted data, the ciphetext.

There are two types of encryption systems: secret-key and public-key systems. In secret-key encryption, also referred to as symmetric cryptography, the same key is used for both encryption and decryption. The most popular secret-key cryptosystem in use today is the Data Encryption Standard (DES, see). In general, the security of a secret-key system depends on the strength of the algorithm and the length of the key. In a brute-force attack, an N bits long key, which implies 2 N possible keys, will take 2 N attempts for the hacker to find the correct key. That is, the longer the key is, the longer it will take for a certain computer to find the correct key among the 2 N possible keys. Besides the key, there is another factor to determine the interval of a successful brute force attack: the speed of each test which relies on the speed of the computer and the computational complexity of the encryption algorithm. Unfortunately in most cases, the longer the key is, the longer it takes to encrypt/decrypt the message, and the more one need to pay for it in terms of cost. To determine the length of a proper key for a certain application, one needs to look at several aspects: the intended security, the current and future computer power, and the speed of the state-of-the-art factoring algorithms. That is, you need a key long enough to be secure but short enough to be computationally feasible and low cost.

On the other hand, in a public-key system, each user has a public key and a private key. The public key maybe made public while the private key remains secret. Encryption is performed with the one key while decryption is done with the other. Today's dominant public key encryption algorithms are factorization based. That is, the algorithms are based on the difficulty of factoring large numbers that are the product of two large prime numbers. One of the most popular public-key encryption algorithms, the RSA public-key cryptosystem, is a typical factorization based algorithm. To break such systems, one need to factor out the large number. Intuitively, the large the number is, the harder it is for a hacker to factor it.

5.6 MODEL OF CRYPTOGRAPHIC SYSTEMS

Cryptography can be used to provide:

- **Confidentiality:** ensure data is read only by authorized parties,
- **Data integrity:** ensure data wasn't altered between sender and recipient,
- **Authentication:** ensure data originated from a particular party.

A cryptographic system (or a cipher system) is a method of hiding data so that only certain people can view it. Cryptography is the practice of creating and using cryptographic systems. Cryptanalysis is the science of analyzing and reverse engineering cryptographic systems. The original data is called plaintext. The protected data is called ciphertext. Encryption is a procedure to convert plaintext into ciphertext. Decryption is a procedure to convert ciphertext into plaintext. A cryptographic system typically consists of algorithms, keys, and key management facilities.

There are two basic types of cryptographic systems: symmetric ("private key") and asymmetric ("public key").

Symmetric key systems require both the sender and the recipient to have the same key. This key is used by the sender to encrypt the data, and again by the recipient to decrypt the data. Key exchange is clearly a problem. How do you securely send a key that will enable you to send other data securely? If a private key is intercepted or stolen, the adversary can act as either party and view all data and communications. You can think of the symmetric crypto system as akin to the Chubb type of door locks. You must be in possession of a key to both open and lock the door.

Asymmetric cryptographic systems are considered much more flexible. Each user has both a public key and a private key. Messages are encrypted with one key and can be decrypted only by the other key. The public key can be published widely while the private key is kept secret. If Alice wishes to send Bob a secret, she finds and verifies Bob's public key, encrypts her message with it, and mails it off to Bob. When Bob gets the message, he uses his private key to decrypt it. Verification of public keys is an important step. Failure to verify that the public key really does belong to Bob leaves open the possibility that Alice is using a key whose associated private key is in the hands of an enemy. Public Key Infrastructures or PKI's deal with this problem by providing certification authorities that sign keys by a supposedly trusted party and make them available for download or verification. Asymmetric ciphers are much slower than their symmetric counterparts and key sizes are generally much larger. You can think of a public key system as akin to a Yale type door lock. Anyone can push the door locked, but you must be in possession of the correct key to open the door.

Cryptography enables you to store sensitive information or transmit it across insecure networks (like the Internet) so that it cannot be read by anyone except the intended recipient.

While cryptography is the science of securing data, cryptanalysis is the science of analyzing and breaking secure communication. Classical cryptanalysis involves an interesting combination of analytical reasoning, application of mathematical tools, pattern finding, patience, determination, and luck. Cryptanalysts are also called attackers.

5.6.1 How Does Cryptography Work

A cryptographic algorithm, or cipher, is a mathematical function used in the encryption and decryption process. A cryptographic algorithm works in combination with a key a word, number, or phrase to encrypt the plaintext.

The same plaintext encrypts to different cipher text with different keys. The security of encrypted data is entirely dependent on two things: the strength of the cryptographic algorithm and the secrecy of the key.

A cryptographic algorithm, plus all possible keys and all the protocols that make it work comprise a cryptosystem. PGP is a cryptosystem.

5.6.2 Symmetric Cryptography

Symmetric cryptography uses a single private key to both encrypt and decrypt data. Any party that has the key can use it to encrypt and decrypt data. They are also referred to as block ciphers.

Symmetric cryptography algorithms are typically fast and are suitable for processing large streams of data.

The disadvantage of symmetric cryptography is that it presumes two parties have agreed on a key and been able to exchange that key in a secure manner prior to communication. This is a significant challenge. Symmetric algorithms are usually mixed with public key algorithms to obtain a blend of security and speed.

5.6.3 Asymmetric, or Public Key, Cryptography

Public-key cryptography is also called asymmetric. It uses a secret key that must be kept from unauthorized users and a public key that can be made public to anyone. Both the public key and the private key are mathematically linked; data encrypted with the public key can be decrypted only by the private key, and data signed with the private key can only be verified with the public key.

The public key can be published to anyone. Both keys are unique to the communication session.

Public-key cryptographic algorithms use a fixed buffer size. Private-key cryptographic algorithms use a variable length buffer. Public-key algorithms cannot be used to chain data together into streams like private-key algorithms can. With private-key algorithms only a small block size can be processed, typically 8 or 16 bytes.

5.7 KEYS

A key is a value that works with a cryptographic algorithm to produce a specific ciphertext. Keys are basically really, really, really big numbers. Key size is measured in bits; the number representing a 1024-bit key is darn huge.

In public key cryptography, the bigger the key, the more secure the ciphertext. However, public key size and conventional cryptography's secret key size are totally unrelated. A conventional 80-bit key has the equivalent strength of a 1024-bit public key. A conventional 128-bit key is equivalent to a 3000-bit public key. Again, the bigger the key, the more secure, but the algorithms used for each type of cryptography are very different and thus comparison is like that of apples to oranges.

While the public and private keys are mathematically related, it's very difficult to derive the private key given only the public key; however, deriving the private key is always possible given enough time and computing power. This makes it very important to pick keys of the right size; large enough to be secure, but small enough to be applied fairly quickly. Additionally, you need to consider who might be trying to read your files, how determined they are, how much time they have, and what their resources might be.

Larger keys will be cryptographically secure for a longer period of time. If what you want to encrypt needs to be hidden formany years, you might want to use a very large key. Of course, who knows how long it will take to determine your key using tomorrow's faster, more efficient computers? There was a time when a 56-bit symmetric key was considered extremely safe. Keys are stored in encrypted form. PGP stores the keys in two files on your hard disk; one for public keys and one for private keys. These files are called keyrings. As you use PGP, you will typically add the public keys of your recipients to your public keyring. Your private keys are stored on your private keyring. If you lose your private keyring, you will be unable to decrypt any information encrypted to keys on that ring.

5.7.1 Key Management and Conventional Encryption

Public key cryptography

The problems of key distribution are solved by public key cryptography, the concept of which was introduced by Whitfield Diffie and Martin Hellman in 1975. (There is now evidence that the British

Secret Service invented it a few years before Diffie and Hellman, but kept it amilitary secret and did nothing with it.)

Public key cryptography is an asymmetric scheme that uses a pair of keys for encryption: a public key, which encrypts data, and a corresponding private, or secret key for decryption. You publish your public key to the world while keeping your private key secret. Anyone with a copy of your public key can then encrypt information that only you can read. Even people you have never met. It is computationally infeasible to deduce the private key from the public key.

Anyone who has a public key can encrypt information but cannot decrypt it. Only the person who has the corresponding private key can decrypt the key.

Figure 5.5: Public key encryption

The primary benefit of public key cryptography is that it allows people who have no preexisting security arrangement to exchange messages securely. The need for sender and receiver to share secret keys via some secure channel is eliminated; all communications involve only public keys, and no private key is ever transmitted or shared. Some examples of public-key cryptosystems are Elgamal (named for its inventor, Taher Elgamal), RSA (named for its inventors, Ron Rivest, Adi Shamir, and Leonard Adleman), Diffie-Hellman (named, you guessed it, for its inventors), and DSA, the Digital Signature Algorithm (invented by David Kravitz).

Because conventional cryptography was once the only available means for relaying secret information, the expense of secure channels and key distribution relegated its use only to those who could afford it, such as governments and large banks (or small children with secret decoder rings).

Public key encryption is the technological revolution that provides strong cryptography to the adult masses. Remember the courier with the locked briefcase handcuffed to his wrist? Public-key encryption puts him out of business (probably to his relief).

5.8 DIGITAL SIGNATURES

A digital signature is a code or verification used to uniquely identify you. By entering in certain information to validate yourself, the code or token is created, allowing it to be used instead of an actual signature.

A major benefit of public key cryptography is that it provides a method for employing digital signatures. Digital signatures enable the recipient of information to verify the authenticity of the information's origin, and also verify that the information is intact. Thus, public key digital signatures provide authentication and data integrity. A digital signature also provides non-repudiation, which means that it prevents the sender from claiming that he or she did not actually send the information. These features are every bit as fundamental to cryptography as privacy, if not more.

A digital signature serves the same purpose as a handwritten signature. However, a handwritten signature is easy to counterfeit. A digital signature is superior to a handwritten signature in that it is nearly impossible to counterfeit, plus it attests to the contents of the information as well as to the identity of the signer.

Some people tend to use signatures more than they use encryption. For example, you may not care if anyone knows that you just deposited $1000 in your account, but you do want to be darn sure it was the bank teller you were dealing with.

The basic manner in which digital signatures are created is illustrated in Figure 5.6. Instead of encrypting information using someone else's public key, you encrypt it with your private key. If the information can be decrypted with your public key, then it must have originated with you.

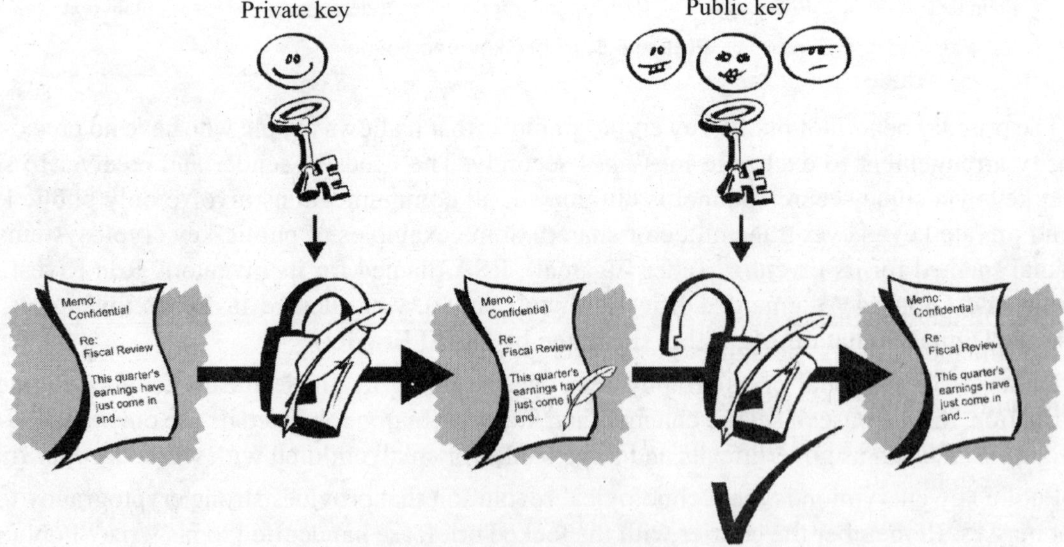

Figure 5.6: Simple digital signatures

5.8.1 What are Digital ID's

Digital ID signature or certificate is an installed file resident on a computer validates who you are. Digital signatures are used by programs on the internet and local to the machines to confirm your identity to any third party concerned. Digital signatures have been confused with electronic signatures. Electronic signatures are scanned copies of a physical written signature.

5.8.2 When do We Need to Verify Identity

New ways of verification are being developed daily. Biometrics and other methods keep getting formulated and incorporated into the information technology industry. One interesting biometric authentication mechanism developed by a leading Japanese biometric company has found a way to get your DNA into a pen. You sign a document and it is digitally scanned. This document then can be scanned in the future to verify its authenticity. Identity should be verified when ever there is doubt of the 3rd party being whom they say they are or when there is personal information at risk. Personal information like credit card details and banking information should be kept safe using digital certification as one of the security layers. Some banking institutions require that a user verifies his/her identity by validating identification credentials using a digital certificate. Important e-mail can also use Digital signatures that verify that the e-mail is from the originating sender and that it has not been tampered with. On many occasions users are unsure if they are dealing with reputable suppliers of institutions. Digital certification gives the user a sense of legitimacy and formalizes the process. It ensure that the company that the user is dealing with has a registration with a trusted authority and that the transaction is guaranteed to be done with the intended parties.

5.8.3 Reasons for Using Digital Security

- It insures by means of verification and validation that the user is whom he/she claims to be. This is done by combine the users credential to the digital certificate and in turn this method uses one point of authentication.
- Digital certificates insure data Integrity giving the user piece of mind that the message or transaction has not been accidentally or maliciously altered. This is done cryptographically.
- Digital certificates ensure confidentiality and ensure that messages can only be read by authorized intended recipients.
- Digital certificates also verify date and time so that senders or recipients can not dispute if the message was actually sent or received.

The components that a digital signature comprise of.

1. **Your public key:** This is the part that any one can get a copy of and is part of the verification system.
2. **Your name and e-mail address:** This is necessary for contact information purposes and to enable the viewer to identify the details.

3. **Expiration date of the public key:** This part of the signature is used to set a shelf life and to ensure that in the event of prolonged abuse of a signature eventually the signature is reset.
4. **Name of the company:** This section identifies the company that the signature belongs too.
5. **Serial number of the Digital ID:** This part is a unique number that is bundled to the signature for tracking ad extra identification reasons.
6. **Digital signature of the CA (certification Authority):** This is a signature that is issued by the authority that issues the certificates.

Figure 5.7(a)

User A is depicted above and has two keys a public key, this key is available to the public for download, and a private key, this key is not available to the public. All keys are used to lock the information in an encrypted mode. The same keys are required to decrypt the data.

Another user can encrypt the data using users A's Public Key. User A will use the Private Key to decrypt the message. Without user A's Private Key the data can not be decrypted. Figure B below depicts the encryption method and decryption method and witch keys are used.

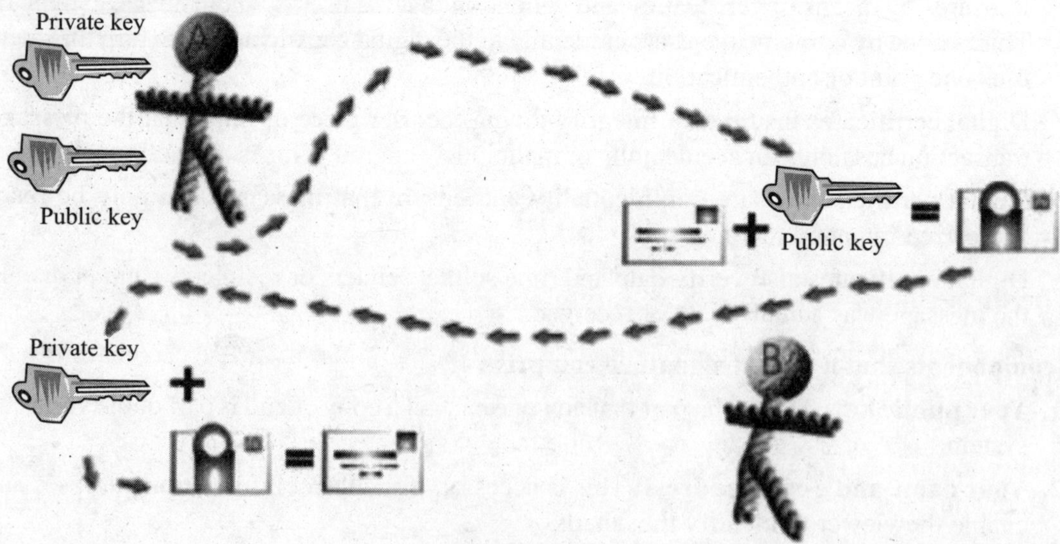

Figure 5.7(b)

Digital signature can be used to make document e-mails and other data private. Big brother is out there and choosing a high encryption mechanism ensures that any one attempting to decrypt the data would find it unviable to attempt decryption.

User A's machine digests the data into a simple string of code after user A's software has encrypted the message digest with his private key. The result is the digital signature. User A's software then appends the digital signature to document. All of the data that was hashed has been signed. User A then passes the digitally signed document to user B.

First user B's software decrypts the signature, using User A's public key then changing it back into a message digest. After the decryption if it has decrypted the data to digest level then verifies that user A in fact did sign the data. To stop fraud certificate authorities have been introduced. Certificate authorities can sign User A's public key, ensuring that no one else uses Bobs information or impersonated his key.

If a user is uncertain of the digital signature it is possible to verify the digital signature with the certificate authority. Signatures can also be revoked if they are abused or if it is suspected that they are abused. When a digital signature is compromised the user that suspects that the certificate is compromised should report the incident to the certificate authority.

The process of checking the validity of digital signature.

- User A sends a signed document to User B.
- To verify the signature on the document, user B's application first uses the certificate authority's public key to check the signature on user A's certificate.
- Successful de-encryption of the certificate proves that the certificate authority created it.
- After the certificate is de-encrypted, user B's software can check if user A is in good standing with the certificate authority and that all of the certificate information concerning user A's identity has not been altered.
- User B's software then takes user A's public key from the certificate and uses it to check user A's signature. If user A's public key de-encrypts the signature successfully, then user B is assured that the signature was created using user A's private key, for the certificate authority has certified the matching public key.
- If the signature is found to be valid, then we know that an intruder didn't try to change the signed content.

5.8.4 The Importance of Private Key Revocation

At times there may be grounds for believing that a private key may have been compromised. This will then result in the key pair being revoked. When a digital signature is revoked the user that is requesting the revoke needs to be verified. If a key is wrongfully revoked legal action can follow.

Digital signatures deliver assurances in the role that the other party will keep their part of the bargain. Knowing the identity of the other party is one way of gaining that assurance. Keys used for digital signatures are very long series of bits, which can be represented as long series of alphanumeric characters. This makes digital signatures unfeasible for an individual to remember. They must consequently be stored in a method which is suitable, portable and protected. The most likely current technology to support such storage is a chip. Smart cards, bios chips, e-prom ships found in cable modems and other types of descrambles are all examples or primitive forms of digital signatures that act as away of identifying user. No form of identification to this date is used more than digital signature to verify the existence of a user and confirmation of credential over the internet. Digital signatures in some form or other are her to stay.

5.8.5 Advantages and Disadvantages of Digital Signatures

Just as with any technology, there will be plus and minuses. This is the way it is with anything, whether it is technology related or not. The advantages of using digital signatures include:

- **Imposter prevention:** By using digital signatures you are eliminating the possibility of committing fraud by an imposter signing the document. Since the digital signature cannot be altered, this makes forging the signature impossible.
- **Message integrity:** By having a digital signature you are in fact proving the document to be valid. You are assuring the recipient that the document is free from forgery or false information.
- **Legal requirements:** Using a digital signature satisfies some type of legal requirement for the document in question. A digital signature takes care of any formal legal aspect of executing the document.

The disadvantages of using digital signatures involve the primary avenue for any business: money. This is because the business may have to spend more money than usual to work with digital signatures including buying certificates from certification authorities and getting the verification software.

5.8.6 Uses of Digital Signatures

As organizations move away from paper documents with ink signatures or authenticity stamps, digital signatures can provide added assurances of the evidence to provenance, identity, and status of an electronic document as well as acknowledging informed consent and approval by a signatory. The United States Government Printing Office (GPO) publishes electronic versions of the budget, public and private laws, and congressional bills with digital signatures. Universities including Penn State, University of Chicago, and Stanford are publishing electronic student transcripts with digital signatures.

Below are some common reasons for applying a digital signature to communications:

Authentication

Although messages may often include information about the entity sending a message, that information may not be accurate. Digital signatures can be used to authenticate the source of messages. When ownership of a digital signature secret key is bound to a specific user, a valid signature shows that the message was sent by that user. The importance of high confidence in sender authenticity is especially obvious in a financial context. For example, suppose a bank's branch office sends instructions to the central office requesting a change in the balance of an account. If the central office is not convinced that such a message is truly sent from an authorized source, acting on such a request could be a grave mistake.

Integrity

In many scenarios, the sender and receiver of a message may have a need for confidence that the message has not been altered during transmission. Although encryption hides the contents of a message, it may be possible to change an encrypted message without understanding it. (Some encryption algorithms, known as nonmalleable ones, prevent this, but others do not.) However, if a message is digitally signed, any change in the message after signature will invalidate the signature. Furthermore, there is no efficient way to modify a message and its signature to produce a new message with a valid signature, because this is still considered to be computationally infeasible by most cryptographic hash functions (see collision resistance).

Non-repudiation

Non-repudiation, or more specifically non-repudiation of origin, is an important aspect of digital signatures. By this property an entity that has signed some information cannot at a later time deny having signed it. Similarly, access to the public key only does not enable a fraudulent party to fake a valid signature. This is in contrast to symmetric systems, where both sender and receiver share the same secret key, and thus in a dispute a third party cannot determine which entity was the true source of the information.

5.8.7 Requirements for Digital Signatures

To establish these conditions, the content creator must digitally sign the content by using a signature that satisfies the following criteria:

- The digital signature is valid. A CA that is trusted by the operating system must sign the digital certificate on which the digital signature is based.
- The certificate that is associated with the digital signature is not expired.
- The signing person or organization (known as the publisher) is trusted by the recipient.
- The certificate associated with the digital signature is issued to the signing publisher by a reputable CA.

Microsoft Office Word 2007, Microsoft Office Excel 2007, and Microsoft Office PowerPoint 2007 detect these criteria for you and warn you if there appears to be a problem with the digital signature. Information about problematic certificates is easily viewed in a certificate task pane that appears in the 2007 Microsoft Office system application. 2007 Office system applications let you add multiple digital signatures to the same document.

5.8.8 How It Works

Assume you were going to send the draft of your business data to your close business partner in another place. You want to give your partner the assurance that it was unchanged from what you sent and that it is really from you.

The sender

You copy-and-paste the data into an e-mail note.

Using special software, you obtain a message hash (mathematical summary) of the data.

You then use a private key that you have previously obtained from a public-private key authority to encrypt the hash.

The encrypted hash becomes your digital signature of the message which will be different each time you send a message.

At the other end, your business partner receives the message

The-receiver

To make sure it's intact and from you, your business partner makes a hash of the received message.

He then uses your public key to decrypt the message hash or summary.

If the hashes match, the received message is valid.

How A digital certificate looks like

-------BEGIN SIGNATURE------

IQB1AwUBMVSiA5QYCuMfgNYjAQFAKgL/

ZkBfbeNEsbthba4BlrcnjaqbcKgNv+a5kr4537y8RCd+RHm

75yYh5xxA1ojELwNhhb7cltrp2V7LlOnAelws4S87UX80cL

BtBcN6AACf11qymC2h+Rb2j5SSU+rmXWru+=QFMx

-------END SIGNATURE------

5.9 ISSUES IN DOCUMENT SECURITY

As organizations move more business processes online, protecting the confidentiality and privacy of information used during these processes, as well as providing authenticity and integrity, are essential. Because many automated processes rely on electronic documents that contain sensitive information, organizations must properly protect these documents. Many information security solutions attempt to protect electronic documents only at their storage location or during transmission. However, these solutions do not provide protection for the entire lifecycle of an electronic document. When the document reaches the recipient, the protection is lost, and the document can be intentionally or unintentionally forwarded to and viewed by unauthorized recipients.

A significantly more effective solution is to protect a document by assigning security parameters that travel with it. Six criteria must be met in order to provide more effective protection for an electronic document throughout its lifecycle:

1. Confidentiality
2. Authorization
3. Accountability
4. Integrity
5. Authenticity
6. Non-repudiation

The requirement of a security regime which addressed these risks are conventionally summarized under four broad headings. For the sender and receiver to be confident in the outcome of their communications, all of these requirement, need to be satisfied.

1. **Confidentially:** This require:
   (a) No observer can access the contents of the message.
   (b) No observer can identify the sender and receiver.
2. **Integrity of message:** This require:
   (a) The message has not been changed or last during transmission.
   (b) The message has not been prevented from reaching the recipient.
   (c) The message has not been reached the recipient twice.
3. **Authentication of the sender and receiver:** This require:
   (a) The sender can be sure that the message reaches the intended recipient and only the intended recipient.
   (b) The recipient can be sure that the message came from the sender and not an imposter. The act by an imposter of sending such a message is referred to as "spoofing".
4. **Non-repudiation by sender and receiver:** This require:
   (a) The sender cannot credibly deny that the message was sent by them.
   (b) The recipient can't credibly deny that the message was receiver by them.

The two major security techniques used to establish these six document security criteria are document control and digital signatures.

5.9.1 Information Security

Thefts of proprietary information are increasing, which can jeopardize revenue, competitive advantage, and customer relationships; generate negative publicity; and result in significant penalties and fines for failure to comply with privacy laws. Many information security solutions attempt to protect electronic documents only at their storage location or during transmission. For example, organizations rely on document management systems and virtual private networks (VPNs) to protect documents. With this approach document security remains a problem because these solutions secure only the communication line or storage site; they do not provide protection for the actual content of an electronic document throughout its lifecycle. When the document reaches the recipient, the protection is lost, and the document can be intentionally or unintentionally forwarded to and viewed by unauthorized recipients. Consequently, many organizations are forced to engage in an inconsistent combination of online and paper processes in which sensitive documents must still be printed and physically delivered to achieve adequate security. As a result, the potential benefits of online processing cannot be fully realized.

5.9.2 How to Provide Document Security

A significantly more effective solution for protecting an electronic document is to assign security parameters that are an integral part of the document itself. The following criteria define persistent document security:

Confidentiality : Who should have access to the document?

Authorization : What permissions does the user have for working with the document?

Accountability : What has the recipient done with the document?

Integrity : How do you know if the document has been altered?

Authenticity : How do you know where the document came from?

Non-repudiation : Can the signatory deny signing the document?

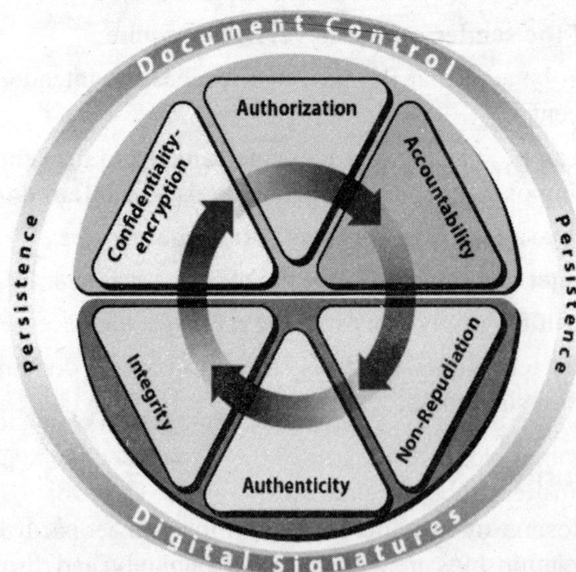

Figure 5.8: Six key criteria for providing persistent document security

Document control provides confidentiality, authorization, and accountability.

5.9.3 Document Control

Confidentiality-encryption

Encryption is the process of transforming information (plaintext) into an incomprehensible form (ciphertext). Encryption is an effective technique for managing document access.

Decryption is the reverse process that transforms ciphertext back to the original plaintext.

Cryptography refers to the two processes of encryption and decryption and its implementation is referred to as a cryptosystem. Popular encryption systems use the concept of keys. An encryption key is data that combines with an encryption algorithm to create ciphertext from plaintext and recover plaintext from ciphertext. Today, security experts widely agree on "Kerckhoff's" principle as the basis of an effective cryptosystem. Kerckhoff's principle states that the key is the only portion of a cryptosystem that must remain secret for the entire system to be secure. If the strength of the cryptosystem relies on the fact that an attacker does not know how the algorithm works, then it is just a matter of time before it can be reverse-engineered and broken.

5.9.4 User Identification and Authentication (UPTU 2010-11)

The modern world needs people with a complex identity who are intellectually autonomous and prepared to cope with uncertainty; who are able to tolerate ambiguity and not be driven by fear into a rigid, single-solution approach to problems, who are rational, foresightful and who look for facts; who can draw inferences and can control their behavior in the light of foreseen consequences, who are altruistic and enjoy doing for others, and who understand social forces and trends.

A computer system comprised of hardware, software, and processes is very often an abstraction of an actual business model that exists in the real world outside the computer system. A financial application, for example, can be considered a model of actual financial relationships between actual organizations and individuals. Every element of the actual financial relationship can be projected onto the computer model (financial application), and then the computer model can be used to determine the outcomes of financial interactions between components of the actual system projected into the computer model.

Actual individuals using a computer system are typically humans (and sometimes applications or services) that exist outside the system. The user ID is a projection of an actual individual (or application or service) into the computer system. The computer system typically uses an abstract object, called a user account, that contains a set of attributes for each actual individual. The object has a name (user ID or logon ID) that is used to represent the abstract object to the system. Additional attributes of the object may include the full name of the actual user, the department for which he is working, his manager and direct reports, extension number, etc. Objects may or may not have credentials as their attributes. Apart from the user ID or logon ID, a security system will typically assign users an internal number (Security Identifier) that is used by the system to refer to the abstract object.

Establishing a unique abstract object in the form of a user account for each individual who will access resources in a computer system is very important. This object is used to identify the user in the system; this object is referred to by the system when user access to information assets is defined, and the system will also trace user actions and record an audit trail referring to the actual user by his abstract object ID. The user ID is therefore the basis for access control and it also helps to implement accountability. Hence, it is essential to have a separate user ID for each user, because each individual has specific access requirements and should be individually kept accountable for his actions.

The process of Authentication is often considered to consist of two distinct phases: (1) identification and (2) (actual) authentication.

Identification provides user identity to the security system. This identity is typically provided in the form of a user ID. The security system will typically search through all the abstract objects that it knows about and find the specific one for the privileges of which the actual user is currently applying. Once this is complete, the user has been identified.

Authentication is the process of validating user identity. The fact that the user claims to be represented by a specific abstract object (identified by its user ID) does not necessarily mean that this is true. To ascertain that an actual user can be mapped to a specific abstract user object in the system, and therefore be granted user rights and permissions specific to the abstract user object, the user must provide evidence to prove his identity to the system. Authentication is the process of ascertaining claimed user identity by verifying user-provided evidence. The evidence provided by a user in the process of user authentication is called a *credential.*

Different systems may require different types of credentials to ascertain user identity, and may even require more than one credential. In computer systems, the credential very often takes the form of a user password, which is a secret known only to the individual and the system. Credentials may take other forms, however, including PIN numbers, certificates, tickets, etc. Once the individual has been authenticated, the system will associate an initial process to the user (a user shell), and the user will be able to launch other processes. All the processes launched by the user access resources (information assets) using the identity of the user, which has already been ascertained by the system.

User identification and authentication are typically the responsibility of the operating system. Before being allowed to create even a single process on a computer, the individual must authenticate to the operating system. Applications and services may or may not honor authentication provided by the operating system, and may or may not require additional authentication upon access to them.

There are typically three components involved in the process of user authentication (Figure):

1. **Supplicant***:* the party in the authentication process that will provide its identity, and evidence for it, and as a result will be authenticated. This party may also be referred to as the authenticating user, or the client.
2. **Authenticator:** the party in the authentication process that is providing resources to the client (the supplicant) and needs to ascertain user identity to authorize and audit user access to resources. The authenticator can also be referred to as the server.
3. **Security authority/database:** storage or mechanism to check user credentials. This can be as simple as a flat file, or a server on the network providing for centralized user authentication, or a set of distributed authentication servers that provide for user authentication within the enterprise or on the Internet.

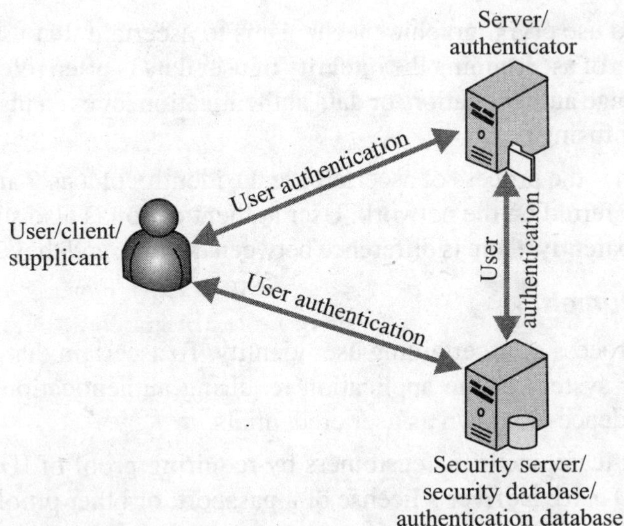

Fig. 5.9: Components of a user authentication system.

In a simple scenario, the supplicant, authenticator, and security database may reside on the same computer. It is also possible and somewhat common for network applications to have the supplicant on one computer and the authenticator and security database collocated on another computer. It is also possible to have the three components geographically distributed on multiple computers. It is important to understand that the three parties can communicate independently with one another. Depending on the authentication mechanism used, some of the communication channels might not be used at least not by an actual dialogue over the network. The type of communication and whether or not it is used depends on the authentication mechanism and the model of trust that it implements.

For example, authentication protocols such as Kerberos will typically involve direct communication between the supplicant and the security server and the supplicant and the authenticator; but with regard to user authentication, there is no direct communication between the authenticator and the security server. Still, messages from the supplicant to the authenticator contain information sent by the security server to the authenticator.

5.9.5 Data Integrity **(UPTU 2010-11)**

An important aspect of cryptography is protecting data integrity from accidental or intentional modification. Accidental data integrity violations include transmission errors, media errors, and noise. Intentional modification generally refers to hacker attacks trying to modify data content while stored on media or in transit.

To provide for data integrity, today's cryptography typically suggests the use of message integrity codes (MICs) that can then be protected with a symmetric or asymmetric key to become message authentication codes Although they are often confused, MACs differ from user authentication.

MACs are meant to use cryptographic mechanisms to ascertain that user data is not modified improperly. The process of ascertaining the integrity of user data is often referred to as data integrity authentication, or message authentication, or data authentication, or even just authentication, which makes it even more confusing.

User authentication is the process of ascertaining the identity of a user and typically takes place before user data is transferred on the network. User authentication is also sometimes referred to as just authentication. Apparently, there is difference between the two, and they should not be confused.

Authentication Document

Authentication is the process of ascertaining user identity. To ascertain that users are who they say they are, the operating system or the application requiring authentication will request evidence from the user. This evidence is known as user credentials.

A bank can authenticate one of its customers by requiring proof of ID, which may include a photo ID, such as an ID card; a driver's license or a passport; or other proof, such as a credit card, a bank statement, a utility bill, etc.

A computer security system may allow for one or more types of credentials as proof of the user's identity. This section discusses the types of credentials that can typically be used in the process of user authentication.

The process of authentication is based on characteristics or unique information that is available to the authenticating parties in the process of user authentication. Authentication credentials fall into one or more of the following categories:

"Something you know." This authentication factor is based on a secret shared between the authenticating parties (the authenticator and the supplicant). Static password authentication schemes are based on the "something you know" factor.

"Something you are." This authentication factor requires the authenticator to authenticate the supplicant based on biometric information, such as fingerprints, retina scan, facial scan, etc. This method relatively closely mimics identification and authentication in legacy security systems, whereby a customer is authenticated by his bank by walking into a branch and showing a photo ID. The client is identified based on his biometric parameters — facial recognition and matching against the photo ID in this instance.

"Something you have." This authentication factor requires the possession of an authentication token, which is an actual object. The authentication token might be a smart card, a key-fob type device, a USB stick, a serial tap, or other object. If a supplicant possesses a token, he is probably who he says he is, so his identity can be ascertained; and as a result, the user can be authenticated.

The use of a single factor to ascertain user identity is very common but not always very secure. Therefore, many systems that require strong user authentication policies implement multiple-factor authentication schemes, whereby the supplicant may be required to provide more than one type of evidence in order to be authenticated. For example, a supplicant may need to provide biometric evidence ("something you are") and a password ("something you know"), or even a password ("something you know"), biometric evidence ("something you are"), and a security token ("something you have").

The use of multiple authentication factors considerably increases the security of a system from a user authentication perspective. If the risk exists that a single-factor authentication system will be compromised, then when a second factor of authentication is taken into consideration, this risk is significantly mitigated. At the same time, it is important to understand that multiple-factor authentication is very likely to increase the time it takes for users to log in. Therefore, users may be resistant to using multiple-factor authentication mechanisms.

User authentication sometimes extends to peer authentication. The server (authenticator) needs to ascertain the identity of the client (supplicant) by means of client authentication, but the client may need to ascertain the identity of the server as well, and make sure that it is talking to the right server and not to an imposter. If the client needs to submit confidential information to the server, or if the client needs to obtain information from the server that is sensitive and must not be tampered with, the client needs to make sure that the server is genuine. When both the client and the server must be authenticated, the process is known as mutual authentication.

5.9.6 Loss of Data Confidentiality/Integrity (UPTU 2010)

Through erroneous actions, IT users can cause or allow loss of data confidentiality/integrity. The consequential damage depends on the sensitivity of the data involved. Examples of such erroneous actions are

- Accidental print-outs containing personal data are not fetched by staff members from the network printer.
- Floppy disks are dispatched without a physical deletion of previously stored data.
- Due to incorrectly administered access rights, a staff member can modify data without being able to assess the critical impact of such a violation of integrity.
- New software is tested using non-anonymous data. Unauthorised staff members thus have access to protected files or confidential information. It is also possible that third parties could have access to this information if the disposal of "test printouts" is not handled correctly

5.9.7 Difference between Secret Information and Confidential Information (UPTU 2010)

'Secret' is something kept or intended to be kept from the knowledge or view of others; not known by others whereas 'confidential' is almost secret only and not to be made known to others, like; confidential letters information, files, letters, etc.

"Secret" is not to be revealed except those for whom it is meant and it is to be kept as secret even afterwards. "Confidential" is meant for the adressees but they can share it with others whom they want to involve.

What Information can be kept Confidential

Confidential or proprietary information can exist in many different forms. It may consist of notes, testing procedures, trade secrets, formulae, test data, specifications, "know-how", software, etc. An important attribute of such information is its unavailability and inaccessibility to the public.

In determining what information the University can agree to keep confidential, it is important to distinguish between information provided by the other party or parties and that which arises from the University performed research. The University can agree to keep someone else's confidential information confidential, however we should not be obligated to keep our own information confidential; this includes the results of research undertaken at the University even if the confidential information was used in to produce the results. All research results must be fully publishable at the discretion of the researcher.

All information received from someone should not be considered confidential by default. Neither should information that is already known by the party receiving it. The obligation of confidentiality should be limited to information that is truly confidential or secret. To reflect this NDAs and CDAS usually include some exceptions to the confidentiality obligation. These exceptions state that the obligation to maintain the confidence would not apply to information: that is already known to or is independently developed by the party to which it is disclosed; is already public or becomes part of the public domain through no fault of the recipient of the information; or is obtained from a third party who is under no obligation to keep the information confidential.

If you are obtaining information from a third party, and there is not a good reason to obligate yourself to keep it confidential, or if you are not prepared to keep it confidential you should not agree to a confidentiality agreement.

5.9.8 Difference between Role of Data Custodians and Role of User

(UPTU 2010-11)

Role of Data Custodians

A Data Custodian is an employee of the University who has administrative and/or operational responsibility over Institutional Data. In many cases, there will be multiple Data Custodians. An enterprise application may have teams of Data Custodians, each responsible for varying functions. A Data Custodian is responsible for the following

(a) **Understanding and reporting on how Institutional Data is stored, processed and transmitted by the University and by third-party Agents of the University.** Understanding and documenting how Institutional Data is being stored, processed and transmitted is the first step toward safeguarding that data. Without this knowledge, it is difficult to implement or validate safeguards in an effective manner. One method of performing this assessment is to create a data flow diagram for a subset of data that illustrates the system(s) storing the data, how the data is being processed and how the data traverses the network. Data flow diagrams can also illustrate security controls as they are implemented. Regardless of approach, documentation should exist and be made available to the appropriate Data Steward.

(b) Implementing appropriate physical and technical safeguards to protect the confidentiality, integrity and availability of Institutional Data.

(c) Data Custodians should work with Data Stewards to gain a better understanding of these requirements. Data Custodians should also document what security controls have been implemented and where gaps exist in current controls. This documentation should be made available to the appropriate Data Steward.

(d) Documenting and disseminating administrative and operational procedures to ensure consistent storage, processing and transmission of Institutional Data.

(e) Documenting administrative and operational procedures goes hand in hand with understanding how data is stored, processed and transmitted. Data Custodians should document as many repeatable processes as possible. This will help ensure that Institutional Data is handled in a consistent manner. This will also help ensure that safeguards are being effectively leveraged.

(f) **Provisioning and deprovisioning access to Institutional Data as authorized by the Data Steward.** Data Custodians are responsible for provisioning and deprovisioning access based on criteria established by the appropriate Data Steward. As specified above, standard procedures for provisioning and deprovisioning access should be documented and made available to the appropriate Data Steward.

(g) **Understanding and reporting on security risks and how they impact the confidentiality, integrity and availability of Institutional Data.**Role of data custodian differ from role of user. Data Custodians should have a thorough understanding of security risks impacting their Institutional Data. For example, storing or transmitting sensitive data in an unencrypted form is a security risk. Protecting access to data using a weak password and/or not patching a vulnerability in a system or application are both examples of security risks. Security risks should be documented and reviewed with the appropriate Data Steward so that he or she can determine whether greater resources need to be devoted to mitigating these risks. This Information Security Office can assist Data Custodians with gaining a better understanding of their security risks.

Role of a Users

For the purpose of information security, a User is any employee, contractor or third-party Agent of the University who is authorized to access University Information Systems and/or Institutional Data. A User is responsible for the following:

(a) **Adhering to policies, guidelines and procedures pertaining to the protection of Institutional Data.** The Information Security Office publishes various policies, guidelines and procedures related to the protection of Institutional Data and Information Systems. They can be found on the Information Security Office website. Business units and/or Data Stewards may also publish their own unique guidelines and procedures. Information on requirements unique to your business unit or a system you have access to can be found by talking to your manager or system administrator.

(b) **Reporting actual or suspected vulnerabilities in the confidentiality, integrity or availability of Institutional Data to a manager or the Information Security Office.**

During the course of day-to-day operations, if a User comes across a situation where he or she feels the security of Institutional Data might be at risk, it should be reported to the Information Security Office. For example, if a User comes across sensitive information on a website that he or she feels shouldn't be accessible, that situation should be reported to the Information Security Office. Additional notifications may be appropriate based on procedures unique to a business unit or defined by a Data Steward. It may be appropriate to notify a local security point of contact that will in turn coordinate with the Information Security Office.

Reporting actual or suspected breaches in the confidentiality, integrity or availability of Institutional Data to the Information Security Office.

5.10 SYSTEM OF KEYS

Two main types of encryption keys include symmetric and asymmetric.

5.10.1 Symmetric Keys

Symmetric key cryptography uses the same key for both encryption and decryption and is very fast and difficult to break with large keys. However, because both parties need the same key for effective communication to occur, key distribution becomes an issue. Today, common symmetric key encryption algorithms are AES, DES, 3DES, and RC4. Adobe products leverage AES (128- and 256-bit) and RC4 (128-bit), as they have evolved into very strong standards.

5.10.2 Asymmetric Keys

Asymmetric key cryptography, also called public key cryptography, uses key pairs for encryption and decryption. For instance, if the first key encrypts the content, then the second key of the pair decrypts the content. Similarly, if the second key is used to encrypt the information, then the first key must be used to decrypt the content. Typically, one key in the pair is labeled as the public key and the other as the private key. An individual keeps the private key secret, while the public key is freely distributed to others who wish to communicate with the individual. When someone wishes to send the individual a confidential message, he or she can encrypt it with the freely available public key and send the ciphertext to the individual. Because the individual is the only one who has the private key, he or she is the only one who can decrypt the content.

Asymmetric keys help solve the key distribution problem, but the algorithms tend to be slower for equivalent strengths. Some common asymmetric algorithms are RSA, DSA, and El Gamal. Adobe leverages RSA (512-, 1024-, and 2048-bit) as it has evolved into a global standard.

5.10.3 Hybrid Encryption

Security systems tend to use a hybrid solution to increase the security and speed of encrypting documents. One approach is to use asymmetric keys to protect the symmetric keys, and then use the symmetric keys for encrypting the information. This technique helps to solve both the key distribution challenge of symmetric key cryptography while solving the performance problem of asymmetric key cryptography. Adobe Acrobat software leverages hybrid approaches so single documents can be protected for multiple recipients, each possessing unique key pairs. The file size is not significantly increased during this method because the entire document does not need to be encrypted for each person. Instead, the document is encrypted with a single symmetric key and that symmetric key is encrypted for each recipient with their respective public key.

5.10.4 Authorization

In addition to managing who can open a document, organizations gain additional protection through authorization. Authorization specifies what a user can do with a document and is achieved via permissions and dynamic document control.

- Permissions govern a user's actions while working with a protected document. Permissions can specify whether or not a recipient who has access to the document is allowed to print or copy content, fill in fields, add comments or annotate the document, insert or remove pages, forward the document, access the document offine, digitally sign the document, and so forth.
- Dynamic document control maintains access rights and permissions assigned to an electronic document once it has been published and distributed. A document's author can make changesto a released document without having to manually redistribute it since the changes are automatically pushed to all existing versions of the document no matter where they reside.

  Using dynamic document control, organizations can manage and monitor electronic document use inside and outside the firewall, online and offine, and across multiple documents. Dynamic document control includes the following capabilities:
- Document expiration and revocation-Post-publication document control can be maintained through the application of expiration dates and the ability to revoke access to a document. For example, an author can send a document that will expire in two weeks so that recipients will not be able to access it once the expiration date has passed. Or, access to a document can be automatically revoked if an authorized recipient leaves the project or changes departments.
- Offine access management-Organizations can manage how long an authorized recipient can access a document offine. Once the specified length of time has passed, the recipient can no longer view the document and must go back online to gain further access. Any access or permission changes that the author has made to the distributed document will be applied when the recipient goes back online.
- Persistent version control Content and document management systems provide an effective mechanism for version control as long as a document stays within the confines of the system. Persistent version control expands on these capabilities by maintaining version control outside the system and offine. It allows document authors to make changes to a document's usage

policies and prevent the obsolete version from being accessed while providing end users with the location of the updated version, no matter where the document resides.

5.10.5 Accountability

Document auditing allows organizations to maintain accountability with regard to the use of protected documents, because they can know precisely:

- How a recipient has used a document
- How often each type of usage occurred
- When that usage occurred

Accountability is achieved when an author can track each recipient's use of a document for each permission assigned (such as allowing a user to fill in fields on a form, print, forward, save a copy, and so forth.) Auditing should include automatic notifications about the use of protected documents. For example, a customer service representative sends a customer a time-critical electronic statement that requires an action on the customer's part, such as a reply or digital signature. Once the customer rceeives the electronic document, the representative is automatically notified when the customer opens it. If the customer fails to open the document, the representative is notified after 24 hours. Alternatively, a customer relationship management (CRM) system can leverage failure notification to initiate an escalation or specific follow-up task by the customer service representative.

5.11 FINGERPRINT

Fingerprint in its narrow sense is an impression left by the friction ridges of a human finger. In a wider use of the term, fingerprints are the traces of an impression from the friction ridges of any part of a human hand. A print from the foot can also leave an impression of friction ridges. A friction ridge is a raised portion of the epidermis on the fingers and toes (digits), the palm of the hand or the sole of the foot, consisting of one or more connected ridge units of friction ridge skin. These are sometimes known as "epidermal ridges" which are caused by the underlying interface between the dermal papillae of the dermis and the interpapillary pegs of the epidermis. These epidermal ridges serve to amplify vibrations triggered, for example, when fingertips brush across an uneven surface, better transmitting the signals to sensory nerves involved in fine texture perception. These ridges also assist in gripping rough surfaces, as well as smooth wet surfaces.

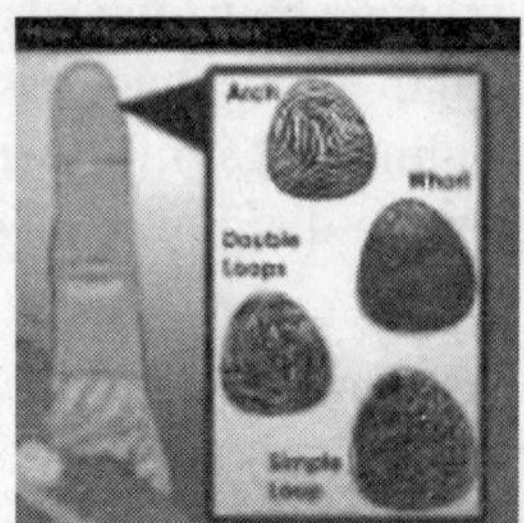

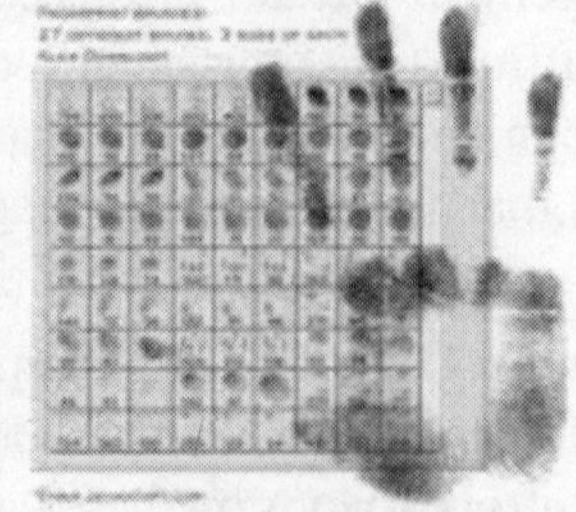
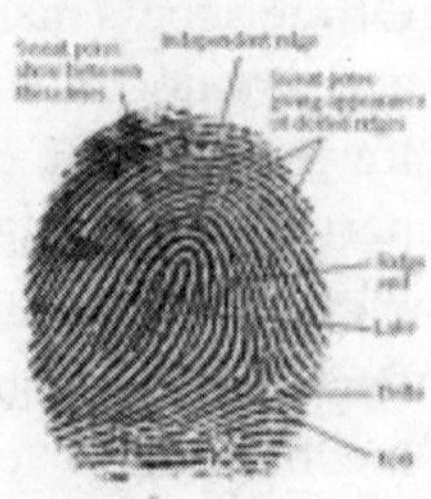

Figure 5.10: Examples of Fingerprint

5.12 FINGERPRINT PATTERNS

There are three main fingerprint patterns: arches, loops and whorls.

Arches are found in about 5% of fingerprint patterns encountered. The ridges run from one side to the other of the pattern, making no backward turn. Ordinarily, there is no delta in an arch pattern but where there a delta, no re-curving ridge must intervene between the core and delta points. There are four types of arch patterns: plain arches, radial arches, ulnar arches and tented arches. Plain arches have an even flow of ridges from one side to the other of the pattern, no "significant up thrusts" and the ridges enter on one side of the impression, and flow out the other with a rise or wave in the center. The ridges of radial arches slope towards the thumb, have one delta and no re-curving ridges. On ulnar arches, the ridges slope towards the little finger, have one delta and no re-curving ridges. Tented arches have an angle, an up thrust, or two of the three basic characteristics of the loop. They don't have the same "easy" flow that plain arches do and particularly have "significant up thrusts" in the ridges near the middle that arrange themselves on both sides of a spine or axis towards which the adjoining ridges converge and appear to form tents.

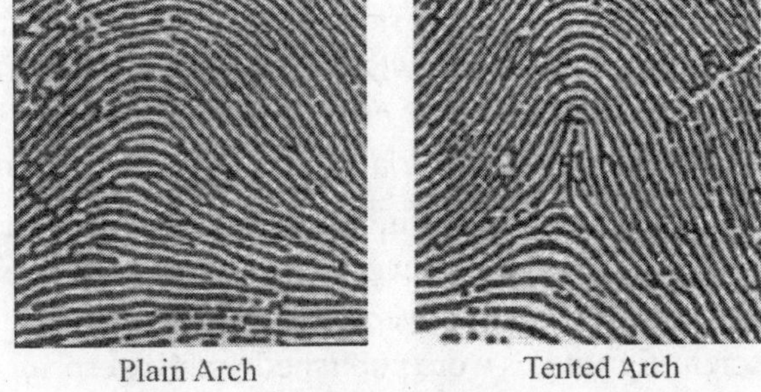

Plain Arch Tented Arch

Figure 5.11

Loops occur in about 60-70 % of fingerprint patterns encountered. One or more of the ridges enters on either side of the impression, re-curves, touches or crosses the line running from the delta to the core and terminates on or in the direction of the side where the ridge or ridges entered. Each loop pattern has is one delta and one core and has a ridge count. Radial loops are named after the radius, a bone in the forearm that joins the hand on the same side as the thumb. The flow of the pattern in radial loops runs in the direction of the radius (toward the thumb). Radial loops are not very common and most of the time radial loops will be found on the index fingers. Ulnar loops are named after the ulna, a bone in the forearm. The ulna is on the same side as the little finger and the flow of the pattern in a ulnar loop runs in the direction of the ulna (toward the little finger).

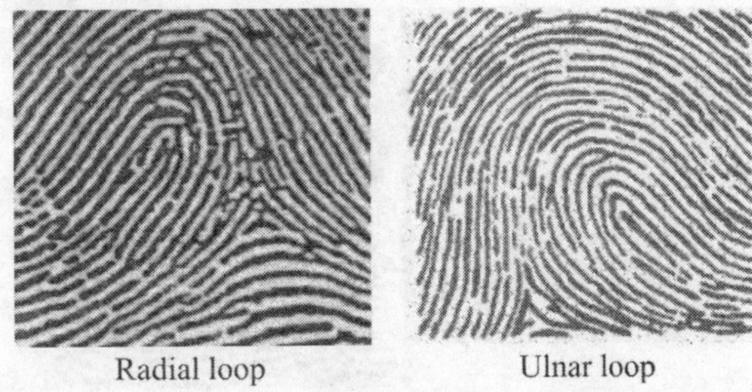

Radial loop Ulnar loop

Figure 5.12

Whorls are seen in about 25-35 % of fingerprint patterns encountered. In a whorl, some of the ridges make a turn through at least one circuit. Any fingerprint pattern which contains 2 or more deltas will be a whorl pattern. There are four types of whorl patterns. Plain whorls consist of one or more ridges which make or tend to make a complete circuit with two deltas, between which an imaginary line is drawn and at least one re-curving ridge within the inner pattern area is cut or touched. Central pocket loop whorls consist of at least one re-curving ridge or an obstruction at right angles to the line of flow, with two deltas, between which when an imaginary line is drawn, no re-curving ridge within the pattern area is cut or touched. Central pocket loop whorl ridges make one complete circuit which may be spiral, oval, circular or any variant of a circle. Double loop whorls consist of two separate and distinct loop formations with two separate and distinct shoulders for each core, two deltas and one or more ridges which make, a complete circuit. Between the two at least one re-curving ridge within the inner pattern area is cut or touched when an imaginary line is drawn. Accidental whorls consist of two different types of patterns with the exception of the plain arch, have two or more deltas or a pattern which possess some of the requirements for two or more different types or a pattern which conforms to none of the definitions.

The beginning of fingerprints goes back to as early as the ancient times. According to historical findings, fingerprints were used on clay tablets for business transactions in ancient Babylon. In China, thumb prints were found on clay seals. But it was in the 19th century that the results of scientific studies were published and fingerprint technology began to be considered more seriously.

Using the1800's scientific studies as a foundation, fingerprint technology was already in use by the beginning of the 20th century. In 1924, FBI(Federal Bureau of Investigation) is already known to have maintained more than 250 million civil files of fingerprints for the purpose of criminal investigation and the identification of unknown casualties. In the late 1960's, fingerprint technology met a great turning point when it gave birth to 'live-scan,' a method to obtain a fingertip image without the use of print ink. When the FBI announced that it planned to stop using paper fingerprint cards inside their new Integrated AFIS (IAFIS) site, it was actually announcing the remarkable breakthrough of today's live-scan technology.

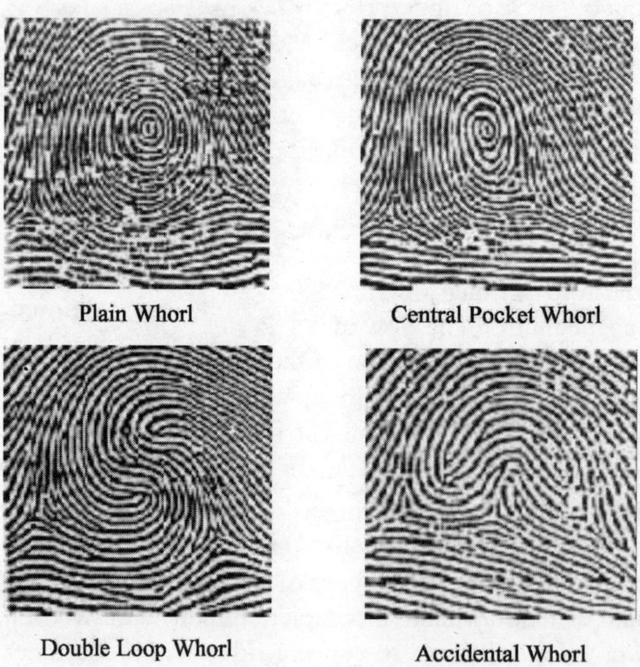

Figure 5.13: History of Fingerprint Technology

But fingerprint identification technology did not stop as a forensic method only. It was officially used for business purposes in 1968 at one security corporation in Wall Street. Fingerprints are now being used as a secure and effective authentication method in numerous fields, including financial, medical, e-commerce and entrance control applications. Modern applications of fingerprint technology rely in large part on the development of exceptionally compact fingerprint sensors.

5.12.1 Why Fingerprints

With increasingly urgent need for reliable security, biometrics is being spotlighted as the authentication method for the next generation. Among numerous biometric technologies, fingerprint authentication has been in use for the longest time and bears more advantages than other biometric technologies do.

Fingerprint authentication is possibly the most sophisticated method of all biometric technologies and has been thoroughly verified through various applications. Fingerprint authentication has particularly proved its high efficiency and further enhanced the technology in criminal investigation for more than a century.

Even features such as a person's gait, face, or signature may change with passage of time and may be fabricated or imitated. However, a fingerprint is completely unique to an individual and stayed unchanged for lifetime. This exclusivity demonstrates that fingerprint authentication is far more accurate and efficient than any other methods of authentication.

Also, a fingerprint may be taken and digitalized by relatively compact and cheap devices and takes only a small capacity to store a large database of information. With these strengths, fingerprint authentication has long been a major part of the security market and continues to be more competitive than others in today's world.

5.12.2 Fingerprint Identification Process

Fingerprint identification process consists of two essential procedures: enrollment and authentication. Taking the following steps completes each procedure:

<Picture 1> Fingerprint Identification Process

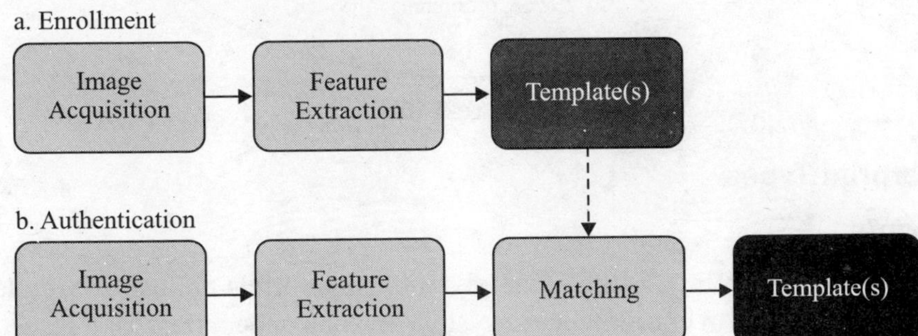

Figure 5.14

As shown in the diagram above, fingerprint identification system compares the input fingerprint image and previously registered data to determine the genuineness of a fingerprint. All the steps described above affect the efficiency of the entire system, but the computational load of the following steps can be reduced to a great extent by acquiring a good-quality fingerprint image in the first step.

5.12.3 Fingerprint Application

Markets for fingerprint technology include entrance control and door-lock applications, fingerprint identification mouses, fingerprint mobile phones, and many others. The fingerprint markets are classified as follows as given in the Figure 5.15.

As the advanced technology enables even more compact fingerprint sensor size, the range of application is extended to the mobile market. Considering the growing phase of the present mobile market, its potential is the greatest of all application markets.

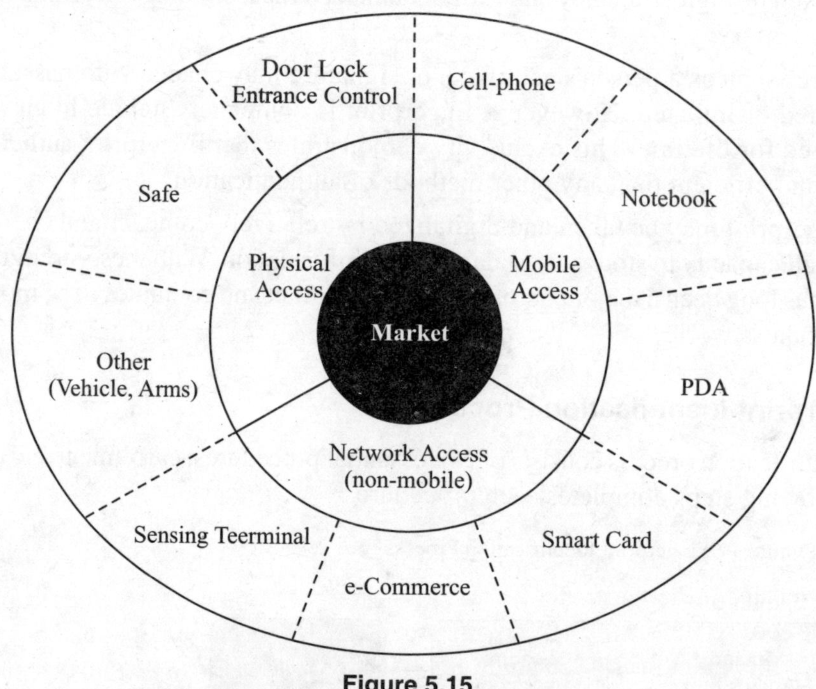

Figure 5.15

5.12.4 Fingerprint Types

Exemplar prints

Exemplar prints, or known prints, is the name given to fingerprints deliberately collected from a subject, whether for purposes of enrollment in a system or when under arrest for a suspected criminal offense. During criminal arrests, a set of exemplar prints will normally include one print taken from each finger that has been rolled from one edge of the nail to the other, plain (or slap) impressions of each of the four fingers of each hand, and plain impressions of each thumb.

Latent prints

Although the word latent means hidden or invisible, in modern usage for forensic science the term latent prints means any chance or accidental impression left by friction ridge skin on a surface, regardless of whether it is visible or invisible at the time of deposition. Electronic, chemical and physical processing techniques permit visualization of invisible latent print residues whether they are from natural sweat on the skin or from a contaminant such as motor oil, blood, ink, paint or some other form of dirt. The different types of fingerprint patterns, such as arch, loop and whorl, will be described below.

Latent prints may exhibit only a small portion of the surface of a finger and this may be smudged, distorted, overlapped by other prints from the same or from different individuals, or any or all of these in combination. For this reason, latent prints usually present an "inevitable source of error in making comparisons," as they generally "contain less clarity, less content, and less undistorted information than a fingerprint taken under controlled conditions, and much, much less detail compared to the actual patterns of ridges and grooves of a finger."

Patent prints

Patent prints are chance friction ridge impressions which are obvious to the human eye and which have been caused by the transfer of foreign material from a finger onto a surface. Some obvious examples would be impressions from flour and wet clay. Because they are already visible and have no need of enhancement they are generally photographed rather than being lifted in the way that latent prints are. An attempt to preserve the actual print is always made for later presentation in court, and there are many techniques used to do this. Patent prints can be left on a surface by materials such as ink, dirt, or blood.

Plastic prints

A plastic print is a friction ridge impression left in a material that retains the shape of the ridge detail. Although very few criminals would be careless enough to leave their prints in a lump of wet clay, this would make a perfect plastic print. Commonly encountered examples are melted candle wax, putty removed from the perimeter of window panes and thick grease deposits on car parts. Such prints are already visible and need no enhancement, but investigators must not overlook the potential that invisible latent prints deposited by accomplices may also be on such surfaces. After photographically recording such prints, attempts should be made to develop other non-plastic impressions deposited from sweat or other contaminates.

Electronic recording

There has been a newspaper report of a man selling stolen watches sending images of them on a mobile phone, and those images included parts of his hands in enough detail for police to be able to identify fingerprint patterns.

5.13 FIREWALL

A **firewall** is a part of a computer system or network that is designed to block unauthorized access while permitting authorized communications. It is a device or set of devices that is configured to permit or deny network transmissions based upon a set of rules and other criteria.

Firewalls can be implemented in either hardware or software, or a combination of both. Firewalls are frequently used to prevent unauthorized Internet users from accessing private networks connected to the Internet, especially intranets. All messages entering or leaving the intranet pass through the firewall, which inspects each message and blocks those that do not meet the specified security criteria.

There are several types of firewall techniques:

1. **Packet filter:** Packet filtering inspects each packet passing through the network and accepts or rejects it based on user-defined rules. Although difficult to configure, it is fairly effective and mostly transparent to its users. It is susceptible to IP spoofing.
2. **Application gateway:** Applies security mechanisms to specific applications, such as FTP and Telnet servers. This is very effective, but can impose a performance degradation.
3. **Circuit-level gateway:** Applies security mechanisms when a TCP or UDP connection is established. Once the connection has been made, packets can flow between the hosts without further checking.
4. **Proxy server:** Intercepts all messages entering and leaving the network. The proxy server effectively hides the true network addresses.

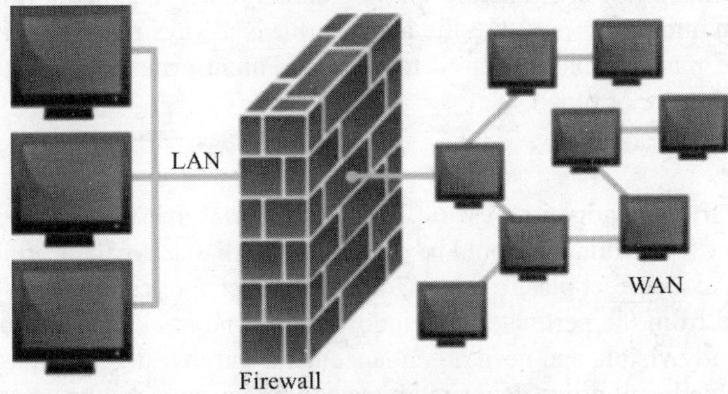

Figure 5.16

5.14 DESIGN AND IMPLEMENTATION ISSUES

5.14.1 What are Some of the Basic Design Decisions in a Firewall

There are a number of basic design issues that should be addressed by the lucky person who has been tasked with the responsibility of designing, specifying, and implementing or overseeing the installation of a firewall.

The first and most important decision reflects the policy of how your company or organization wants to operate the system: is the firewall in place explicitly to deny all services except those critical to the mission of connecting to the Net, or is the firewall in place to provide a metered and audited method of ``queuing'' access in a non-threatening manner? There are degrees of paranoia between these positions; the final stance of your firewall might be more the result of a political than an engineering decision.

The second is: what level of monitoring, redundancy, and control do you want? Having established the acceptable risk level (i.e., how paranoid you are) by resolving the first issue, you can form a checklist of what should be monitored, permitted, and denied. In other words, you start by figuring out your overall objectives, and then combine a needs analysis with a risk assessment, and sort the almost always conflicting requirements out into a laundry list that specifies what you plan to implement.

The third issue is financial. We can't address this one here in anything but vague terms, but it's important to try to quantify any proposed solutions in terms of how much it will cost either to buy or to implement. For example, a complete firewall product may cost between $100,000 at the high end, and free at the low end. The free option, of doing some fancy configuring on a Cisco or similar router will cost nothing but staff time and a few cups of coffee. Implementing a high end firewall from scratch might cost several man-months, which may equate to $30,000 worth of staff salary and benefits. The systems management overhead is also a consideration. Building a home-brew is fine, but it's important to build it so that it doesn't require constant (and expensive) attention. It's important, in other words, to evaluate firewalls not only in terms of what they cost now, but continuing costs such as support.

On the technical side, there are a couple of decisions to make, based on the fact that for all practical purposes what we are talking about is a static traffic routing service placed between the network service provider's router and your internal network. The traffic routing service may be implemented at an IP level via something like screening rules in a router, or at an application level via proxy gateways and services.

The decision to make is whether to place an exposed stripped-down machine on the outside network to run proxy services for telnet, FTP, news, etc., or whether to set up a screening router as a filter, permitting communication with one or more internal machines. There are benefits and drawbacks to both approaches, with the proxy machine providing a greater level of audit and, potentially, security in return for increased cost in configuration and a decrease in the level of service that may be provided (since a proxy needs to be developed for each desired service). The old trade-off between ease-of-use and security comes back to haunt us with a vengeance.

5.14.2 What are the Basic Types of Firewalls

Conceptually, there are three types of firewalls:

1. Network layer
2. Application layer
3. Hybrids

They are not as different as you might think, and latest technologies are blurring the distinction to the point where it's no longer clear if either one is ``better" or ``worse." As always, you need to be careful to pick the type that meets your needs.

Which is which depends on what mechanisms the firewall uses to pass traffic from one security zone to another. The International Standards Organization (ISO) Open Systems Interconnect (OSI) model for networking defines seven layers, where each layer provides services that ``higher-level" layers depend on. In order from the bottom, these layers are physical, data link, network, transport, session, presentation, application.

The important thing to recognize is that the lower-level the forwarding mechanism, the less examination the firewall can perform. Generally speaking, lower-level firewalls are faster, but are easier to fool into doing the wrong thing.

These days, most firewalls fall into the ``hybrid" category, which do network filtering as well as some amount of application inspection. The amount changes depending on the vendor, product, protocol and version, so some level of digging and/or testing is often necessary.

5.14.3 Network Layer Firewalls

These generally make their decisions based on the source, destination addresses and ports in individual IP packets. A simple router is the ``traditional" network layer firewall, since it is not able to make particularly sophisticated decisions about what a packet is actually talking to or where it actually came from. Modern network layer firewalls have become increasingly sophisticated, and now maintain internal information about the state of connections passing through them, the contents of some of the data streams, and so on. One thing that's an important distinction about many network layer firewalls is that they route traffic directly though them, so to use one you either need to have a validly assigned IP address block or to use a ``private internet" address block . Network layer firewalls tend to be very fast and tend to be very transparent to users.

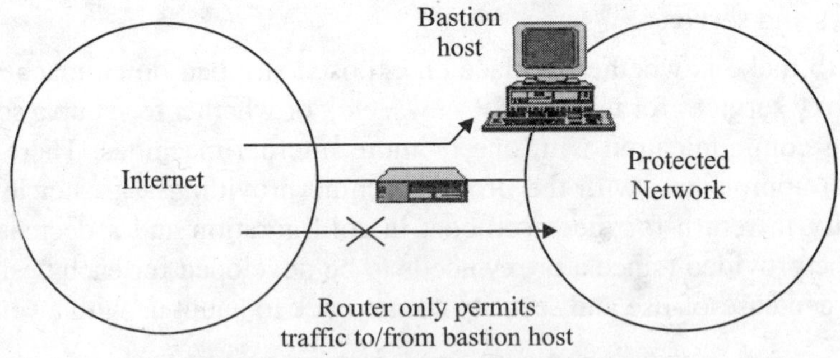

Figure 5.17: Screened Host Firewall

In Figure 5.16, a network layer firewall called a ``screened host firewall" is represented. In a screened host firewall, access to and from a single host is controlled by means of a router operating at a network layer. The single host is a bastion host; a highly-defended and secured strong-point that (hopefully) can resist attack.

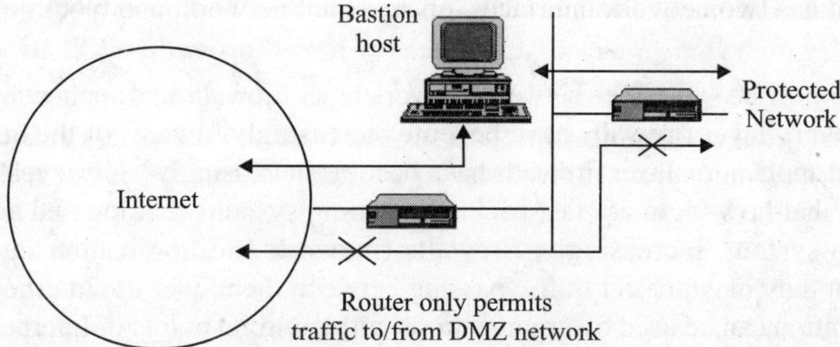

Figure 5.18: Screened Subnet

Example Network layer firewall: In Figure 5.17, a network layer firewall called a ``screened subnet firewall'' is represented. In a screened subnet firewall, access to and from a whole network is controlled by means of a router operating at a network layer. It is similar to a screened host, except that it is, effectively, a network of screened hosts Application layer firewalls

These generally are hosts running proxy servers, which permit no traffic directly between networks, and which perform elaborate logging and auditing of traffic passing through them. Since the proxy applications are software components running on the firewall, it is a good place to do lots of logging and access control. Application layer firewalls can be used as network address translators, since traffic goes in one ``side'' and out the other, after having passed through an application that effectively masks the origin of the initiating connection. Having an application in the way in some cases may impact performance and may make the firewall less transparent. Early application layer firewalls such as those built using the TIS firewall toolkit, are not particularly transparent to end users and may require some training. Modern application layer firewalls are often fully transparent. Application layer firewalls tend to provide more detailed audit reports and tend to enforce more conservative security models than network layer firewalls.

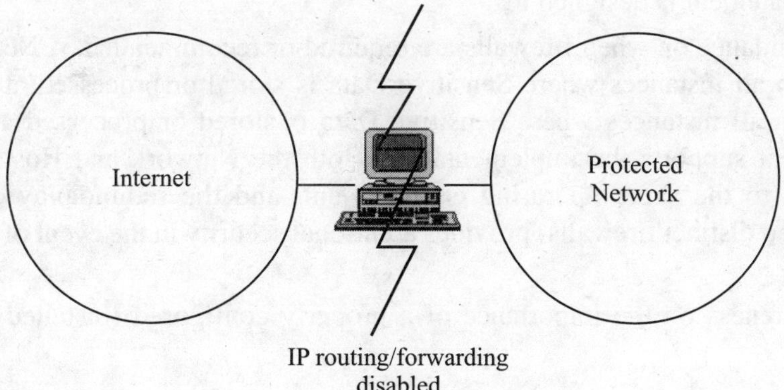

Figure 5.19: Dual Homed Gateway

Example Application layer firewall: In Figure 5.18, an application layer firewall called a "dual homed gateway" is represented. A dual homed gateway is a highly secured host that runs proxy software. It has two network interfaces, one on each network, and blocks all traffic passing through it.

Most firewalls now lie someplace between network layer firewalls and application layer firewalls. As expected, network layer firewalls have become increasingly "aware" of the information going through them, and application layer firewalls have become increasingly ``low level" and transparent. The end result is that now there are fast packet-screening systems that log and audit data as they pass through the system. Increasingly, firewalls (network and application layer) incorporate encryption so that they may protect traffic passing between them over the Internet. Firewalls with end-to-end encryption can be used by organizations with multiple points of Internet connectivity to use the Internet as a "private backbone" without worrying about their data or passwords being sniffed.

5.15 FIREWALL POLICY

A firewall is an appliance (a combination of hardware and software) or an application (software) designed to control the flow of Internet Protocol (IP) traffic to or from a network or electronic equipment. Firewalls are used to examine network traffic and enforce policies based on instructions contained within the Firewall's Ruleset. Firewalls represent one component of a strategy to combat malicious activities and assaults on computing resources and network-accessible information. Other components include, but are not limited to, antivirus software, intrusion detection software, patch management, strong passwords/passphrases, and spyware detection utilities.

Firewalls are typically categorized as either "Network" or "Host": a Network Firewall is most often an appliance attached to a network for the purpose of controlling access to single or multiple hosts, or subnets; a Host Firewall is most often an application that addresses an individual host (e.g., personal computer) separately. Both types of firewalls (Network and Host) can be and often are used jointly.

This policy statement is designed to:

- Provide guidance on when firewalls are required or recommended. A Network Firewall is required in all instances where Sensitive Data is stored or processed; a Host Firewall is required in all instances where Sensitive Data is stored or processed and the operating environment supports the implementation. Both the Network and Host Firewalls afford protection to the same operating environment, and the redundancy of controls (two separate and distinct firewalls) provides additional security in the event of a compromise or failure.
- Raise awareness on the importance of a properly configured (installed and maintained) firewall.

SUMMARY

Cryptography is the science of using mathematics to encrypt and decrypt data. Cryptography enables you to store sensitive information or transmit it across insecure networks (like the Internet) so that it cannot be read by anyone except the intended recipient.

Data that can be read and understood without any special measures is called plaintext or clear text. The method of disguising plaintext in such a way as to hide its substance is called encryption. Encrypting plaintext results in unreadable gibberish called cipher text. You use encryption to ensure that information is hidden from anyone for whom it is not intended, even those who can see the encrypted data. The process of reverting cipher text to its original plaintext is called decryption.

Encryption techniques have become the immediate solution to protect information against third parties. These techniques required that data and information should be encrypted with some sort of mathematical algorithm where only the party that shares the information could possible decrypt to use the information. This phenomenon has long existed and is not fully reliable which pose danger to the information sharing. However, many method of encryption emerge to serve the need of the emergent trend of rapid technological advancement. These emergent techniques were more reliable and are fast in operation and performance wise.

Encryption uses a systematic or step-by-step procedure called an algorithm to convert data or the text of an original message, known as plaintext, into ciphertext, its encrypted form.

Cryptographic algorithms normally require a string of characters called a key to encrypt or decrypt data. Those who possess the key and the algorithm can encrypt the plaintext into ciphertext and then decrypt the ciphertext back into plaintext.

Cryptologists engage in an unending competition to create stronger cryptographic techniques and to break them. Many recent cryptography techniques are nearly unbreakable even with the most powerful computers. These systems produce ciphertext that appears to be random characters. These systems resist most existing methods for deciphering back into plaintext.

Asymmetric key encryption uses different keys for encryption and decryption. These two keys are mathematically related and they form a key pair. One of these two keys should be kept private, called private-key, and the other can be made public (it can even be sent in mail), called public-key. Hence this is also called Public Key Encryption.

Cryptography can be used to provide:

- **Confidentiality :** ensure data is read only by authorized parties,
- **Data integrity :** ensure data wasn't altered between sender and recipient,
- **Authentication :** ensure data originated from a particular party.

A cryptographic system (or a cipher system) is a method of hiding data so that only certain people can view it. Cryptography is the practice of creating and using cryptographic systems. Cryptanalysis is the science of analyzing and reverse engineering cryptographic systems. The original data is called plaintext. The protected data is called ciphertext. Encryption is a procedure to convert plaintext into ciphertext. Decryption is a procedure to convert ciphertext into plaintext. A cryptographic system typically consists of algorithms, keys, and key management facilities.

A digital signature is a code or verification used to uniquely identify you. By entering in certain information to validate yourself, the code or token is created, allowing it to be used instead of an actual signature.

A major benefit of public key cryptography is that it provides a method for employing digital signatures. Digital signatures enable the recipient of information to verify the authenticity of the information's origin, and also verify that the information is intact. Thus, public key digital signatures provide authentication and data integrity. A digital signature also provides non-repudiation, which means that it prevents the sender from claiming that he or she did not actually send the information. These features are every bit as fundamental to cryptography as privacy, if not more.

EXERCISES

1. What is cryptographic system. Discuss it with its types.
2. Explain the model of cryptographic system.
3. What are the different concept in cryptography.
4. What do you understand by public and private key encryption.
5. What are the issues in document security.
6. What are system of keys, public key cryptography.
7. What is digital signature.
8. How does digital signature work.
9. What are the basic requirement of digital signature.
10. What are finger print.
11. Define firewall with it design and implementation issues, and policies.

CHAPTER 6

Network Security

6.1 INTRODUCTION

In the field of networking, the specialist area of network security consists of the provisions and policies adopted by the network administrator to prevent and monitor unauthorized access, misuse, modification, or denial of the computer network and network-accessible resources.

6.1.1 The First Step to Information Security

The terms network security and information security are often used interchangeably. Network security is generally taken as providing protection at the boundaries of an organization by keeping out intruders (hackers). Information security, however, explicitly focuses on protecting data resources from malware attack or simple mistakes by people within an organization by use of data loss prevention (DLP) techniques. One of these techniques is to compartmentalize large networks with internal boundaries.

6.2 NETWORK SECURITY CONCEPTS

Network security starts from authenticating the user, commonly with a username and a password. Since this requires just one thing besides the user name, i.e. the password which is something you 'know', this is sometimes termed one factor authentication. With two factor authentication something you 'have' is also used (e.g. a security token or 'dongle', an ATM card, or your mobile phone), or with three factor authentication something you 'are' is also used (e.g. a fingerprint or retinal scan).

Once authenticated, a firewall enforces access policies such as what services are allowed to be accessed by the network users. Though effective to prevent unauthorized access, this component may fail to check potentially harmful content such as computer worms or Trojans being transmitted over the network. Anti-virus software or an intrusion prevention system (IPS) help detect and inhibit the action of such malware. An anomaly-based intrusion detection system may also monitor the network and traffic for unexpected (i.e. suspicious) content or behavior and other anomalies to protect resources, e.g. from denial of service attacks or an employee accessing files at strange times. Individual events occurring on the network may be logged for audit purposes and for later high level analysis.

Communication between two hosts using a network could be encrypted to maintain privacy.

Honeypots, essentially decoy network-accessible resources, could be deployed in a network as surveillance and early-warning tools as the honeypot will not normally be accessed. Techniques used by the attackers that attempt to compromise these decoy resources are studied during and after an attack to keep an eye on new exploitation techniques. Such analysis could be used to further tighten security of the actual network being protected by the honeypot.

6.2.1 Network Security Model (NSM)

The proposed Network Security Model (NSM) is a seven layer model that divides the daunting task of securing a network infrastructure into seven manageable sections. The model is generic and can apply to all security implementation and devices. The development of the NSM is important because unity is needed in securing networks, just as unity was needed in the architecture of networks with the development of the OSI model. When an attack on a network has succeeded it is much easier to locate the underlying issue and fix it with the use of the NSM.

(1) Physical
(2) VLAN
(3) ACL
(4) Software
(5) User
(6) Administrative
(7) IT Department

The Network Security Model

6.2.2 Why do We Need a Network Security Model

A well structured NSM will give the security community a way to study, implement, and maintain network security that can be applied to any network. In study, it can be used as a tool to breakdown network security into seven simple layers with a logical process.

Traditional books have always presented network security in an unorganized fashion where some books cover issues that other books may completely neglect. In implementation, it can be used by network architects to insure that they are not missing any important security details while designing a network. In maintaining existing networks it can be used to develop maintenance schedules and lifecycles for the security of the existing network. It can also be used to detect where breaches have occurred so that an attack can be mitigated.

The NSM is beneficial to all types of professionals. Let us not forget professionals who are transitioning into positions previously held by other network security professionals. Currently, learning what security techniques are implemented on a network and which ones have not can be a daunting task when the basic security structure of the network is unclear. The NSM provides that basic structure. It provides the new professional with the knowledge to discover what has been implemented and what has not been implemented from a security standpoint. Without an NSM, the network security community faces potential chaos as professionals continue to implement their own versions of secure networks without adequate structure. Understanding the NSM Seven Layer Model: The Physical Layer

6.2.3 What is the Physical Layer

The physical layer's primary focus is on physical security. Physical security is applied to prevent attackers from accessing a facility to gain data stored on servers, computers, or other mediums.

Physical security is the first chosen layer because it is a breaking point for any network. In any scenario providing other devices, such as firewalls, will not help your security if the physical layer is attacked. For this reason we can say that if the layers below the physical layer fail the physical layer has failed as well because the attacker would be able to manipulate data as if they had breached the facility. Physical security comes in many forms including site design, access control devices, alarms, or cameras. The physical layer is one of the easiest layers to secure because it does not require advanced technical concepts to do so. A company can be hired to install an alarm system, or an employee can be hired to stand as a security guard.

6.2.4 Elements of the Physical Layer

The first form of physical security consists of site design. Site design includes features that are placed on the land around the exterior of the building. Some of these devices include fencing, barbed wire, warning signs, metal or concrete barriers, and flood lights. These forms of security are not always practical unless the facility contains highly sensitive data.

The second form of physical security consists of access control devices. Access control devices include gates, doors, and locks that are either mechanical or electronic. Locks may seem archaic but they are actually the most cost effective way to increase security.

Locked doors should be placed before all areas which can either contain hosts or potentially contain hosts.

The third form of physical security is an alarm. Alarms are one of the most important features to include in the physical network security. This will provide an immediate signal that can alert the CIO or network security administrator as well as the local law enforcement that someone has entered an area that should not have been accessed.

The fourth and final form of physical security is a camera. If someone breaking in sees a camera, they are usually deterred because being caught on camera makes them easy to identify and prosecute by the police. It is the best way to determine how, where, and when physical access was obtained. This can be useful in determining what course of action should be taken in order to mitigate an attack. How many cameras are placed in an area should be determined by the security of that area and the cost.

6.2.5 What is the VLAN Layer

The VLAN layer deals with the creation and maintenance of Virtual Local Area Networks. VLANs are used to segment networks for multiple reasons. The primary reason that you make VLANs is to group together common hosts for security purposes. For example, putting an accounting department on a separate VLAN from the marketing department is a smart decision because they should not share the same data. This breaks the network up into less secure and more secure areas. In the next section we will be discussing the implementation of VLANs.

6.2.6 What is the ACL Layer

The ACL layer is focused on the creation and maintenance of Access Control Lists. ACLs are written on both routers and firewalls. ACLs are created to allow and deny access between hosts on different networks, usually between VLANs. This makes them absolutely indispensable in the area of network security. By setting up strong access control lists, a network security professional can stop many attacks before they begin. Setting up ACLs can seem a very daunting task. There are many things to take into consideration such as return traffic or everyday traffic that is vital to operations.

These are the most important ACLs that a network security professional creates. If they are not created properly, the ACL may allow unauthorized traffic, but deny authorized traffic.

6.2.7 What is the Software Layer

The software layer is focused on keeping software up to date with upgrades and patches in order to mitigate software vulnerabilities.

Network security professionals should know what software is running on their hosts and what patch level they are currently running at to ensure that if something has happened that they can remove any unwanted software accordingly and know what vulnerabilities currently exist or have existed recently. They should also know what each new patch will do to the system it will be installed on.

6.2.8 What is the User Layer

The user layer focuses on the user's training and knowledge of security on the network. The user should understand basic concepts in network security. They should also learn what applications should not be run or installed on their system; likewise they should have an idea of how their system runs normally. We will cover how their knowledge of network security can assist the network security professional in determining if there is an issue on the network and if so, what that issue possibly is.

6.2.9 What is the Administrative Layer

The administrative layer focuses on the training of administrative users. The administrative layer includes all members of management.

It is much like the user layer except dealing with a higher level of secure data on the network. Like the user layer, administrative users should be trained on what applications should not be installed on their systems and have an understanding of how their systems run normally. They should also be trained to identify problems with the user layer. Such as recognizing an employee that installs Peer-to- Peer against security policy.

6.2.10 What is the IT Department Layer

The IT department layer contains all of the network security professionals, network technicians, architects, and support specialists. These are all of the people that make a network operational, and maintain the network, and all of the hosts that reside on that network. The IT department layer is like the administrative layer except the IT department has accounts to access any device on the network. For example, an IT department user can have read, write, and modify access to a database table structure, where an administrator or user only has read, write, and modify access to the records within that table structure.

6.3 PERIMETER PROTECTION

The enterprise network often provides employees with a connection to the Internet from the corporate headquarters campus. It is usually centralized in order to more easily protect a single interface to the public world. That's exactly where perimeter control solution such as firewalls and intrusion-detection systems (IDSs) are generally deployed to prevent malicious intrusion of unauthorized persons. It is highly recommended that firewalls be implemented at every site within an enterprise to secure internal and external traffic, and at every point of interconnection with the Internet (e.g. even a remote PC). In some cases, it is appropriate to integrate this functionality with secure IP services gateways used also for remote office and remote access IP-VPNs.

Firewalls provide a perimeter defense against unauthorized access-an essential first step when planning for Internet access. Firewalls come in various sizes and capabilities, fitting many specific network requirements depending on their point of use. An emerging trend is to use new, multi-gigabit firewalls to interconnect segments of the campus LAN, which keeps departments separate and enables communication only through firewall security policies. An IDS monitors the network to identify unauthorized users or suspicious patterns of utilization. Most IDS applications compare network traffic and host log entries to match data signatures and host address profiles indicative of hackers. Intrusion-detection software identifies traffic patterns that indicate the presence of unauthorized users. Suspicious activities trigger administrator alarms and other configurable responses. BTC Networks partners with best-of-breed companies such as Internet Security Systems (ISS) to offer specialty solutions for intrusion-detection.

Content inspection via content filtering and anti-virus systems. These tools provide essential protections for remote and local computing, ASIC-based Network Anti-virus solution can be used to secure the network from different kinds of viruses and blended threats that are of major concern for network managers nowadays.

Load-balancing. Firewalls and VPNs are compute-intensive applications and can become bottlenecks to network performance. Load balancing using an application switch mitigates this problem by distributing traffic among multiple active devices, enabling many firewalls/VPNs to operate in parallel.

In the digital world, perimeter protection is any system's first line of defense against compromise. Perimeter solutions are designed to allow an organization to draw lines around their assets and enforce them while maintaining high availability to the functionality their users need. With the vast and diverse number of services and network architectures in organizations, perimeter solutions range from firewall, ACL Router, and VPN technologies to match an organizations needs.

Firewall Solutions

Firewalls are perhaps one of the oldest and most trusted solutions used to enforce the lines that draw a network's perimeter. While not being a new idea, the technology found in today's firewall is on the cutting edge to support and protect network services. In order to provide robust security, a firewall must track and control the flow of communication passing through it. State information - derived from past communications and other applications - is an essential factor in making the control decision for new communication attempts and is one of the features of an effective firewall solution. Firewalls must be able to ensure that all network communications adhere to relevant protocol standards and are used properly. Any traffic that does not adhere to protocol standards may put business applications at risk. Firewalls play an important role in ensuring that non-compliant network traffic does not pass the outside perimeters.

ACL Router Solutions

High availability networks and internal segmentation requires a solution that can provide effective security while maintaining high speed access requirements. ACL Routers provide security in a firmware solution, capable of delivering effective security through the management of access control lists defining your users and networks, while delivering high performance in access its networks. Including features that allow a company to define virtual local are networks and manage security based on these definitions, ACL routers help an organization a cost effective means of segmentation with a maintenance nightmare.

VPN Solutions

Virtual Private networks have become an increasingly more cost effective means of connecting trusted networks and clients to the services they require, while maintaining privacy and protection over the Internet. VPN Solutions use tested and secure encryption to provide high performance tunneling to users and/or networks. With the increase of discovered vulnerabilities and steady rise of security incidents each year, VPN technology has become a necessary solution in providing secure network access of organizational services without their exposure. Just as the services and assets of an organization are dynamic, perimeter solutions are designed to be practical to maintain as the networks they protect do. Enter Edge does more than simply provide these technologies to clients on a per hock basis. We join our client's IT staff in finding the best solution to meet our client's specific needs and requirements.

6.4 NETWORK SECURITY DIMENSION

6.4.1 Security Management

Security management for networks is different for all kinds of situations. A small home is an office would only require basic security while large businesses will require high maintenance and advanced software and hardware to prevent malicious attacks from spamming.

6.4.2 Small Homes

- A basic firewall like COMODO Internet Security or a unified threat management system.
- For Windows users, basic Antivirus software like AVG Antivirus, ESET NOD32 Antivirus, Kaspersky, McAfee, Avast!, Zone Alarm Security Suite or Norton AntiVirus. An anti-spyware program such as Windows Defender or Spybot-Search and Destroy would also be a good idea. There are many other types of antivirus or anti-spyware programs out there to be considered.
- When using a wireless connection, use a robust password. Also try to use the strongest security supported by your wireless services, such as WPA2 with AES eneryption.
- If using Wireless: Change the default SSID network name, also disable SSID Broadcast; as this function is unnecessary for home use. (However, many security experts consider this to be relatively useless.
- Enable MAC Address filtering to keep track of all home network MAC devices connecting to your router.
- Assign STATIC IP addresses to network devices.
- Disable ICMP ping on router.
- Review router or firewall logs to help identify abnormal network connections or traffic to the internet.
- Use passwords for all accounts.
- Have multiple accounts per family member, using non-administrative accounts for day-to-day activities. Disable the guest account (Control Panel > Administrative Tools > Computer Management > Users).
- Raise awareness about information security to children.

6.4.3 Medium Businesses

- A fairly strong firewall or Unified Threat Management System.
- Strong Antivirus software and Internet Security Software.
- For authentication, use strong passwords and change it on a bi-weekly/monthly basis.
- When using a wireless connection, use a robust password.
- Raise awareness about physical security to employess.
- Use an optional network analyzer or network monitor.
- An enlightened administrator or manager.

6.4.4 Large Businesses

- A strong firewall and proxy to keep unwanted people out.
- A strong Antivirus software package and Internet Security Software package.
- For authentication, use strong passwords and change it on a weekly/bi-weekly basis.
- When using a wireless connection, use a robust password.
- Exercise physical security precautions to employees.
- Prepare a network analyzer or network monitor and use it when needed.
- Implement physical security management like closed circuit television for entry areas and restricted zones.
- Security fencing to mark the company's perimeter.
- Fire extinguishers for fire-sensitive areas like server rooms and security rooms.
- Security guards can help to maximize security.

6.4.5 School

- An adjustable firewall and proxy to allow authorized users access from the outside and inside.
- Strong Antivirus software and Internet Security Software packages.
- Wireless connections that lead to firewalls.
- Children's Internet Protection Act Compliance.
- Supervision of network to guarantee updates and changes based on popular site usage.
- Constant supervision by teachers, librarians, and administrators to guarantee protection against attacks by both internet and sneakernet sources.

6.4.6 Large Government

- A strong firewall and proxy to keep unwanted people out.
- Strong Antivirus software and Internet Security Software suites.
- Strong encryption.

- Whitelist authorized wireless connection, block all else.
- All network hardware is in secure zones.
- All host should be on a private network that is invisible from the outside.
- Put web servers in a DMZ, or a firewall from the outside and from the inside.
- Security fencing to mark perimeter and set wireless range to this.

6.5 NETWORK SECURITY ARCHITECTURE

In Network Security Architecture there are three defined network phases - from a basic secure network, to an autonomic network that provides enhanced situational awareness and reduces the need for human intervention, to an authenticated network that can automatically adjust its security posture to individual users.

The objective of the architecture is to create the framework that guides security technology evolution and to serve as a model for customers' security planning strategies as they evolve their networks.

This architectural framework evolves through three phases: basic, autonomic, and authenticated. This three-phase evolution, however, is not strictly sequential, since customers may achieve different levels of security at different times in their networks, based on their own unique requirements. Rather, these phases should be viewed as different maturity levels with associated functionality that, in some cases, already exists in solutions. As networks and solutions evolve from today's primary focus on "keeping the bad guys out," we can expect increased focus on taking human involvement out of the attack-response process and on "enabling the good."

In each of the three phases, the architecture maps across the three key network domains: the applications that run on the network; the network itself; and the various connected user devices, including wired and wireless, handheld and desktop.

Securing the network domain involves defending the network from attacks and protecting device-management and network-management traffic, and includes:

Network perimeter protection of key security zones:

- safeguarding the network interior from insider attacks, and providing a secondary layer of defense and detection for perimeter protection;
- authentication and integrity of signaling control and management traffic, such as user provisioning, network routing, and topology control data; and
- encryption of sensitive data, such as user passwords, security configuration data, and lawful intercept configuration data.

Network boundaries, defined by zones of trust, need to be protected from intrusions and attacks. This protection is accomplished by sanitizing and selectively allowing connections to cross zone boundaries, and is supplemented by monitoring network traffic patterns within the zones to detect anomalies and attack patterns.

6.5.1 Phase One: Basic secure network

The first "basic" phase of the Network Security Architecture focuses mainly on "keeping the bad guys out," which means ensuring that unauthorized users as well as malicious and unsolicited traffic is kept out of sensitive zones in the network. It also means protecting valuable data stored on the network from compromise, whether accidental or deliberate. In the basic secure network (Figure 6.1), components across all three domains (application, network, and device) work together using a "layered defense" approach to address different kinds of threats, and to ensure that there is no single point of security failure.

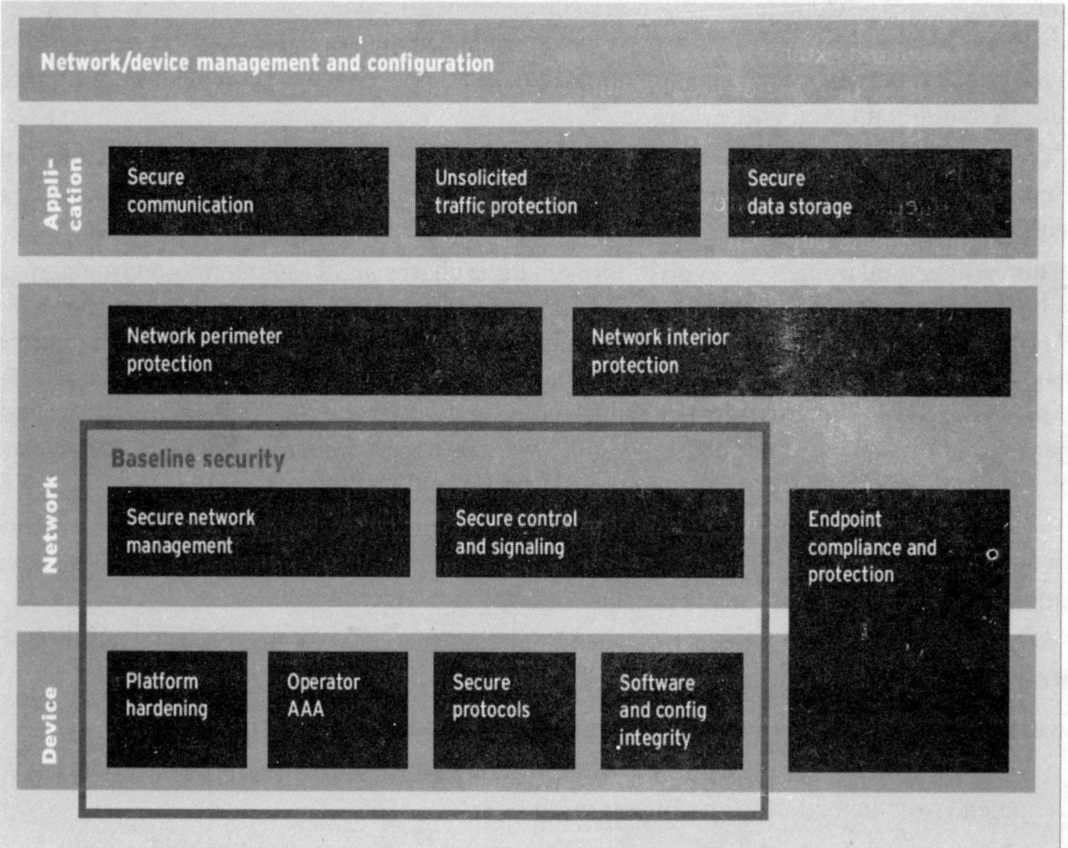

Figure 6.1: Phase One - Basic Secure Network

At the application domain, what users care about most is that their valuable data - credit card numbers, personal address books, documents, and financial records as examples - is stored securely in the network, accessible only by authorized users, protected from accidental or malicious loss, and properly backed up, as well as transported in an equally secure manner. In the basic phase, solutions that address the network domain focus on protecting both the perimeter and interior of the network. Solutions to protect the network perimeter include enforcing network segmentation - by providing various types of protection with firewalls, deep packet inspection, intrusion prevention/ detection, malware scanning, and content inspection - at the boundaries of network zones. Protecting the network interior involves enabling detection and mitigation of threats that originate inside secure network zones, as well as providing a secondary defense for threats that make it through perimeter defenses. In addition, the basic phase provides endpoint security, giving network operators the ability to set security policies that will be enforced on devices before allowing them to join the network. If a device fails a compliance check, the device may be admitted with restricted access (i.e., quarantined), it may be sent to a remediation portal (to update malware definitions and re-scan, for example), or it may be blocked from the network altogether.

6.5.2 Phase Two: Autonomic Network

The next phase of the architecture focuses on reducing the complexity and need for human involvement in day-to-day security management activities. In a world where security attacks can impact the reliability of the network within seconds, the network needs to have the intelligence and inherent situational awareness to be able to automatically protect itself and recover from threats, on a second-by-second basis. As well, the network needs to be able to automatically adapt as more and more applications actively seek to directly control the network configuration. For instance, an application that sets up a peer-to-peer whiteboard or other collaboration session, or a videoconference session, needs to signal the network to dynamically allocate more bandwidth or other resources to ensure quality of service. In such cases, the network must be able to quickly and automatically recognize those application requests that are legitimate and compliant with the network policy and those that are not.

An autonomic network, then, is able to respond without human intervention more quickly to attacks across all three domains (device, network, and application) to contain any damage immediately and operate seamlessly under many different attack conditions.

An autonomic network can also automatically adjust to the needs of specific applications to create an optimal operating environment for them. Furthermore, such a network will provide more meaningful and actionable security reporting to operators.

The ultimate goal in Phase Two is to implement a common approach through which network elements and applications alike can generate and report relevant events to a centralized event correlation and remediation function that is responsible for collecting, normalizing, and processing network-wide security events (Figure 6.2). With this information provided on a real-time basis, the network can reliably identify attack patterns and anomalies, effectively detect and mitigate such attacks as distributed denial of service (DDoS) and coordinated hacking attempts, reconfigure network devices in real time, and take corrective actions to protect key resources.

A security information manager (SIM) function is central to realizing autonomic network capabilities. This function enables the intelligent correlation of events across the entire network, followed by autonomic action under attack circumstances. The SIM function would then report both the correlated information and network response, in real time, to network security operators.

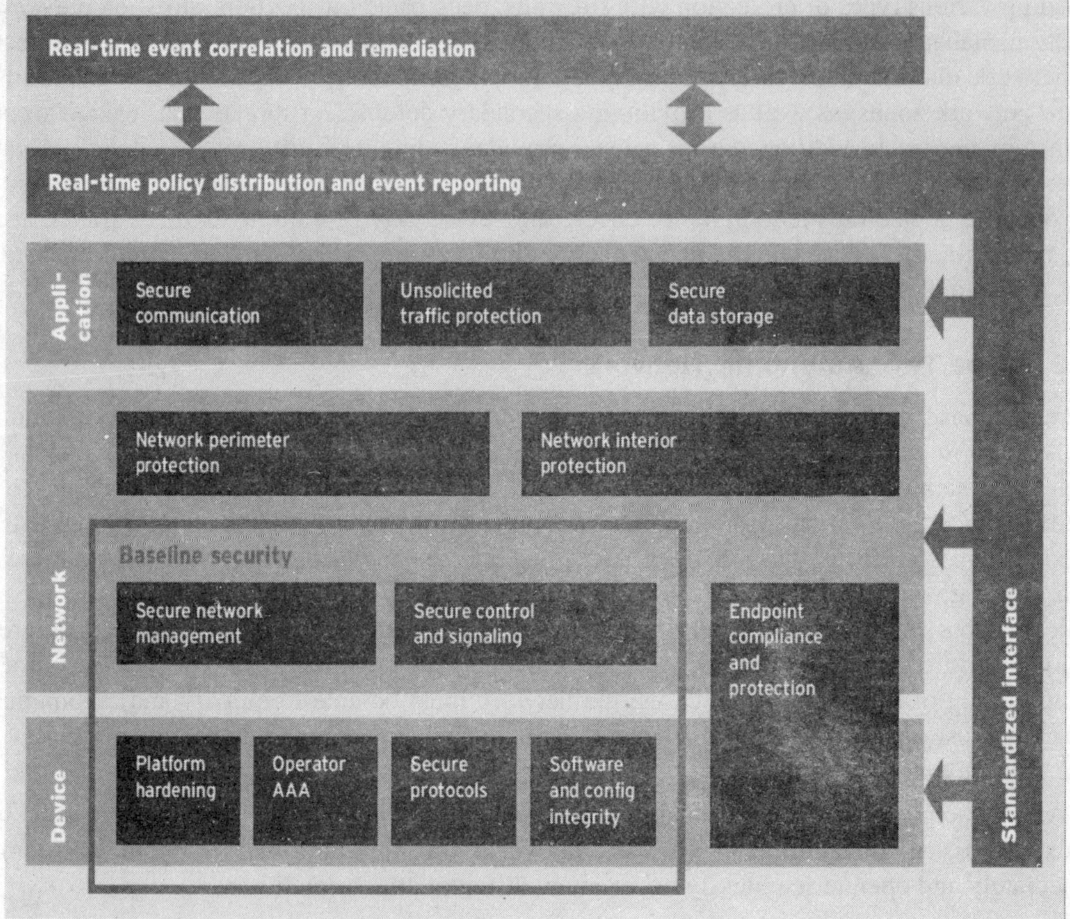

Figure 6.2: Phase Two - Autonomic network

This capability would serve to simplify the information with which security operators need to contend, by eliminating false positives, correlating and normalizing related information, and presenting the most meaningful view for the given audience.

In this way, network personnel can obtain a meaningful real-time report of the state of their network security "health," enabling them to monitor the working conditions of their various defenses and alerting them when any part of the security system fails.

6.5.3 Phase Three: Authenticated network

As more mobile users use a variety of devices to access the network, the traditional concept of a physical perimeter no longer applies: in many cases, the perimeter is, effectively, wherever the users are. Thus, the third phase of the architecture focuses on tying together traditional network security approaches with network awareness of both the user's access device and the user's physical environment, to bring an entirely new dimension to network security.

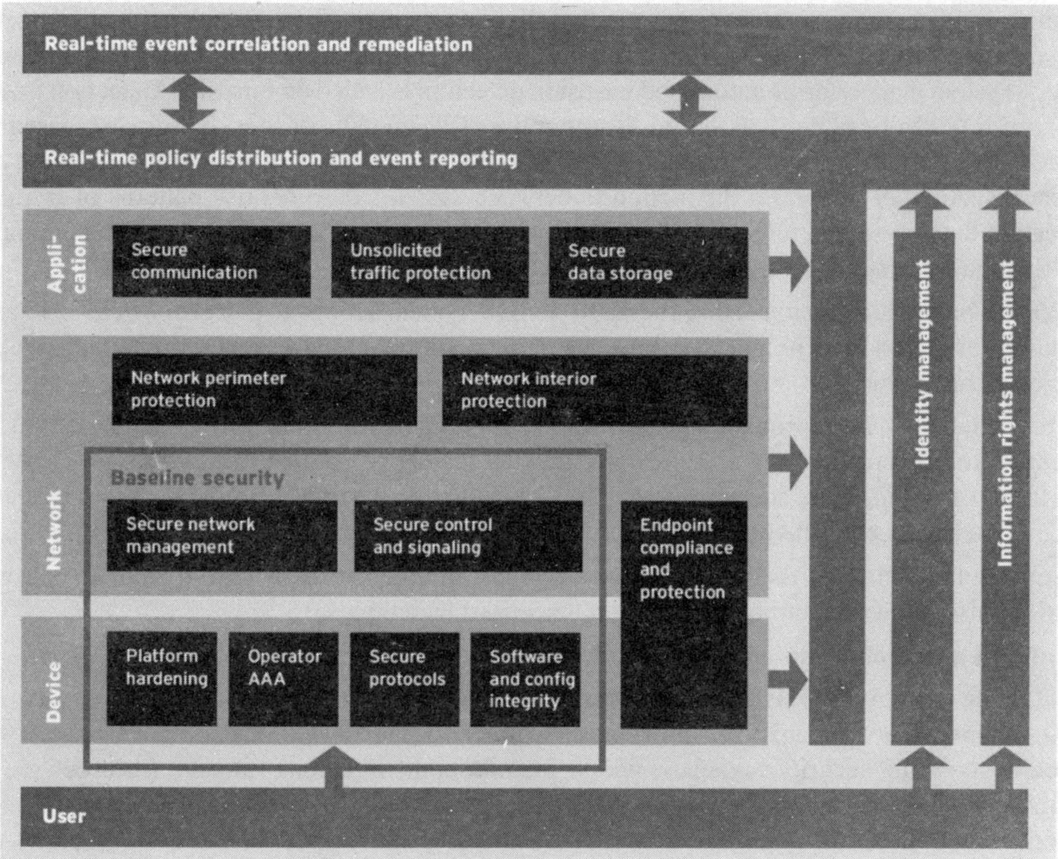

Figure 6.3: Phase Three – Authenticated network

In other words, Phase Three involves enabling the network to recognize who users are, what devices they are using at any given time, and where they are located. Phase Three also involves enabling the network to adjust its security posture to individual users, determine which security policies to enforce given the particular circumstances under which a user is accessing the network, and allow users to access only that information to which they are entitled under the circumstances.

Enabling these capabilities are two fundamental new elements introduced in Phase Three: identity management, and information rights management (Figure 6.3).

6.6 INTRUSION DETECTION

In Information Security, intrusion detection is the act of detecting actions that attempt to compromise the confidentiality, integrity or availability of a resource. When Intrusion detection takes a preventive measure without direct human intervention, then it becomes an Intrusion-prevention system.

Intrusion detection can be performed manually or automatically. Manual intrusion detection might take place by examining log files or other evidence for signs of intrusions, including network traffic. A system that performs automated intrusion detection is called an Intrusion Detection System (IDS). An IDS can be either host-based, if it monitors system calls or logs, or network-based if it monitors the flow of network packets. Modern IDSs are usually a combination of these two approaches. Another important distinction is between systems that identify patterns of traffic or application data presumed to be malicious (misuse detection systems), and systems that compare activities against a 'normal' baseline (anomaly detection systems).

When a probable intrusion is discovered by an IDS, typical actions to perform would be logging relevant information to a file or database, generating an email alert, or generating a message to a pager or mobile phone.

Determining what the probable intrusion actually is and taking some form of action to stop it or prevent it from happening again are usually outside the scope of intrusion detection. However, some forms of automatic reaction can be implemented through the interaction of Intrusion Detection Systems and access control systems such as firewalls.

Some authors classify the identification of attack attempts at the source system as extrusion detection (also known as outbound intrusion detection) techniques.

Intrusion prevention is an evolution of intrusion detection.

Intrusion detection (ID) is a type of security management system for computers and networks. An ID system gathers and analyzes information from various areas within a computer or a network to identify possible security breaches, which include both intrusions (attacks from outside the organization) and misuse (attacks from within the organization). ID uses vulnerability assessment (sometimes refered to as scanning), which is a technology developed to assess the security of a computer system or network.

Intrusion detection functions include:

- Monitoring and analyzing both user and system activities
- Analyzing system configurations and vulnerabilities
- Assessing system and file integrity
- Ability to recognize patterns typical of attacks
- Analysis of abnormal activity patterns
- Tracking user policy violations

ID systems are being developed in response to the increasing number of attacks on major sites and networks, including those of the Pentagon, the White House, NATO, and the U.S. Defense Department. The safeguarding of security is becoming increasingly difficult, because the possible technologies of attack are becoming ever more sophisticated; at the same time, less technical ability is required for the novice attacker, because proven past methods are easily accessed through the Web.

Typically, an ID system follows a two-step process. The first procedures are host-based and are considered the passive component, these include: inspection of the system's configuration files to detect inadvisable settings; inspection of the password files to detect inadvisable passwords; and inspection of other system areas to detect policy violations. The second procedures are network-based and are considered the active component: mechanisms are set in place to reenact known methods of attack and to record system responses.

6.6.1 The Need for Intrusion Detection

Intrusion prevention measures, such as encryption and authentication, can be used in ad-hoc networks to reduce intrusions, but cannot eliminate them. For example, encryption and authentication cannot defend against compromised mobile nodes, which often carry the private keys. Integrity validation using redundant information, such as those being used in secure routing also relies on the trust-worthiness of other nodes, which could likewise be a weak link for sophisticated attacks.

The history of security research has taught us a valuable lesson no matter how many intrusion prevention measures are inserted in a network, there are always some weak links that one could exploit to break in. Intrusion detection presents a second wall of defense and it is a necessity in any high-survivability network.

In summary, mobile computing environment has inherent vulnerabilities that are not easily preventable. To secure mobile computing applications, we need to deploy intrusion detection and response techniques, and further research is necessary to adapt these techniques to the new environment, from their original applications index wired network. In this paper, we focus on a particular type of mobile computing environment called mobile ad-hoc networks and propose a new model for intrusion detection and response for this environment.

We will first give a background on intrusion detection, then present our new architecture, followed by an experimental study to evaluate its feasibility.

6.7 NEED FOR NETWORK MONITORING FOR INTRUSION DETECTION

In the world of intrusion detection, we tend to focus on detecting attacks and clearly anomalous activity. However, another important component of a complete intrusion detection solution is basic network monitoring and traffic analysis. Network monitoring collects information on connections, while traffic analysis allows us to see what services are being used on a network and to compare that against the activity that we should be seeing. This allows us to identify unauthorized services being used within a network, as well as gaps in network perimeter defenses. By combining basic network monitoring and traffic analysis with other intrusion detection methods, you can establish better overall security. In this article, I will present an introduction to network monitoring and traffic analysis.

An intrusion detection solution that simply looks for attacks is missing a key component: the identification of unauthorized and undesirable traffic that is not obviously malicious. Such traffic could be generated by misconfigured equipment, or a host that is providing or using unauthorized services, either accidentally or purposely. Perhaps a mistake in a firewall rule set is allowing certain types of external traffic to enter your internal network. Perhaps trojans are communicating through

IRC. If you are unaware that these problems exist, you are providing easy targets for attackers. This may lead to more intrusion attempts and a higher chance of a successful intrusion occurring. So identifying unauthorized traffic can be critical to providing and maintaining a good level of security for your environment.

6.7.1 Network Monitoring

In order to perform basic network monitoring, you need to collect information on traffic at various points within your network. Although you definitely want to pay attention to your network borders, you should also look at purely internal traffic. If you have internal hosts providing unauthorized services for other internal hosts, you will miss this traffic if you only look at your borders. Various tools, including sniffers and packet capture utilities (such as tcpdump) and some intrusion detection systems (such as NFR Security's NID) and Internet Security Systems (ISS's) RealSecure), can be used to gather the appropriate information on traffic.

When you are preparing to collect data on network traffic, it's very important to get only the minimum information needed. Unless you are in an environment with a very low volume of traffic, trying to store the headers and contents of every packet will be far too resource-intensive. Besides, you can do initial traffic analysis simply by looking at a handful of the characteristics of packets and ignoring the packets' payloads altogether. Later, you can gather detailed information on particular services or hosts that require further investigation. One note of caution on this - by ignoring payloads, you will be unable to verify that the communications occurring on that port match the expected service. For example, a Trojan could use TCP port 21, making it appear during your analysis that FTP activity is occurring.

In most environments, you will want to focus your analysis on TCP, UDP and ICMP traffic. Of course, you may also be interested in identifying protocols other than these that are in use on your network. But for the sake of our discussion, we will stick to these three protocols, as we are primarily interested in what TCP and UDP-based services are being used. The most fundamental elements you should examine during traffic analysis are:

- Source and destination IP addresses.
- For TCP or UDP traffic, the source and destination ports.
- For ICMP traffic, only the contents of Destination Unreachable (ICMP type 3) messages. These will be useful in identifying failed and blocked connection attempts.

You'll want to collect these traffic elements for a period of time. Depending on the volume of traffic that you see, you might start by collecting traffic for a few minutes, hours or days. Remember that the collection can be very resource-intensive, so it's best to start with a small sample and then collect larger samples later as resources permit. It's a good idea to either collect information over a long period of time or to do short collections repeatedly and on different days and times to get a more accurate sampling of data. This also allows you to create a baseline of sorts. It is very important to realize that by doing monitoring periodically, you cannot be sure that you are catching everything going on. You will only catch activity that occurs during the monitoring period.

Depending on what tools you have in your environment, you may be able to capture information on TCP traffic by packet or by connection. Ideally, you'd like to do both. By looking at TCP connections, you'll see what traffic is being permitted. However, if you only look at successful connections, you are missing valuable information on failed connections. Capturing data on TCP packets and querying it to reveal unsuccessful connections (those that lack the full TCP three-way handshake), as well as examining the contents of ICMP Destination Unreachable messages, can provide additional valuable data for analysis.

There are four different types of TCP activity that we should consider:

- **Successful connection:** three-way handshake is completed successfully.
- **Failed connection:** client gets no response to a connection attempt. The client often does two or three retries with brief delays between each.
- **Blocked connection:** client gets a negative response to a connection attempt, such as a TCP RST packet or an ICMP host unreachable or port unreachable packet.
- **Aborted connection:** three-way handshake is started but never completed (client crashed, network connection was lost, etc.) In most cases, you should ignore these, unless you're seeing large numbers of these.

6.7.2 Traffic Analysis

Once you've collected information from a particular point on your network for a period of time, the real fun begins - performing traffic analysis on the data. You should approach this differently depending on what your environment is like. If you permit everything that isn't explicitly denied, then you should look for those items that are explicitly denied. If you deny everything that isn't explicitly permitted, then you'll need to look for those items that aren't explicitly permitted. Of course, in many environments, no single person will know what activity is really unauthorized, particularly on a server-by-server or host-by-host basis. In those cases, your best approach may be to create a report that shows all types of activity occurring; then consult with the appropriate people to determine which activity is unauthorized.

When you are starting your traffic analysis, you should use a statistical approach. You certainly don't want to look at each packet; instead, you should focus on discovering which servers and ports are being used. So we want to know that there was an IRC connection from client X to your primary DNS server, but during the initial analysis, we don't care how many times that connection occurred, or how many packets were sent in that connection. Likewise, with a connectionless protocol such as UDP, we are initially interested in knowing what server ports were used, but not how many packets each received. By summarizing the activity and ignoring the finer details, we can reduce the amount of material for analysis to a manageable amount. Once we find the most significant details, we can return to the original traffic data to get more information.

At this stage, you're going to want to do some data validation on the IP addresses. Any traffic that has suspicious or improper IP addresses should be examined more closely. For example, packets coming from the Internet should not have reserved IP addresses. You should also check to confirm that all addresses for internal hosts are in your defined internal IP ranges. This sounds simple, but in some environments, there are many different IP ranges in use, and it may be difficult to develop an accurate list of valid internal IP addresses. Checking internal addresses can help you in identifying misconfigured or unauthorized equipment and other items that need to be investigated. The IP address information may also be added to your network intrusion detection system so that it will alert when improper IP addresses are used.

There are many different ways that we can look at the data. One way that we can use the data is to find port scans and host scans against your internal hosts, particularly those that might occur over a long period of time. This can be done by sorting the data by client, then looking at how many server ports it attempts to contact, or how many different servers it attempts to contact. Those with the highest values should be investigated further to explain the activity. When using data for this purpose or others described here, you're certainly not going to be able to view it all manually. Instead, you should put the data into a database and use queries to crunch the numbers and produce a report for you.

One difficulty you will encounter is how to handle UDP packets. Because UDP is connectionless, it is often unclear which host is the server and which is the client. You can try to query the data in order to find out which host sent the first UDP packet to the other, but this may be difficult, and it will produce some inaccurate results because it will miss packets sent before the monitoring begins. You may achieve better results by sorting the data by source host and by destination host. If you find a host that always uses the same UDP port number when communicating with several other hosts, it's a fairly safe bet that it's acting as a server. You'll need to indicate in your database which entries are client to server and which are server to client.

When you're ready to analyze the traffic, there are many different ways to begin. One method would be to separate the UDP traffic and TCP connections and connection attempts into three groups:

- External client and internal server. In most cases, the source addresses and ports are irrelevant; all you will want to examine initially are the destination addresses and ports.
- Internal client and internal server. Although you'll want to focus on destination addresses and ports, source addresses may also be quite important.
- Internal client and external server. If outgoing connections are unrestricted in your environment, you can skip this data when performing your analysis. If outgoing connections are restricted, you will probably want to focus most on the destination ports.

The ICMP traffic should be placed into the same groups, except that the destination address of the ICMP packets should be aligned with the TCP client address.

Within each group, sort the TCP information by server port or by server address and server port. This will show you what services are being used and what servers are running them. If you aren't familiar with any of the port numbers, there are many good references on the Internet that can tell you what typically listens at that port number.

Next Steps

Once you determine that suspicious or unauthorized activity is occurring, obviously you will want to determine why the activity is occurring. You may want to use the original traffic logs to get more information involving the services and hosts in question. If your perimeter security devices are permitting traffic through that they shouldn't, you'll want to review firewall rule sets, router ACL's and the like. If hosts are providing unauthorized services, you'll want to check those hosts for misconfiguration or signs of compromise, depending on the situation.

Based on the results of the traffic analysis and subsequent investigations, you should tune your intrusion detection sensors. This might include items such as:

- Alerting on traffic from internal hosts that use unauthorized addresses
- Alerting when a host uses or attempts to use an unauthorized service
- Alerting when a host attempts to connect to particular internal or external hosts
- Optimizing by enabling or disabling code that performs full analysis on particular protocols or services, in order to save IDS sensor resources.

By adding basic network monitoring and traffic analysis to your existing intrusion detection framework, you can improve the overall security of your environment. Network monitoring and traffic analysis are certainly useful as an auditing method, and they can permit you to reduce the chance that a successful intrusion will occur. They can also assist you in tuning your intrusion detection sensors more effectively.

Due to a growing number of intrusion events and also because the Internet and local networks have become so ubiquitous, organizations are increasingly implementing various systems that monitor IT security breaches. This is the second article devoted to these systems. The previous article dealt with IDS categorization and architecture. At this point we will provide further in depth guidance. This includes an overview of the classification of intrusion detection systems and fundamental concepts of IDS methodology: audit trail analysis and on-the-fly processing as well as anomaly detection and signature detection approaches. We will also discuss the primary intrusion detection techniques.

Primarily, an IDS is concerned with the detection of hostile actions. This network security tool uses either of two main techniques (described in more detail below). The first one, anomaly detection, explores issues in intrusion detection associated with deviations from normal system or user behavior. The second employs signature detection to discriminate between anomaly or attack patterns (signatures) and known intrusion detection signatures. Both methods have their distinct advantages and disadvantages as well as suitable application areas of intrusion detection.

When considering the area being the source of data used for intrusion detection, another classification of intrusion detection systems can be used in terms of the type of the protected system. There is a family of IDS tools that use information derived from a single host (system) host based IDS (HIDS) and those IDSs that exploit information obtained from a whole segment of a local network (network based IDS, i.e. NIDS).

6.7.3 Two Primary Types of HIDS can be Distinguished

Systems that monitor incoming connection attempts. These examine host-based incoming and outgoing network connections. These are particularly related to the unauthorized connection attempts to TCP or UDP ports and can also detect incoming portscans.

- Systems that examine network traffic (packets) that attempts to access the host. These systems protect the host by intercepting suspicious packets and looking for aberrant payloads (packet inspection).
- Systems that monitor login activity onto the networking layer of their protected host (Host Sentry). Their role is to monitor log-in and log-out attempts, looking for unusual activity on a system occurring at unexpected times, particular network locations or detecting multiple login attempts (particularly failed ones).
- Systems that monitor actions of a super-user (root) who has the highest privileges (Log Check). IDS scans for unusual activity, increased super-user activity or actions performed at particular times, etc.
- Systems that monitor file system integrity (Tripwire, AIDE). Tools that have this ability (integrity checker) allow the detection of any changes to the files that are critical for the operating system.
- Systems that monitor the system register state (Windows platform only). They are designed to detect any illegal changes in the system register and alert the system administrator to this fact.
- Kernel based intrusion detection systems. These are especially prevalent within Linux (LIDS, Open Wall). These systems examine the state of key operating system files and streams, preventing buffer overflow, blocking unusual interprocess communications, preventing an intruder from attacking the system. In addition, they can block a part of the actions undertaken by the super-user (restricting privileges).

The HIDS reside on a particular computer and provide protection for a specific computer system. They are not only equipped with system monitoring facilities but also include other modules of a typical IDS, for example the response module (see Part I of the cycle).

HIDS products such as Snort, Dragon Squire, Emerald expert-BSM, NFR HID, Intruder Alert all perform this type of monitoring.

The network-based type of IDS (NIDS) produces data about local network usage. The NIDS reassemble and analyze all network packets that reach the network interface card operating in promiscuous mode. They do not only deal with packets going to a specific host - since all the machines in a network segment benefit from the protection of the NIDS. Network-based IDS can also be installed on active network elements, for example on routers.

Since intrusion detection (for example flood-type attack) employs statistical data on the network load, a certain type of dedicated NIDS can be separately distinguished, for example, those that monitor the traffic (Novell Analyzer, Microsoft Network Monitor).

The IDS can operate as standalone, centralized applications or integrated applications that create a distributed system. The latter have a particular architecture with autonomous agents that are able to take preemptive and reactive measures and even to move over the network. The AAFID architecture of these systems has been presented in Part I of the cycle.

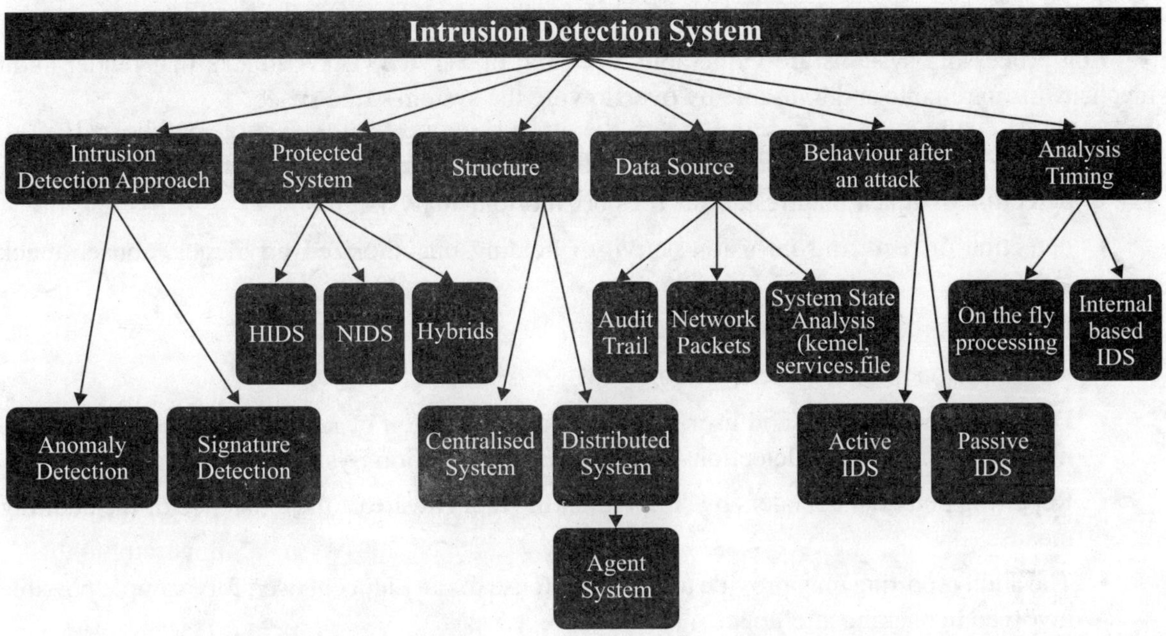

Figure 6.4: Classification of Intrusion Detection Systems

6.7.4 Audit trail processing vs. on-the-fly processing

Intrusion detection systems can run on either a continuous or periodic feed of information (Real-time IDS and Interval-based IDS respectively) and hence they use two different intrusion detection approaches. **Audit trail analysis** is the prevalent method used by periodically operated systems. In contrast, the IDS deployable in real-time environments are designed for online monitoring and analyzing system events and user actions.

6.7.5 Audit Trail Processing

There are many issues related to audit trail (event log) processing. Storing audit trail reports in a single file must be avoided since intruders may use this feature to make unwanted changes. It is far better to keep a certain number of event log copies spread over the network, though it would imply adding some overheads to both the system and network.

Further, from the functionality point of view, recording every event possible means a noticeable consumption of system resources (both the local system and network involved). Log compression, instead, would increase the system load. Specifying which events are to be audited is difficult because certain types of attacks may pass undetected. It is also difficult to predict how large audit files can be - through experience one can only make a rough estimate. Also, an appropriate setting of a storage period for current audit files is not a straightforward task. In general, this depends on a specific IDS solution and its correlation engine. Certainly, archive files should be stored as copies for retrieval analysis purposes.

Log processing systems are vulnerable to Denial of Service (DoS) attacks that render audit mechanisms unreliable and unusable by overflowing the system's free space.

The main reasons for having an audit function include:

- detection of attack manifestations for post-mortem analysis;
- detection of recurring intrusion activity (yielding unauthorized privileges, abuse, attack attempts);
- identification of successful intruders;
- identification of own system weaknesses;
- Development of access and user signatures and definition of network traffic rules that are important for anomaly detection-based Intrusion Detection Systems.
- Repelling potential intruders by simply making them aware of the existence of the auditing means.
- The audit reporting may provide a form of defense for an innocent user, for example possible involved in hacking attempts.
- The log event-based IDS method needs to have the following capabilities:
- Allowing of parameterization for easy recording of system event logs and user activities,
- Providing an option of self-disengagement of logging mechanisms in the event of insufficient space or DoS attacks;
- Audit trail processing using additional mechanisms (aggregation, artificial intelligence, and data mining) because of large file sizes,
- A reasonable minimum system resource consumption for auditing purposes.

Examples of intrusion detection systems that use audit trail processing are:

- SecureView that checks logs produced by CheckPoint Firewall-1
- CMDS (Computer Misuse Detection System). With its built-in expert system, it analyzes all event logs to recognize abnormal user behavior.
- ACID (Analysis Console for Intrusion Databases) - is a PHP-based analysis engine to search and process a database of incidents generated by various security tools such as IDSs, firewalls and network traffic analyzers. ACID has a user query builder, which can analyze packets down to their payload, in order to find identical alerts among databases, which match certain criteria. It can also manage alerts and generate a variety of statistics.

6.7.6 On-the fly processing

With on the fly processing, an IDS performs online verification of system events. Generally, a stream of network packets is constantly monitored constantly. With this type of processing, intrusion detection uses the knowledge of current activities over the network to sense possible attack attempts (it does not look for successful attacks in the past).

Given the computation complexity, the algorithms that are used here are limited to quick and efficient procedures that are often algorithmically simple. This is due to a compromise between the main requisite - attack detection capability and the complexity of data processing mechanisms used in the detection itself.

At the same time, construction of an on-the-fly processing IDS tool requires a large amount of RAM (buffers) since no data storage is used. Therefore, such an IDS may sometime miss packets, because realistic processing of too many packets is not available.

The amount of data collected by the detector is small since it views only buffer contents. Hence, only small portions of information can be analyzed for searching certain values or sequences.

The main method used in real-time detecting is simply looking for character strings in the transport layer packets (3. and 4.), particularly in their headers. This may be done by monitoring IP addresses that initiate connections, or by checking for misappropriate TCP/IP flag combination (to capture packets that do not match known standards). An example of packet pathology is when both the source and destination port addresses are set to 21. This is not compliant with FTP specifications since the source port number must be greater than 1024. Another example may be 0 Value Service-type, a packet with SYN and FIN flags both set, mismatch in numbering of sequences or acknowledgements, ACK value set to a non-zero number with the ACK flag not set, etc.

As a contrast with standard inspection methods, only selective packets in a data stream get inspected, and the inspection process only looks for "state" information, such as whether a packet contains malicious code.

A somewhat different method is applied in the application layer analysis (FTP, POP3, HTTP, etc.). Application-based IDS employ so-called standard packet inspection to analyze the TCP packet payload (headers are excluded). With this method, only selective, correlated packets in a data stream get examined and the inspection process looks for information about whether a packet matches typical packets (commands) of a given protocol. Thus, POP3 denial of service vulnerability is exploited by saturating POP3 server with multiple requests to execute a command. Here, the attack signature is developed by the number of commands sent by a given system and by establishing the alarm threshold. The method assumes that anomalies found in packet inspection, checking of packet size and threshold values are manifestations of a denial of service attack, also at the transport layer, for example Ping of Death attack. Another example of standard packet inspection IDSs include detecting email viruses before they get to email boxes by looking for matching email titles or attachment names. One may also search for malicious code which may compromise the system if it is attacked by, for example, buffer overflow exploits looking for signatures that monitor the user session status to disallow, for example, listing of directory structure on a FTP server before a successful user login. A drawback of the high layer analysis approach lies in the fact that it is time-consuming and operating environment-dependent (application layer protocols that vary from operating system to operating system).

The real-time based IDSs offer the following advantages:

- they excel at detecting attacks in progress and even responding to (blocking) them;
- the ability to cover network-inherent security holes associated with vulnerability to many types of attacks, particularly DoS, which cannot be detected using a common audit trail analysis approach-network traffic analysis is needed here;
- the system resources are less consumed than in the case of audit trail processing.

Disadvantages include:

- Source identification is accomplished based on the network address derived from the packet (not, for example, with using the network ID[1]). The source address may be spoofed, making attacks harder to trace and respond to automatically.
- That they cannot handle encrypted packets thereby not providing essential information required for intrusion detection.
- Since the analytical module uses a limited portion of source information (buffer content only), its detection capability is limited.
- A continuous scanning of network traffic reduces the network throughout the segment on which the IDS sits. This is of particular importance when an IDS tool is deployed near the firewall.

6.7.7 Anomaly vs. Signature Detection

Intrusion detection systems must be capable of distinguishing between normal (not security-critical) and abnormal user activities, to discover malicious attempts in time. However translating user behaviors (or a complete user-system session) in a consistent security-related decision is often not that simple - many behavior patterns are unpredictable and unclear (Fig. 2). In order to classify actions, intrusion detection systems take advantage of the anomaly detection approach, sometimes referred to as behavior based or attack signatures i.e. a descriptive material on known abnormal behavior (signature detection)], also called knowledge based.

Behaviour

Figure 6.5: Behavior of the user in the system

6.7.8 Normal Behavior Patterns Anomaly Detection

Normal behavior patterns are useful in predicting both user and system behavior. Here, anomaly detectors construct profiles that represent normal usage and then use current behavior data to detect a possible mismatch between profiles and recognize possible attack attempts.

In order to match event profiles, the system is required to produce initial user profiles to train the system with regard to legitimate user behaviors. There is a problem associated with profiling: when the system is allowed to "learn" on its own, experienced intruders (or users) can train the system to the point where previously intrusive behavior becomes normal behavior. An inappropriate profile will be able to detect all possible intrusive activities. Furthermore, there is an obvious need for profile updating and system training which a difficult and time-consuming task is.

Given a set of normal behavior profiles, everything that does not match the stored profile is considered to be a suspicious action. Hence, these systems are characterized by very high detection efficiency (they are able to recognize many attacks that are new to the system), but their tendency to generate false alarms is generally a problem.

Advantages of this anomaly detection method are: possibility of detection of novel attacks as intrusions; anomalies are recognized without getting inside their causes and characteristics; less dependence of IDSs on operating environment (as compared with attack signature-based systems); ability to detect abuse of user privileges.

The biggest disadvantages of this method are:

- A substantial false alarm rate. System usage is not monitored during the profile construction and training phases. Hence, all user activities skipped during these phases will be illegitimate.
- User behaviors can vary with time, thereby requiring a constant update of the normal behavior profile database (this may imply the need to close the system from time to time and may also be associated with greater false alarm rates).
- The necessity of training the system for changing behavior makes a system immune to anomalies detected during the training phase (false negative).

6.7.9 Misbehavior Signatures - Signature Detection

Systems possessing information on abnormal, unsafe behavior (attack signature-based systems) are often used in real-time intrusion detection systems (because of their low computational complexity).

The misbehavior signatures fall into two categories:

- **Attack signatures:** they describe action patterns that may pose a security threat. Typically, they are presented as a time-dependent relationship between series of activities that may be interlaced with neutral ones.
- **Selected text strings:** signatures to match text strings which look for suspicious action (for example - calling /etc/passwd).

Any action that is not clearly considered prohibited is allowed. Hence, their accuracy is very high (low number of false alarms). Typically, they do not achieve completeness and are not immune to novel attacks.

There are two main approaches associated with signature detection (already mentioned in the section describing real-time detectors):

- Verification of the pathology of lower layer packets- many types of attacks (Ping of Death or TCP Stealth Scanning) exploit flaws in IP, TCP, UDP or ICMP packets. With a very simple verification of flags set on specific packets it is possible to determine whether a packet is legitimate or not. Difficulties may be encountered with possible packet fragmentation and the need for re-assembly. Similarly, some problems may be associated with the TCP/IP layer of the system being protected. It is well known that hackers use packet fragmentation to bypass many IDS tools.
- Verification of application layer protocols - many types of attacks (WinNuke) exploit programming flaws, for example, out-of-band data sent to an established network connection. In order to effectively detect such attacks, the IDS must have implemented many application layer protocols.

The signature detection methods have the following advantages: very low false alarm rate, simple algorithms, easy creation of attack signature databases, easy implementation and typically minimal system resource usage.

Some disadvantages:

- Difficulties in updating information on new types of attacks (when maintaining the attack signature database updated as appropriate).
- They are inherently unable to detect unknown, novel attacks. A continuous update of the attack signature database for correlation is a must.
- Maintenance of an IDS is necessarily connected with analyzing and patching of security holes, which is a time-consuming process.
- The attack knowledge is operating environment-dependent, so misbehavior signature-based intrusion detection systems must be configured in strict compliance with the operating system (version, platform, applications used etc.)
- They seemed to have difficulty handling internal attacks. Typically, abuse of legitimate user privileges is not sensed by the system as a malicious activity (because of the lack of information on user privileges and attack signature structure).

Commercially offered IDS products often use the signature detection method for two reasons. Firstly, it is easier for a given signature to be associated with a known attack abstraction and to assign a name to an attack, e.g. Ping of Death, which is used worldwide (a suitable signature can be attached to the installation version), than the normal behavior of a certain John Brown in an organization. Secondly, the attack signature database must be updated regularly (by adding signatures of newly discovered attacks and exploits), which may create a fairly good source of income for vendors of IDS tools. A database update is at the same time a less cumbersome task than that associated with the change of typical user behavior profiles. In the latter case, a temporary closing down of the system may be required, what cannot be tolerated on certain applications.

The example below presents an attack signature taken from the Snort program that detects ping ICMP packets larger than 800 bytes, incoming from an external network and associated with any port:

Parameter Pattern Matching

The third method of intrusion detection is subtler than the two mentioned earlier. It reasons on the fact, that system administrators monitor various systems and network attributes (not necessarily targeting security issues). As a rule, information obtained in this way has a constant specific environment. This method involves the use of day-to-day operational experience of the administrators as the basis for detecting anomalies. It can be considered as a special case of Normal Profile Methods. The difference lies in the fact that a profile here is part of the human knowledge.

This is a very powerful technique, since it allows intrusions based on unknown type attacks. The system operator can detect subtle changes that are not obvious to the operator himself. Its inherent disadvantage is connected with the fact that humans can process and hence understand only a limited portion of information at a time, what means that certain attacks may pass undetected.

Data processing techniques used in intrusion detection systems:

Depending on the type of approach taken in intrusion detection, various processing mechanisms (techniques) are employed for data that is to reach an IDS. Below, several systems are described briefly:

- **Expert systems**, these work on a previously defined set of rules describing an attack. All security related events incorporated in an audit trail are translated in terms of if-then-else rules. Examples are Wisdom & Sense and Computer Watch (developed at AT&T).
- **Signature analysis:** Similarly to expert System approach, this method is based on the attack knowledge. They transform the semantic description of an attack into the appropriate audit trail format. Thus, attack signatures can be found in logs or input data streams in a straightforward way. An attack scenario can be described, for example, as a sequence of audit events that a given attack generates or patterns of searchable data that are captured in the audit trail. This method uses abstract equivalents of audit trail data. Detection is accomplished by using common text string matching mechanisms. Typically, it is a very powerful technique and as such very often employed in commercial systems.
- **Colored Petri Nets:** The Colored Petri Nets approach is often used to generalize attacks from expert knowledge bases and to represent attacks graphically. Purdue University's IDIOT system uses Colored Petri Nets. With this technique, it is easy for system administrators to add new signatures to the system. However, matching a complex signature to the audit trail data may be time-consuming. The technique is not used in commercial systems.
- **State-transition analysis:** Here, an attack is described with a set of goals and transitions that must be achieved by an intruder to compromise a system. Transitions are represented on state-transition diagrams.
- **Statistical analysis approach:** This is a frequently used method (for example SECURENET). The user or system behavior (set of attributes) is measured by a number of variables over time. Examples of such variables are: user login, logout, number of files accessed in a period of time, usage of disk space, memory, CPU etc. The frequency of updating can vary from a few minutes to, for example, one month. The system stores mean values for each

variable used for detecting exceeds that of a predefined threshold. Yet, this simple approach was unable to match a typical user behavior model. Approaches that relied on matching individual user profiles with aggregated group variables also failed to be efficient. Therefore, a more sophisticated model of user behavior has been developed using short- and long-term user profiles. These profiles are regularly updated to keep up with the changes in user behaviors. Statistical methods are often used in implementations of normal user behavior profile-based Intrusion Detection Systems.

- **Neural Networks:** Neural networks use their learning algorithms to learn about the relationship between input and output vectors and to generalize them to extract new input/output relationships. With the neural network approach to intrusion detection, the main purpose is to learn the behavior of actors in the system (e.g., users, daemons). It is known that statistical methods partially equate neural networks. The advantage of using neural networks over statistics resides in having a simple way to express nonlinear relationships between variables, and in learning about relationships automatically. Experiments were carried out with neural network prediction of user behaviors. From the results it has been found that the behavior of UNIX super-users (roots) is predictable (because of very regular functioning of automatic system processes). With few exceptions, behavior of most other users is also predictable. Neural networks are still a computationally intensive technique, and are not widely used in the intrusion detection community.
- **User intention identification:** This technique (that to our knowledge has only been used in the SECURENET project) models normal behavior of users by the set of high-level tasks they have to perform on the system (in relation to the users' functions). These tasks are taken as series of actions, which in turn are matched to the appropriate audit data. The analyzer keeps a set of tasks that are acceptable for each user. Whenever a mismatch is encountered, an alarm is produced.
- **Computer immunology:** Analogies with immunology has lead to the development of a technique that constructs a model of normal behavior of UNIX network services, rather than that of individual users. This model consists of short sequences of system calls made by the processes. Attacks that exploit flaws in the application code are very likely to take unusual execution paths. First, a set of reference audit data is collected which represents the appropriate behavior of services, then the knowledge base is added with all the known "good" sequences of system calls. These patterns are then used for continuous monitoring of system calls to check whether the sequence generated is listed in the knowledge base; if not an alarm is generated. This technique has a potentially very low false alarm rate provided that the knowledge base is fairly complete. Its drawback is the inability to detect errors in the configuration of network services. Whenever an attacker uses legitimate actions on the system to gain unauthorized access, no alarm is generated.
- **Machine learning:** This is an artificial intelligence technique that stores the user-input stream of commands in a vectorial form and is used as a reference of normal user behavior profile. Profiles are then grouped in a library of user commands having certain common characteristics.

- **Data mining** generally refers to a set of techniques that use the process of extracting previously unknown but potentially useful data from large stores of data. Data mining method excels at processing large system logs (audit data). However they are less useful for stream analysis of network traffic. One of the fundamental data mining techniques used in intrusion detection is associated with decision trees. Decision tree models allow one to detect anomalies in large databases. Another technique refers to segmentation, allowing extraction of patterns of unknown attacks. This is done by matching patterns extracted from a simple audit set with those referred to warehoused unknown attacks. A typical data mining technique is associated with finding association rules. It allows one to extract previously unknown knowledge on new attacks or built on normal behavior patterns. Anomaly detection often generates false alarms. With data mining it is easy to correlate data related to alarms with mined audit data, thereby considerably reducing the rate of false alarms.

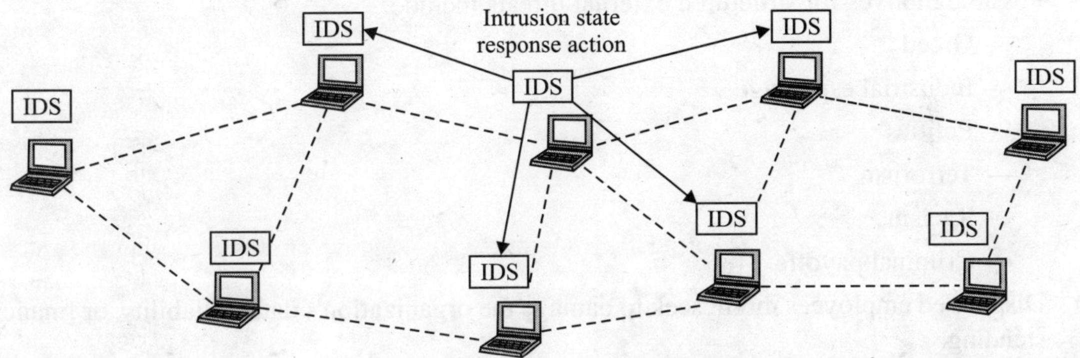

Figure 6.6: IDS Architecture

6.8 UNDERSTANDING NETWORK ATTACKS

A network attack can be defined as any method, process or means used to maliciously attempt to compromise the security of the network.

There are a number of reasons why an individual(s) would want to attack corporate networks. The individuals performing network attacks are commonly referred to as network attackers or hackers or crackers.

A few different types of malicious activities performed by network attackers and hackers are summarized here:

- Illegally using user accounts and privileges.
- Stealing hardware.
- Stealing software.
- Running code to damage systems.
- Running code to damage and corrupt data.

- Modifying stored data.
- Stealing data.
- Using data for financial gain or for industrial espionage
- Performing actions that prevent legitimate authorized users from accessing network services and resources.
- Performing actions to deplete network resources and bandwidth.

A few reasons why network attackers attempt to attack corporate networks are listed here:

- Individuals seeking fame or some sort of recognition. Script kiddies usually seek some form of fame when they attempt to crash Web sites and other public targets on the Internet. A script kiddie could also be looking for some form of acceptance or recognition from the hacker community or from black hat hackers.
- Possible motives for structured external threats include:
  - Greed
  - Industrial espionage
  - Politics
  - Terrorism
  - Racism
  - Criminal payoffs
- Displeased employees might seek to damage the organization's data, reliability, or financial standing.
- There are though some network attackers that simply enjoy the challenge of trying to compromise the security systems of highly secured networks. These types of attackers simply see their actions as a means by which existing security vulnerabilities can be exposed.

Network attacks can be classified into the following four types of attacks:

- Internal threats
- External threats
  - Unstructured threats
  - Structured threats

Threats to the network can be initiated from a number of different sources, hence the reason why network attacks are classified as either external network attacks/threats, or internal network attacks/threats:

- **External threats:** External threats or network attacks are carried out by individuals with no assistance from internal employees or contractors. These attacks are typically performed by a malicious experienced individual, a group of experienced individuals, an experienced malicious organization, or by inexperienced attackers (script kiddies). External threats are usually performed by using a predefined plan and the technologies (tools) or techniques of the attacker(s). One of the main characteristics of external threats is that it usually involves scanning and gathering information. You can therefore detect an external attack by scrutinizing existing firewall logs. You can also install an Intrusion Detection System to quickly identify external threats.

- **External threats can be further categorized into either structured threats or unstructured threats:**
  - — **Structured external threats:** These threats originate from a malicious individual, a group of malicious individual(s) or from a malicious organization. Structured threats are usually initiated from network attackers that have a premeditated thought on the actual damages and losses which they want to cause. Possible motives for structured external threats include greed, politics, terrorism, racism and criminal payoffs. These attackers are highly skilled on network design, the methods on avoiding security measures, Intrusion Detection Systems (IDSs), access procedures, and hacking tools. They have the necessary skills to develop new network attack techniques and the ability to modify existing hacking tools for their exploitations. In certain cases, the attacker could be assisted by an internal authorized individual.
  - — **Unstructured external threats:** These threats originate from an inexperienced attacker, typically from a script kiddie. A script kiddie is the terminology used to refer to an inexperienced attacker who uses cracking tools or scripted tools readily available on the Internet, to perform a network attack. Script kiddies are usually inadequately skilled to create the threats on their own. Script kiddies can be considered as being bored individuals seeking some form of fame by attempting to crash Web sites and other public targets on the Internet.

- **External attacks can also occur either remotely or locally:**
  - — **Remote external attacks:** These attacks are usually aimed at the services which an organization offers to the public. The various forms which remote external attacks can take are listed here:
    - * Remote attacks aimed at the services available for internal users. This remote attack usually occurs when there is no firewall solution implemented to protect these internal services.
    - * Remote attacks aimed at locating modems to access the corporate network.
    - * Denial-of-service (DoS) attacks to place an exceptional processing load on servers in an attempt to prevent authorized user requests from being serviced.
    - * War-dialing of the corporate private branch exchange (PBX).
    - * Attempts to brute force password authenticated systems.
  - — **Local external attacks:** These attacks typically originate from situations where computing facilities are shared, and access to the system can be obtained.

- Internal threats: Internal attacks originate from dissatisfied or unhappy inside employees or contractors. Internal attackers have some form of access to the system and usually try to hide their attack as a normal process. For instance, internal disgruntled employees have local access to some resources on the internal network already. They could also have some administrative rights on the network. One of the best means to protect against internal attacks is to implement an Intrusion Detection System, and to configure it to scan for both external and internal attacks. All forms of attacks should be logged and the logs should be reviewed and followed up.

With respect to network attacks, the core components which should be included when you design network security are:

- Network attack prevention.
- Network attack detection.
- Network attack isolation.
- Network attack recovery.

6.8.1 What is Hacking

The terminology, hacking, was initially used to refer to the process of finding solutions to rather technical issues or problems. These days, hacking is used to refer to the process whereby intruders maliciously attempt to compromise the security of corporate networks to destroy, interpret or steal confidential data; or to prevent an organization from operating.

Different terminology is used to refer to criminal hacking:

- Cracking
- Cybercrime
- Cyberespionage
- Phreaking

To access a network system, the intruder (hacker) performs a number of activities:

- **Footprinting:** This is basically the initial step in hacking a corporate network. Here the intruder attempts to gain as much information on the targeted network by using sources which the public can access. The aim of footprinting is to create a map of the network to determine what operating systems, applications and address ranges are being utilized, and to identify any accessible open ports. The methods used to footprint a network are listed here:
  - — Access information publicly available on the company Web site to gain any useful information.
  - — Try to find any anonymous File Transfer Protocol (FTP) sites and intranet sites which are not secured.
  - — Gather information on the domain name of the company and the IP address block being used.
  - — Test for hosts in the IP address block of the network. Tools such as Ping or Flping are typically used.

— Using tools such as Nslookup, the intruder attempts to perform Domain Name System (DNS) zone transfers.

— A tool such as Nmap is used to find out what the operating systems are which are being used.

— Tools such as Tracert are used to find routers and to collect subnet information.

- Port scanning: Port scanning or simply scanning, is the process whereby which intruders collect information on the network services on a target network. Here, the intruder attempts to find open ports on the target system.

  The different scanning methods used by network attackers are:

  — **Vanilla scan/SYNC scan:** TCP SYN packets are sent to the ports of each address in an attempt to connect to all ports. Port numbers 0 - 65,535 are utilized.

  — **Strobe scan:** Here, the attacker attempts to connect to a specific range of ports which are typically open on Windows based hosts or UNIX/Linux based hosts.

  — **Sweep:** A large set of IP addresses are scanned in an attempt to detect a system that has one open port.

  — **Passive scan:** Here, all network traffic entering or leaving the network is captured and traffic is then analyzed to determine what the open ports are on the hosts within the network.

  — **User Datagram Protocol (UDP) scan:** Empty UDP packets are sent to the different ports of a set of addresses to determine how the operating responds. Closed UDP ports respond with the Port Unreachable message when any empty UDP packets are received. Other operating systems respond with the Internet Control Message Protocol (ICMP) error packet.

  — **FTP bounce:** To hide the location of the attacker, the scan is initiated from an intermediary File Transfer Protocol (FTP) server.

  — **FIN scan:** TCP FIN packets that specify that the sender wants to close a TCP session are sent to each port for a range of IP addresses.

- **Enumeration:** The unauthorized intruder uses a number of methods to collect information on applications and hosts on the network, and on the user accounts utilized on the network. Enumeration is particularly successful in networks that contain unprotected network resources and services:

  — Network services that are running but which are not being utilized.

  — Default user accounts which have no passwords specified.

  — Guest accounts which are active.

- **Acquiring access:** Access attacks are performed when an attacker exploits a security weakness so that he/she can obtain access to a system or the network. Trojan horses and password hacking programs are typically used to obtain system access. When access is obtained, the intruder is able to modify or delete data; and add, modify or remove network resources.

The different types of access attacks are listed here:

- Unauthorized system access entails the practice of exploiting the vulnerabilities of operating systems, or executing a script or a hacking program to obtain access to a system.
- Unauthorized privilege escalation is a frequent type of attack. Privilege escalation occurs when an intruder attempts to obtain a high level of access like administrative privileges to gain control of the network system.
- Unauthorized data manipulation involves interpreting, altering and deleting confidential data.

- **Privilege escalation:** When an attacker initially gains access to the network, low level accounts are typically used. Privilege escalation occurs when an attacker escalates his/her privileges to obtain a higher level of access, like administrative privileges, in order to gain control of the network system.

  The privilege escalation methods used by attackers are listed here:

  - The attacker searches the registry keys for password information.
  - The attacker can search documents for information on administrative privileges.
  - The attacker can execute a password cracking tool on targeted user accounts.
  - The attacker can use a Trojan in an attempt to obtain the credentials of a user account that has administrative privileges.

- **Install backdoors:** A hacker can also implement a mechanism such as some form of access granting code with the intent of using it at some future stage. Backdoors are typically installed by attackers so that they can easily access the system at some later date. After a system is compromised, you can remove any installed backdoors by reinstalling the system from a backup which is secure.
- **Removing evidence of activities:** Attackers typically attempt to remove all evidence of their activities.

6.8.2 What are Hackers or Network Attackers

A hacker or network attacker is someone who maliciously attacks networks, systems, computers, applications; and who captures, corrupts, modifies, steals or deletes confidential company information.

A hacker can refer to a number of different individuals who perform activities aimed at hacking systems and networks, and it can also refer to individuals who perform activities that have nothing to do with criminal activity:

- Programmers who hack complex technical problems to come up with solutions.
- Script kiddies who use readily available tools on the Internet to hack into systems.
- Criminal hackers who steal or destroy company data.

- Protesting activists who deny access to specific Web sites as part of their protesting strategy.

Hackers these days are classified according to the hat they wear. This concept is illustrated below:

- Black hat hackers are malicious or criminal hackers who hack at systems and computers to damage data or who attempt to prevent businesses from rendering their services. Some black hat hackers simply hack security protected systems to gain prestige in the hacking community.
- White hat hackers are legitimate security experts who are trying to expose security vulnerabilities in operating system platforms. White hat hackers have the improvement of security as their motive. They do not damage or steal company data, nor do they seek any fame. These security experts are usually quite knowledgeable on the hacking methods utilized by black hat hackers.
- Grey hat hacker: These are individuals who have motives between that of black hat hackers and white hat hackers.

6.8.3 The Common Types of Network Attacks

While there are many different types of network attacks, a few can be regarded as the more commonly performed network attacks. These network attacks are discussed in this section of the Article:

- Data modification or data manipulation pertains to a network attack where confidential company data is interpreted, deleted, or modified. Data modification is successful when data is modified without the sender actually being aware that it was tampered with.

  A few methods of preventing attacks aimed at compromising data integrity are listed here:

  — Use digital signatures to ensure that data has not been modified while it is being transmitted or simply stored.

  — Implement access control lists (ACLs) to control which users are allowed to access your data.

  — Regularly back up important data.

  — Include specific code in applications that can validate data input.
- **Eavesdropping:** This type of network attack occurs when an attacker monitors or listens to network traffic in transit, and hen interprets all unprotected data. While you need specialized equipment and access to the telephone company switching facilities to eavesdrop telephone conversations, all you need to eavesdrop on an Internet Protocol (IP) based network is a sniffer technology to capture the traffic being transmitted. This is basically due to the Transmission Control Protocol/Internet Protocol (TCP/IP) protocol being an open architecture which transmits unencrypted data over the network.

  A few methods of preventing intruders from eavesdropping on the network are listed here:

— Implement Internet Protocol Security (IPSec) to secure and encrypt IP data before it is sent over the network.

— Implement security policies and procedures to prevent attackers from attaching a sniffer on the network.

— Install antivirus software to protect the corporate network from Trojans. Trojans are typically used to discover and capture sensitive, valuable information, such as user credentials.

- IP address spoofing or IP spoofing or identity spoofing: IP address spoofing occurs when an attacker assumes the source Internet Protocol (IP) address of IP packets to make it appear as though the packet originated from a valid IP address. The aim of an IP address spoofing attack is to identify computers on a network. The majority of IP networks utilize the IP address of the user to verify identities, and routers also typically ignore source IP addresses when routing packets. Routers use the destination IP addresses to forward packets to the intended destination network.

  These factors could enable an attacker to bypass a router and to launch a number of subsequent attacks, including:

  — Initiation of a denial of service (DoS) attacks.

  — Initiation of man-in-the-middle (MITM) attacks to hijack sessions.

  — Redirect traffic.

  A few methods of preventing IP address spoofing attacks are listed here:

  — Encrypt traffic between routers and external hosts.

  — Define ingress filters on routers and firewalls to stop inbound traffic where the source address is from a trusted host on the internal network

- **Sniffer attacks:** Sniffing refers to the process used by attackers to capture and analyze network traffic. The contents of packets on a network are analyzed. The tools which attackers use for sniffing are called sniffers or more correctly, protocol analyzers. While protocol analyzers are really network troubleshooting tools, they are also used by hackers for malicious purposes. Sniffers are used to monitor, capture and obtain network information, such as passwords and valuable customer information. When an individual has physical access to a network, he/she can easily attach a protocol analyzer to the network and then capture traffic. Remote sniffing can also be performed and is typically used by network attackers.

  There are protocol analyzers or sniffers available for most networking technologies including:

  — Asynchronous Transfer Mode (ATM)

  — Ethernet

  — Fiber Channel

  — Serial connections

  — Small Computer System Inter-face (SCSI)

  — Wireless

There are a number of common sniffers which are used by network security administrators and malicious hackers:

— Dsniff

— Ethereal

— Etherpeek

— Network Associates's Sniffer

— Ngrep

— Sniffit

— Snort

— Tcpdump

— Windump

To protect against sniffers, implement Internet Protocol Security (IPSec) to encrypt network traffic so that any captured information cannot be interpreted.

- **Password attacks:** Password based attacks or password crackers are aimed at guessing the password for a system until the correct password is determined. One of the primary security weaknesses associated with password based access control is that all security is based on the user ID and password being utilized. But who is the individual using the credentials at the keyboard? There are some of the older applications that do not protect password information. The password information is simply sent in clear or plain text - no form of encryption is utilized! Remember that network attackers can obtain user ID and password information and can then pose as authorized users and attack the corporate network. Attackers can use dictionary attacks or brute force attacks to gain access to resources with the same rights as the authorized user. A big threat would be present if the user has some level of administrative rights to certain portions of the network. An even bigger threat would exist if the same password credentials are used for all systems. The attacker would then have access to a number of systems.

  There are two ways in which password based attacks are performed:

  — **Online cracking:** The network attacker sniffs network traffic to seize authentication sessions in an attempt to capture password based information. There are tools which are geared at sniffing out passwords from traffic.

  — **Offline cracking:** The network attacker gains access to a system with the intent of gaining access to password based information. The attacker then runs some password cracker technology to decipher valid user account information.

  A dictionary attack occurs when all the words typically used for passwords are attempted to detect a password match. There are some technologies that can generate a number of complex word combinations and variations. Modern operating systems only stores passwords in an encrypted format. To obtain password credentials, you have to have administrative credentials to access the system and information. Operating systems these days also support password policies. Password policies can be used to define how passwords are managed, and to define the characteristics of passwords which are considered acceptable.

Password policy settings can be used to specify and enforce a number of rules for passwords:

— Define whether passwords are simple or complex.

— Define whether password history is maintained.

— Define the minimum length for passwords.

— Define the minimum password age.

— Define the maximum password age.

— Define whether passwords are stored using reversible encryption or irreversible encryption.

Account lockout policies should be implemented if your environment is particularly vulnerable to threats arising from passwords which are being guessed. Implementing an account lockout policy ensures that the account of a user is locked after an individual has unsuccessfully tried for several times to provide the correct password. The important factor to remember when defining an account lockout policy is that you should implement a policy that permits some degree of user error, but that also prevents hackers from using your user accounts.

The following password and account lockout settings are located in the Account Lockout Policy area in Account Policies:

— **Account lockout threshold:** This setting controls the number of times after which an incorrect password attempt results in the account being locked out of the system.

— **Account lockout duration:** This setting controls the duration that an account which is locked, remains locked. A setting of 0 means that an administrator has to manually unlock the locked account.

— **Reset account lockout counter after:** This setting determines the time duration that must pass subsequent to an invalid logon attempt occurring prior to the reset account lockout counter being reset.

• **Brute force attack:** Brute force attacks simply attempt to decode a cipher by trying each possible key to find the correct one. This type of network attack systematically uses all possible alpha, numeric, and special character key combinations to find a password that is valid for a user account. Brute force attacks are also typically used to compromise networks that utilize Simple Mail Transfer Protocol (SNMP). Here, the network attacker initiates a brute force attack to find the SNMP community names so that he/she can outline the devices and services running on the network.

A few methods of preventing brute force attacks are listed here:

— Enforce the use of long password strings.

— For SNMP use long, complex strings for community names.

— Implement an intrusion detection system (IDS). By examining traffic patterns, an IDS is capable of detecting when brute force attacks are underway.

- **Denial of Service (DoS) attack:** A DoS attack is aimed at preventing authorized, legitimate users from accessing services on the network. The DoS attack is not aimed at gathering or collecting data. It is aimed at preventing the normal use of computers or the network by authorized, legitimate users. The SYN flood from 1996 was the earliest form of a DoS attack which exploited a vulnerability of the Transmission Control Protocol (TCP). A DoS attack can be initiated by sending invalid data to applications or network services until the server hangs or simply crashes. The most common form of a DoS attack is TCP attacks.

  DoS attacks can use either of the following methods to prevent authorized users from using the network services, computers, or applications:

  — Flood the network with invalid data until traffic from authorized network users cannot be processed.

  — Flood the network with invalid network service requests until the host providing that particular service cannot process requests from authorized network users. The network would eventually become overloaded.

  — Disrupt communication between hosts and clients through either of the following methods:

  * Modification of system configurations.

  * Physical destruction of the network. Crashing a router for instance would prevent users from accessing the system.

  There are a number of tools easily accessible and available on the Internet which can be used to initiate DoS attacks:

  — Bonk

  — LAND

  — Smurf

  — Teardrop

  — WinNuke

  A network attacker can increase the enormity of a DoS attack by initiating the attack against a single network from multiple computers or systems. This type of attack is known as a distributed denial of service (DDoS) attack. Network administrators can experience great difficulty in fending off DDoS attacks, simply because blocking all the attacking computers, can also result in blocking authorized users.

  The following measures can be implemented to protect a network against DoS attacks:

  — Implement and enforce strong password policies.

  — Back up system configuration data regularly.

  — Disable or remove all unnecessary network services.

— Implement disk quotas for your user and service accounts.

— Configure filtering on your routers and patch operating systems.

The following measures can be implemented to protect a network against DDoS attacks:

— Limit the number of ICMP and SYN packets on router interfaces.

— Filter private IP addresses using router access control lists.

— Apply ingress and egress filtering on all edge routers.

- Man-in-the-middle (MITM) attack: A man-in-the-middle (MITM) attack occurs when a hacker eavesdrops on a secure communication session and monitors, captures and controls the data being sent between the two parties communicating. The attacker attempts to obtain information so that he/she can impersonate the receiver and sender communicating.

  For a man-in-the-middle (MITM) attack to be successful, the following sequence of events has to occur:

  — The hacker must be able to obtain access to the communication session to capture traffic when the receiver and sender establish the secure communication session.

  — The hacker must be able to capture the messages being sent between the parties and then send messages so that the session remains active.

There are some public key cryptography systems, such as Diffie-Hellman (DH) key exchange which are rather susceptible to man-in-the-middle attacks. This is due to the Diffie-Hellman (DH) key exchange using no authentication.

6.8.5 What are Viruses

A virus can be defined as a malicious code which affects and infects files on a system. Numerous instances of the files are then recreated. Viruses usually lead to some sort of data loss, and/or system failure.

There are numerous methods by which a virus can get into a system:

- Through infected floppy disks.
- Through an e-mail attachment infected with the virus.
- Through downloading software infected with the virus.

A few common types of viruses are listed here:

- **Boot sector viruses:** These are viruses that infect a hard-drive's master boot record. The virus is then loaded into memory whenever the system starts or is rebooted.
- **File viruses or program viruses or parasitic viruses:** These are viruses that are attached to executable programs. Whenever the particular program is executed, the viruses are loaded into memory.
- **Multipartite viruses:** These are viruses which are a combination of a boot sector virus and a file virus.

- **Macro viruses:** These are viruses that are written in macro languages utilized by applications, of which Microsoft Word is one. Macro viruses usually infect systems through e-mail.
- **Polymorphic viruses:** These viruses can be considered as being the more difficult viruses to fend against because they can modify their code. Virus protection software often finds polymorphic viruses harder to detect and remove.

If you discover that a virus has infected your system, use the recommendations listed here:

- Scan each of your systems to gauge how infected your infrastructure is.
- To prevent the virus from spreading any further. You should immediately disconnect all infected systems.
- All infected systems should be installed from a clean backup copy, that is, a back up which was taken when the system was clean from virus infections.
- Inform the antivirus vendor so that the vendor's virus signature database is updated accordingly.

A few methods of protecting your network infrastructure against viruses are listed here:

- Install virus protection software on systems.
- Regularly update all installed virus protection software.
- Regularly back up systems after they have been scanned for viruses, and are considered clean from virus infection.
- Your users should be educated to not open any e-mail attachments which were sent from individuals they do not recognize.

6.8.6 What are Worms

As mentioned previously, a virus is a form of malicious code that infects files on the system. A worm on the other hand is an autonomous code that propagates over a network, targeting hard drive space and processor cycles. Worms not only infects files on one system but can propagate to other systems on the network. The purpose of a worm is to deplete available system resources. Hence the reason why a worm makes copies of itself over and over and over. Worms basically make copies of itself or replicate until available memory is used, bandwidth is unavailable, and legitimate network users are no longer able to access network resources or services.

There are a few worms that are sophisticated enough to corrupt files, render systems un-operational, and even steal data. These worms usually have one or numerous viral codes.

A few previously encountered worms are listed here:

- Te ADMw0rm worm took advantage of a buffer overflow in Berkeley Internet Name Domain (BIND).
- The Code Red worm utilized a buffer overflow vulnerability in Microsoft Internet Information Services (IIS) version 4 and IIS version 5.

- The LifeChanges worm exploited a Microsoft Windows weakness which allowed scrap shell files to be utilized for running arbitrary code.
- The LoveLetter worm used a Visual Basic Script to replicate or mass mail itself to all individuals in the Windows address book.
- The Melissa worm utilized a Microsoft Outlook and Outlook Express vulnerability to mass mail itself to all individuals in the Windows address book.
- The Morris worm exploited a Sendmail debug mode vulnerability.
- The Nimda worm managed to run e-mail attachments in Hypertext Markup Language (HTML) messages through the exploitation of HTML IFRAME tag.
- The Slapper worm exploited an Apache Web server platform buffer overflow vulnerability.
- The Slammer worm exploited a buffer overflow vulnerability on un-patched machines running Microsoft SQL Server.

6.8.7 What are Trojan Horses

A Trojan horse or simply Trojan, is a file or e-mail attachment which is disguised as being a friendly, legitimate file. When executed though, the file corrupts data and can even install a backdoor which hackers can utilize to access the network.

A Trojan horse differs to a virus or worm in the following ways:

- Trojan horses disguise themselves as friendly programs. Viruses and worms are much more obvious in their actions.
- Trojan horses do not replicate like worms and viruses do.

A few different types of Trojan horses are listed here:

- Keystroke loggers monitor the keystrokes that a user types and then e-mails the information to the network attacker.
- Password stealers are disguised as legitimate login screens which wait for users to provide their passwords so that they can be stolen by hackers. Password stealers are aimed at discovering and stealing system passwords for hackers.
- Remote administration tools (RATs) are used by hackers to gain control over the network from some remote location.
- Zombies are typically used to initiate distributed denial of service (DDoS) attacks on the hosts within a network.

6.8.8 Predicting Network Threats

To protect your network infrastructure, you need to be able to predict the types of network threats to which it is vulnerable. This should include an analysis of the risks that each identified network threat imposes on the network infrastructure.

A model known as STRIDE is used by security experts to classify network threats:

- **Spoofing identity:** These are attacks that are aimed at obtaining user account information. Spoofing identity type attacks typically affect data confidentiality.
- **Tampering with data:** These are attacks that are aimed at modifying company information. Data tampering usually ends up in affecting the integrity of data. A man-in-the-middle attack is a form of data tampering.
- **Repudiation:** Repudiation takes place when a user performs some form of malicious action on a resource and then later denies carrying out that particular activity. Network administrators usually have no evidence which they can use to back up their suspicions.
- **Information disclosure:** Here, private and confidential information is made available to individuals who should not have access to the particular information. Information disclosure usually impacts data confidentiality and network resource confidentiality.
- **Denial of service:** These attacks affect the availability of company data and network resources and services. DoS attacks are aimed at preventing legitimate users from accessing network resources and data.
- **Elevation of privilege:** Elevation of privilege occurs when an attacker escalates his/her privileges to obtain a high level of access like administrative privileges, in an attempt to gain control of the network system.

6.8.9 Identifying Threats to DHCP Implementations

A few threats specific to DHCP implementations are listed here:

- Because the IP address number in a DHCP scope is limited, an unauthorized user could initiate a denial of service (DoS) attack by requesting or obtaining a large numbers of IP addresses.
- A network attacker could use a rogue DHCP server to offer incorrect IP addresses to your DHCP clients.
- A denial of service (DoS) attack can be launched through an unauthorized user performing a large number of DNS dynamic updates via the DHCP server.
- Assigning DNS IP addresses and WINS IP addresses through the DHCP server increases the possibility of hackers using this information to attack your DNS and WINS servers.

Protect your DHCP environment from network attacks, use the following strategies:

- Implement firewalls
- Close all open unused ports
- If necessary, use VPN tunnels.
- You can use MAC address filters.

6.8.10 Identifying Threats to DNS Implementations

A few threats specific to DNS implementations:

- Denial of service (DoS) attacks occurs when DNS servers are flooded with recursive queries in an attempt to prevent the DNS server from servicing legitimate client requests for name resolution. A successful DoS attack can result in the unavailability of DNS services, and in the eventual shut down of the network.
- In DNS, footprinting occurs when an intruder intercepts DNS zone information. When the intruder has this information, the intruder is able to discover DNS domain names, computer names, and IP addresses which are being used on the network. The intruder then uses this information to decide on which computers he/she wants to attacks.
- **IP Spoofing:** After an intruder has obtained a valid IP address from a footprinting attack, the intruder can use the IP address to send malicious packets to the network, or access network services. The intruder can also use the valid IP address to modify data.
- In DNS, a redirection attack occurs when an intruder is able to make the DNS server forward or redirect name resolution requests to the incorrect servers. In this case, the incorrect servers are under the control of the intruder. A redirection attack is achieved by an intruder corrupting the DNS cache in a DNS server that accepts unsecured dynamic updates.

To protect an external DNS implementation from network attacks, use the following list of recommendations:

- DNS servers should be placed in a DMZ or in a perimeter network.
- Access rules and packet filtering should be configured firewalls to control both source and destination addresses and ports.
- Host your DNS servers on different subnets and ensure that the DNS servers have different configured routers.
- Install the latest service packs on your DNS servers
- All unnecessary services should be removed.
- Secure zone transfer data by using VPN tunnels or IPSec.
- Ensure that zone transfer is only allowed to specific IP addresses.
- For Internet facing DNS servers, disable recursion, disable dynamic updates, and enable protection against cache pollution
- You can use a stealth primary server to update secondary DNS servers which are registered with ICANN.

6.8.11 Identifying Threats to Internet Information Server (IIS) servers (Web servers)

The security vulnerabilities of the earlier versions of Internet Information Server (IIS), including IIS version 5, were continuously patched up by service packs and hotfixes available from Microsoft. Previously when IIS was installed, all services were enabled and started; all service accounts had high system rights; and permissions were assigned to the lowest levels. This basically meant that the IIS implementation was vulnerable to all sorts of attacks from hackers. Microsoft introduced the Security Lockdown Wizard in an attempt to address the security loopholes and vulnerabilities which existed in the previous versions of IIS. The Security Lockdown Wizard in IIS 6 has been included in the Web Service Extensions (WSE).

IIS is installed in locked-down mode with IIS 6. The only feature immediately available is to access static content. You actually need to utilize the WSE feature in the IIS Manager console tree to manually enable IIS to run applications and its features. By default, all applications and extensions are prohibited from running.

To protect IIS servers from network attacks, use the following recommendations:

- To prevent hackers from using default account names, all default account names, including the Administrator account and Guest account should be changed. You should utilize names for these accounts which are difficult to guess.
- To prevent a hacker from compromising Active Directory should the Web server be compromised, the Web server should be a stand-alone server or a member of a forest, other than the forest which is used by the private network.
- All the latest released security updates, service packs, and hotfixes should be applied to the Web server.
- All sample applications should be removed from a Web server. A few sample application files are installed by default with IIS 5.0.
- All unnecessary services should be removed or disabled. This would ensure that network attackers cannot exploit these services to compromise the Web server.
- Disable the utilization of parent paths. Hackers typically attempt to access unauthorized disk subsystem areas through parent paths.
- Apply security to each content type. Content should be categorized into separate folders, based on content type. You should then apply discretionary access control lists for each content type you have identified.
- To protect commonly attacked ports, use IPSec.
- To protect the secure areas of the Web server, use the Secure Socket Layer (SSL) protocol.
- To detect hacking activity, implement an intrusion detection system (IDS).
- A few recommendations for writing secure code for ASP or ASP.NET applications are summarized here:
  - — ASP pages should not contain any hard-coded administrator account names and administrator account passwords.
  - — Sensitive and confidential information and data should not be stored in hidden input fields on Web pages and in cookies.
  - — Verify and validate form input prior to it being processed.

— Do not use information from HTTP request headers to code decision branches for applications.

— Be wary of buffer overflows generated by unsound coding standards.

— Use Secure Sockets Layer (SSL) to encrypt session cookies.

6.8.12 Identifying Threats to Wireless Networks

A few threats specific to DNS implementations:

- **Eavesdropping attacks:** The hacker attempts to capture traffic when it is being transmitted from the wireless computer to the wireless access point (WAP).
- **Masquerading:** Here, the hacker masquerades as an authorized wireless user to access network resources or services.
- **Denial of service (DoS) attacks:** The network attacker attempts to prevent authorized wireless users from accessing network resources by using a transmitter to block wireless frequencies.
- **Man-in-the-middle attacks:** If an attacker successfully launches a man-in-the-middle attack, the attacker could be able to replay, and modify wireless communications.
- **Attacks at wireless clients:** The attacker starts a network attack at the actual wireless computer which is connected to an untrusted wireless network.

To protect wireless networks from network attacks, use the following strategies:

- Administrators should require all wireless communications to be authenticated and encrypted. The common technologies used to protect wireless networks from security threats are Wired Equivalent Privacy (WEP), Wi-Fi Protected Access (WPA), and IEEE 802.1X authentication
- Regularly apply all firmware updates to your wireless devices.
- Place the wireless network in a wireless demilitarized zone (WDMZ). A router or firewall should isolate the private corporate network from the WDMZ. DHCP should not be used in the wireless demilitarized zone.
- To ensure a high level of wireless security, your wireless devices should support 802.1X authentication using Extensible Authentication Protocol (EAP) authentication; Temporal Key Integrity Protocol (TKIP); and use IPSec to secure communication between the AP and the RADIUS server.
- The default administrative password utilized to manage the AP should be a complex, strong password.
- The SSID should not contain the name of the company, the address of the company, and any other identification-type information
- You should not utilize shared key encryption because it can lead to the compromise of the WEP keys.
- To protect the network from site survey mechanisms, disable SSID broadcasts.

6.8.13 Determining Security Requirements for Different Data Types

When determining security requirements for different data types it is often helpful to categorize data as follows:

- **Public data:** This category includes all data which is already publicly available on the company's Web site or news bulletins. Because the data is already publicly available, no risk is typically associated with the data being stolen. You do however need to maintain and ensure the integrity of public data.
- **Private data:** Data that falls within this category is usually well-known within your organization's environment but is not well-known to the outside public. A typical example of data that falls within this category is data on the corporate intranet.
- **Confidential data:** Data that falls within this category is data such as private customer information that should be protected from unauthorized access. The organization would almost always suffer some sort of loss if confidential data is intercepted.
- **Secret data:** This is data which can be considered more confidential and sensitive in nature than confidential data. Secret data consists of trade secrets, new product and business strategy information, and patent information. Secret data should have the highest levels of security.

6.8.14 Creating an Incidence Response Plan

The terminology, incident response, refers to planned actions in response to a network attack or any similar event that affects systems, networks and company data. An Incident Response plan is aimed at outlining the response procedures that should take place when a network is being attacked or security is being compromised.

The Incident Response plan should assist an organization with dealing with the incident in an orderly manner. Reacting to network attacks by following a planned approach defined by a security policy is the better approach.

These security policies should clearly define the following:

- The response to follow for each different type of incident.
- The individual(s) who are responsible for dealing with these incidents.
- The escalation procedures which should be followed.

An Incident Response plan can be divided into the following four steps:

- **Response:** Determine how network attacks and security breaches will be dealt with.
- **Investigation:** Determine how the attack occurred, why the specific attack occurred, and the extent of the attack.
- **Restoration:** All infected systems should be taken offline and then restored from a clean backup.
- **Reporting:** The network attack or security breach should be reported to the appropriate authorities.

Before you attempt to determine the existing state of a machine that is being attacked, it is recommended that you first record the information listed here:

- The name of the machine.
- The IP address of the machine.
- The installed operating system, operating system version, and installed service packs.
- All running processes and services.
- List all parties that are dependent on the server. These are the individuals which you need to inform of the current situation.
- Obtain the following valuable information:
  - Application event log information.
  - System event log information.
  - Security event log information.
  - All other machine specific event logs, such as DNS logs, DHCP logs, or File Replication logs.
- Record all information which indicates malicious activities. This should include:
  - All files that have been modified, corrupted, or deleted.
  - All unauthorized processes running.
- Try to identify and record the source of the network attack.

6.9 VIRTUAL PRIVATE NETWORK

A virtual private network (VPN) is the extension of a private network that encompasses links across shared or public networks like the Internet. A VPN enables you to send data between two computers across a shared or public internetwork in a manner that emulates the properties of a point-to-point private link. The act of configuring and creating a virtual private network is known as virtual private networking.

To emulate a point-to-point link, data is encapsulated, or wrapped, with a header that provides routing information allowing it to traverse the shared or public transit internetwork to reach its endpoint. To emulate a private link, the data being sent is encrypted for confidentiality. Packets that are intercepted on the shared or public network are indecipherable without the encryption keys. The portion of the connection in which the private data is encapsulated is known as the tunnel. The portion of the connection in which the private data is encrypted is known as the virtual private network (VPN) connection.

VPN connections allow users working at home or on the road to connect in a secure fashion to a remote corporate server using the routing infrastructure provided by a public internetwork (such as the Internet). From the user's perspective, the VPN connection is a point-to-point connection between the user's computer and a corporate server. The nature of the intermediate internetwork is irrelevant to the user because it appears as if the data is being sent over a dedicated private link.

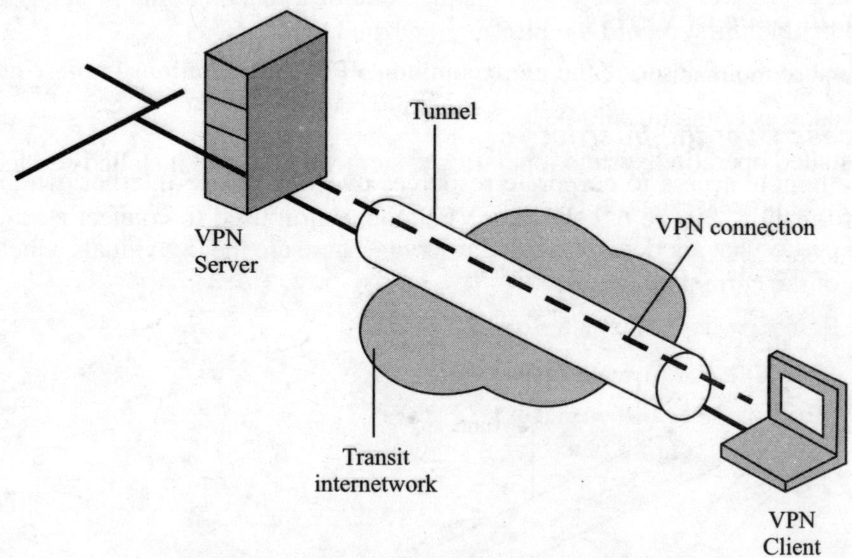

Figure 6.7: Virtual Private Network Connection

VPN technology also allows a corporation to connect to branch offices or to other companies over a public internetwork (such as the Internet), while maintaining secure communications. The VPN connection across the Internet logically operates as a wide area network (WAN) link between the sites.

In both of these cases, the secure connection across the internetwork appears to the user as a private network communication despite the fact that this communication occurs over a public internetwork hence the name virtual private network.

VPN technology is designed to address issues surrounding the current business trend toward increased telecommuting and widely distributed global operations, where workers must be able to connect to central resources and must be able to communicate with each other.

To provide employees with the ability to connect to corporate computing resources, regardless of their location, a corporation must deploy a scalable remote access solution. Typically, corporations choose either an MIS department solution, where an internal information systems department is charged with buying, installing, and maintaining corporate modem pools and a private network infrastructure; or they choose a value-added network (VAN) solution, where they pay an outsourced company to buy, install, and maintain modem pools and a telecommunication infrastructure.

Neither of these solutions provides the necessary scalability, in terms of cost, flexible administration, and demand for connections. Therefore, it makes sense to replace the modem pools and private network infrastructure with a less expensive solution based on Internet technology so that the business can focus on its core competencies. With an Internet solution, a few Internet connections through Internet service providers (ISPs) and VPN server computers can serve the remote networking needs of hundreds or thousands of remote clients and branch offices.

6.9.1 Common Uses of VPNs

The next few subsections describe the more common VPN configurations in more detail.

Remote Access Over the Internet

VPNs provide remote access to corporate resources over the public Internet, while maintaining privacy of information. Figure 6.9 shows a VPN connection used to connect a remote user to a corporate intranet.

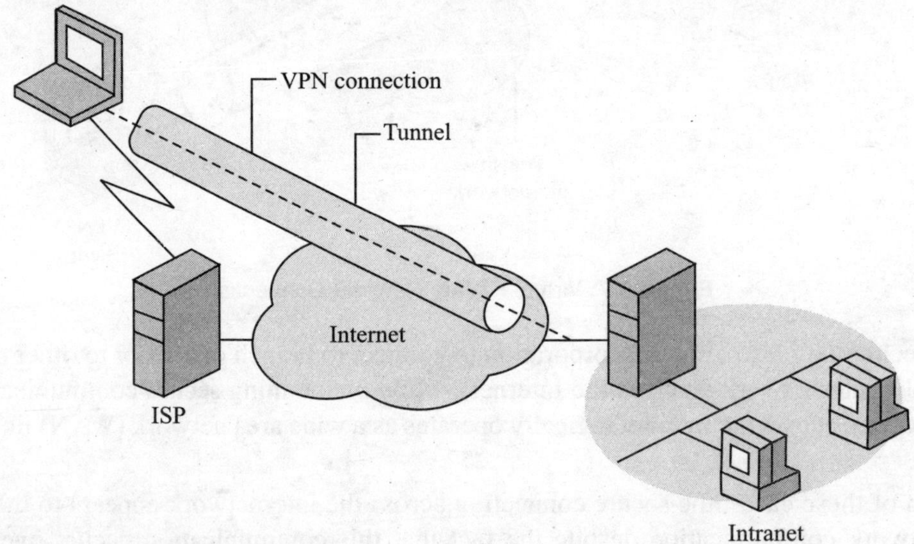

Figure 6.8: Using a VPN connection to connect a remote client to a private intranet

Rather than making a long distance (or 1-800) call to a corporate or outsourced network access server (NAS), the user calls a local ISP. Using the connection to the local ISP, the VPN software creates a virtual private network between the dial-up user and the corporate VPN server across the Internet.

Connecting Networks Over the Internet

There are two methods for using VPNs to connect local area networks at remote sites:

- **Using dedicated lines to connect a branch office to a corporate LAN.** Rather than using an expensive long-haul dedicated circuit between the branch office and the corporate hub, both the branch office and the corporate hub routers can use a local dedicated circuit and local ISP to connect to the Internet. The VPN software uses the local ISP connections and the Internet to create a virtual private network between the branch office router and corporate hub router.
- **Using a dial-up line to connect a branch office to a corporate LAN.** Rather than having a router at the branch office make a long distance (or 1-800) call to a corporate or outsourced

NAS, the router at the branch office can call the local ISP. The VPN software uses the connection to the local ISP to create a VPN between the branch office router and the corporate hub router across the Internet.

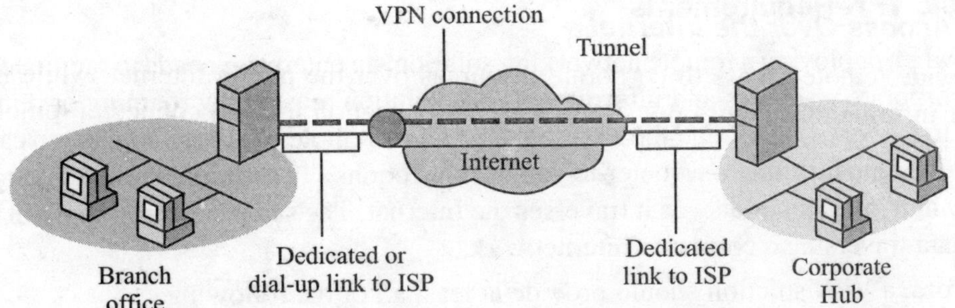

Figure 6.9: Using a VPN connection to connect two remote sites

In both cases, the facilities that connect the branch office and corporate offices to the Internet are local. The corporate hub router that acts as a VPN server must be connected to a local ISP with a dedicated line. This VPN server must be listening 24 hours a day for incoming VPN traffic.

Connecting Computers over an Intranet

In some corporate internetworks, the departmental data is so sensitive that the department's LAN is physically disconnected from the rest of the corporate internetwork. Although this protects the department's confidential information, it creates information accessibility problems for those users not physically connected to the separate LAN.

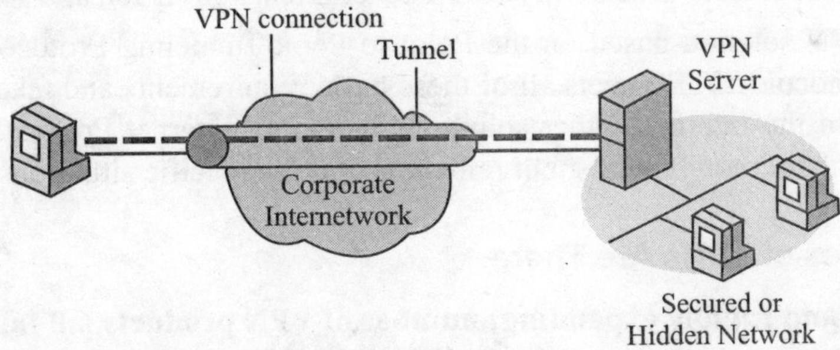

Figure 6.10: Using a VPN connection to connect to a secured or hidden network

VPNs allow the department's LAN to be physically connected to the corporate internetwork but separated by a VPN server. The VPN server is not acting as a router between the corporate network and the department LAN. A router would connect the two networks, allowing everyone access to the sensitive LAN. By using a VPN, the network administrator can ensure that only those users on the corporate internetwork who have appropriate credentials (based on a need-to-know policy within the company) can establish a VPN with the VPN server and gain access to the protected resources of the department. Additionally, all communication across the VPN can be encrypted for data confidentiality. Those users who do not have the proper credentials cannot view the department LAN.

6.9.2 Basic VPN Requirements

Typically, when deploying a remote networking solution, an enterprise needs to facilitate controlled access to corporate resources and information. The solution must allow roaming or remote clients to connect to LAN resources, and the solution must allow remote offices to connect to each other to share resources and information (router-to-router connections). In addition, the solution must ensure the privacy and integrity of data as it traverses the Internet. The same concerns apply in the case of sensitive data traversing a corporate internetwork.

Therefore, a VPN solution should provide at least all of the following:

- **User Authentication.** The solution must verify the VPN client's identity and restrict VPN access to authorized users only. It must also provide audit and accounting records to show who accessed what information and when.
- **Address Management.** The solution must assign a VPN client's address on the intranet and ensure that private addresses are kept private.
- **Data Encryption.** Data carried on the public network must be rendered unreadable to unauthorized clients on the network.
- **Key Management.** The solution must generate and refresh encryption keys for the client and the server.
- **Multiprotocol Support.** The solution must handle common protocols used in the public network. These include IP, Internetwork Packet Exchange (IPX), and so on.

An Internet VPN solution based on the Point-to-Point Tunneling Protocol (PPTP) or Layer Two Tunneling Protocol (L2TP) meets all of these basic requirements and takes advantage of the broad availability of the Internet. Other solutions, including Internet Protocol Security (IPSec), meet only some of these requirements, but remain useful for specific situations.

6.9.3 What Types of VPNs Are There (UPTU 2010-11)

Despite the large (and rapidly expanding) number of VPN products, all fall into three broad categories: hardware-based systems, firewall-based VPNs and standalone VPN application packages.

Most hardware-based VPN systems are encrypting routers. They are secure and easy to use, since they provide the nearest thing to "plug and play" encryption equipment available. They provide the highest network throughput of all VPN systems, since they don't waste processor overhead in running an operating system or other applications. However, they may not be as flexible as software based systems. The best hardware VPN packages offer software-only clients for remote installation, and incorporate some of the access control features more traditionally managed by firewalls or other perimeter security devices.

Firewall-based VPNs take advantage of the firewall's security mechanisms, including restricting access to the internal network. They also perform address translation; satisfy requirements for strong authentication; and serve up real-time alarms and extensive logging. Most commercial firewalls also "harden" the host operating system kernel by stripping out dangerous or unnecessary services, providing additional security for the VPN server. OS protection is a major plus, since very few VPN application vendors supply guidance on OS security. Performance may be a concern, especially if the firewall is already loaded — however, some firewall vendors offer hardware-based encryption processors to minimize the impact of VPN management on the system.

Software-based VPNs are ideal in situations where both endpoints of the VPN are not controlled by the same organization (typical for client support requirements or business partnerships), or when different firewalls and routers are implemented within the same organization. At the moment, standalone VPNs offer the most flexibility in how network traffic is managed. Many software-based products allow traffic to be tunneled based on address or protocol, unlike hardware-based products, which generally tunnel all traffic they handle, regardless of protocol. Tunneling specific traffic types is advantageous in situations where remote sites may see a mix of traffic —some that needs transport over a VPN (such as entries to a database at headquarters) and some that doesn't (such as Web surfing). In situations where performance requirements are modest (such as users connecting over dial-up links), software-based VPNs may be the best choice.

But software-based systems are generally harder to manage than encrypting routers. They require familiarity with the host operating system, the application itself, and appropriate security mechanisms. And some software VPN packages require changes to routing tables and network addressing schemes.

Be aware that as the VPN market evolves, the distinctions between VPN architectures are becoming less clearly defined. Some hardware vendors have added software clients to their product offerings, and extended their server capabilities to include some of the security features more "traditionally" offered by software or firewall-based VPNs. A few stand-alone products have added support for hardware-based encryptors to improve their performance. And for all types of VPNs, further implementation of the proposed IPSec protocol is making it easier (not trivial) to mix and match VPN products. So bear in mind that these VPN categories are becoming less meaningful as time goes on.

Router based vpn

Broadband Routers with VPN Servers

Until recently, VPN server hardware was VERY expensive. As home networks become more sophisticated, the demand for home level VPN's increase. At the end of 2001, the home network industry responded by adding VPN servers into some broadband routers. These products are often priced at under $300 (us) and some are as inexpensive as $170.

VPN functionality is very processor intensive and most broadband routers have somewhat slow processors in them. Broadband router based VPN servers are often limited in throughput because of their microprocessors. Most have a maximum VPN throughput of around .6Mbps or 600Kbps.

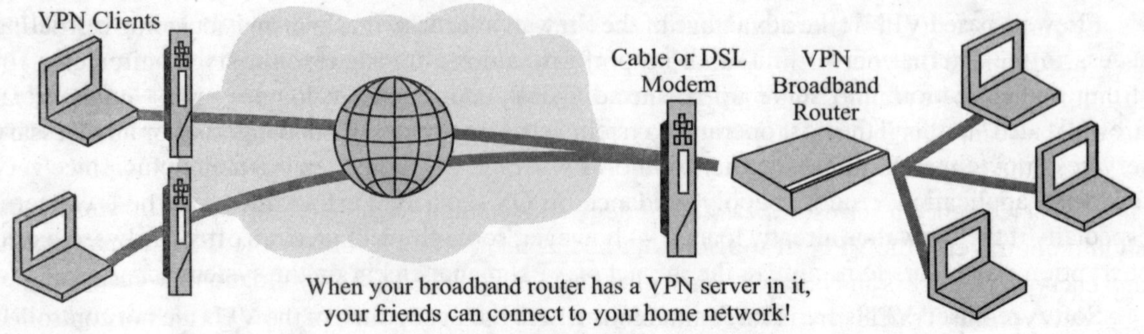

Figure 6.11

6.10 NEED OF VPN

As internal corporate networks grow and telecommuting/remote offices become more commonplace, companies are turning to virtual private networks (VPNs) to provide access to internal corporate resources. A VPN is a collection of private data and voice networks utilizing the public communications infrastructure. VPNs operate on the premise of tunnels, which protect the data inside from external threats, utilizing predetermined parameters.

The goal of a VPN is to offer the same services to both internal and authorized external personnel, while at the same time minimizing overhead costs. The need for point-to-point leased lines can be virtually eliminated when a VPN is implemented properly.

There are numerous vendors that offer a variety of VPN capable equipment. Several offer a variety of routers, firewalls, remote access clients and concentrators that support very scalable VPN implementations. IP Security (IPSec) is the most dominant of all secure VPN technologies and is a standards-based method of providing integrity to data transmitted over IP. IPSec provides layer 3 encryption of data packets and utilizes various checks and balances to ensure data integrity. Key management and security associations, the IPSec parameters between devices, are negotiated utilizing the Internet key exchange.

The Internet offers a wide variety of opportunities and resources, but they do not come without inherent risks. These risks, as well as the need to protect sensitive information, are what drives the need for VPNs. The following three items may explain the need of VPN.

1. **Data privacy:** Traffic traversing the Internet is unencrypted and can be viewed by unauthorized parties between the source and destination. This may be acceptable in many instances, but there are times when confidential information may be compromised.
2. **Data integrity:** While it may not be detrimental if unauthorized persons or entities could read your general e-mail, it could be problematic if they could access and possibly modify more sensitive documents, bank transactions, etc.
3. **Identity theft:** Hackers are becoming more creative in their techniques, and identity theft is becoming more prevalent. No secure data such as credit card numbers.

Social Security numbers and bank account numbers may give people the information they need to take on your identity and, in turn, gain access to your confidential information. The solution needs to be planned and implemented diligently. Defining exactly what types of information need to be secured is the first step. Certain traffic, such as remote file and mail requests, may need to access the corporate Internet, whereas World Wide Web (WWW) requests do not.

VPNs reference a series of permit-and deny statements to determine which traffic should and should not traverse the VPN. If traffic is marked as interesting, it follows the IPSec encapsulation and encryption process and is forwarded to the other end of the tunnel for validation, de-encapsulation and decryption. Traffic that is not interesting will be routed in clear text, based on current implemented policies.

Another popular implementation is the use of remote access clients. These clients have software installed on PCs, laptops or PDAs and are able to securely access internal resources. Typically the software is very inexpensive and is a more-than-adequate solution for remote salespersons, managers, IT staff and executives.

Network and information security are becoming increasingly more important in corporate environments. VPNs offer another level of defense against unauthorized access to confidential information while still maintaining flexibility and scalability.

There are still instances in which point to- point links make sense and are necessary, but in many cases, having a virtual point-to-point network is both cost effective and secure.

6.10.1 How does VPN work

Virtual private networks (VPN) are a secure way for businesses and companies to communicate via the Internet. They assure the tightest of security and are not open to traffic from the public. Remote users and multiple sites of users can be connected through a direct private pathway. The installation of a VPN alters the need for a WAN (wide area network), simplifies the companies' network needs, provides extended telecommute opportunities and opens up the possibility for global networking. Building a secure VPN requires reliability, scalability and management of the network and policies designed to run the network. VPN's can be managed by the company or contracted to a VPN provider.

The world has changed a lot in the last couple of decades. Instead of simply dealing with local or regional concerns, many businesses now have to think about global markets and logistics. Many companies have facilities spread out across the country or around the world, and there is one thing that all of them need: A way to maintain fast, secure and reliable communications wherever their offices are.

Until fairly recently, this has meant the use of **leased lines** to maintain a **wide area network** (WAN). Leased lines, ranging from ISDN (integrated services digital network, 128 Kbps) to OC3 (Optical Carrier-3, 155 Mbps) fiber, provided a company with a way to expand its private network beyond its immediate geographic area. A WAN had obvious advantages over a public network like the Internet when it came to reliability, performance and security. But maintaining a WAN, particularly when using leased lines, can become quite expensive and often rises in cost as the distance between the offices increases.

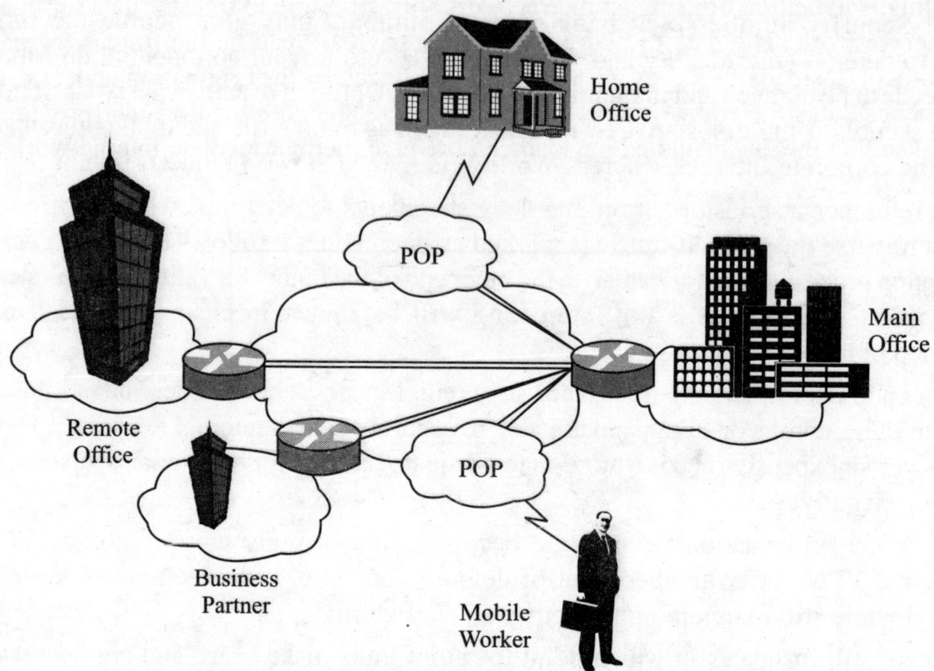

Figure 6.12: Image courtesy Cisco Systems, Inc.

As the popularity of the Internet grew, businesses turned to it as a means of extending their own networks. First came intranets, which are password-protected sites designed for use only by company employees. Now, many companies are creating their own **VPN (virtual private network)** to accommodate the needs of remote employees and distant offices.

A typical VPN might have a main LAN at the corporate headquarters of a company, other LANs at remote offices or facilities and individual users connecting from out in the field.

Basically, a VPN is a private network that uses a public network (usually the Internet) to connect remote sites or users together. Instead of using a dedicated, real-world connection such as leased line, a VPN uses "virtual" connections routed through the Internet from the company's private network to the remote site or employee. In this article, you will gain a fundamental understanding of VPNs, and learn about basic VPN components, technologies,tunneling and security.

6.11 USE OF TUNNELING WITH VPN

Tunneling is the transmission of data intended for use only within a private, usually corporate network through a public network in such a way that the routing nodes in the public network are unaware that the transmission is part of a private network. Tunneling is generally done by encapsulating the private network data and protocol information within the public network transmission units so that the private network protocol information appears to the public network as data. Tunneling allows the use of the Internet, which is a public network, to convey data on behalf of a private network

Tunneling is a method of using an internetwork infrastructure to transfer data for one network over another network. The data to be transferred (or payload) can be the frames (or packets) of another protocol. Instead of sending a frame as it is produced by the originating node, the tunneling protocol encapsulates the frame in an additional header. The additional header provides routing information so that the encapsulated payload can traverse the intermediate internetwork.

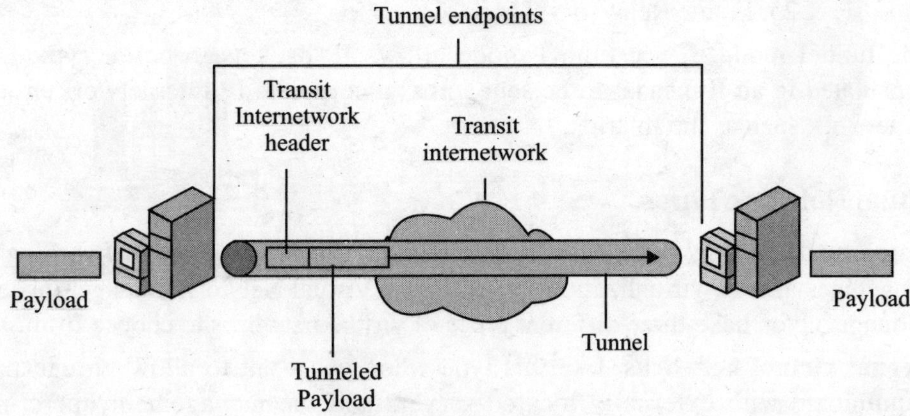

Figure 6.13: Tunneling

The encapsulated packets are then routed between tunnel endpoints over the internetwork. The logical path through which the encapsulated packets travel through the internetwork is called a tunnel. Once the encapsulated frames reach their destination on the internetwork, the frame is decapsulated and forwarded to its final destination. Tunneling includes this entire process (encapsulation, transmission, and decapsulation of packets).

The transit internetwork can be any internetwork-the Internet is a public internetwork and is the most widely known real world example. There are many examples of tunnels that are carried over corporate internetworks. And while the Internet provides one of the most pervasive and cost-effective internetworks, references to the Internet in this paper can be replaced by any other public or private internetwork that acts as a transit internetwork.

Tunneling technologies have been in existence for some time. Some examples of mature technologies include:

- **SNA tunneling over IP internetworks.** When System Network Architecture (SNA) traffic is sent across a corporate IP internetwork, the SNA frame is encapsulated in a UDP and IP header.
- **IPX tunneling for Novell NetWare over IP internetworks.** When an IPX packet is sent to a NetWare server or IPX router, the server or the router wraps the IPX packet in a UDP and IP header, and then sends it across an IP internetwork. The destination IP-to-IPX router removes the UDP and IP header and forwards the packet to the IPX destination.

New tunneling technologies have been introduced in recent years. These newer technologies-which are the primary focus of this paper-include:

- Point-to-Point Tunneling Protocol (PPTP). PPTP allows IP, IPX, or NetBEUI traffic to be encrypted, and then encapsulated in an IP header to be sent across a corporate IP internetwork or a public IP internetwork such as the Internet.
- Layer Two Tunneling Protocol (L2TP). L2TP allows IP, IPX, or NetBEUI traffic to be encrypted, and then sent over any medium that supports point-to-point datagram delivery, such as IP, X.25, Frame Relay, or ATM.
- IPSec tunnel mode. IPSec tunnel mode allows IP packets to be encrypted, and then encapsulated in an IP header to be sent across a corporate IP internetwork or a public IP internetwork such as the Internet.

6.11.1 Virtual Network Types

You can create virtual networks on the server running Hyper-V to define various networking topologies for virtual machines and the virtualization server. Using Virtual Network Manager (accessed from Hyper-V Manager), you have three different types of virtual networks to choose from.

- **External virtual networks.** Use this type when you want to allow virtual machines to communicate with externally located servers and the management operating system (sometimes referred to as the parent partition). This type also allows virtual machines on the same physical server to communicate with each other.
- **Internal virtual networks.** Use this type when you want to allow communication between virtual machines on the same physical server and virtual machines and the management operating system. An internal virtual network is a virtual network that is not bound to a physical network adapter. It is commonly used to build a test environment where you need to connect to the virtual machines from the management operating system.
- **Private virtual networks.** Use this type when you want to allow communication only between virtual machines on the same physical server. A private virtual network is a virtual network without a virtual network adapter in the management operating system. Private virtual networks are commonly used when you want to isolate virtual machines from network traffic in the management operating system and in the external networks.

You can use VPN connections whenever you need a secure point-to-point connection to connect users or networks. Typical VPN connections are either Internet-based or intranet-based. This section covers:

- Internet-based VPNs
- Intranet-based VPNs

6.11.2 Internet-based VPNs

By using an Internet-based VPN connection, you can avoid long-distance and 1-800 telephone charges while taking advantage of the global availability of the Internet.

Remote access over the Internet

Rather than making a long distance or 1-800 call to a corporate or outsourced network access server (NAS), a remote access client can call a local ISP. By using the established physical connection to the local ISP, the remote access client initiates a VPN connection across the Internet to the organization's VPN server. Once the VPN connection is created, the remote access client can access the resources of the private intranet. The following illustration shows remote access over the Internet.

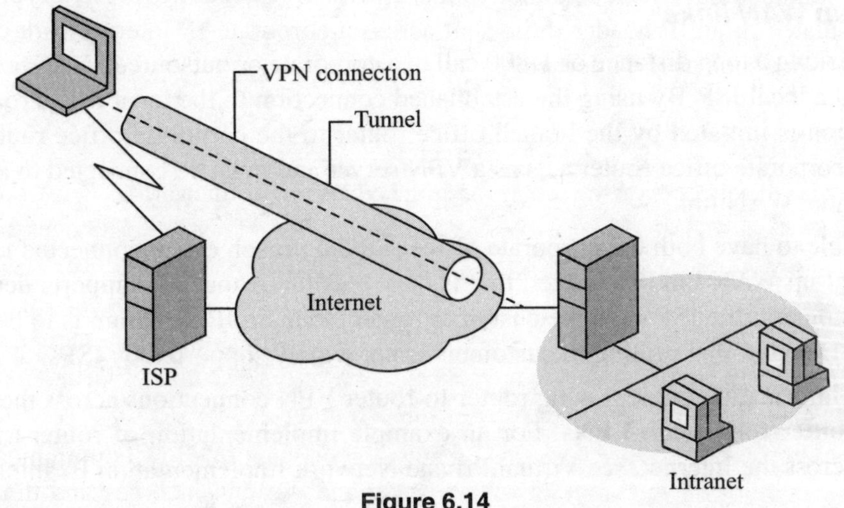

Figure 6.14

For more information on deploying remote access VPN connections across the Internet, see **Deploying VPNs for Remote Access**. For an example implementation of a remote access VPN connection across the Internet, see Virtual Private Network Implementation Examples.

Connecting networks over the Internet

When networks are connected over the Internet, a router forwards packets to another router across a VPN connection. This is known as a router-to-router VPN connection. To the routers, the VPN operates as a data-link layer link.

The following illustration shows connecting networks over the Internet.

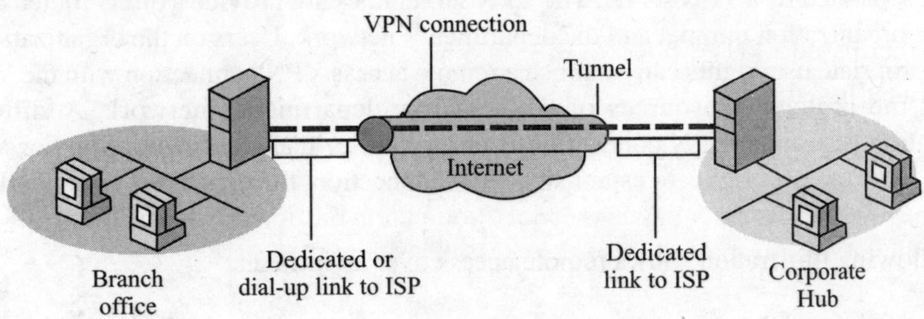

Figure 6.15

Using dedicated WAN links

Rather than using an expensive long-distance dedicated WAN link between branch offices, the branch office routers are connected to the Internet by using local dedicated WAN links to a local ISP. A router-to-router VPN connection is then initiated by either router across the Internet. Once connected, routers can forward directed or routing protocol traffic to each other by using the VPN connection.

Using dial-up WAN links

Rather than making a long distance or 1-800 call to a corporate or outsourced NAS, a branch office router can call a local ISP. By using the established connection to the local ISP, a router-to-router VPN connection is initiated by the branch office router to the corporate office router across the Internet. The corporate office router acts as a VPN server and must be connected to a local ISP by using a dedicated WAN link.

It is possible to have both the corporate office and the branch office connected to the Internet by using a dial-up WAN link. However, this is only feasible if the ISP supports demand-dialing routing to customers--the ISP calls the customer router when an IP datagram is to be delivered to the customer. Demand-dial routing to customers is not widely supported by ISPs.

For more information on deploying router-to-router VPN connections across the Internet, see **Deploying Router-to-Router VPNs**. For an example implementation of router-to-router VPN connections across the Internet, see Virtual Private Network Implementation Examples.

6.11.3 Intranet-based VPNs

The intranet-based VPN connection takes advantage of IP connectivity on an organization intranet.

Remote access over an intranet

On some organization intranets, the data of a department, such as a human resources department, is so sensitive that the department's network is physically disconnected from the rest of the organization's intranet. While this protects the department's data, it creates information acccssibility problems for those users who are not physically connected to the separate network.

With a VPN connection, the department's network is physically connected to the organization intranet but separated by a VPN server. The VPN server does not provide a direct routed connection between the organization intranet and the department's network. Users on the organization intranet with the appropriate user rights can establish a remote access VPN connection with the VPN server and access the protected resources of the sensitive department's network. Additionally, all communication across the VPN connection is encrypted for data confidentiality. For those users who do not have the user rights to establish a VPN connection, the department's network is hidden from view.

The following illustration shows remote access over an intranet.

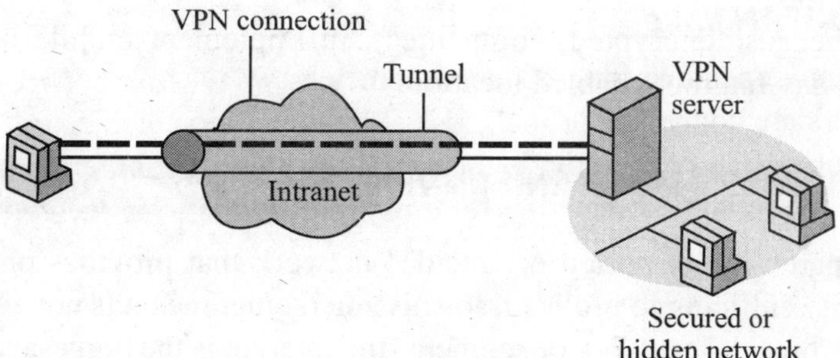

Figure 6.16

For more information on deploying remote access VPN connections across an intranet, see Deploying VPNs for Remote Access.

Connecting networks over an intranet

You can also connect two networks over an intranet by using a router-to-router VPN connection. Organizations with departments in separate locations, whose data is highly sensitive, may use a router-to-router VPN connection to communicate with each other.

For example, the finance department might need to communicate with the human resources department to exchange payroll information. The finance department and the human resources department are connected to the common intranet with computers that can act as VPN routers. Once the VPN connection is established, users on computers on either network can exchange sensitive data across the corporate intranet.

The following illustration shows connecting networks over an intranet.

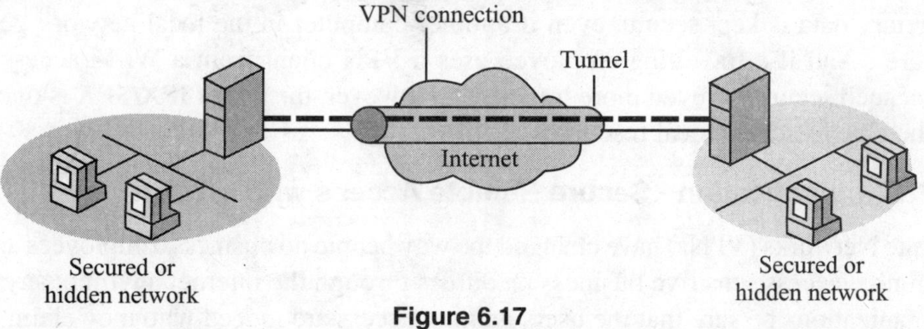

Figure 6.17

For more information on deploying router-to-router VPN connections across an intranet, see Deploying Router-to-Router VPNs.

Why should I use VPN? Nowadays most corporate offices operate through a computer network. Most offices also use the Internet, whether for research, e-mail or other communications. Although network firewalls prevent most attacks from outsiders seeking to breach into the network using the Internet, they also prevent remote users to access essential data. That's where VPN comes in. By ensuring that only properly configured and authenticated users can access network data, and that this data is secure because encrypted, companies can implement mobile network access and telecommuting from any Internet-enabled location.

6.12 AUTHENTICATION-MECHANISM (VPN)

VPN involves two parts: the protected or "inside" network that provides physical security and administrative security sufficing to protect transmission (sometimes it is not always the case), and a less trustworthy or "outside" network or segment (the internet is the biggest "jungle"). Generally, a Firewall sits between a remote user's workstation or Client and the host Network or Server . As the user's client establishes the communication with the firewall, the client may pass Authentication data to an authentication service inside the perimeter. A known trusted person, sometimes only when using trusted devices, can be provided with appropriate security privileges to access resources not available to general users.

Many VPN client programs can be configured to require that all IP traffic must pass through the tunnel while the VPN is active, for better security. From the user's perspective, this means that while the VPN client is active, all access outside their employer's secure network must pass through the same firewall as would be the case while physically connected to the office ethernet. This reduces the risk that an attacker might gain access to the secured network by attacking the employee's laptop: to other computers on the employee's home network, or on the public internet, it is as though the machine running the VPN client simply does not exist. Such security is important because other computers local to the network on which the client computer is operating may be untrusted or partially trusted. Even with a home network that is protected from the outside internet by a firewall, people who share a home may be simultaneously working for different employers over their respective **VPN** connections from the shared home network. Each employer would therefore want to ensure their proprietary data is kept secure, even if another computer in the local network gets infected with Malware . And if a travelling employee uses a VPN client from a Wi-Fi access point in a public place, such security is even more important. However, the use of IPX/SPX is one way users might still be able to access local resources.

6.12.1 VPN Authentication - Secure Remote Access with eToken

Virtual Private Networks (VPNs) have changed the way people do business. Employees and business partners can now access sensitive business resources through the internet anytime, anywhere. But how can organizations be sure that the users gaining access are indeed who they claim to be?

VPNs ensure privacy by providing a private tunnel through the Internet for remote access to the network. For full security, your VPN must be enhanced with a reliable user authentication mechanism, securing the end points of the VPN.

User name and password authentication is not enough - this method is weak and highly susceptible to hacking, cracking, keyloggers, and other attacks. It only takes one compromised password for your organization to lose control over who gains network access. Strong user authentication with a VPN provides true secure remote access for today's world.

6.12.2 eToken Provides the Best Secure Access to Your VPN

Together with our world class solution partners, eToken provides a highly robust and secure VPN solution, enabling:

- Strong user VPN authentication using varied methods, including certificates and one-time passwords
- Secure access from any platform, including unparalleled support for certificate-based access on Windows, Linux, and Mac OS platforms
- Rapid and easy deployment with Token Management System (TMS): a single system managing the entire solution

6.13 THE FOUR TYPES OF VPN SECURE DIALOG

The most important part of a VPN solution is security. The very nature of VPNs putting private data on public networks raises concerns about potential threats to that data and the impact of data loss. A Virtual Private Network must address all types of security threats by providing security services in the areas of:

6.13.1 Authentication (Access Control)

Authentication is the process of ensuring that a user or system is who the user claims to be. There are many types of authentication mechanisms, but these mechanisms all work off of one or more of the following principles: something you know (a login name, a password), something you have (a token, a card key), something you are (fingerprint, retinal scan). Weak authentication makes use of one of these components, usually a simple login/password sequence. Strong authentication combines at least two authentication components from different areas.

6.13.2 Presentation (Privacy /Encryption)

Encryption is based on two components: an algorithm and a key. A cryptographic algorithm is a mathematical function that combines data with the string of digits contained in a key to produce encrypted text. There are several major types of encryption of varying degrees of complexity, as measured by lengths (bits) of cryptographic keys. Examples: Advanced Encryption Standard (AES), RSA, Elliptic Curve Cryptosystems (ECC).

6.13.3 Transportation (Data Integrity)

The modification of data packets in a network is an attack on data integrity. Message authentication is the procedure used to verify that received messages come from the alleged source and have not been altered.

6.13.4 Non repudiation (Correct Message Reception) (UPTU 2010)

Non-repudiation is a means to verify that an electronic message has been sent and received by the specified parties. This protects both parties to ensure that neither the sender nor the recipient can later claim the transaction did not take place. This is vital not only when dealing with contracts, but also for online sales of digital goods such as music.

Non-repudiation refers to a state of affairs where the purported maker of a statement will not be able to successfully challenge the validity of the statement or contract. The term is often seen in a legal setting wherein the authenticity of a signature is being challenged. In such an instance the authenticity is being "repudiated".

Non-repudiation is the concept of ensuring that a contract, especially one agreed to via the Internet, cannot later be denied by one of the parties involved. In today's global economy, where face-to-face agreements are often not possible, non-repudiation is becoming extremely important to commerce.

With regards to digital security, non-repudiation means that it can be verified that the sender and the recipient were, in fact, the parties who claimed to send or receive the message, respectively. In other words, non-repudiation of *origin* proves that data has been sent, and non-repudiation of *delivery* proves it has been received. Traditional methods such as seals or signatures are vulnerable to forgery. Digital transactions are also potentially subject to fraud, such as when computer systems are broken in to or infected with trojan horses or viruses. Participants can potentially claim such fraud to attempt to repudiate a transaction.

In reference to digital security, *nonrepudiation* means to ensure that a transferred message has been sent and received by the parties claiming to have sent and received the message. Nonrepudiation is a way to guarantee that the sender of a message cannot later deny having sent the message and that the recipient cannot deny having received the message.

Nonrepudiation can be obtained through the use of:

- digital signatures — function as a unique identifier for an individual, much like a written signature.
- confirmation services — the message transfer agent can create digital receipts to indicated that messages were sent and/or received.
- timestamps — timestamps contain the date and time a document was composed and proves that a document existed at a certain time.

For e-Commerce and other electronic transactions, including ATMs (cash machines), all parties to a transaction must be confident that the transaction is secure; that the parties are who they say they are (authentication), and that the transaction is verified as final. Systems must ensure that a party cannot subsequently repudiate (reject) a transaction. To protect and ensure digital trust, the parties to such systems may employ Digital Signatures, which will not only validate the sender, but will also 'time stamp' the transaction, so it cannot be claimed subsequently that the transaction was not authorised or not valid etc.

Nonrepudiation is the assurance that someone cannot deny something. Typically, nonrepudiation refers to the ability to ensure that a party to a contract or a communication cannot deny the authenticity of their signature on a document or the sending of a message that they originated.

To repudiate means to deny. For many years, authorities have sought to make repudiation impossible in some situations. You might send registered mail, for example, so the recipient cannot deny that a letter was delivered. Similarly, a legal document typically requires witnesses to signing so that the person who signs cannot deny having done so.

On the Internet, a digital signature is used not only to ensure that a message or document has been electronically signed by the person that purported to sign the document, but also, since a digital signature can only be created by one person, to ensure that a person cannot later deny that they furnished the signature.

Since no security technology is absolutely fool-proof, some experts warn that a digital signature alone may not always guarantee nonrepudiation. It is suggested that multiple approaches be used, such as capturing unique biometric information and other data about the sender or signer that collectively would be difficult to repudiate.

Email nonrepudiation involves methods such as email tracking that are designed to ensure that the sender cannot deny having sent a message and/or that the recipient cannot deny having received it.

6.14 SECURITY CONCERN IN VPN

A firewall provides a strong barrier between your private network and internet. You can set firewalls to restrict the number of open ports, what type of packets are passed through and which protocols are allowed through.

While the potential savings and employee productivity increases that come with a remote-access VPN is significant and attractive to business, advance consideration must be given to the initial efforts required to plan, implement and monitor the technology. These considerations should be documented and addressed within security policy and additionally it is recommended by cisco that security policies be in place prior to be deployment of any security technology and also supporting the implementation of security policy to address VPN. It is important to note that while the VPN connection offers secure connectivity between the client PC and the corporate n/w it does not offer personal security features to the client, or protect it from outside attack from sources such as internet.

The VPN connection is in place to provide data confidentiality and integrity as well as authentication services. To reduce exposure to the corporate network, VPN users should be prevented from opening a VPN session to the corporate office, and leaving the connection established. This is of particular concern to remote users with broadband internet access due to the always on nature of the connection.

Security policy should address the VPN session connect time of the VPN clients and require that a session be terminated after a prescribed period of idle time has elapsed.

VPNs serve as gateways into corporate infrastructure and as such, security is a critical component of any SSL VPN offering. So important are the security-related capabilities of SSL VPN products that the differences in the security features set across products often determine which SSL VPN an enterprise will choose to deploy.

VPN security falls into three categories:

1. **Authentication and Authorization:** Users gain access to valuable information and systems through the SSL VPN. Because of this, it is critical to ensure that only authorized users access resources through the SSL VPN and that individual users access only those resources that they are supposed to access.
2. **Endpoint Security:** Endpoint security is sometimes known as Client-Side Security or Browser-Side Security. It refers to technology implemented to prevent any security-related problems occurring on devices used to access resources via the SSL VPN. It is important to realize that as opposed to earlier remote-access technologies, SSL VPN technology allows access from machines not known to be secure and as such, the endpoint concerns are different from the endpoint issues present in older remote-access scenarios.
3. **Server-Side Security:** Server-Side security, sometimes known as Network Security, refers to protecting internal corporate resources including the SSL VPN server itself from falling victim to any form of compromise.

Throughout our detailed review of these areas, it is important to keep in mind that SSL VPN products differ widely on how security is implemented. Each product does not necessarily offer all the features discussed, and due to product design and capability differences, some of the security issues may not even be pertinent when certain products are deployed. One should also be aware that some of the security functions described below are often implemented through the integration of third-party products with the core SSL VPN offering sometimes by the SSL VPN vendor and sometimes by the implementer. In any case, the remainder of this chapter describes the security concerns associated with SSL VPN technology and some approaches to addressing them.

Authentication is generally required to access secure data or enter a secure area. The requestor for access or entry shall authenticate himself based on proving authentically his identity by means of

- What are requestor individually knows as a secret, such as a password or a Personal Identification Number (PIN), or
- What the requesting owner uniquely has, such as a passport or an ID-card, or
- What the requesting bearer individually is, such as biometric data, like a fingerprint or the face geometry.

Two-factor authentication means using any independent two of these authentication methods (password + PIN) to increase the assurance that the bearer has been authorized to access secure systems. The owner of secure data or the operator of such secure systems is implementing two-factor authentication for laptops first because of the inherent security risks in mobile computers, to make it more difficult for unauthorized persons to use a "found" laptop to access secure data or systems. With mobile phones or smart phones, the quality of the problem does not change: A lost or left phone shall not be activated to enable the finder for unauthorised access to secure data or system. Multi-factor authentication hence means two or more of the authentication factor required for being authenticated.

Types of Two-factor Authentication

1. **Tokens:** One form of 'something you have' is the smart cad and USB tokens. Difference between the smart card and USB token are diminishing; both technologies include a microcontroller, an OS, a security application, and a secured storage area.
2. **Wireless tokens:** A new quality of tokens has been developed to ease the authentication process without keying character sequences and with automatic pairing of authentication factors. Presumed the bearer of the authentication factors prepares himself in good separation from other similar entities, the achieved pairing status may be maintained for all the daytime and especially during worktime without repetition of the pairing process.

6.15 NEED OF INTRUSION MONITORING AND DETECTION

An Intrusion Detection System is software and 1 or hardware designed to detect unwanted attempts at accessing, manipulating and/or disability of computer systems, mainly through a network, such as Internet.

IDS monitors network traffic and monitors for suspicious activity and alert the system or network administration. In some cases the IDS may also respond to anomalous are malicious traffic by taking action such as blocking the user cer source IP address pour accessing the ????.

IDS come in a variety of "flavours" and approach the goal of detecting suspicious traffic in different ways. There are network based (NIPS) and host based (HIDS) intrusion detection system. There are IDS that detect based on looking for specific signatures of known threats, similar to the way antivirus software typically detects and protects against malware and there are IDS that detect based on comparing traffic patterns against a baseline and looking for anomalius.

6.15.1 NIDS

A network intrusion detection system is an intrusion detection system that tries to detect malicious activity such as denial of service attacks part scans as even attempts to crack into computers by monitoring network traffic.

6.15.2 HIDS

A hart based IDS monitoring all or parts of the dynamic behaviour and the state of a computer system. Much as a NIDS will dynamically inspect network packets, a HIDS might detect which program accesses what resources and discover that, for exa, a work-processer has suddenly and inexplicably started modifying the system password database.

6.15.3 Signature Based

It attempt the detect attacks based on known "signature" or patterns. This similar to the way most antivirus s/w detects malware.

6.15.4 Anomaly Based

An IDS which is anomaly based will monitor network traffic and computer it against an established baseline. The baseline will identify what is "normal" for that network what sort of bandwidth is generally used. What protocols are used. What pcut and devices generally connect to each other and alert the administrator aruser when traffic is detected which is anomalous, or significantly different, that the baseline.

SUMMARY

Network security starts from authenticating the user, commonly with a username and a password. Since this requires just one thing besides the user name, i.e. the password which is something you 'know', this is sometimes termed one factor authentication. With two factor authentication something you 'have' is also used (example. a security token or 'dongle', an ATM card, or your mobile phone), or with three factor authentication something you 'are' is also used (example, a fingerprint or retinal scan).

Once authenticated, a firewall enforces access policies such as what services are allowed to be accessed by the network users. Though effective to prevent unauthorized access, this component may fail to check potentially harmful content such as computer worms or Trojans being transmitted over the network. Anti-virus software or an intrusion prevention system (IPS)[3] help detect and inhibit the action of such malware. An anomaly-based intrusion detection system may also monitor the network and traffic for unexpected (i.e. suspicious) content or behavior and other anomalies to protect resources, example, from denial of service attacks or an employee accessing files at strange times. Individual events occurring on the network may be logged for audit purposes and for later high level analysis.

The enterprise network often provides employees with a connection to the Internet from the corporate headquarters campus. It is usually centralized in order to more easily protect a single interface to the public world. That's exactly where perimeter control solution such as firewalls and intrusion-detection systems (IDSs) are generally deployed to prevent malicious intrusion of unauthorized persons. It is highly recommended that firewalls be implemented at every site within an enterprise to secure internal and external traffic, and at every point of interconnection with the Internet (e.g. even a remote PC). In some cases, it is appropriate to integrate this functionality with secure IP services gateways used also for remote office and remote access IP-VPNs.

In Network Security Architecture there are three defined network phases - from a basic secure network, to an autonomic network that provides enhanced situational awareness and reduces the need for human intervention, to an authenticated network that can automatically adjust its security posture to individual users.

The objective of the architecture is to create the framework that guides security technology evolution and to serve as a model for customers' security planning strategies as they evolve their networks.

In Information Security, intrusion detection is the act of detecting actions that attempt to compromise the confidentiality, integrity or availability of a resource. When Intrusion detection takes a preventive measure without direct human intervention, then it becomes an Intrusion-prevention system.

Intrusion detection can be performed manually or automatically. Manual intrusion detection might take place by examining log files or other evidence for signs of intrusions, including network traffic. A system that performs automated intrusion detection is called an Intrusion Detection System (IDS). An IDS can be either host-based, if it monitors system calls or logs, or network-based if it monitors the flow of network packets. Modern IDSs are usually a combination of these two approaches. Another important distinction is between systems that identify patterns of traffic or application data presumed to be malicious (misuse detection systems), and systems that compare activities against a 'normal' baseline (anomaly detection systems).

In order to perform basic network monitoring, you need to collect information on traffic at various points within your network. Although you definitely want to pay attention to your network borders, you should also look at purely internal traffic. If you have internal hosts providing unauthorized services for other internal hosts, you will miss this traffic if you only look at your borders. Various tools, including sniffers and packet capture utilities (such as tcpdump) and some intrusion detection systems (such as NFR Security's NID) and Internet Security Systems (ISS's) RealSecure), can be used to gather the appropriate information on traffic.

When you are preparing to collect data on network traffic, it's very important to get only the minimum information needed. Unless you are in an environment with a very low volume of traffic, trying to store the headers and contents of every packet will be far too resource-intensive. Besides, you can do initial traffic analysis simply by looking at a handful of the characteristics of packets and ignoring the packets' payloads altogether. Later, you can gather detailed information on particular services or hosts that require further investigation. One note of caution on this - by ignoring payloads, you will be unable to verify that the communications occurring on that port match the expected service. For example, a Trojan could use TCP port 21, making it appear during your analysis that FTP activity is occurring.

EXERCISES

1. What do you understand by network security.
2. Explain the different types of firewall.
3. What is intrusion detection. Explain it with its need and types,
4. What is network security model.
5. What are different types of h/w attacks.
6. What is virtual network.
7. Explain different types of VPN.
8. What is authentication mechanism.
9. Explain the use of tunneling with VPN.
10. Explain various types of VPN protocols.
11. What are the security concern in VPN.

UNIT – 4

CHAPTER 7

Security Metrics

7.1 WHAT IS SECURITY METRICS

In today's information technology world, there is a growing need for security solutions: information systems are more and more vulnerable because of the increased complexity and interconnection of insecure components and networks. Even though appropriate security approaches can be found, the resulting security level often remains unknown. It is a widely accepted principle that an activity cannot be managed well if it cannot be measured. Information security (IS) metrics offers work as a research field.

A growing number of security solutions are used in today's information technology world. However, the achieved security level is often unclear. There is not much research about what kind of information security metrics are used in Finnish industry and state institutions. Therefore, the aim of this study was to investigate the issues focused especially on the development and use of the metrics within production processes. The topics cover what kind of techniques are used in implementation and analysis of these metrics, how useful these metrics are for an organization, and what the future targets for the use of information security metrics are.

The aim is to reveal how development and implementation of the metrics is carried out in the organisations. In addition, the techniques used in implementation and analysis of metrics, as well as their usefulness and future targets are studied. Technical metrics and risk assessment metrics are commonly used, but there is a need to measure individual expertise as well as to automate and rationalize measurements. Most of the organisations do not use IS metrics as a process. However, there are intentions to implement an IS metrics process, as well as to integrate the IS metrics process into quality and business processes. Legislation, customers and technical development especially affect the future development of IS metrics.

The following questions guide the security metrics study:

- What is the definition of information security metrics?
- What kind of classifications and categorizations offer for IS metrics?

- What kind of methods and techniques are proposed for IS metrics?
- What is the direction of IS metrics research and development?
- What can we expect as the outcome of the experimental phase of this study, the interviews?

7.1.1 Information Security Metrics Concept

A few basic concepts are defined in order to understand the application of the concept of metrics in the IS area.

It defines the purpose of information security as "to ensure business continuity and minimise business damage by preventing and minimising the impact of security incidents". Information security is defined as the protection of information for confidentiality, integrity and availability. These dimensions can be explained as follows:

- **Confidentiality:** information is accessible only to those authorised to have access,
- **Integrity:** accuracy and completeness of information and computer software is safeguarded, and
- **Availability:** authorised users have access to information and associated assets when required.

7.2 SECURITY METRICS CLASSIFICATIONS

In order to understand how different IS can be constructed, one must take a look at definitions and constructions proposed in the literature for the security metrics model along with various classifications and categorizations for IS. According to Katzke, a security metrics model consists of three components:

- The object being measured,
- The security objectives, i.e. the "measuring rod" that the object is being measured against, and
- The method of measurement.

The model is illustrated in Figure 1, as well as how the security objectives are divided into:

- Security requirements, such as specifications, standards, control objectives and CC- (Common Criteria, 1999) Protection Profiles,
- Best practises,
- Security base lines,
- Due diligence, i.e. security management based on experience, and
- Maturity models like SSE-CMM (Systems Security Engineering Capability Maturity Model, 2003) and IA-CMM (INFOSEC Assessment CapabilityMaturity Model, 2003).

7.2.1 Methods of Measurement Include

- Direct testing (like functional, red team/penetration),
- Evaluation (for example with Common Criteria),
- Assessment (like risk/vulnerability assessment),
- Accreditation,
- Training/education/level of competence and
- Observation of system performance, such as intrusion detection.

Lindqvist categorize the security guidelines according to the audience for whom they offer the most advantage. They claim that, for vendors and manufacturers, the functionality of the system and the development process have been the target of standards specify criteria against which security evaluations can be made. In their opinion, baseline security documents have been created for producers to set a minimum set of requirements for security features that an information technology should possess. Security policies are useful to managers, operators and users of information technology system, because they need to follow certain rules in order to minimise potential threats. In this context, standards mostly mean guidelines and codes of practices.

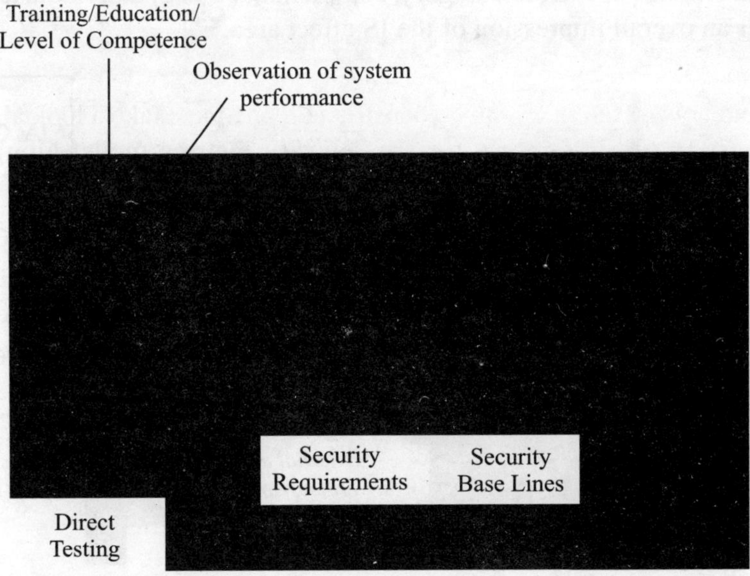

Figure 7.1: Security metrics model according to Katzke (2001).

Jonsson sorts the methods of measurement into the following techniques: risk analysis, certification and measures of the intrusion process.

- **Risk analysis** is an estimation of the probability of specific intrusions and their consequences and costs, and it can be thought of as a trade-off to the corresponding costs for protection,

- **Certification** is the classification of the system in classes based on design characteristics and security mechanisms, "The `better' the design is, the more secure the system.", and
- **Measure on the intrusion process** is a statistical measure of a system based on the effort it takes to make an intrusion. "The harder it is to make an intrusion, the more secure the system".

The security metrics model can be seen as an abstraction in Henning's definition: it divides IS* into four categories:

- Technical,
- Organizational,
- Operational IS

Henning emphasizes that some viewpoints are excluded from this classification, i.e. individual IS(describing individual expertise) and environmental IS(describing security-relevant aspects of an organisation's or operation's environment, in particular, threats). Figure 2 clarifies this abstraction and binds the IS to the process. The model is considered from the perspectives of "type of object", which means IS, "purpose", in other words how the IS is to be used, and "intended audience", which means the people who primarily use the information gained by the use of IS. However, Table 1 presents the main features of each IS category, complemented with individual and environmental IS in order to offer an overall impression of the IS effect area.

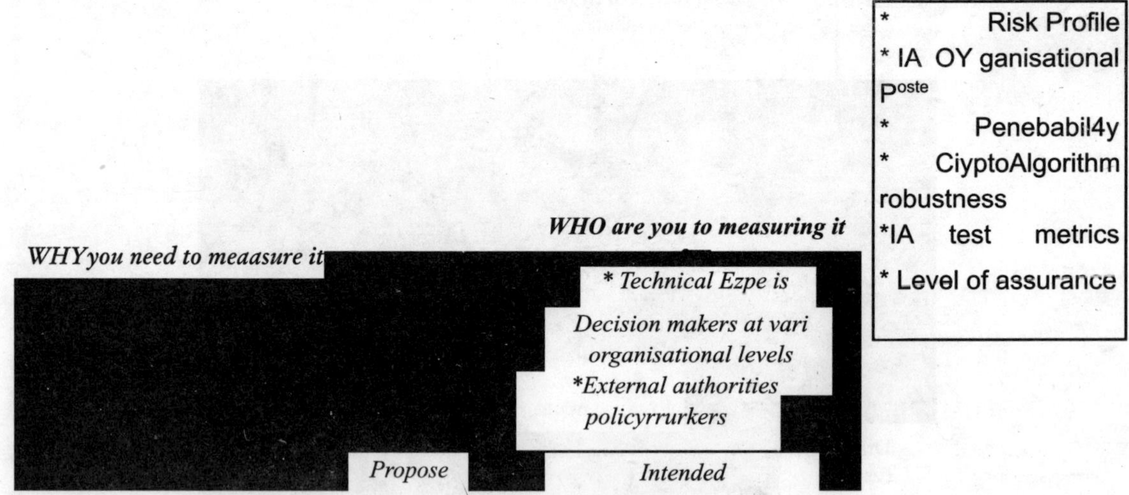

Figure 7.2: Characterisation of IS.

The purpose for which the IS are being developed can be divided into decision support and mandated reporting of IS status or posture. According to Figure 7.2, IS can be used to describe, compare and predict the behavior and attributes of a system or its components.

Swanson offer a different classification in their Security Metrics Guide:

- Implementation metrics to measure implementation of security policy,

- Effectiveness/efficiency metrics to measure results of security services delivery, and
- Impact metrics to measure business or mission impact of security events.

Miettinen divides metrics into qualitative and quantitative. Qualitative metrics use discrete variables and measurement is thus conducted by assessing. Examples of qualitative metrics are measuring the criticalness of a corporation's activity, measuring the level of management's IS awareness, and personnel and risk assessment. Quantitative metrics use numeric measures, such as probabilities, percentages, ratios and numbers. Quantitative values are gained by measuring technical issues, the costs resulting from activities and the number of development acts.

7.2.2 Technical Information Security Metrics

Technical IS can be used to describe, and hence compare, technical objects. This includes algorithms, specifications, architectures and alternative designs, products, and as-implemented systems at different stages of the system life cycle. Thus technical metrics represents quantitative metrics using Miettinen's classification.

Intrusion detection metrics is a typical example of technical IS for which a reasonable amount of research can be found. This research details intrusion detection systems (IDS), which, due to their technical nature, can be modelled and parameterised for further modularising and quantifying.

7.2.3 Organizational Information Security Metrics

Organizational IS are for describing and tracking the effectiveness of organisational programs and processes, such as the percentage of personnel trained in security and the percentage of systems accredited. Thus, organisational IS* represent both quantitative and qualitative metrics in Miettinen's (1999) model. One example of this is the study by Kajava & Leiwo (1994) about information security staff in organisations. They discuss the approach to measure the amount of IS staff and its applicability in Finland, based on research carried out in the U.S. by Wood (1989). They point out that the size of an organization is a relative concept when interpreting these kinds of results, as a staff size of 2500 people is not small in Finland, even though this is the case in the U.S. This is why using this kind of IS as an indicator of the state of IS requires common sense, yet can be one important indicator about investment in IS.

Commercial organisations aim mainly at the use of metrics to resolve the effectiveness of organisational programs and processes, as well as the amount and quality needed for security actions. Governmental units mainly measure how well the organization meets the requisite mandates (reporting metrics). The IS metrics for these organisations often serves as a tool for decision support. The difference between the aims of these sectors can result in different needs for IS.

A similarity for both sectors is that both usually have a functioning security program for the IT modernization process, which comprises the same steps: requirements, approvals, development and installation. There are also established procedures for both sectors that include approval points as well as IS integrated into any program/business case. Both rely on auditors, penetration testing and configuration management procedures. The difference is that government procurements are constrained by national and organisational policies and architectures (policy-driven), while the commercial enterprises rely on the personal judgments of the security practitioner (profit-driven). Due diligence on the part of the individuals is expected and forms the basis for management approval in commercial units, while the government approval process is more structured

7.2.4 Operational Information Security Metrics

Henning (2001) refers to the use of operational IS as to describe and manage the risks to operational environments, including as-used systems and operating practises. Operational IS* are hence mainly risk assessment metrics for which their component metrics related to asset values, impact severity, threats, vulnerabilities and effectiveness of security measures. But they also represent the number of advisories responded to, the time devoted to patch installation and the percentages of systems patched that are assessment components.

In order to manage and measure operational attributes, it must be understood what constitutes the organisation's operational environment: controllable areas, external areas and assumable or predictable matters. Controllable areas consist of physical, procedural and personnel security measures, as well as information systems owned or operated by the organization. External areas consist of systems that have an interface with the organisation's own systems, or systems that the organisation's own system is dependent on.

Table 7.1: IS classification according to Henning (2001) with complementary qualities.

	Tech. IS	Org.IS	Oper.IS	Brainst.	Indiv.IS	Env. IS
Describe	Technical Objects	Effectiveness of programs and processes of the organisation	Risks to operational environments including as-used systems and operating practises	Synthesis, cross-track issues and big-picture concerns	Individual expertise	Security relevant aspects of the environment of organisation or operation
Example	Logs	Percentage of systems accredited	Asset values	Combination of other 3 IS* into one framework	Awareness or educational level of an employee	Threats caused by functioning in environment
Challenges	May contain a lot of useless data, often need to be filtered and rationalised	Require viewpoint of the whole organisation, not necessarily directly applicable in other organisations	Require that the operational environment and its effects are understood, this can often be just assessed	Require viewpoint of the whole system life cycle	Difficult to level on the organisation scale	Possibly difficult to model functions of an environment, can contain unexpected factors and combinations

7.2.5 Problems in Application of Metrics in Information Security

There are a few disturbing factors that may be faced when applying metrics in the area of information security. Some concluded problems are illustrated in Figure 7.3.

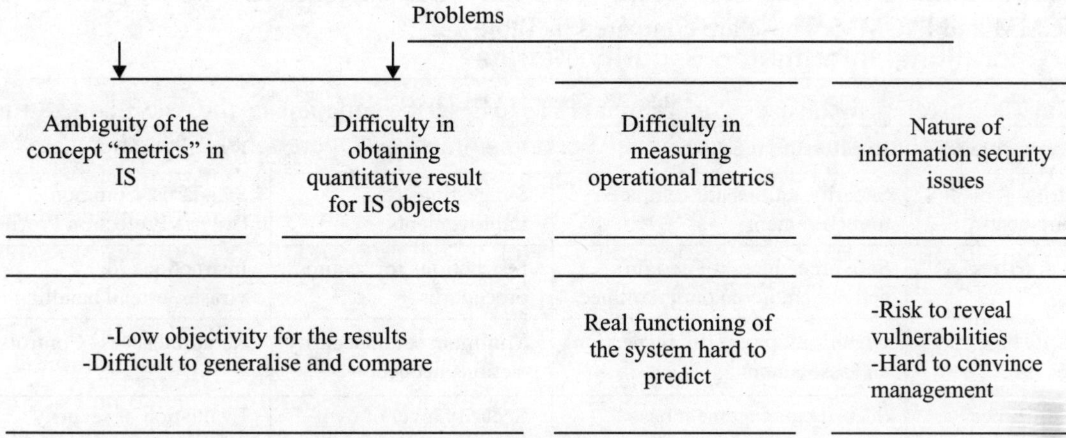

Figure 7.3: Problems related to IS metrics

7.2.6 Nature of Information Security Issues

The purpose of measuring information security is ultimately to be aware of the current security level. This process reveals the strengths of the system, but also the vulnerabilities, which require some kind of reaction. The reaction may sometimes be as simple as leaving vulnerabilities as they are, that is, fixing them might be less valuable than taking the risk caused by the vulnerability. Often the cost of a certain threat is hard to define. This mechanism, which is part of the risk analysis process, is using security metrics itself, but the object might also be other types of IS metrics.

The concept of metrics is overlapping and complex. In organisations where the management is not aware of IS issues, it might be extremely hard to convince them to invest in better security. What makes things worse is that security issues are invisible. The better the security is, the more invisible IS becomes in an organisation's life. Therefore, investments in security do not show visible results in daily life, and this is why there may be pressure to reduce investment in security if "nothing happens".

Often the measurement process may require outside knowledge, for example, in audit sessions, or long-term commitment from the staff. This itself may become too high a risk for the organisation compared to the benefits gained by the use of effective metrics. Human factors are considerable for any IS, and the competitive benefit of gaining access to the organisation's precious information, its weaknesses, and strengths may become too attractive for some people. The information, when in the wrong hands, can even be devastating to the trustworthiness of the company (Kajava & Leiwo, 1994). Therefore, many organisations may ask themselves: "can we afford good security?"

7.2.7 Security Objectives

Using the classification from Katzke (2001), security objectives can be divided into the following: security requirements (such as specifications, standards, control objectives and Common Criteria Protection Profiles), best practises, security base lines, due diligence and maturity models like SSE-CMM and IACMM. These are compared in Table 7.2.

Table 7.2: Security Objectives

Security objective	Application method	Expected result	Example
Security requirements	Security actions are compared to requirement	Suggestions for improvements	Standards, Common Criteria Protection Profiles
Best practises	Safe procedures for certain activity are given or determined	Instructions for secure procedures	Instructions for viruses, e-mail handling
Security base Lines	Organisation security inspection and assessment	Minimum set of security actions needed	Required access Controls
Due diligence	Security management based on expertise	Security level of own organisation or business partner	Evaluation of security controls
Maturity models	Security practises are inspected and compared to the model	Explicit security level	SSE-CMM

7.2.8 Security Requirements

IS can be considered one quality factor of the organisation's products and services. Therefore, many common factors can be found when considering security issues and organisation's quality actions. The standards used in quality assessment can act as a model when developing information security quality issues, since quality standards have been implemented and tested for a much longer period of time, and far more broadly in industry organisations than have security standards, and the development is therefore further advanced.

Finnish State Administration gives a broad IS instruction set that covers all IS subareas. The instructions have been developed by VAHTI (Valtionhallinnon Tietoturvallisuuden Kehitysohjelma, 2004). It helps to ensure and backup IS in organisations under the supervision of State Administration. Its development targets are, for example, virus protection, ensuring information systems, management of log data and e-mail and issues concerning electronic services.

Malcolm Baldrige criteria are standard for self-assessment in order to measure and improve organisation excellence. The criteria is divided into seven sub-areas, 1) leadership, 2) strategic planning, 3) customer and target focus, 4) measurement, analysis and knowledge management, 5) human resource focus, 6) process management and 7) business results. Details defined in the sub-areas are detected in the target organisation and evaluated against the criteria.

The Goal Question Metric (GQM) Approach (Basili et al., 1994) is based upon the assumption that for an organisation to measure in a purposeful way it must first specify the goals for itself and its projects. Then, it must trace those goals to the data that are intended to define those goals operationally and finally provide a framework for interpreting the data with respect to the stated goals. Thus the organisation's informational needs have to be clarified, so that they can be quantified whenever possible, and the quantified information can be analysed regarding whether or not the goals have been achieved. Figure 7.4 illustrates the GQM process:

- **Conceptual level (GOAL):** Goal is defined for an object.
- **Operational level (QUESTION):** A set of questions is used to characterise the way the assessment/achievement of a specific goal is going to be performed based on some characterisation model.
- **Quantitative level (METRIC):** A set of data is associated with every question in order to answer it in a quantitative way.

Figure 7.4: S. GQMprocess (Basili et al., 1994)

Common criteria (CC, 1999) are a "catalogue or dictionary of requirements" for constructing the basis for evaluation of the security properties of IT products and systems. It comprises Protection Profiles (PP) and Security Targets (ST). Their concepts differ from each other in that PP are implementation-independent and ST are implementation-specific. Therefore, ST can be considered to be security objectives as well, only targeted for a different audience (product vendors and implementers). CC present a similar concept described earlier in this paper, namely "security objectives", which is the main element of PP and ST. In CC the security objective is described as to "reflect the intent to counter identified threats and address any identified organisational security policies and assumptions".

CC defines security functional requirements and security assurance requirements. Functional requirements define the desired security behaviour, while assurance requirements enable an assessment of the trustworthiness in the effective implementation of the specified security measures. CC exclude the following security features: evaluation criteria pertaining to administrative security measures not directly related to the IT security measures, evaluation of the technical physical aspects of IT security specifically, evaluation methodology or the administrative and legal framework under which the criteria may be applied by evaluation authorities, procedures for use of evaluation results in product or system accreditation or as the subject of criteria for the assessment of the inherent qualities of cryptographic algorithms. Figure 7.5 depicts the major elements that form the context for evaluations.

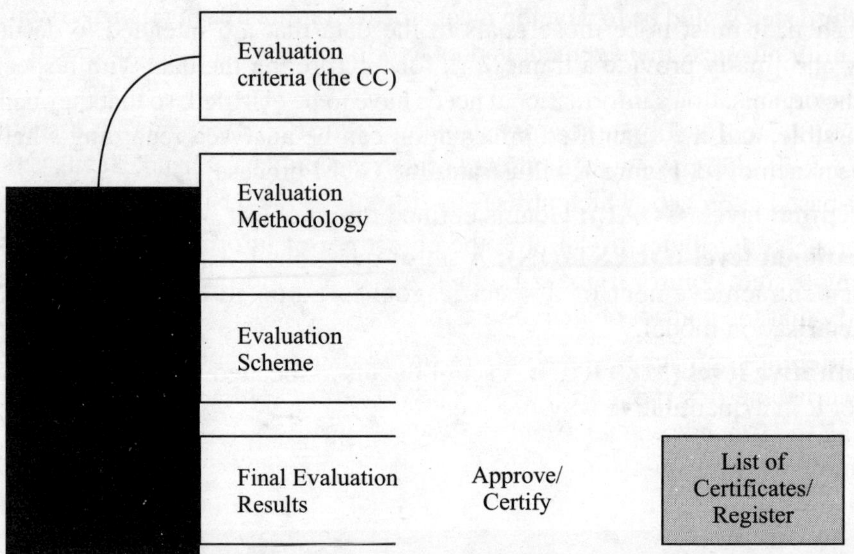

Figure 7.5: Evaluation context of the Common Criteria (Common Criteria, 1999)

7.2.9 Building a Security Metrics Program

Payne (2001) proposes seven key steps for guiding the process of building a security metrics program. They are:

- Defining the metrics program goals and objectives,
- Deciding what metrics to generate,
- Developing strategies for generating the metrics,
- Establishing benchmarks and targets,
- Determining how the metrics will be reported,
- Creating an action plan and acting on it, and
- Establishing a formal program review/refinement cycle.

Another approach, the NIST's metrics program by Swanson et al. (2003), consists of the four independent components: Results-Oriented Metrics Analysis, Quantifiable Performance Metrics, Practical Security Policies and Procedures, and Strong Upper-Level Management Support.

Leach's (2003) definition is much more abstract, but it recognises the key problems in the IS* development area well. He suggests four steps to be taken when aiming towards better IS* solutions:

- The first would be to take a fresh approach in a sense that one should have an attitude towards learning to interpret data in a reliable way, not according to beliefs,
- The second step would be to develop a framework for describing the security characteristics of threats and solutions in terms that can be quantified. The essential aspect pointed out here is that "we need an agreed definition of what the security dimensions are and what their yardsticks should be so that our security terms can be quantified",

- The third step would be to develop mechanisms for quantifying risk aversion and how much insecurity business management is prepared to tolerate for a given system or environment, and
- The fourth step, "calibrate security steel, our security components", is essentially the easiest part once the appropriate methods and practises would be at hand. Bayuk (2000) presents an audit-based approach, which utilises audit steps as the basis for metrics.

Her approach contributes to defining the objectives of information security controls and the corresponding system control framework, then processing the audit steps that cover both, i.e. the steps to verify that the control objectives are met.

These different approaches are examples of the many methods available for constructing an effective security metrics program. Despite the differences, they all agree on the importance of understanding the framework and establishing the security objectives that are to be measured and met by the metrics.

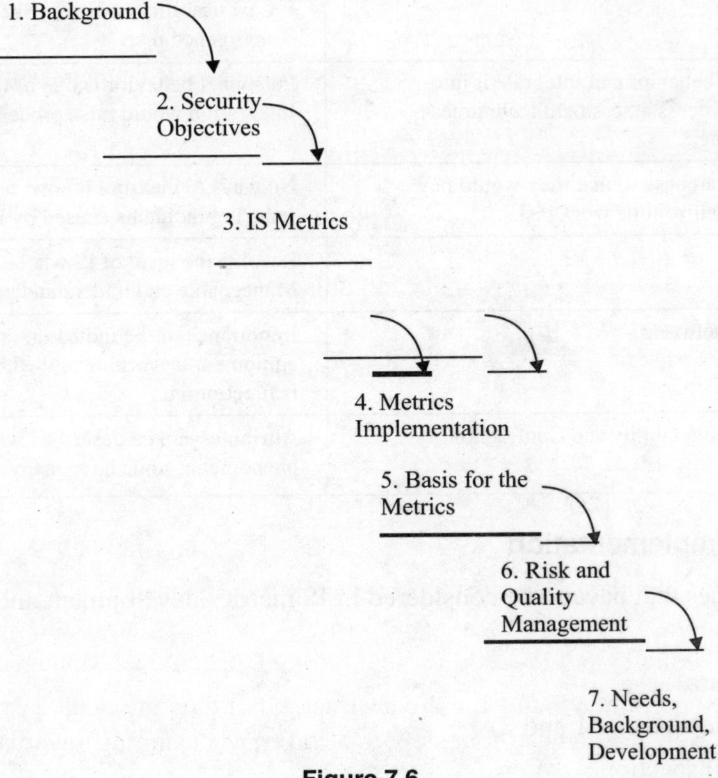

Figure 7.6

7.2.10 What Kind of Security Objectives Cause the Need for IS Metrics

The origin of state institutions' security objectives is usually a compromise of their own action group recommendations and the legislation directions. The most common objectives that cause the need for IS metrics is the effect on the personnel IS behaviour and ensuring the business goal and fulfilment, as presented in Table 7.3.

Table 7.3: Security objectives causing a need for information security metrics.

Security objectives	**Related issues**
State institutions	
Confidentiality, access control monitoring, Integrity	Protection of existing information
Maturity of the IS processes, responsibility assignment, reporting activities	Pervasive IS process
Industry organizations	
Measurement of work practices	System administrators are big risks. • Skills good, but the morale can be low. • Low usability caused by laziness, inexpericnce, negligence feats
Measure personnel behavior and integrate it into the used business process assessment techniques in quality monitoring.	Personnel behavior is one of the greatest risks. Integration would raise process effectiveness.
Raise personnel awareness so that they would pay attention to IS in their routine work tasks.	No ways to measure it now; benefits gained by reducing incidents caused by ignorance.
Enable business	Resolve the level of IS where incidents are Manageable and understandable.
Availability of the network	Importance of the indicators: resolve which equipment is working and whether the network is functioning.
Integrity/accuracy, availability and Confidentiality	Attributes can be described with certain phenomena; some have many aspects.

7.2.11 Metrics Implementation

There are four issues that have to be considered in IS metrics development and implementation:

1. Meaning
2. Who measures
3. Methods (depends on 1 and 2)
4. Classes of inspection

A problem in metrics implementation is the absence of processes. Interviewees are not that worried about the kind of metrics they lack, but rather the process concerning the current metrics use, or the lack thereof. It can be concluded that even though there are a variety of different measurement technologies or methods are applied, they cannot be considered as useful as if they were applied as a process-like manner. The most hindering factors in this seem to especially be the lack of readiness or ignorance of the top management to commit to IS issues, together with an absence of documentation caused by unclear or inappropriate responsibilities. This indicates that the personnel involved should have the right expertise. Futhermore, metrics use should be part of quality thinking and corporate management, so that it would become a part of yearly planning. Responsible persons should be at least somewhat aware of IS issues:

Table 7.4: Metrics implementation in organisations as a process.

Metric process in the organization	Problems and requirements
	State institutions
• **Firewall, virus control** and server-side administration (e-mail control), metrics process restricted to using standards • **Two-sided actions** with partners involving process activities (e.g. reporting) -* improvement strategies -* learning process • **Cyclic evolutionary process** model: theory and practise combined	• Inside business units the process is not Well managed because of the **complexity of the environment.**
	Industry organizations
• The process is an essential concept because "unless it is a process, it is random", and can not be improved	• Processes are not documented, it is Unclear how things are applied in production *responsibilities open • Has to be integrated into quality and management, problem finding metrics

Table 7.5: Responsibility division for metrics implementation in organisations.

Government	Industry
• Normal division like the normal IS division	• Division in site-level and in production according to certain functionalities, on the architectural level. Both geographical and architectural level based on the location
• Operational staff of IS and data communications techniques (5-10 people)	• Every process has an owner, who is responsible for an adequate level and the functionality of the process
• Centralised IT department maintaining vulnerability table managed by system administrators, vulnerability tool development within units, information security group responsible for risk analysis	• IS design and maintenance responsibility with system administrators, responsibility for measuring how well instructions are followed is difficult
• Administrative group responsible as a unit: implementation and design knowledge and tasks, ideas for changes from user response	

In general, the problem is that IS metrics are not applied as processes. There are some processes implemented, but they do not cover the whole system. In addition to this, some IS metrics processes can be hard to point out, not to mention integrate into the system. Factors that affect the metrics process evolution are legislation restrictions and responsibility questions.

Table 7.6: IS metrics process development

Opinions and experiences regarding the IS metrics process	Problems and development suggestions
State institutions	
• System scanning embedded, easy: networks planned and not public no legislation problems	• **Aim:** embed processes in quality management processes, part of the quality manual tailored requirements analys is standard -* basis for IS
• **Corporate tolerance concept** will most likely affect how processes are embedded. "...so that in the future, the CEO most likely has to give warrant, he himself has to sign the contract."	• Biggest challenge to get measurement embedded no means or operation models.
• Pressures to improve processes in a way that the work processes built can be supervised in order to prevent misuse.	• In some network-related activities legislation deterrent or problematic.
Industry Organisations	
Physical side (access control): easily a embedded in actual work (education and motivation) as **immaterial equirements** like hard to see the presence comes along by knowledge	Certificate not a complete solution, way for an organisation to fmd a suitable level of requirements analysis and to prove IS level.

7.2.12 Need for IS metrics

The most common need is to have a constantly developing metrics system. Many respondents emphasise and justify the importance of a process. The process would enhance the definition of IS issues and update the policy when history data produced comparison material. The problem is the contradiction between IS and user privacy; there is the need to preserve valuable information by strict procedures, but at the same time the aim is to offer usability and gain confidence from users.

Table 7.7: Needs for IS metrics

Need for metrics	Type of metrics	Original type
Customer expects high-quality services with IS as an expectation value need for means that show the IS quality level of the service	Organisational	S
Logs and their analysis need development (rationalisation), detection of what launched applications, what equipment connected to the network	Technical, organisational	S
Detecting listening computers protocol firewall does not help much.	Technical	S

Audit methods that could be sustained continuously, self-directing method that could be used, for example, continuously as a part of normal work process and included as internal auditing concepts	Technical, operational	S
New personnel should be educated, including security managers that have not worked with the metrics. Through meetings and educational events	Organisational, individual	S
Complex systems -*reality and policies separate - need for measurement system that checks how and whether policy is derived from business, are the IS risks managed, how well the policy adheres to the actual processes or structures -*policy can be adjusted easily	Technical, organisational, operational	S
Need in administration. The process of IS: from business strategy, proceeding through IS policy to IS strategy -*objectives. But how to measure IS work executed within business processes, via guidelines, procedures and policies -*a tool for quality control	Organisational, operational	I
Optimal system protection level with risk and business analysis, checking it with some points	Operational	I
Measure every day IS work within processes, who is obeying instructions	Operational, individual	I

Table 7.8: Useful metrics for the organisations and affecting factors.

What measures organisations need	Affecting factors
State institutions	
Common standard	IS emphasises a process more than a product.
IS culture	Different audiences have different views. And yet it is included in all policies. "Enemy inside"
Technical tools	Only parts that are easily predictable can be automated.
To get the spectrum that comes from different tasks so well profiled that illegal actions could be separated from there	Different zones in the system "outside you can do anything but the closer you get to the kernel the more restricted it becomes, tools, protocols, policies."
Data concurrently from several metrics	The more sensors provide combined and analysed data, the better picture of the whole situation every moment or on every time scale. Data rewind, checkpoints
Usability metrics: to be able to measure the capacity of a functioning production system	Notification when the usability of the system is so low that is has to be replaced by another system "we are constantly losing time, and in business money."
Measure all OSI 7 layers and the 7`h layer, the application layer, in several ways at several points	A need for a covered checkpoint system
Measure network in a way that user privacy is not threatened	Network availability is a primary target.
Absolute metrics whether the computer is broken into or not.	One viewpoint to intrusion detection

Virus tracing and localisation in the computers in the network	Includes the questions of privacy, tracing people
User behaviour	Complex systems, people might not even know they have threatened IS instructions
Industry	
User behaviour	Privacy protection issues
Personnel behaviour	Probably one of the main issues
Education	Customers not very aware of IS issues dpen & on the corporation size whether they Demand documentation -*sales personnel should be educated.
Automation of IS metrics	Checkpoints to the system that can be measured.
The minimum IS metrics amount required	Determined at all times to minimise the costs
IS metrics use should be integrated into business management	Otherwise it will be experienced as an extra cost, a trouble that does not promote business.
Absolute security in a product, process, premises or practises	Absolute modelling, not necessarily exact, but accurate enough
Self-learning SW	SW can learn from its own functioning and spend endless time testing itself, which can never be done with human work.
Staff IS behaviour, not only awareness	No need for technical tools or system solutions

A well-managed security metrics program requires effective documentation management. Documentation concerning security policies and procedures has to be constantly updated and close to the implemented practises. The dialogue between theory and practise is optimally a cyclic process, where the significance of tacit knowledge is understood and used as a source for the development and updating of documentation. Again, the allocation of responsibility affects the success of this process.

In terms of technical metrics, there is need for automation, rationalization and self-learning. In order to rationalize resource management, the minimum amount of needed metrics has to be measured. The rationalization could be implemented with automated tools that inspect the system's state and priorities actions. Furthermore, routine tasks could be automated with appropriate systems. This would all help to justify the need for attention to a pervasive information security process, as savings could be achieved by rationalization.

Institute of Standards and Technology (NIST) define metrics as tools designed to facilitate decision-making and improve performance and accountability through collection, analysis, and reporting of relevant performance-related data. Metrics are simply a standard or system of measurement. In this case, it is a standard for measuring security, specifically measuring an organization's security posture. Although there are some published standards for measuring security, ideally security metrics should be adjusted and tuned to fit a specific organization or situation.

It helps to understand what metrics are by drawing a distinction between metrics and measurements. Measurements provide single-point-in-time views of specific, discrete factors, while metrics are derived by comparing to a predetermined baseline two or more measurements taken over time.3 Measurements are generated by counting; metrics are generated from analysis.4 In other words, measurements are objective raw data and metrics are either objective or subjective human interpretations of those data.

Good metrics are those that are SMART, i.e. specific, measurable, attainable, repeatable, and time-dependent, according to George Jelen of the International Systems Security Engineering Association. Truly useful metrics indicate the degree to which security goals, such as data confidentiality, are being met, and they drive actions taken to improve an organization's overall security program. Distinguishing metrics meaningful primarily to those with direct responsibility for security management from those that speak directly to executive management interests and issues is critical to development of an effective security metrics program.

7.3 THE BENEFITS OF SECURITY METRICS

A team of more than 150 government, private, and academic experts worked to reach consensus on an initial set of security outcome and practice metrics. These metrics cover the following business functions:

Application Security

- Number of Applications
- Percentage of Critical Applications
- Risk Assessment Coverage
- Security Testing Coverage

Configuration Change Management

- Mean-Time to Complete Changes
- Percent of Changes with Security Review
- Percent of Changes with Security Exceptions

Financial

- Information Security Budget as % of IT Budget
- Information Security Budget Allocation

Incident Management

- Mean-Time to Incident Discovery
- Incident Rate
- Percentage of Incidents Detected by Internal Controls
- Mean-Time Between Security Incidents
- Mean-Time to Recovery

Patch Management

- Patch Policy Compliance
- Patch Management Coverage
- Mean-Time to Patch

Vulnerability Management

- Vulnerability Scan Coverage
- Percent of Systems Without Known Severe Vulnerabilities
- Mean-Time to Mitigate Vulnerabilities
- Number of Known Vulnerability Instances

A widely accepted management principle is that an activity cannot be managed if it cannot be measured. Security falls under this rubric. Metrics can be an effective tool for security managers to discern the effectiveness of various components of their security programs, the security of a specific system, product or process, and the ability of staff or departments within an organization to address security issues for which they are responsible. Metrics can also help identify the level of risk in not taking a given action, and in that way provide guidance in prioritizing corrective actions. Additionally, they may be used to raise the level of security awareness within the organization.

Finally, with knowledge gained through metrics, security managers can better answer hard questions from their executives and others, such as:

- Are we more secure today than we were before?
- How do we compare to others in this regard?
- Are we secure enough?

7.3.1 Why Metrics Generation Is Difficult

Many in the security industry will agree that the number of successful security attacks an organization has experienced is not necessarily an indication of how secure that organization is. Luck plays a major role and how does one measure luck, So a security manager needs to look beyond the organization's security incident record for indicators of security strength. There are further complications they need to keep in mind, however, in their search for meaningful metrics.

As a case in point, asset value, threat, and vulnerability are critical elements of overall risk and are (or should be) weighed in most decisions having to do with security. Each of these elements poses difficulties when trying to incorporate them into a useful security metric. Asset value is the easiest of these three elements to measure; however, certain aspects of value, such as a company's good reputation, are hard, if not impossible, to quantify. Some believe that threat cannot be measured at all, since it is the potential for harm, although survey results and other information gathered from external sources could be useful in quantifying threat at a high level. Some progress is being made in objectively measuring vulnerability , at least for specific types networked computer devices. For example, the Center for Internet Security has established benchmarks and developed automated tools to detect levels of computer system vulnerabilities. Measurements of other facets of vulnerability, such as degree of understanding of security issues among computer users, remain somewhat subjective.

Security metrics are also hard because the discipline itself is still in the early stages of development There is not yet a common vocabulary and not many documented best practices to follow. Those pursuing the development of a security metrics program should think of themselves as pioneers and be prepared to adjust strategies as experience dictates.

7.4 BUILDING A SECURITY METRICS PROGRAM WITH ITS CLASSIFICATION

To facilitate understanding and acceptance at all levels of a new security metrics program, it is advisable to ground the program in process improvement frameworks that are already familiar to the organization. The Dupont Corporation, for example, bases its program on the popular "Six Sigma Breakthrough Strategy", a marketed management process that focuses on defect elimination. The First Union Corporation ties its metrics program to corporate security standards compliance. A representative of Bear, Stearns and Company espouses an audit-based approach that verifies compliance with industry standard control objectives as well as locally defined standards. Regardless of the underlying framework, the seven key steps below could be used to guide the process of establishing a security metrics program.

1. Define the metrics program goal(s) and objectives
2. Decide which metrics to generate
3. Develop strategies for generating the metrics
4. Establish benchmarks and targets
5. Determine how the metrics will be reported
6. Create an action plan and act on it, and
7. Establish a formal program review/refinement cycle

This seven-step methodology should yield a firm understanding of the purpose of the security metrics program, its specific deliverables, and how, by whom, and when these deliverables will be provided. The steps are briefly described below, and outcome examples, where appropriate, are provided.

Step 1: Define the metrics program goal(s) and objectives

Because developing and maintaining a security metrics program could take considerable effort and divert resources away from other security activities, it is critical that the goal(s) and objectives of the program be well-defined and agreed upon up front. Although there is no hard and fast rule about this, a single goal that clearly states the end toward which all measurement and metrics gathering efforts should be directed is a good_approach. Statements of objective should indicate high-level actions that must be collectively accomplished to meet the goal(s). An action plan should be directly derivable from these statements.

A few objectives for the goal above, for example, might be:

(a) To base the security metrics program on process improvement best practices within our company.

(b) To leverage any relevant measurements currently being collected.

(c) To communicate metrics in formats custom-tailored to various audiences.

(d) To involve stakeholders in determining what metrics to produce.

Step 2: Decide which metrics to generate

Any underlying corporate framework for process improvement, as discussed at the beginning of this section, could dictate what metrics are needed. For example, a "Six Sigma" approach would focus on security processes for which defects could be detected and managed, and Step 2 of building a metrics program would, therefore, be to identify those specific security processes. A compliance-based approach would assess how closely established security standards are being followed. In this case, Step 2 would identify those standards for which compliance should be tracked. In the absence of any preexisting framework, a top-down or a bottom-up approach for determining which metrics might be desirable could be used. The top-down approach starts with the objectives of the security program, and then works backward to identify specific metrics that would help determine if those objectives are being met, and lastly measurements needed to generate those metrics. For example:

Top-down Approach

(a) Define/list objectives of the overall security program. Example objective: To reduce the number of virus infections within the company by 30% by 2002.

(b) Identify metrics that would indicate progress toward each objective. Example metric: Current ratio of virus alerts to actual infections as compared to the baseline 2000 figure.

(c) Determine measurements needed for each metric. Example measurement: Number of virus alerts issued to the organization by month Example measurement: Number of virus infections reported The bottom-up approach entails first defining which security processes, products, services, etc. are in place that can be or already are measured, then considering which meaningful metrics could be derived from those measurements, and finally assessing how well those metrics link to objectives for the overall security program. To illustrate:

Bottom-up Approach

(a) Identify measurements that are/could be collected for this process Example measurement: Average number of Level 1 vulnerabilities detected per server by department using our xyz scanning tool.

(b) Determine metrics that could be generated from the measurements Example metric: Change in number of critical vulnerabilities detected on servers by department since last reporting period.

(c) Determine the association between the derived metrics and established objectives of the overall security program. Example objective: To reduce the level of detectable vulnerabilities on servers in every department within the company.

The top-down approach will more readily identify the metrics that should be in place given the objectives of the overall security program, while the bottom-up approach yields the most easily obtainable metrics. Both approaches assume that overall security program objectives have already been established. If they have not been, defining these high-level objectives is obviously important and a prerequisite.

Step 3: Develop Strategies for Generating the Metrics

Now that what is to be measured is well understood, strategies for collecting needed data and deriving the metrics must be developed. These strategies should specify the source of the data, the frequency of data collection, and who is responsible for raw data accuracy, data compilation into measurements, and generation of the metric. Although a formal risk assessment is one method for collecting some of the data that might be needed, experts disagree on its value for generating metrics. One line of thought is that quantitative risk assessment provides "close enough" metrics, while another is that risk assessments are not standardized and are too subjective and speculative to provide good comparative metrics over time. There are, however, other suggested sources of data, such as help desk logs, system logs, firewall logs, audit reports, and user surveys. Early on there were few automated tools available to make data collection, analysis, and reporting cost-effective, but in recent years products have been introduced into the marketplace to make these activities more viable.

Step 4: Establish benchmarks and targets

In this step appropriate benchmarks would be identified and improvement targets set. Benchmarking is the process of comparing one's own performance and practices against peers within the industry or noted "best practice" organizations outside the industry. Not only does this process provide fresh ideas for managing an activity, but also can provide comparative data needed to make metrics more meaningful. Benchmarks also help establish achievable targets for driving improvements in existing practices. A security manager should consult industry-specific data resources for possible benchmarks and best practices, but also may find national and global metrics provided by SecurityStats.com, CIO Magazine, and other services and publications helpful.

Step 5: Determine how the metrics will be reported

Obviously, no security metrics efforts are worthwhile if the results are not effectively communicated. While conventional management wisdom on disseminating information of this nature should prevail, current security metrics literature does reveal some guidance in this area. One analyst, for example, cautions that over-simplification in the name of clarity is a mistake. Executives are accustomed to dealing with financial and other trend lines, so complex security-related data can be valuable to this group if presented well. Graphic representations are particularly effective. Some metrics may be meaningful only to the security manager and staff and should not be distributed further. Security managers may, however, use other metrics to help trigger needed remedial actions with the organization. For example, a widely distributed metric, such as one that shows levels of vulnerability for each department in the organization, might spawn healthy competition among departments to become the least vulnerable department by the next reporting period a security manager's dream! In any case, the context, format, frequency, distribution method, and responsibility for reporting metrics should be defined up front, so that the end product can be visualized early on by those who will be involved in producing the metrics and those who will be using them for decision-making.

Step 6: Create an action plan and act on it

Now it is time to get the real work done. The action plan should contain all tasks that need to be accomplished to launch the security metrics program, along with expected completion dates and assignments. As mentioned in Step 1, action items should be directly derivable from the objectives. Documenting the linkage of actions in the plan to these objectives is useful, so that no one will lose sight of why a given action is important. In the same manner that software should be developed, it is critical to include a testing process in the plan. Deficiencies in collected data may, for example, prove some metrics unusable and require reexamination of what is to bc mcasurcd and how.

Step 7: Establish a formal program review/refinement cycle

Formal, regular reexamination of the entire security metrics program should be built into the overall recess. Is there reason to doubt the accuracy of any of the metrics? Are the metrics useful in determining new courses of action for the overall security program? How much effort is it taking to generate the metrics? Is the value derived worth that effort? These and other questions like them will be important to answer during the review process. A fresh scan of security metrics standards and best practices within and outside the industry should also be conducted to help identify new developments and opportunities to fine-tune the program.

7.4.1 Conclusion

The task of developing a security metrics program may seem daunting to some, but it need not be. The seven-step methodology can guide development of very simple metrics programs, as well as highly ambitious ones. In fact, some individuals with experience in security metrics recommend that simple starts be made. They advise managers to do what is easy, cheap, fast, and leverage existing measures and metrics.

The important thing to keep in mind is that the metrics generated should be useful enough to drive improvement in the overall security program and to help prove the value of that program to the organization as a whole.

The purpose of this guide is to provide an overview of the current state of security metrics as well as suggestions for developing a metrics program. The following are noteworthy related standards or initiatives that may provide further insight and guidance:

- The International Systems Security Engineering Association's SSE-CMM Project
- The National Institute of Standards and Technology's IT Security Assessment Framework

- The National Institute of Standards and Technology's Security Metrics Guide for Information Technology Systems
- The Department of Defense's Information Assurance Readiness Project
- The ISO standard for Common Criteria

7.5 INFORMATION SECURITY AND LAW

7.5.1 Information Security

Thefts of proprietary information are increasing, which can jeopardize revenue, competitive advantage, and customer relationships; generate negative publicity; and result in significant penalties and fines for failure to comply with privacy laws.

Many information security solutions attempt to protect electronic documents only at their storage location or during transmission. For example, organizations rely on document management systems and virtual private networks (VPNs) to protect documents. With this approach document security remains a problem because these solutions secure only the communication line or storage site; they do not provide protection for the actual content of an electronic document throughout its lifecycle. When the document reaches the recipient, the protection is lost, and the document can be intentionally or unintentionally forwarded to and viewed by unauthorized recipients. Consequently, many organizations are forced to engage in an inconsistent combination of online and paper processes in which sensitive documents must still be printed and physically delivered to achieve adequate security. As a result, the potential benefits of online processing cannot be fully realized.

Information security is rapidly emerging as one of the most critical legal and public relations issues facing companies today. As the series of highly-publicized security breaches over the past few years has demonstrated, it is in many respects a time bomb waiting to explode.

The problem stems from the fact that, in today's business environment, virtually all of a company's daily transactions and all of its key records are created, used, communicated, and stored in electronic form using networked computer technology.

Most business entities are, quite literally, fully dependent upon information technology and an interconnected information infrastructure. This has, of course, provided companies with tremendous economic benefits, including significantly reduced costs and increased productivity.

Information security professionals work within an enterprise to protect it from all non-physical threats to the integrity and availability of its data and systems. Performing this function draws security professionals into simultaneous, ongoing relationships between the enterprise on the one hand and, successively on the other, the enterprise's employees and other agents, its customers, suppliers, competitors, government officials and regulators, to say nothing of unidentified and sometimes unidentifiable actors.

Each article in the series deals with information security in a particular context. The first article (below) addresses the legal framework for protection of information systems and the role of information security professionals in the creation of trade secret interests, one type of intellectual property. The articles that follow will discuss the law of achieving and maintaining a secure working environment, the criminal law aspects of information security, and the impact of national defense law and regulations on information security. Throughout the series, the focus will be on providing information that security professionals can bring to bear to improve the security of the people and businesses who depend on them.

7.5.2 Part One: Protecting Private Sector Systems; Information Security Professionals and Trade Secrets

Information security professionals work to protect both an enterprise's information technology systems and the enterprise's information itself. These functions are obviously related, and in practice, the division between them may be a bit artificial, but the division is helpful for organizing an introduction to the relevant body of law. Our discussion focuses primarily on the legal framework for the protection of information systems because the two functions most closely associated with information security professionals - protection from hackers and infection by viruses - occur at a systems level. The article ends with a comment on the role that security professionals play in the acquisition and maintenance of legal rights in trade secrets.

In 2003, it is traditional, and may even be cliché, to describe the Internet as a "network of networks," but the definition remains true and it is helpful for understanding a fundamental legal point. The Internet neither perceives nor respects jurisdictional boundaries between states or between the United States and other countries. The networks that collectively form the Internet allow us to exchange information with people across any border or borders we wish. That capability is, after all, one of the fundamental advantages of being online. In legal terms, that means that network security is an issue that bears on the interstate and foreign commerce of the United States. The Constitution of the United States gives the Congress the right to regulate interstate and foreign commerce, and so it is no surprise to find that the primary sources of United States law for the protection of networks are federal statutes.

7.5.3 Computer Fraud and Abuse Act (CFAA)

The starting point for a discussion of the current United States law of information security is the Computer Fraud and Abuse Act, 18 U.S.C.§ 1030 (the "CFAA"). The CFAA was originally enacted solely as a computer crime statute, but in its present form, it imposes both civil and criminal liability for a wide variety of acts that compromise the security of public and private sector computer systems. By the time this series concludes, we will have given the CFAA a fairly comprehensive review. For now, let's focus on the provisions that form the legal backbone for the protection of private sector systems.

The core provisions of the CFAA apply to "protected computer[s]," a term that the act defines in sweeping terms. Under the CFAA, the term "protected computer" means "a computer:

(a) "exclusively for the use of a financial institution or the United States Government, or, in the case of a computer not exclusively for such use, used by or for a financial institution or the United States Government and the conduct constituting the offense affects that use by or for the financial institution or the Government;" or

(b) "which is used in interstate or foreign commerce or communication [.]"

The CFAA imposes liability on anyone who:

1. Intentionally accesses a protected computer without authorization or in excess of authority, and by doing so, steals anything of value, other than the use of the computer itself, where that computer use is worth less than $5,000 in any one year period ;
2. Knowingly transmits a program, code or instruction, and as a result, intentionally causes damage, without authorization, to a protected computer ;
3. Intentionally accesses a protected computer without authorization, and as a result, causes damage, recklessly or otherwise ;
4. Knowingly traffics illegally in passwords or other access credentials that allow unauthorized access to a computer, if that traffic effects interstate or foreign commerce or the computer is used by or for the United States government ;
5. Threatening to damage a protected computer with intent to extort anything of value; or
6. Attempts to do any of the above.

7.5.3 DMCA - The Digital Millennium Copyright Act

The Digital Millennium Copyright Act, 17 U.S.C. §1201- 05 (the "DMCA"), provides that "[n]o person shall circumvent a technological measure that effectively controls access to a work protected under this title [the Copyright Law]," and goes on to prohibit the "manufacture, import, offer to the public, provide, or otherwise traffic in any technology, product, service, device, component, or part thereof, that - (A) is primarily designed or produced for the purpose of circumventing a technological measure that effectively controls access to [a copyrighted work]; (B) has only limited commercially significant purpose or use other than to circumvent a technological measure that effectively controls access to [a copyrighted work]; or (C) is marketed by that person or another acting in concert with that person with that person's knowledge for use in circumventing a technological measure that effectively controls access to [a copyrighted work]." The DMCA defines the term "circumvent a technological measure" [to] mean[] to descramble a scrambled work, to decrypt an encrypted work, or otherwise to avoid, bypass, remove, deactivate, or impair a technological measure, without the authority of the copyright owner. 17 U.S.C. §1201 (a). This provision of the DMCA assists licensors of digitized copyrighted works in restricting access to those who obtain access to it lawfully and are therefore entitled to decrypt the work.

It is important to note that the DMCA imposes liability for the removal of technological devices, regardless of whether or how those responsible then treat the formerly protected copyrighted works. Unauthorized uses of those works might or might not constitute infringement. Liability for infringement, if any, would arise separately, under the pertinent provisions of the Copyright Law.

The DMCA focuses on the circumvention of technological measures specified, regardless of whether infringement occurs.

7.5.4 State Laws - Filling the Gaps Left by CFAA and DMCA

As important as they are, the CFAA and the DMCA do not provide a comprehensive legal response to the entire range of possible system security violations. In certain cases, evidence satisfying the $5,000 damage threshold for an action for economic relief under the CFAA may be difficult or impossible to come by, and the applicability of the DMCA is expressly restricted to the protection of copyrighted works. In such circumstances, state laws, both those specifically aimed at information security and common law concepts developed long before the information age, may fill the gaps. A survey of state computer crime laws is far beyond the scope of this series, but it is worthwhile to address one example of how state law supplements the federal statutory provisions discussed above.

Let's begin with the idea that at a basic level, a secure system enables its proprietors to control when and how the system's resources are used. To assert control, system proprietors set terms and conditions for access, and users obtain access to users only when, and for as long as, they agree to abide by those terms. When access restrictions or limitations are exceeded, the system operator loses control of some portion of the resources it would otherwise have to respond to user needs. In theory, this loss of control results in an injury, even if the proportion of the resources involved is small and difficult to quantify. The CFAA may not be terribly helpful in this situation. No data has been lost, nothing has been corrupted, and the prospect of meeting the $5,000 damage threshold seems remote.

7.5.5 Proprietary Information - Information Security Professionals and Trade Secrets

The law provides a variety of theories through which legal rights in certain kinds of information may arise. Many, but not all, information based resources fall within the four categories of intellectual property: (1) trade secret, (2) trademark and service mark, (3) copyright; and (4) patent. Information security professionals do important work in protecting information based resources of all types, but they have a particular relationship with trade secrets that merits attention.

State law is the primary source of rights in trade secrets. At this writing, forty-three (43) states and the District of Columbia have adopted the Uniform Trade Secrets Act ("UTSA"), which means that they have decided to adopt a common legal approach to the law of trade secrets and that variations between them, if any, will be minor . The UTSA defines a "trade secret" to mean "information, including a formula, pattern, compilation, program, device, method, technique, or process, that: (i) derives independent economic value, actual or potential, from not being generally known to, and not being readily ascertainable by proper means by, other persons who can obtain economic value from its disclosure or use, and (ii) is the subject of efforts that are reasonable under the circumstances to maintain its secrecy. UTSA, § 1. Even in states that have not adopted the UTSA, trade secret protection generally requires some element of secure and restricted access to the information in question".

As the UTSA definition of "trade secret" makes clear, and as the term itself implies, the law will only permit a party to control information as its trade secret only if the information involved is, in fact, secret. This means that security professionals play a direct role to play in the actual creation and maintenance of trade secret interests.

In short, the working environment for security professionals is a maelstrom. In determining which aspect of this multi-faceted environment needs your immediate attention, the law can help. Whether in the courts or in legislatures or agencies, the law addresses individual claims or interests more or less one at a time. As such, the way the law treats a particular topic provides one point of focus that may help you allocate effort and resources to best effect.

Security is the sum of all measures taken to prevent loss of any kind. Loss can occur because of user error, defects in code, malicious acts, hardware failure, and acts of nature. Holistic computer security uses a number of methods to prevent these events, but is primarily focused on preventing user error and malicious acts.

Security is the antithesis of convenience generally, the more secure something is, the less convenient it is. Think about this in the context of your life: think of how easy it would be if you could just walk up and push a button to start your car without worrying about keys or paying for car insurance. But the risk of theft and accidents makes these two security measures mandatory. Meanwhile, advanced technology like remote key fobs for cars is making automotive security easier, just like biometric scanners can make logging on computers both more secure and less annoying at the same time. Computer security is not complicated. It may seem that way, but the theory behind computer security is relatively simple. Hacking methods fall into just a few categories. And solutions to computer security problems are actually rather straightforward.

7.5.6 Security Principles

Computer security is based on the same concepts that physical security is: trust, knowledge of a secret to prove authenticity, possession of a key to open locks, and legal accountability. The metaphors are so apt that most computer security mechanisms even have the same names as their physical counterparts.

7.5.7 Trust

All computer security springs from the concept of inherent or original trust. Just like a child inherently trusts its parents, a secure computer system inherently trusts those who set it up. While this may seem rather obvious, it is an important concept because it is the origination of all subsequent security measures. There's more inherent trust in computer security than simply the original establishment of a system. For example, you trust that there are no "backdoors" in the software you use that could be exploited by a knowledgeable person to gain access. You trust that the login screen that you are looking at is actually the system's true login screen and not a mimic designed to collect your password and then pass it to a remote system. Finally, you trust that the designers of the system have not made any serious mistakes that could obviate your security measures.

7.5.8 Authentication

Authentication is the process of determining the identity of a user. Forcing the user to prove that they know a secret that should be known only to the actual user proves that the user is who they say they are.

User accounts are associated with some form of secret, such as a password, PIN, biometric hash, or with a device like a **smart card** that contains a larger, more secure password than a human could remember. To the system, there is no concept of a human; there is only a secret, information tied to that secret, and information to which that secret has access.

Authentication is only useful in so far as it is accurate. Passwords are probably the least reliable form of authentication in common use today, but they're also the most easily implemented-they require no special hardware and no sophisticated algorithms for basic use. However, they are easily guessed, and even when they're carefully chosen it's still possible to simply guess the entire range of possible passwords on many systems in short order.

A less common but more secure method of authentication is to physically possess a unique key. This is analogous to most physical locks. In computer security systems, "keys" are actually large numbers generated by special algorithms that incorporate information about the user and which are stored on removable media like smart cards. The problem with keys is that, like physical keys, they can be lost or stolen. However, when combined with a password they are very secure and difficult to thwart.

Another form of authentication provides inherent identification by using a physical property of the user. This is called biometric authentication, and it relies upon unique and unchangeable physical properties of a human, such as handwriting characteristics, fingerprints, facial characteristics, and so forth. Biometric authentication is the most reliable form of authentication because it's easy to use, nearly impossible to fake, and can't be circumvented by users even if they wanted to. Some forms of biometric authentication are easier to "forge" than others, and naïve implementations can sometimes be easily faked. But when well implemented, biometric authentication is the most secure form of authentication and the only form that can be truly said to uniquely and unmistakably identify a user.

7.5.9 Chain of Authority

During the installation of a security system, the original administrator will create the root or additional administrative accounts. From that original account, all other accounts, keys, and certificates spring. Every account on a system, even massive systems containing millions of accounts, spring from this chain of authority. The concept of chains of authority isn't often discussed because it is inherent in a secure system.

Certificate systems are also based on a chain of authority. Consider the case of separate businesses that do a lot of work together. It would be convenient if users from Business Alpha could automatically log on to computers at Business Beta. But because these two systems have two different chains of authority, there's no way for Business Alpha to trust that users who say they are from Business Beta actually are. This problem is solved by having both businesses and trust a third-party trust provider, or a company that specializes in verifying identity and creating secure certificates that can be used to prove identity to foreign systems. As long as both businesses trust the same trust provider, they are rooted in the same chain of authority and can trust certificates that are generated by that trust provider. Trust Providers are the digital equivalent of a Notary Public.

7.5.10 Accountability

Accountability is where the secret meets the user. Users don't try to circumvent security because their identity would be known and they would be held legally accountable for their actions. It is accountability that prevents illegal behavior, rather than access controls.

In pure accountability-based systems, no access control mechanisms are present. Users simply know that their every action is being logged, and since their identity is known and their activities are tracked, they won't do things that could jeopardize their position (unless something happens to make them no longer care).

The problem with accountability-based systems is two-fold-they only work if identity can't be faked, and there are rare occasions where users lose their inhibitions. Without access control, these rare users can destroy the entire system. For these reasons, accountability-based security is normally used to augment access control systems rather than to replace them.

7.6 INTELLECTUAL PROPERTY RIGHTS (IPR) LAW IN INDIA (UPTU-2010)

Intellectual property rights is a legal concept that confers rights to owners and creators of the work, for their intellectual creativity. Such rights can be granted for areas related to literature, music, invention etc, which are used in the business practices. In general, the intellectual property law offers exclusionary rights to the creator or inventor against any misappropriation or use of work without his/her prior knowledge. Intellectual property law establishes an equilibrium by granting rights for limited duration of time.

Every nation has framed their own intellectual property laws. But on international level it is governed by the World Intellectual Property Organization (WIPO). The Paris Convention for the Protection of Industrial Property in 1883 and the 'Berne Convention for the Protection of Literary and Artistic Works' in 1886 were first conventions which have recognized the importance of safeguarding intellectual property. Both the treaties are under the direct administration of the WIPO. The WIPO convention lays down following list of the activities or work which are covered by the intellectual property rights -

- Industrial designs
- Scientific discoveries
- Protection against unfair competition
- Literary, artistic and scientific works
- Inventions in all fields of human endeavor
- Performances of performing artists, phonograms and broadcasts

- Trademarks, service marks and commercial names and designations
- All other rights resulting from intellectual activity in the industrial, scientific, literary or artistic fields.

Types of Intellectual Property Rights

Intellectual Property Rights signifies to the bundle of exclusionary rights which can be further categorized into the following heads-

- **Copyright:** Copyright, one of the form of intellectual property right, offers exclusive rights for protecting the authorship of original & creative work like dramatic, musical and literary in nature.
- **Patent:** A patent is termed as the exclusionary rights given by the government or the authorized authority to its inventor for a particular duration of time, in respect of his invention. It is the part of the intellectual property right.
- **Trademark:** The trademark or trade mark, symbolized as the â„¢ and ®, is the distinctive sign or indication which is used for signifying some kind of goods or/and services and is distinctively used across the business.
- **Trade Secrets:** Trade secret points towards a formula, pattern, any instrument, design which is kept confidential and through which any business or trade can edge over its rival and can enjoy economic gain.
- **Utility Model:** The utility model is the intellectual property right for protecting the inventions. It is somehow described as the statutory monopoly which is bestow upon for the fixed duration of time in exchange to the inventor.
- **Geographical Indication:** Geographical Indication (GI) signifies to the name or sign, used in reference to the products which are corresponding to the particular geographical area or somewhat related to the origin like town, region or nation.
- **Industrial Design Rights:** Industrial design rights are defined as the part of the intellectual property rights which confers the rights of exclusivity to the visual designs of objects which are generally not popular utilitarian.

Advantages of Intellectual Property Rights

Intellectual property rights help in providing exclusive rights to creator or inventor, thereby induces them to distribute and share information and data instead of keeping it confidential. It provides legal protection and offers them incentive of their work. Rights granted under the intellectual property act helps in socio and economic development.

India has defined the establishment of statutory, administrative and judicial framework for protecting the intellectual property rights in the Indian territory, whether they connotes with the copyright, patent, trademark, industrial designs or with other parts.

Tuning with the changing industrial world, the intellectual property rights have continued to strengthen its position in the India. In 1999, the government has passed the important legislation in relation to the protection of intellectual property rights on the terms of the worldwide practices and in accordance to the India's obligations under the Trade Related Aspects of Intellectual Property Rights. It consists of -

- The Patents(Amendment) Act, 1999 which was passed on 10th March, 1999 in the Indian Parliament for amending the Patents Act of 1970 which in turns facilitate to establish the mail box system for filing patents and accords with the exclusive marketing rights for the time period of 5 years.
- The Trade Marks Bill, 1999 was passed in the India parliament during the winter session for replacing the Trade and Merchandise Marks Act, 1958. It was passed on 23rd December, 1999.
- The Copyright(Amendment) Act, 1999 was passed by both upper house and lower house of the Indian parliament and was later on signed by the Indian president on 30th December, 1999.
- The suigeneris legislation was approved by both houses of the Indian parliament on 23rd December, 1999 and was named as the Geographical Indications of Goods (Registration & Protection) Bill, 1999.
- The Industrial Designs Bill, 1999 was passed in the Upper House of the Indian parliament for replacing the Designs Act, 1911.
- The Patents (Second Amendment) Bill, 1999 was introduced in the upper house of the parliament for further amending the Patents Act 1970 and making it compliance with the TRIPS.

Along with the above legislative measures, the Indian government has introduced several changes for streamlining and bolstering the intellectual property administration system in the nation. Several projects concerning to the modernizing of the patent information services and trademark registry have been undergone with the help of the World Intellectual Property Organization/ United Nations Development Programmed.

In India, the Intellectual Property Rights (IPR) of computer software is covered under the Copyright Law. Accordingly, the copyright of computer software is protected under the provisions of Indian Copyright Act 1957. Major changes to Indian Copyright Law were introduced in 1994 and came into effect from 10 May 1995. These changes or amendments made the Indian Copyright law, one of the toughest in the world.

The amendments to the Copyright Act introduced in June 1994 were in themselves, a landmark in the India's copyright arena. For the first time in India, the Copyright Law clearly explained:

- the rights of a copyright holder
- position on rentals of software
- the rights of the user to make backup copies
- and most importantly the amendments imposed heavy punishment and fines for infringement of copyright of software.

Because most software is easy to duplicate and the copy is usually as good as original, the Copyright Act was greatly in demand. According to this Act, the infringer can be tried under both civil and criminal law.

According to section 16 of this Act, it is illegal to make or distribute copies of copyrighted software without proper or specific authorization. The only exception is provided by section 52 of the Act, which allows a backup copy purely as a temporary protection against loss, distribution or damage to the original copy. The 1994 amendment to the Copyright Act also prohibits the sale or hiring, or any offer for sale or hire of any copy of the computer program without specific authorization of the Copyright holder.

A civil and criminal action may be instituted for injunction, actual damages (including infringer's profits) or statutory damages per infringement etc. With these amendments, even the criminal penalties have substantially increased. Section 63 B, stipulates a minimum jail term of 7 days which can be extended up to 3 years. The Act further states the fine ranging from Rs. 50,000 to 2,00,000.

Government agencies have been very actively participating in protecting of the rights of the copyright holder. Both Ministry of Information Technology and Ministry of Human Resource Development have been active in incorporating amendments to the Indian Copyright Act. These agencies are now helping the law enforcing agencies e.g. the Police in enforcing the law. Today, NASSCOM officers and those of these government agencies are committed to enforce copyright laws and eradicate the menace of software piracy.

The Anti-Piracy raids facilitated by NASSCOM and Business Software Alliance (BSA) over the last few years in metros as well as smaller cities have already had salutary effect. The law enforcing authorities too supported these raids actively.

7.7 PATENT LAW

Patent law is a specific area of law that encompasses the legal regulation, jurisprudence, and enforcement of specific intellectual property rights known as patent rights. A patent is a government issued right granted to individuals or groups that protects their original inventions from being made, used, or sold by others without their permission for a set period of time. While patents can be legally obtained without the use of an attorney, an attorney who specializes in patent law can help ensure that their client's patent is enforceable by law. Because patent law pertains to intellectual property, which is like any other property in that it can be legally sold, exchanged, traded, or abandoned, the finer points of patent law are frequently amended as technology changes. This is another reason why an attorney specializing in patent law is of significant use to those seeking a patent.

7.8 COPYRIGHT LAW

Copyright is a set of exclusive rights granted by the law of a jurisdiction to the author or creator of an original work, including the right to copy, distribute and adapt the work. Exceptions and limitations to these rights strive to balance the public interest in the wide distribution of the material produced and to encourage creativity. Exceptions include fair dealing and fair use, and such use does not require the permission of the copyright owner. All other uses require permission and copyright owners can license or permanently transfer or assign their exclusive rights to others. Copyright does not protect ideas, only their expression or fixation. In most jurisdictions, copyright arises upon fixation and does not need to be registered. Copyright protection applies for a specific period of time, after which the work is said to enter the public domain.

The first copyright statute was the British Statute of Anne of 1709, the full title of which was: "An Act for the Encouragement of Learning, by vesting the Copies of Printed Books in the Authors or purchasers of such Copies, during the Times therein mentioned". Initially copyright only applied to published books, but over time copyright was extended to other uses, such as translations and derivative works. Copyright now covers a wide range of works, including maps, dramatic works, paintings, photographs, sound recordings, motion pictures and computer programs. Today, copyright laws have been standardized to some extent through international and regional agreements such as the Berne Convention and the European copyright directives. Although there are consistencies among nations' copyright laws, each jurisdiction has separate and distinct laws and regulations covering copyright. National copyright laws on licensing, transfer and assignment of copyright still vary greatly between countries and copyrighted works are licensed on a territorial basis. Some jurisdictions also recognize moral rights of creators, such as the right to be credited for the work. "Indian work" means a literary, dramatic or musical work,

- The author of which is a citizen of India; or
- Which is first published in India; or
- The author of which, in the case of an unpublished work is, at the time of the making of the work, a citizen of India.

The U.S. Congress first exercised its power to enact copyright legislation with the Copyright Act of 1790. The Act secured an author the exclusive right to publish and vend "maps, charts and books" for a term of 14 years, with the right of renewal for one additional 14 year term if the author was still alive. The act did not regulate other kinds of writings, such as musical compositions or newspapers and specifically noted that it did not prohibit copying the works of foreign authors. The vast majority of writings were never registered - between 1790 and 1799, of approximately 13,000 titles published in the United States, only 556 works were registered.

Copyright law has been modified many times since to encompass new technologies such as music recording, to extend the duration of protection, and to make other changes. U.S. courts have interpreted this clause of the Constitution to say that the ultimate purpose of copyrights is to encourage the production of creative works for the public benefit, and that therefore the interests of the public are primary over the interests of the author when the two conflict. These rulings have since been formalized into fair use laws and decisions. Certain attempts by copyright owners to restrict uses beyond the rights provided for by copyright law may also subject them to the copyright misuse doctrine, preventing enforcement against infringers.

7.9 LEGAL ISSUE IN DATA MINING

"Data mining" is defined in many different ways, but most have in common the elements of searches of one or more databases of personally identifiable information by or on behalf of the government. Data mining in the antiterrorism context usually involves third-party data that have been provided voluntarily, purchased or seized by the government, or reported to the government in compliance with routine reporting requirements. It may also involve the use of data previously collected by the government for other purposes.

Data mining is a promising tool in the fight against terrorism. It already plays a number of important roles in counter terrorism including locating known suspects, identifying and tracking suspicious financial and other transactions, and facilitating background checks. Rapid increases in the power and speed of computing technologies, the capacity of data storage, and the reach of networks have added exponentially to both the volume of data available for possible use and the ability of the government to meaningfully examine them. As a result, as discussed elsewhere in this volume, new data mining applications are likely to play increasingly important roles in fighting terrorism.

Government data mining also poses significant issues for individual privacy and other civil liberties. Proposals for enhanced government data mining have provoked serious controversy, beginning with the first large-scale computerized government benefits databases created by the then-Department of Health, Education and Welfare. More recently, public concern over proposals for Total Information Awareness and second-generation Computer Assisted Passenger Profiling was sufficient to block at least public development of these systems.

One of the major contributors to the controversies over government data mining is the absence of clear legal standards. Forty years ago the lack of relevant law was understandable: the technologies were new, their capacity was largely unknown, and the types of legal issues they might raise were novel. Today, it is inexplicable and threatens to undermine both privacy and security.

7.10 PLAGIARISM (UPTU 2010-11)

Plagiarism refers to the use of another's information, language, or writing, when done without proper acknowledgment of the original source. Essential to an act of plagiarism is an element of dishonesty in attempting to pass off the plagiarized work as original. Plagiarism is not necessarily the same as copyright infringement, which occurs when one violates copyright law. Like most terms from the area of intellectual property, plagiarism is a concept of the modern age and not really applicable to medieval or ancient works. An example of plagiarism would be copying this definition and pasting straight into a report.

Plagiarism is derived from two Latin words; plagiarius which means an abductor, and plagiare which means to steal. According to Random House Compact Unabridged Dictionary, plagiarism is defined as "use or close imitation of the language and thoughts of another author and the representation of them as one's own original work." It is also considered as violation of scholarly ethics and intellectual property by many academicians.

Reasons of Plagiarism

Most of the views and the discussions on the reasons of plagiarism also elaborate the fact that most of the people are not aware of the different types of plagiarism. You can take the example of a person who is going to write a research paper and he includes the statistical analysis of the other writer to show his own conclusions, although he is not claiming that data as his own but because of the lack of poor referencing he can be liable for copyrights. Plagiarism does not only include the copy of the words but also the copy of expressions, ideas, and many other creative tasks.

Types of Plagiarism

There are different types of plagiarism based on the intensity of plagiarism and some of them are as follows:

1. Minimal Plagiarism: It is type of plagiarism, which is most common in the educational sector and in this plagiarism the person do plagiarism by substituting the synonyms and editing the original text.
2. Substantial Plagiarism: Adding more details in the text and just changing the patterns of the text leads to substantial plagiarism.
3. Complete plagiarism: Without making any change in the data and presenting it as your own is the complete plagiarism. On the other hand there are the some other types of plagiarism, which must be never forgotten while coming up with any written article or idea like:

Academic and journalistic plagiarism is an age old practice. However, Internet plagiarism is now rampant with the advent of the Internet, and plagiarism has taken many new forms. Now it is just about cut, copy, and paste, or a little rephrasing. But copy it is!

Full Plagiarism: Content that has been presented as own, without any changes made to the language, thoughts, flow, and even punctuation is known as full plagiarism. Many academicians believe that is generally the work of people who are incompetent in the particular subject, or are just plain lazy to make an effort.

Partial Plagiarism: When the presented content is a combination of two to three different sources, where the use of rephrasing and synonyms is rampant, then it is known as partial plagiarism. Here, the author uses some originality, but inadequacy of knowledge on the particular subject is a common reason for the occurrences of partial plagiarism.

Minimalistic Plagiarism: Here, the plagiarist authors someone else concept, ideas, thought, or opinions in their own words and in a different flow. Although many do not regard this as plagiarism (probably the one's who do it!), it is considered as stealing some ones study or thoughts. Minimalistic plagiarism involves a lot of paraphrasing.

Source Citation: When complete source information with quotes is provided, it does not amount to plagiarism. However, the definition of a complete source citation varies vastly. Some writers quote the source's name, but give no other accessible information. While some conveniently give false references, some just merge their information with an original piece of writing. A ghost writer is a perfect example of a plagiarist. Here the writer feels free to source information and reproduce it as their own.

Self-plagiarism: This form of plagiarism is perhaps most contested as "it is " and "is not". Using one's own work, fully or partially, or even the same thought and re-writing it, is known as self-plagiarism by many. Publishing the same material through different mediums without referencing it correctly is a very common habit among many writers. The content on many websites are perfect examples of self-plagiarism.

According to professor Paul Brian's opinion posted on the Internet Humanist Forum, "self-plagiarism, or the recycling of an old work in a new guise is also a theft since the author leads the book-buyer to think that there is a new book of his on the market. The author is misleading his/her readers." "Self-plagiarism is fraud if not outright theft".

Plagiarism is a personal ethical issue. Knowing what it is, and learning ways to not only detect and prevent plagiarized content, but also how self-plagiarism happens will a go a long way in promoting and preserving authenticity and originality.

SUMMARY

In today's information technology world, there is a growing need for security solutions: information systems are more and more vulnerable because of the increased complexity and interconnection of insecure components and networks. Even though appropriate security approaches can be found, the resulting security level often remains unknown. It is a widely accepted principle that an activity cannot be managed well if it cannot be measured. Information security (IS) metrics offers work as a research field.

A growing number of security solutions are used in today's information technology world. However, the achieved security level is often unclear. There is not much research about what kind of information security metrics are used in Finnish industry and state institutions. Therefore, the aim of this study was to investigate the issues focused especially on the development and use of the metrics within production processes. The topics cover what kind of techniques are used in implementation and analysis of these metrics, how useful these metrics are for an organization, and what the future targets for the use of information security metrics are.

EXERCISE

1. What is security metrics. Explain it with its benefits.
2. What do you understand by information security.
3. What are laws. Explain all the laws.
4. Classified security metrics.
5. What are legal issues in data mining security.

CHAPTER 8

Ethical Issues

Before discussing ethical issues we first come to know about what is ethics and what does the mean of issue.

8.1 ETHICS

Ethics is a general term for what is often described as the "science (study) of morality". In philosophy, ethical behavior is that which is "good" or "right." The Western tradition of ethics is sometimes called **moral philosophy**. This is one part of value theory (axiology) the other part is aesthetics of the four major branches of philosophy, alongside metaphysics, epistemology, and logic. Ethics (also known as moral philosophy) is a branch of philosophy which seeks to address questions about morality; that is, about concepts such as good and bad, right and wrong, justice, and virtue.

Ethics (also known as **moral philosophy**) is a branch of philosophy that addresses questions about morality that is, concepts such as good and evil, right and wrong, virtue and vice, justice, etc.

Major branches of ethics include:

- Meta-ethics, about the theoretical meaning and reference of moral propositions and how their truth-values (if any) may be determined;
- Normative ethics, about the practical means of determining a moral course of action;
- Applied ethics, about how moral outcomes can be achieved in specific situations;
- Moral psychology, about how moral capacity or moral agency develops and what its nature is; and
- Descriptive ethics, about what moral values people actually abide by.

8.2 ISSUE

Issues are about what is right and what is wrong. An example would be whether or not it is right to use genetic engineering, to have an abortion, legalize euthanasia etc. These are ethical ISSUES because there is disagreement about what is right and what is wrong.

8.3 ETHICAL ISSUES

The foundations of all secure systems are the moral principles and practices and the professional standards of all employ-ees of the organization, i.e., while people are part of the solution, they are also most of the problem. The following issues are examples of security problems which an organization may have to deal with:

8.3.1 Ethics and Responsible Decision-Making

The foundation of all security systems is formed by moral principles and practices of those people involved and the standards of the profession. That is, while people are part of the solution, they are also most the problem. Security problems with which an organization may have to deal include: responsible decision-making, confidentiality, pri-vacy, piracy, fraud & misuse, liability, copyright, trade secrets, and sabotage. It is easy to sensationalize these topics with real horror stories; it is more difficult to deal with the underlying ethical issues involved.

The student should be made aware of his individual responsibility in making ethical decisions associated with infor-mation security.

8.3.2 Confidentiality and Privacy

Computers can be used symbolically to intimidate, deceive or defraud victims. Attorneys, government agencies and businesses increasingly use mounds of computer generated data quite legally to confound their audiences. Criminals also find useful phony invoices, bills and checks generated by the computer. The computer lends an ideal cloak for carrying out criminal acts by imparting a clean quality to the crime.

The computer has made the invasion of our privacy a great deal easier and potentially more dangerous than before the advent of the computer. A wide range of data are collected and stored in computerized files related to individu-als. These files hold banking information, credit information, organizational fund raising, opinion polls, shop at home services, driver license data, arrest records and medical records. The potential threats to privacy include the improper commercial use of computerized data, breaches of confidentiality by releasing confidential data to third parties, and the release of records to governmental agencies for investigative purposes.

The basic law that protects our privacy is the Fourth Amendment to the United States Constitution, which mandates that people have a right to be secure in homes and against unreasonable search and seizure. In addition, many laws have been enacted to protect the individual from having damaging information stored in computerized databases.

8.3.3 Piracy

Software piracy is the unauthorized reproduction of copyrighted software. The unauthorized copying may be done for personal use, business use, or it may be done to sell copies of the pirated software. The problem can be found wherever computers are used: in businesses, schools, libraries, and homes. The Business Software Alliance puts it bluntly when they point out that making unauthorized copies of software or downloading unauthorized copies of software via the Internet is against the law (Anonymous 2001 a). The problem of making illegal software copies has been recognized in the computer industry for decades and has increased to match the growing use of computers (Wood 1998).

Microcomputer software presents a particular problem since many individuals are involved in the use of this soft-ware. Section 117 of the copyright laws, specifically the 1980 amendment, deals with a law that addresses the prob-lem of backup copies of software. This section states that users have the right to create backup copies of their soft-ware. That is, users may legally create a backup copy of software if it is to be held in archive. Many software com-panies provide a free backup copy to users that precludes the need for to users purchase software intended to defeat copy protection systems and subsequently create copies of their software. If the software purchased is actually leased, you may in fact not even be able to make backup copies of the software. The distinction between leasing and buying is contained within the software documentation. The copyright statement is also contained in the software documentation. The copyright laws regarding leased material state that the leasor may say what the leaseholder can and cannot do with the software. So it is entirely up to the owner of the software as to whether or not users may make backup copies of the software. At a time when federal laws relating to copyright protection are evolving, sev-eral states are considering legislation that would bar unauthorized duplication of software.

The software industry is prepared to do battle against software piracy. The courts are dealing with an increasing number of lawsuits concerning the protection of software. Large software publishers have established the Software Protection Fund to raise between $500,000 and $1 million to promote anti-piracy sentiment and to develop addi-tional protection devices.

8.3.4 Fraud and Misuse

The computer can create a unique environment in which unauthorized activities can occur. Crimes in this category have many traditional names including theft, fraud, embezzlement, extortion, etc. Computer related fraud includes the introduction of fraudulent records into a computer system, theft of money by electronic means, theft of financial instruments, theft of services, and theft of valuable data.

8.3.5 Liability

Under the UCC, an express warranty is an affirmation or promise of product quality to the buyer and becomes a part of the basis of the bargain. Promises and affirmations made by the software developer to the user about the nature and quality of the program can also be classified as an express warranty. Programmers or retailers possess the right to define express warranties. Thus, they have to be realistic when they state any claims and predictions about the ca-pabilities, quality and nature of their software or hardware. They should consider the legal aspects of their affirma-tive promises, their product demonstrations, and their product description. Every word they say may be as legally effective as though stated in writing. Thus, to protect against liability, all agreements should be in writing. A dis-claimer of express warranties can free a supplier from being held responsible for any informal, hypothetical state-ments or predictions made during the negotiation stages.

Implied warranties are also defined in the United States by the UCC. These are warranties that are provided automatically in every sale. These warranties need not be in writing nor do they need to be verbally stated. They insure that good title will pass to the buyer, that the product is fit for the purpose sold, and that it is fit for the ordinary purposes for which similar goods are used (merchantability)..

8.3.6 Patent and Copyright Law

A patent can protect the unique and secret aspect of an idea. It is very difficult to obtain a patent compared to a copyright (please see discussion below). With computer software, complete disclosure is required; the patent holder must disclose the complete details of a program to allow a skilled programmer to build the program. Moreover, a United States software patent will be unenforceable in most other countries.

Copyright law provides a very significant legal tool for use in protecting computer software, both before a security breach and certainly after a security breach. This type of breach could deal with misappropriation of data, computer programs, documentation, or similar material. For this reason the information security specialist will want to be fa-miliar with basic concepts of to copyright law.

The United States, United Kingdom, Australia, and other countries have now amended or revised their copy-right legislation to provide explicit laws to protect computer program. Copyright law in the United States is governed by the Copyright Act of 1976 that preempted the field from the states. Formerly, the United States had a dual state and federal system. In other countries, such as Canada, the courts have held that the un-revised Copyright Act is broad enough to protect computer programs. In many of these countries the reform of copyright law is actively underway.

8.3.7 Trade Secrets

A trade secret protects something of value and usefulness. This law protects the unique and secret aspects of ideas, known only to the discoverer or his confidants. Once disclosed the trade secret is lost as such and can only be pro-tected under one of the following laws. The application of trade secret law is very important in the computer field, where even a slight head start in the development of software or hardware can provide a significant competitive ad-vantage.

8.3.8 Sabotage

The computer can be the object of attack in computer crimes such as the unauthorized use of computer facilities, al-ternation or destruction of information, data file sabotage and vandalism against a computer system. Computers have been shot, stabbed, short-circuited and bombed.

It is easy to sensationalize these topics with real horror stories; it is more difficult to deal with the underlying ethical issues involved.

8.3.8.1 Data Theft in Cyber Space – Issues and Laws

The rapid development of Information technology poses new challenges before the law. These challenges are not confined to any single traditional legal category but arise in, for example, Criminal Law, Intellectual Property Law, Contract and Tort. One such challenge is the growing menace of "Data Theft". It is the term used when any information in the form of data is illegally copied or taken from a business or other individual without his knowledge or consent.

8.3.8.2 Data as a Valuable Asset

Data is a valuable asset in this modern era of Information Technology (IT). Data is an important raw-material for Call Centers and I.T. Companies. Data has also become an important tool and weapon for Corporate to capture larger market shares. Due to the importance of Data in this new era, its security has become a major issue with the I.T. industry. The piracy of data is a threat, faced by the I.T. players, who spend millions to compile or buy data from the market. Their profits depend upon the security of their Data.

8.4 ISSUES IN DATA AND SOFTWARE PRIVACY

The major issue regarding Data Theft is its International character, for example Systems may be accessed in USA, the data manipulated in China and the consequences felt in India. The result of this ability is that different sovereignties, jurisdictions, laws and rules will come into play which again is an issue in itself. Further, collection of evidence in such circumstances become another issue as investigation in three different countries, all of whom may not be in talking terms, is almost impossible and poor technical know-how of our cops adds to the woes. Also, the lack of coordination between different investigating agencies and a not-so-sure extradition process is another head ache. However the biggest of all these issues is the lack of specific laws in the country dealing with this crime, so even if the culprit is caught he can easily get away by picking and choosing any of the of various loopholes in our law.

8.4.1 Does India have Sufficient Laws

The problem of data theft which has emerged as one of the major cyber crimes worldwide has attracted little attention of law makers in India. Unlike U.K which has The Data Protection Act, 1984 there is no specific legislation in India to tackle this problem, though India boasts of its Information Technology Act, 2000 to address the ever growing menace of cyber crimes, including data theft. The truth is that our IT Act, 2000 is not well equipped to tackle such crimes. The various provisions of the IT Act, 2000 which deal with the problem to some extent are briefly discussed below.

Section 43:- This section provides protection against destruction and unauthorized access of the computer system by imposing heavy penalty up to one crore. The unauthorized downloading, extraction and copying of data are also covered under this section. Clause 'C' of this section imposes penalty for unauthorized introduction of computer viruses of contaminants. Clause 'G' provides penalties for assisting the unauthorized access.

Section 65:- This section provides for computer source code. If anyone knowingly or intentionally conceals, destroys, alters or causes another to do as such shall have to suffer imprisonment of up to 3 years or fine up to 2 lakh rupees. Thus protection has been provided against tampering of computer source documents.

Section 66:- Protection against hacking has been provided under this section. As per this section, hacking is defined as any act with an intention to cause wrongful loss or damage to any person or with the knowledge that wrongful loss or damage will be caused to any person and information residing in a computer resource must be either destroyed, deleted, altered or its value and utility get diminished. This section imposes the penalty of imprisonment of up to three years or fine up to two lakh rupees or both on the hacker.

Section 70:- This section provides protection to the data stored in the protected system. Protected systems are those computers, computer system or computer network to which the appropriate government, by issuing gazette information in the official gazette, declared it as a protected system. Any access or attempt to secure access of that system in contravention of the provision of this section will make the person accessed liable for punishment of imprisonment which may extend to ten years and shall also be liable to fine.

Section 72:- This section provides protection against breach of confidentiality and privacy of the data. As per this, any person upon whom powers have been conferred under IT Act and allied rules to secure access to any electronic record, book, register, correspondence, information document of other material discloses it to any other person, shall be punished with imprisonment which may extend to two years or with fine which may extend to one lakh rupees or both.

8.5 WHAT IS CYBER CRIME

Online activities are just as vulnerable to crime and can compromise personal safety just as effectively as common everyday crimes. Lawmakers, law enforcement, and individuals need to know how to protect themselves and the persons for which they are responsible. You can see by the explanations of various cyber crimes below that the crimes have existed long before computers and the internet were made available to the general public. The only difference involves the tools used to commit the crime.

Cyber crime is the latest and perhaps the most complicated problem in the cyber world. "Cyber crime may be said to be those species, of which, genus is the conventional crime, and where either the computer is an object or subject of the conduct constituting crime" . "Any criminal activity that uses a computer either as an instrumentality, target or a means for perpetuating further crimes comes within the ambit of cyber crime".

A generalized definition of cyber crime may be " unlawful acts wherein the computer is either a tool or target or both" The computer may be used as a tool in the following kinds of activity- financial crimes, sale of illegal articles, pornography, online gambling, intellectual property crime, e-mail spoofing, forgery, cyber defamation, cyber stalking. The computer may however be target for unlawful acts in the following cases- unauthorized access to computer/ computer system/ computer networks, theft of information contained in the electronic form, e-mail bombing, data didling, salami attacks, logic bombs, Trojan attacks, internet time thefts, web jacking, theft of computer system, physically damaging the computer system.

8.5.1 Distinction Between Conventional and Cyber Crime

There is apparently no distinction between cyber and conventional crime. However on a deep introspection we may say that there exists a fine line of demarcation between the conventional and cyber crime, which is appreciable. The demarcation lies in the involvement of the medium in cases of cyber crime. The sine qua non for cyber crime is that there should be an involvement, at any stage, of the virtual cyber medium.

8.5.1.1 Reasons For Cyber Crime

Hart in his work " The Concept of Law" has said 'human beings are vulnerable so rule of law is required to protect them'. Applying this to the cyberspace we may say that computers are vulnerable so rule of law is required to protect and safeguard them against cyber crime. The reasons for the vulnerability of computers may be said to be:

1. **Capacity to store data in comparatively small space:** The computer has unique characteristic of storing data in a very small space. This affords to remove or derive information either through physical or virtual medium makes it much more easier.
2. **Easy to access:** The problem encountered in guarding a computer system from unauthorised access is that there is every possibility of breach not due to human error but due to the complex technology. By secretly implanted logic bomb, key loggers that can steal access codes, advanced voice recorders; retina imagers etc. that can fool biometric systems and bypass firewalls can be utilized to get past many a security system.
3. **Complex:** The computers work on operating systems and these operating systems in turn are composed of millions of codes. Human mind is fallible and it is not possible that there might not be a lapse at any stage. The cyber criminals take advantage of these lacunas and penetrate into the computer system.
4. **Negligence:** Negligence is very closely connected with human conduct. It is therefore very probable that while protecting the computer system there might be any negligence, which in turn provides a cyber criminal to gain access and control over the computer system.

5. **Loss of evidence:** Loss of evidence is a very common & obvious problem as all the data are routinely destroyed. Further collection of data outside the territorial extent also paralyses this system of crime investigation.

   (a) ***Children and adolescents between the age group of 6 – 18 years – CYBER CRIMINALS:*** The cyber criminals constitute of various groups/ category. This division may be justified on the basis of the object that they have in their mind. The following are the category of cyber criminals-

   The simple reason for this type of delinquent behaviour pattern in children is seen mostly due to the inquisitiveness to know and explore the things. Other cognate reason may be to prove themselves to be outstanding amongst other children in their group. Further the reasons may be psychological even. E.g. the Bal Bharati (Delhi) case was the outcome of harassment of the delinquent by his friends.

   (b) ***Organised hackers:*** These kinds of hackers are mostly organised together to fulfil certain objective. The reason may be to fulfil their political bias, fundamentalism, etc. The Pakistanis arc said to bc one of the best quality hackers in the world. They mainly target the Indian government sites with the purpose to fulfil their political objectives. Further the NASA as well as the Microsoft sites is always under attack by the hackers.

   (c) ***Professional hackers / crackers:*** Their work is motivated by the colour of money. These kinds of hackers are mostly employed to hack the site of the rivals and get credible, reliable and valuable information. Further they are ven employed to crack the system of the employer basically as a measure to make it safer by detecting the loopholes.

   (d) ***Discontented employees:*** This group include those people who have been either sacked by their employer or are dissatisfied with their employer. To avenge they normally hack the system of their employee.

8.5.2 Mode and Manner of Commiting Cyber Crime

1. **Unauthorized access to computer systems or networks / Hacking:** This kind of offence is normally referred as hacking in the generic sense. However the framers of the information technology act 2000 have no where used this term so to avoid any confusion we would not interchangeably use the word hacking for 'unauthorized access' as the latter has wide connotation.
2. **Theft of information contained in electronic form:** This includes information stored in computer hard disks, removable storage media etc. Theft may be either by appropriating the data physically or by tampering them through the virtual medium.
3. **Email bombing:** This kind of activity refers to sending large numbers of mail to the victim, which may be an individual or a company or even mail servers there by ultimately resulting into crashing.
4. **Data diddling:** This kind of an attack involves altering raw data just before a computer processes it and then changing it back after the processing is completed. The electricity board faced similar problem of data diddling while the department was being computerised.

5. **Salami attacks:** This kind of crime is normally prevalent in the financial institutions or for the purpose of committing financial crimes. An important feature of this type of offence is that the alteration is so small that it would normally go unnoticed. E.g. the Ziegler case wherein a logic bomb was introduced in the bank's system, which deducted 10 cents from every account and deposited it in a particular account.
6. **Denial of Service attack:** The computer of the victim is flooded with more requests than it can handle which cause it to crash. Distributed Denial of Service (DDoS) attack is also a type of denial of service attack, in which the offenders are wide in number and widespread. E.g. Amazon, Yahoo.
7. **Virus / worm attacks:** Viruses are programs that attach themselves to a computer or a file and then circulate themselves to other files and to other computers on a network. They usually affect the data on a computer, either by altering or deleting it. Worms, unlike viruses do not need the host to attach themselves to. They merely make functional copies of themselves and do this repeatedly till they eat up all the available space on a computer's memory. E.g. love bug virus, which affected at least 5 % of the computers of the globe. The losses were accounted to be $ 10 million. The world's most famous worm was the Internet worm let loose on the Internet by Robert Morris sometime in 1988. Almost brought development of Internet to a complete halt.
8. **Logic bombs:** These are event dependent programs. This implies that these programs are created to do something only when a certain event (known as a trigger event) occurs. E.g. even some viruses may be termed logic bombs because they lie dormant all through the year and become active only on a particular date (like the Chernobyl virus).
9. **Trojan attacks:** This term has its origin in the word 'Trojan horse'. In software field this means an unauthorized programme, which passively gains control over another's system by representing itself as an authorised programme. The most common form of installing a Trojan is through e-mail. Example, a Trojan was installed in the computer of a lady film director in the U.S. while chatting. The cyber criminal through the web cam installed in the computer obtained her nude photographs. He further harassed this lady.
10. **Internet time thefts:** Normally in these kinds of thefts the Internet surfing hours of the victim are used up by another person. This is done by gaining access to the login ID and the password. E.g. Colonel Bajwa's case- the Internet hours were used up by any other person. This was perhaps one of the first reported cases related to cyber crime in India. However this case made the police infamous as to their lack of understanding of the nature of cyber crime.
11. **Web jacking:** This term is derived from the term hi jacking. In these kinds of offences the hacker gains access and control over the web site of another. He may even mutilate or change the information on the site. This may be done for fulfilling political objectives or for money. E.g. recently the site of MIT (Ministry of Information Technology) was hacked by the Pakistani hackers and some obscene matter was placed therein. Further the site of Bombay crime branch was also web jacked. Another case of web jacking is that of the

'gold fish' case. In this case the site was hacked and the information pertaining to gold fish was changed. Further a ransom of US $ 1 million was demanded as ransom. Thus web jacking is a process where by control over the site of another is made backed by some consideration for it.

8.5.3 Classification of Cybercrime

The subject of cyber crime may be broadly classified under the following three groups. They are-

1. **Against Individuals**
   (a) their person &
   (b) their property of an individual
2. **Against Organization**
   (a) Government
   (b) Firm, Company, Group of Individuals.
3. **Against Society at large:** The following arc the crimes, which can be committed against the followings group

   Against Individuals:
   (i) Harassment via e-mails.
   (ii) Cyber-stalking.
   (iii) Dissemination of obscene material.
   (iv) Defamation.
   (v) Unauthorized control/access over computer system.
   (vi) Indecent exposure
   (vii) Email spoofing
   (viii) Cheating & Fraud

   Against Individual Property:
   (i) Computer vandalism.
   (ii) Transmitting virus.
   (iii) Netrespass
   (iv) Unauthorized control/access over computer system.
   (v) Intellectual Property crimes
   (vi) Internet time thefts

   Against Organization:
   (i) Unauthorized control/access over computer system
   (ii) Possession of unauthorized information.
   (iii) Cyber terrorism against the government organization.
   (iv) Distribution of pirated software etc.

Against Society at large:

(i) Pornography (basically child pornography).

(ii) Polluting the youth through indecent exposure.

(iii) Trafficking

(iv) Financial crimes

(v) Sale of illegal articles

(vi) Online gambling

(vii) Forgery

8.5.4 Types of Cyber Crime

Assault by Threat – threatening a person with fear for their lives or the lives of their families or persons whose safety they are responsible for (such as employees or communities) through the use of a computer network such as email, videos, or phones.

Child Pornography – the use of computer networks to create, distribute, or access materials that sexually exploit underage children.

Cyber Contraband – transferring illegal items through the internet (such as encryption technology) that is banned in some locations.

Cyber laundering – electronic transfer of illegally-obtained monies with the goal of hiding its source and possibly its destination.

Cyber stalking – express or implied physical threats that creates fear through the use of computer technology such as email, phones, text messages, webcams, websites or videos.

Cyber terrorism – premeditated, usually politically-motivated violence committed against civilians through the use of, or with the help of, computer technology.

Cyber theft – using a computer to steal. This includes activities related to: breaking and entering, DNS cache poisoning, embezzlement and unlawful appropriation, espionage, identity theft, fraud, malicious hacking, plagiarism, and piracy. Examples include:

1. **Advertising or soliciting prostitution through the internet.** It is against the law to access prostitution through the internet (including in the state of Nevada in the United States) because the process of accessing the internet crosses state and sometimes national borders. This is a violation of the federal Digital Millennium Copyright Act http://www.copyright.gov/legislation/dcma.pdf.
2. **Drug Sales.** Both illegal and prescription drug sales through the internet are illegal except as a customer through a state licensed pharmacy based in the United States http://www.fda.gov.
3. **Computer-based fraud.** Fraud is different from theft because the victim voluntarily and knowingly gives the money or property to the criminal but would not have if the criminal did not misrepresent themselves or their offering. Fraud is a lie. If someone leads you on

or allows you to believe something that is false to benefit them, they are lying and this is fraud. You become a victim when you voluntarily surrender monies or property based on their misrepresentation or lie. Losing money from computer crime can be especially devastating because often it is very difficult to get the money back. Examples are: scams and altering data to get a benefit, suchas removing arrest records from the police station server, changing grades on the school computer system or deleting speeding tickets from driving records.

4. **Online Gambling**. Gambling over the internet is a violation of American law because the gambling service providers require electronic payment for gambling through the use of credit cards, debit cards, electronic fund transfers which is illegal with the Unlawful Internet Gambling Enforcement Act http://frwebgate.access.gpo.gov/cgi-bin/getdoc.cgi?dbname=109_cong_bills&docid=f:h4411eh.txt.pdf

8.5.4.1 Cybertresspass

Someone accesses a computer's or network's resources without the authorization or permission of the owner but does not alter, disturb, misuse, or damage the data or system. This is hacking for the purpose of entering an electronic network without permission. Examples might include:

1. Using a wireless internet connection at a hotel at which you are staying and accessing the hotel's private files without disturbing them because they are available.
2. Reading email, files, or noting which programs are installed on a third-party's computer system without permission just for fun, because you can. This is sometimes called Snooping.

8.5.4.2 Cyber Vandalism

Damaging or destroying data rather than stealing or misusing them (as with cyber theft) is called cyber vandalism. This can include a situation where network services are disrupted or stopped. This deprives the computer/network owners and authorized users (website visitors, employees) of the network itself and the data or information contained on the network. Examples:

- Entering a network without permission and altering, destroying, or deleting data or files.
- Deliberately entering malicious code (viruses, Trojans) into a computer network to monitor, follow, disrupt, stop, or perform any other action without the permission of the owner of the network.
- Attacking the server of the computer network (DDoS attack) so the server does not perform properly or prevents legitimate website visitors from accessing the network resources with the proper permissions.

8.5.5 Prevention Methods

1. **Firewalls**
2. **Frequent password changing**
3. **Safe surfing**

4. Frequent virus checks

5. Email filters

1. Firewalls

These are programs, which protect a user from unauthorized access attacks while on a network. They provide access to only known users, or people who the user permits.

2. Frequent Password Changing

With the advent of multi-user systems, security has become dependent on passwords. Thus one should always keep passwords to sensitive data secure. Changing them frequently, and keeping them sufficiently complex in the first place can do this.

3. Safe surfing

This is a practice, which should be followed by all users on a network.

Safe surfing involves keeping ones e-mail address private, not chatting on open systems, which do not have adequate protection methods, visiting secure sites. Accepting data from only known users, downloading carefully, and then from known sites also minimizes risk.

4. Frequent Virus Checks

One should frequently check ones computer for viruses and worms. Also any external media such as floppy disks and CD ROMS should always be virus checked before running.

5. Email Filters

These are programs, which monitor the inflow of mails to the inbox and delete automatically any suspicious or useless mails thus reducing the chances of being bombed or spoofed.

8.5.6 Information Security and Cyber Law

Everyday people are busier then they were yesterday. With people being so busy it makes it harder to pay bills or do any kind of shopping. This is no longer an issue if you have access to the internet and the many things it has to offer you.

Since the internet is drawing in more people daily for using, it is also drawing crime in. The crimes on the internet are mounting daily. There are many different kinds of crimes that are done for different reasons. Some crimes like hacking are done so a person can have bragging rights. Other crimes are done in order to get a person personal information so it can be resold on the black market.

Let's take things a step farther so you will understand the different types of internet crimes. There are computer intrusions which mean bots, worms, viruses, spyware, malware and hacking. Computer intrusions have been known to take down complete systems in many different organizations. Sometimes it is another organization knocking the competition out for a while. Other times it is someone wanting to brag that they hacked into a major system and disrupted things and made the system crash.

Child pornography is growing at a rapid place on the internet. With the child pornography there are more pedophiles that are showing up on the internet. The pedophiles are trying to lure children in to meeting them. If a child is going to be on the internet it is always best to take precautions and restrict where they can and cannot go. This will help to keep them safe from lurking criminals.

These are just a few of the internet crimes that are committed around the clock. There are laws in place to handle internet crimes. These crimes are dealt with just like a crime that was not committed on the internet. There will be steep fines and even jail time if a persons is caught doing any type of crime on the internet.

A thing to remember is the person will have criminal records if they are charged with an internet crime. Criminal records follow a person around for the rest of their lives and can make it hard to do certain things. People have many reasons to look at persons records from curiosity to jobs. The records are easy to view online any time of day or night. A person only needs to know where to go in order to search criminal records and they can see every crime a person has ever committed.

The next time you are online and thinking about doing something to another person, you better think twice. Just because another person cannot see you or does not know who you are does not mean they cannot track you. Everything on the internet can be tracked one way or another. A crime will be dealt with even if it was committed on the internet. There could be steep fines and even mandatory jail time. It just depends what the person is being charged with.

8.5.7 Cyber Law Issues in E-Business Management

Consumer protection laws for cyberspace differ from country to country and court judgments passed in one country are often unenforceable in another country. This makes it difficult for online consumers to protect their rights. The increasing rate of cyber crime all over the world has made governments realize the need for cyber laws. In 1986, the CFAA were passed in the US to prosecute hackers.

The Act can be applied to any individual if he tries to access a system without having the required authorization. Another serious crime in cyberspace is credit card fraud. Credit card abuse laws have declared that disclosing, using and distributing credit card information of one individual to another with the intention to defraud, is a crime.

The US law declares that the possession of software to generate codes (that can help obtain the code of a stolen credit card) is a crime. The trading of pirated software is a billion dollar business. The web facilitates free trafficking of illegal copies of copyrighted software.

Many countries have framed laws to deal with software piracy. It is illegal to advertise or transfer or download copies of pirated software on the web. Hackers send harmful viruses over the Internet which can destroy data and cause huge losses to organizations. The cyber laws of many countries impose heavy penalties and imprisonment on people responsible for spreading viruses.

The ECP Act seeks to protect the privacy of users and businesses by declaring it illegal to intercept the communication on the Internet without any authorization. Some of the problems faced by companies marketing their products and services on the web are volatility, trust, and locus.

Online players operate in a highly volatile environment because of precarious consumer demands. The revenues, share prices, and customer response to a website may rise to peak at some points of time and may dwindle later. Customer confidence is vital for e-commerce players.

They have to sustain and enhance customer confidence by offering user-friendly features and deploying advanced technology and security systems. The locus of an online customer is not restricted to a desktop computer. He may access the same website from different devices such as a mobile phone, PDA, or laptop at different times. An online player needs to provide the best quality of services to the customer irrespective of the medium he uses to access the company.

The major technical problems faced by online players are differences in application platforms, problems in communication and scarcity of skills. Online players also need to deal with legal issues regarding similarity in domain names, website content, and features. In the absence of a uniform regulatory framework for e-commerce, businesses are finding it difficult to combat cyber crime. Public and private agencies, and businesses across the world have to work together to form comprehensive and uniform laws that are universally enforceable

8.5.8 Overview of Indian IT Act

The set of laws that are enforceable in India are known as Indian laws. The provisions of modern Indian laws are based on the stipulations of the English common law. Several legislations passed by the British Government in India, during the British rules, are still applicable. However, they have been amended to suit the modern times. Also, the Indian laws are influenced by the legislations of Western nations.

The primary sources of laws in India are the Constitution of India and the laws passed by authorized government bodies. Also, the President and the State Governors are empowered to issue ordinance. Another important source of Indian laws is the verdicts or judgments passed by the Supreme Courts, High Courts and Tribunals. Only a few Indian laws are in compliance with the guidelines provided by the United Nations on critical issues; this includes environmental pollution and human rights laws.

Key Branches of Indian Laws

Indian labour laws

Indian labor laws are laws that govern the employment conditions, labor issues and industrial disputes in India. The primary objective of labor laws is to protect the interest of employers and workers. Important labor laws in India include:

- The Payment of Bonus Act, 1965.
- The Industrial Dispute Act, 1947
- The Wages Act, 1948
- The Employees State Insurance Act, 1948
- The Equal Remuneration Act, 1976

- The Factories Act, 1948
- The Child Labour Act, 1986

Personal Laws

Personal laws in India are applicable to individuals by virtue of their religion. The three fundamental branches of personal laws are Muslim laws, Hindu law, and Christian laws. Personal laws primarily govern the litigations related to personal matters, such as marriage, divorce, succession, adoption and guardianship.

Civil Laws

The working of Civil Courts in India is governed by the Civil Procedure Code (CPC). The CPC lays down guidelines to file civil court cases, requisite court fees, legal rights of the complainant and the defendant and power of the Civil Courts exercised to issue orders.

Criminal Laws

The Indian Penal Code (IPC) that came into effect in 1862 is applicable to the whole of India. It is known as Ranbir Penal Code (RPC) in the State of Jammu and Kashmir. It is applicable on all Indian citizens who commit any criminal offence.

8.5.9 Data Pprivacy and Protection

Information privacy, or **data privacy** is the relationship between collection and dissemination of data, technology, the public expectation of privacy, and the legal and political issues surrounding them.

Privacy concerns exist wherever personally identifiable information is collected and stored - in digital form or otherwise. Improper or non-existent disclosure control can be the root cause for privacy issues. Data privacy issues can arise in response to information from a wide range of sources, such as:

- Healthcare records
- Criminal justice investigations and proceedings
- Financial institutions and transactions
- Biological traits, such as genetic material
- Residence and geographic records
- Ethnicity

The challenge in data privacy is to share data while protecting personally identifiable information. The fields of data security and information security design and utilize software, hardware and human resources to address this issue.

Maintaining of data bases is not as much difficult task as maintaining its integrity, so in this era the most concerned debate is going on to innovate a perfect method of data protection. With the advancement in technological development, there took place a transition in the standard of crimes. In the present era most of the crimes are being done by the professionals through the easiest medium i.e. computers and electronic gadgets. Just by the single click, the criminals are able to get the secured information. The lust of information is acting as a catalyst in the growth of cyber crimes.

It is the very big headache for the business houses, financial institutions and the governmental bodies so as to give adequate protection to their huge databases. In the absence of any particular stringent law relating to data protection, the miscreants are gaining expertise in their work day by day.

Though this world simplified our life style but it left certain anomalies in procurement of its object which resulted in involuntary disclosure of data. This can be analyzed from theses illustrations:

1. On every login to the e-mail account in the cyber cafes, the electronic trail of password remained left there unsecured.
2. On every use of credit card for purchasing purpose, the trail of brand preference, place of shopping etc. left behind.
3. On every login to internet, there left behind an electronic trail enabling website owners and advertising companies to get access to the preference and choices of the users by tracking them.
4. Employees are under seizing, as employers routinely use software to access employee's e-mail and their move.
5. Phone call signals of the police are easily tracked by the naxalites enabling them to know about the police plans.
6. Source code theft is the most preferred act of the miscreants.
7. Unsolicited e-mails are also a usual practice of gathering personal information of the users.
8. Movement across the web can be tracked by placing cookies and then retrieving such a way that allows building detailed profile of the user's interest, spending habits and lifestyle.
9. Through hacking, the hackers can whimsically alter anyone's account.

Thus it can be easily pointed out that how easy we are providing room to the miscreants to enhance and simplify their acts and how safe is it to avail the services of the digital world.

Data protection under foreign law

Many countries other than India have their data protection laws as a separate discipline. They have well framed and established laws, exclusively for the data protection.

Data protection under Indian Law

Our constitution has provided the law relating to privacy under the scope of Article 21. Its interpretation is found insufficient to provide adequate protection to the data. In the year 2000, effort has been made by our legislature to embrace privacy issues relating to computer system under the purview of IT Act, 2000. This Act contains certain provisions which provide protection of stored data. In the year 2006, our legislature has also introduced a bill known as 'The Personal Data Protection Bill' so as to provide protection to the personal information of the person.

Law of contract

These days' companies are relying on the contract law as a useful means to protect their information. The corporate houses enters into several agreements with other companies, clients, agencies or partners to keep their information secured to the extent they want to secure it. Agreements such as 'non circumvention and non-disclosure' agreements, 'user license' agreements, 'referral partner' agreements etc. are entered into by them which contains confidentiality and privacy clauses and also arbitration clauses for the purpose of resolving the dispute if arises. These agreements help them in smooth running of business. BPO companies have implemented processes like BS 7799 and the ISO 17799 standards of information security management, which restrict the quantity of data that can be made available to employees of BPO and call centers.

Indian Penal Code

It imposes punishment for the wrongs which were expected to occur till the last decade. But it failed to incorporate within itself the punishment for crimes related to data which has become the order of the day.

The Personal Data Protection Bill, 2006

Upon the footprints of the foreign laws, this bill has been introduced in the Rajya Sabha on December 8th 2006. The purpose of this bill is to provide protection of personal data and information of an individual collected for a particular purpose by one organization, and to prevent its usage by other organization for commercial or other purposes and entitle the individual to claim compensation or damages due to disclosure of personal data or information of any individual without his consent and for matters connected with the Act or incidental to the Act. Provisions contained in this Act are relating to nature of data to be obtained for the specific purpose and the quantum of data to be obtained for that purpose. Data controllers have been proposed to be appointed to look upon the matters relating to violation of the proposed Act.

U.K Law

U.K. parliament framed its Data Protection Act (DPA) in the year 1984 which thereafter repealed by the DPA of 1998. This Act is basically instituted for the purpose of providing protection and privacy of the personal data of the individuals in UK. The Act covers data which can be used to identify a living person. This includes names, birthday, anniversary dates, addresses, telephone numbers, fax numbers, e-mail addresses etc. It applies only to the data which is held or intended to be held, on computers or other equipments operating automatically in response to instructions given for that purpose or held in a relevant filing system.

As per the Act, the persons and organizations which store personal data must register with the information commissioner, which has been appointed as the government official to oversee the Act. The Act put restrictions on collection of data. Personal data can be obtained only for one or more specified and lawful purposes, and shall not be further processed in any manner incompatible with that purpose or purposes. The personal data shall be adequate, relevant, and not excessive in relation to the purpose or purposes for which they are processed.

U.S Law

Though both U.S and the European Union focus on enhancing privacy protection of their citizens, U.S takes a different approach to privacy from that of the European Union. US adopted the sectoral approach that relies of mix of legislation, regulation, and self regulation. In U.S, data are grouped into several classes on the basis of their utility and importance. Thereafter, accordingly a different degree of protection is awarded to the different classes of data.

Several Acts were also passed in order to stabilize the data protection laws in the United States. The privacy Act was passed in the year 1974 which provided for establishing standards for when it is reasonable, ethical and justifiable for government agencies to compare data in different databases. Another Electronic Communications Privacy Act was passed for restricting the interception of electronic communications and prohibiting the access to stored data without the consent of the user or the communication service.

Further the Children's Online Privacy Protection Act was passed by the US Congress in October 1998 requiring website operators to obtain parental consent before obtaining personal information from children, and a Consumer Internet Privacy Protection Act required an ISP to get permission of the subscriber before disclosing his personal information to third parties.

However, the existing federal laws is not suffice to cover the broad range of issues and circumstances that make the new digital environment a threat to personal privacy. Furthermore, the US Government has been reluctant to impose a regulatory burden on Electronic Commerce activities that could hamper its development and has looked for an answer in self regulation.

8.5.10 Domain Name

A **domain name** is an identification label that defines a realm of administrative autonomy, authority, or control in the Internet. Domain names are also hostnames that identify Internet Protocol (IP) resources such as web sites. Domain names are formed by the rules and procedures of the Domain Name System (DNS).

Domain names are used in various networking contexts and application-specific naming and addressing purposes. They are organized in subordinate levels (subdomains) of the DNS root domain, which is nameless. The first-level set of domain names are the top-level domains (TLDs), including the generic top-level domains (gTLDs), such as the prominent domains com, net and org, and the country code top-level domains (ccTLDs). Below these top-level domains in the DNS hierarchy are the second-level and third-level domain names that are typically open for reservation by end-users that wish to connect local area networks to the Internet, run web sites, or create other publicly accessible Internet resources. The registration of these domain names is usually administered by domain name registrars who sell their services to the public.

Individual Internet host computers use domain names as host identifiers, or hostnames. Hostnames are the leaf labels in the domain name system usually without further subordinate domain name space. Hostnames appear as a component in Uniform Resource Locators (URLs) for Internet resources such as web sites (e.g., en.wikipedia.org).

Domain names are also used as simple identification labels to indicate ownership or control of a resource. Such examples are the realm identifiers used in the Session Initiation Protocol (SIP), the DomainKeys used to verify DNS domains in e-mail systems, and in many other Uniform Resource Identifiers (URIs).

An important purpose of domain names is to provide easily recognizable and memorizable names to numerically addressed Internet resources. This abstraction allows any resource (e.g., website) to be moved to a different physical location in the address topology of the network, globally or locally in an intranet. Such a move usually requires changing the IP address of a resource and the corresponding translation of this IP address to and from its domain name.

Domain names are often referred to simply as *domains* and domain name registrants are frequently referred to as *domain owners*, although domain name registration with a registrar does not confer any legal ownership of the domain name, only an exclusive right of use.

8.5.11 Issues in Ethical Hacking

Before jumping into Ethical hacking and hacking tips and tricks, it is direly needed to know what is **ethical hacking** all about and why do you need this and where you need this? You must know such aspects before you put yourselves into ethical hacking. Just assume that you are in need of accessing your own security parameters of your system, to fix several issues related to it. If you do this, it's also a kind of ethical hacking because all you want to do is to ensure your own safety and security of your information systems no matter whether you are a corporate owner or a home based user. Security is must.

So now I successfully explained without any details that *ethical hacking* is some kind of security testing and related parameters. So you would ask that how should Government know whether I am an ethical hacker or a black hat one. So that makes the definition al little lengthier. That is, testing your security related issues legally. So you need not worry about legal concerns if you really start in the right way. This is not at all the complete definition of ethical hacking and I cannot provide you a scientific or technical explanation just like Wikipedia does. So this hub is to make you know what is ethical hacking and not about the geeky definition to note down. Just make yourselves familiar with ethical hacking.

In order to fix your security related issues, you must think like a hacker, a real black hat hacker. And that makes ethical hacking risky sometimes. But if you are well aware about the above mentioned issues, then you need not worry about anything. Remember that ethical hacking should be explained in series of articles and it requires a lot of time to do that. So I am very happy to share with you what I have learned so far about ethical hacking. And It's my duty to admit that I am not an expert in this filed and I am not working in any of these departments. It's just one of my passions. That's all.

So here, everything is a kind of trial and error method to make sure your won systems are secure. And there are occasions where somebody hires you to do this job. Then also, ethical hacking is that itself. At this time, you should be well prepared with the sensitive issues as you are doing it for somebody else. Just stay tuned for my hubs about ethical hacking in more detail. And I hope you got a brief idea about the very term.

SUMMARY

Computers can be used symbolically to intimidate, deceive or defraud victims. Attorneys, government agencies and businesses increasingly use mounds of computer generated data quite legally to confound their audiences. Criminals also find useful phony invoices, bills and checks generated by the computer. The computer lends an ideal cloak for carrying out criminal acts by imparting a clean quality to the crime.

The computer has made the invasion of our privacy a great deal easier and potentially more dangerous than before the advent of the computer. A wide range of data are collected and stored in computerized files related to individu-als. These files hold banking information, credit information, organizational fund raising, opinion polls, shop at home services, driver license data, arrest records and medical records. The potential threats to privacy include the improper commercial use of computerized data, breaches of confidentiality by releasing confidential data to third parties, and the release of records to governmental agencies for investigative purposes.

The basic law that protects our privacy is the Fourth Amendment to the United States Constitution, which mandates that people have a right to be secure in homes and against unreasonable search and seizure. In addition, many laws have been enacted to protect the individual from having damaging information stored in computerized databases.

Online activities are just as vulnerable to crime and can compromise personal safety just as effectively as common everyday crimes. Lawmakers, law enforcement, and individuals need to know how to protect themselves and the persons for which they are responsible. You can see by the explanations of various cyber crimes below that the crimes have existed long before computers and the internet were made available to the general public. The only difference involves the tools used to commit the crime.

Cyber crime is the latest and perhaps the most complicated problem in the cyber world. "Cyber crime may be said to be those species, of which, genus is the conventional crime, and where either the computer is an object or subject of the conduct constituting crime" . "Any criminal activity that uses a computer either as an instrumentality, target or a means for perpetuating further crimes comes within the ambit of cyber crime".

A generalized definition of cyber crime may be " unlawful acts wherein the computer is either a tool or target or both" The computer may be used as a tool in the following kinds of activity-financial crimes, sale of illegal articles, pornography, online gambling, intellectual property crime, e-mail spoofing, forgery, cyber defamation, cyber stalking. The computer may however be target for unlawful acts in the following cases- unauthorized access to computer/ computer system/ computer networks, theft of information contained in the electronic form, e-mail bombing, data didling, salami attacks, logic bombs, Trojan attacks, internet time thefts, web jacking, theft of computer system, physically damaging the computer system.

EXERCISE

1. How can you build security into software life cycle.
2. What do you mean by ethics.
3. What is data privacy.
4. What are the various types of cyber crime.
5. How are cyber crimes different from conventional crime.
6. What is issues in data and software privacy.

Question Bank

Information Security and Cyber Laws

1. State the critical characteristics of information.
2. List the components used in security models.
3. Name the counter measures on threats.
4. Differentiate between threats and attacks.
5. Mention the benefits of risk management.
6. State the roles involved in Risk management.
7. Name the people affected in security policy.
8. State the pros of Visa international security model.
9. List any two IDS. Mention its category of classification
10. what are the basic functions of access control devices?
11. What is SDLC? Illustrate the security of SDLC.
12. What are the different types of cryptanalytic attacks?
13. Discuss the Legal, Ethical and Professionalism issues during security investigation.
14. What is risk Management?
15. State the methods of identifying and assessing risk management.
16. Discuss the process of assessing and controlling risk management issues.
17. Compare and contrast the ISO 17700 with BS7799 NIST security models.
18. Briefly explain the NIST SECURITY MODEL
19. List the styles of architecture security models.
20. What is intrusion detection system?

21. What is cryptography?
22. Discuss the authentication models used in cryptography.
23. Write notes on the control devices used in security design.
24. Explain multilevel and multilateral security.
25. What are physiological biometric techniques?
26. How to protect e-commerce systems.
27. What do you understand by Unix operating system security?
28. What do you understand by Sandboxing and proof carrying code.
29. What are the most common attacks.
30. What is Digital Signature?
31. What is Asymmetric cryptography.
32. What is Fault tolerance & fault recovery.
33. What is an information system?
34. What are the different type of IS?
35. What is distributed Information System?
36. What is VPN?
37. What is tunneling with VPN?
38. What are the security challenges in mobile devices?
39. What is confidentiality?
40. What is integrity?
41. What is authentication?
42. What is non-repudiation?
43. Explain threat and attack.
44. What are the different type of network attacks & threats?
45. What is Firewall?
46. Explain the different type of Firewall?
47. What is symmetric key cryptography?
48. What is asymmetric key cryptography?
49. What is distributed Information System?
50. What is ecommerce?
51. What are the various types of ecommerce?
52. What are the various security threats to ecommerce?
53. What is need of physical security?
54. What are the deferent disasters and controls?

55. What are Virtual Organizations?
56. Write down the advantages of Virtual Organizations.
57. What is Electronic Data Interchange?
58. What are credit cards?
59. What are the various steps in processing the credit cards?
60. What are biometric systems?
61. What is e-cash?
62. What are the various types of e-cash?
63. What are Ethics?
64. What are the various Ethical Issues?
65. What is Data Privacy?
66. What are the various types of Cyber Crime?
67. How are cyber crimes different from conventional crime?
68. What are security metrics?
69. What are the benefits of security metrics?
70. What do you understand by Information Security?
71. Discuss IPR.
72. What is Patent Law?
73. What is Copyright Laws?
74. How can you build Security into Software Life Cycle?
75. What are intrusion detection systems?
76. What are the various types of intrusion detection systems?
77. What are the various types of VPN protocols?
78. What is the use of tunneling with VPN?
79. What are the Security Concerns in VPN?
80. How to manage a firewall?
81. What is a Denial of Service attack?
82. What is a "spoofed" packet?
83. What is a SYN Flood?
84. What do you do if you are a victim of a DoS?
85. What is GPG/PGP?
86. What is SSH?
87. What is SSL?
88. How do you create certificates?

89. What would you do if you discovered a UNIX or Network device on your network has been compromised?
90. What would you do if you discovered a Windows system on your network has been compromised?
91. What is DNS Hijacking?
92. What is a log host?
93. What is IDS or IDP?
94. Why are proxy servers useful?
95. What is web-caching?
96. What is a digital envelope?
97. What are typical key spaces for symmetric ciphers?
98. What are typical key spaces for asymmetric ciphers?
99. What are the three types of security policies?
100. What would you do if you encountered a security incident?
101. How can you protect against viruses?
102. How can you protect yourself and your company from social engineering?
103. Explain multilevel and multilateral security.
104. Explain electronic banking.
105. What are physiological biometric techniques?
106. How to protect e-commerce systems.
107. What do you understand by Unix operating system security
108. What do you understand by Sandboxing and proof carrying code.
109. What are the most common attacks.
110. What do you understand by Digital Signature
111. What do you understand by Asymmetric cryptography.
112. What do you understand by Fault tolerance & fault recovery.
113. What is an information system? What are the different type of IS?
114. What do you understand by distributed Information System?
115. What is VPN? Explain the use of tunneling with VPN.
116. What are the security challenges in mobile devices?
117. Explain with example the concept of confidentiality, integrity, authentication and non-repudiation.
118. Explain threat and attack. What are the different type of network attacks & threats?
119. What are Digital Signature?

120. What is Firewall? Explain the different type of Firewall?

121. What do you understand by symmetric key cryptography?

122. What do you understand by asymmetric key cryptography?

123. What do you understand by distributed Information System?

124. What do you understand by ecommerce? What are the various types of ecommerce?

125. What are the various security threats to ecommerce?

126. What is need of physical security? What are the deferent disasters and controls?

127. What are Virtual Organizations? Write down the advantages of Virtual Organizations.

128. Explain the Electronic Data Interchange.

129. What are credit cards and what are the various steps in processing?

130. What are biometric systems?

131. What do you understand by e-cash?

132. What do you understand by Ethics?

133. What are the various Ethical Issues?

134. What is Data Privacy?

135. What are the various types of Cyber Crime/

136. How are cyber crimes different from conventional crime?

137. What are security metrics?

138. What are the benefits of security metrics?

139. What do you understand by Information Security?

140. Discuss IPR.

141. Explain Patent Law?

142. What are Copyright Law?

143. How can you build Security into Software Life Cycle.

144. What are intrusion detection systems?

145. What are the various types of intrusion detection systems?

146. What are the various types of VPN protocols?

147. What is the use of tunneling with VPN?

148. What are the Security Concerns in VPN?

149. Describe, genrally, how to manage a firewall

150. What is a Denial of Service attack?

151. What is a "spoofed" packet?

152. What is a SYN Flood?

153. What do you do if you are a victim of a DoS?

154. What is GPG/PGP?

155. What is SSH?

156. What is SSL? How do you create certificates?

157. What would you do if you discovered a UNIX or Network device on your network has been compromised?

158. What would you do if you discovered a Windows system on your network has been comrpromised?

159. What is DNS Hijacking?

160. What is a log host?

161. What is IDS or IDP, and can you give me an example of one?

162. Why are proxy servers useful?

163. What is web-caching?

164. What is a digital envelope ?

165. What are typical key spaces for symmetric and asymmetric ciphers?

Model Papers

MODEL PAPER –I

Q.1 What do you understand by distributed Information System?

Q.2 Explain with example the concept of confidentiality, integrity, authentication and non-repudiation.

Q.3 What is VPN? Explain the use of tunneling with VPN.

Q.4 What are the security challenges in mobile devices?

Q.5 What do you understand by ecommerce? What are the various types of ecommerce?

Q.6 What are the various security threats to ecommerce?

Q.7 What is need of physical security? What are the deferent disasters and controls?

Q.8 What are Virtual Organizations? Write down the advantages of Virtual Organizations.

MODEL PAPER –II

Q.1 What are Digital Signature?

Q.2 What is Firewall? Explain the different type of Firewall?

Q.3 What do you understand by symmetric key cryptography?

Q.4 Explain the Electronic Data Interchange.

Q.5 What are credit cards and what are the various steps in processing?

Q.6 What is an information system? What are the different type of IS?

Q.7 What do you understand by distributed Information System?

Q.8 What is VPN? Explain the use of tunneling with VPN.

MODEL PAPER –III

Q.1 Attempt any two of the following.

(a) What is an information system? What are the different type of IS?

(b) What do you understand by distributed Information System?

(c) Explain with example the concept of confidentiality, integrity, authentication and non-repudiation.

Q.2 Attempt any two of the following.

(a) What do you understand by ecommerce? What are the various types of ecommerce?

(b) What are biometric systems?

(c) What are Virtual Organizations? Write down the advantages of Virtual Organizations.

Q.3 Attempt any two of the following.

(a) What are biometric systems?

(b) What are Virtual Organizations? Write down the advantages of Virtual Organizations.

(c) Explain the Electronic Data Interchange.

Q.4 Attempt any two of the following.

(a) What are Digital Signature?

(b) What is Firewall? Explain the different type of Firewall?

(c) What do you understand by symmetric key cryptography?

Q.5 Attempt any two of the following.

(a) What are credit cards and what are the various steps in processing?

(b) What is VPN? Explain the use of tunneling with VPN.

(c) What do you understand by e-cash? What are the various types of e-cash.

MODEL PAPER –IV

Q.1 Attempt any two of the following.

(a) What do you understand by ecommerce? What are the various types of ecommerce?

(b) What are biometric systems?

(c) What are Virtual Organizations? Write down the advantages of Virtual Organizations.

Q.2 Attempt any two of the following.

(a) What are biometric systems?

(b) What are Virtual Organizations? Write down the advantages of Virtual Organizations.

(c) Explain the Electronic Data Interchange.

Q.3 Attempt any two of the following.

(a) What is an information system? What are the different type of IS?

(b) What do you understand by distributed Information System?

(c) Explain with example the concept of confidentiality, integrity, authentication and non-repudiation.

Q.4 Attempt any two of the following.

(a) What are credit cards and what are the various steps in processing?

(b) What is VPN? Explain the use of tunneling with VPN.

(c) What do you understand by e-cash? What are the various types of e-cash.

Q.5 Attempt any two of the following.

(a) What are Digital Signature?

(b) What is Firewall? Explain the different type of Firewall?

(c) What do you understand by symmetric key cryptography?

M.C.A
(Sem. V) Odd Semester Theory Examination 2010-11
Information Security and Cyber Laws

Time : 3 Hours *Total Marks* : 100

Note: Attempt **all** questions

1. Attempt any ***two*** parts of the following: **(10 × 2 = 20)**

   (a) What are Information Systems? What are global information sysems? Explain how internet and web services are affecting information system from user's perspective. List various architectures for information systems.

   (b) What do you mean by information security? Differentiate between information level threat and network level threats. Discuss the security issues in mobile and wireless computing.

   (c) What are networking devices? Give the definition of following?

   (i) Routers

   (ii) Bridge

   (iii) Switch

   (iv) Hub

2. Attempt any ***two*** parts of the following: **(10 × 2 = 20)**

   (a) What do you mean by loss of data integrity and confidentiality to organization? Explain with a suitable example how data integrity and confidentiality is critical to various business organizations. What are differences in confidential and secret information? What method the organizations use to protect confidentiality and secrecy of information?

   (b) What is virtual organization? How virtual organization works? Explain with an example what business model they follow and what payment mechanism are integrated with them.

   (c) What are electronic payment instruments? Discuss with example how e-cash, credit cards and debit cards are used in electronic payments.

3. Attempt any ***two*** parts of the following: **(10 × 2 = 20)**

   (a) What do you mean by Physical Security? Explain with a suitable example how physical security is important for information systems and organizations. Discuss various physical entry control mechanism used in the organizations.

   (b) What are Biometrics? Discuss various physiological characteristics that are used for Biometric based Identifications? Comment on the interoperability, economic and social issues involved in biometrics.

   (c) What do you mean by framework for information security? Discuss various security models and framework standards used now a days.

4. Attempt any ***two*** parts of the following: **(10 × 2 = 20)**
   (a) What are differences in digital signature and finger print? Discuss various requirements of a digital signature systems and explain how these requirements are fulfilled by a system of digital signature.
   (b) What are Virtual Private Networks? Discuss various types of VPN architecture and explain the differences in firewall based VPNs and router based VPNs.
   (c) What do you mean by security audits? Discuss various types of security audits.
5. Attempt any ***two*** parts of the following: **(10 × 2 = 20)**
   (a) What are cyber crimes? In the light of IT Act, discuss what measures has been taken by the Government to stop crimes in cyber space.
   (b) What are intellectual property rights? Discuss how patents are obtained and what agencies are involved in the patent.
   (c) Write short notes on following:
      (i) Software piracy
      (ii) Plagiarism

B.Tech

(Sem. V) Odd Semester Theory Examination 2010-11

Information Security and Cyber Laws

Time : 2 Hours | *Total Marks* : 50

Note: Attempt **all** questions

1. Attempt any ***four*** parts: **(4 × 3 = 12)**

   (a) What are Information Systems? Explain how distributed information systems help global organizations?

   (b) What are Decision Support Systems? Discuss major functional requirement of a Decision Support System.

   (c) What are security threats in Mobile Computing? Explain how are they dealt?

   (d) What do you mean by Information Security? Distinguish between Information level threats and network level threats.

   (e) What do you mean by RFID? How RFID can be used in Mobile Commerce and Information Asset Protection?

   (f) Explain different roles involved in managing information as 'asset'. How does the role of custodian differ from the role of user?

2. Attempt any ***four*** parts: **(4 × 3 = 12)**

   (a) What do you mean by Electronic Commerce? What are benefits of Electronic Commerce for business firms? What precaution must be taken to ensure confidentiality of the document sent over the network?

   (b) What do you mean by Payment Instruments used in Electronic Commerce? Explain the difference in Credit and Debit cards.

   (c) What do you mean by access control to an information resource? Discuss differences in authentication and user identification.

   (d) What do you mean by Biometric data? Discuss the advantages of Biometrics over traditional authentication methods.

   (e) What do you mean by Physical Security for information systems? What physical security measures are generally used for typical information system resources?

   (f) What are legal challenges in deployment of Biometric in public domain applications?

3. Attempt any ***four*** parts: **(4 × 3 = 12)**

   (a) What are Electronic Payment Systems? Compare electronic payment system on Internet with conventional payment mechanisms.

   (b) List broad activities involved in settlement of a business transaction in E-Commerce. List issues related to safety of business transaction on Web.

(c) What are objective, requirement and threats in a Cryptographic System? What do you mean by Non-repudiation in such systems? Discuss the issue of Integrity and authentication of the documents.

(d) What is Digital Signature? How Digital Signatures are related to Public Key Cryptographic Systems?

(e) What do you mean by Virtual Private Networks? Discuss authentication mechanism used in Virtual Private Networks.

4. Write short note on any ***two*** of the following: **(2 × 7 = 14)**

(a) Intellectual Property Rights

(b) Ethical and Legal Issues in Data and Software Piracy

(c) Types of Cyber Crimes

Index

K

L

M

N

O

P